The Architects of International Relations

Based on extensive archival research, this book provides a new and stimulating history of International Relations (IR) as an academic discipline. Contrary to traditional accounts, it argues that IR was not invented by Anglo-American men after the First World War. Nor was it divided into neat theoretical camps. To appreciate the twists and turns of early IR scholarship, the book follows a diverse group of men and women from across Europe and beyond who pioneered the field since 1914. Like architects, they *built* a set of institutions (university departments, journals, libraries, etc.), but they also *designed* plans for a new world order (draft treaties, petitions, political commentary, etc.). To achieve these goals, they interacted closely with the League of Nations and its bodies for intellectual cooperation, until the Second World War put an end to their endeavour. Their story raises broader questions about the status of IR well beyond the inter-war period.

JAN STÖCKMANN is a lecturer in Modern History at Helmut-Schmidt-Universität, Hamburg. His research has appeared in *The International History Review*, the *Review of International Studies*, and *Past & Present*.

T0371542

The Architects of International Relations

Building a Discipline, Designing the World, 1914–1940

JAN STÖCKMANN

Helmut-Schmidt-Universität, Hamburg

CAMBRIDGE
UNIVERSITY PRESS

Shaftesbury Road, Cambridge CB2 8EA, United Kingdom

One Liberty Plaza, 20th Floor, New York, NY 10006, USA

477 Williamstown Road, Port Melbourne, VIC 3207, Australia

314–321, 3rd Floor, Plot 3, Splendor Forum, Jasola District Centre, New Delhi – 110025, India

103 Penang Road, #05–06/07, Visioncrest Commercial, Singapore 238467

Cambridge University Press is part of Cambridge University Press & Assessment,
a department of the University of Cambridge.

We share the University's mission to contribute to society through the pursuit of
education, learning and research at the highest international levels of excellence.

www.cambridge.org
Information on this title: www.cambridge.org/9781009055130

DOI: 10.1017/9781009053341

First published 2022
First paperback edition 2024

A catalogue record for this publication is available from the British Library

Library of Congress Cataloging-in-Publication data
Names: Stöckmann, Jan, 1989– author.
Title: The architects of international relations : building a discipline, designing the world,
    1914–1940 / Jan Stöckmann, Hamburg.
Description: Cambridge ; New York, NY : Cambridge University Press, [2022] |
    Includes index.
Identifiers: LCCN 2021058042 (print) | LCCN 2021058043 (ebook) |
    ISBN 9781316511619 (hardback) | ISBN 9781009055130 (paperback) |
    ISBN 9781009053341 (epub)
Subjects: LCSH: International relations–History–20th century. | International
    relations–Study and teaching–Europe. | International relations–Study and teaching. |
    BISAC: POLITICAL SCIENCE / International Relations / General
Classification: LCC JZ1305 .S75 2022 (print) | LCC JZ1305 (ebook) | DDC
    327.09–dc23/eng/20211214
LC record available at https://lccn.loc.gov/2021058042
LC ebook record available at https://lccn.loc.gov/2021058043

ISBN   978-1-316-51161-9   Hardback
ISBN   978-1-009-05513-0   Paperback

For My Grandparents

Contents

Acknowledgements

This book is a revised and extended version of my dissertation that I completed in 2017 at the University of Oxford. First and foremost, I would like to thank my supervisor, Patricia Clavin, for her thoughtful guidance throughout the entire process. Patricia was a sharp-minded reader, a warm-hearted supporter, and a good-humoured commentator on academia, politics, and life in general – a rare combination that I found truly inspiring. It was thanks to her rigorous and caring supervision that I was able to defend the dissertation in front of two brilliant scholars of international relations and history – Andrew Hurrell and Joe Maiolo. They made plenty of valuable comments and asked important questions, some of which I hope to have addressed in the present volume.

During my doctoral research, I was generously supported by the German National Academic Foundation (*Studienstiftung*) and the German Academic Exchange Service (DAAD). I also benefitted from travel grants and stipends by the Europaeum, the Rockefeller Archive Center, the University of Oxford, and New College, Oxford. I am very grateful for their financial support as well as their gentle reminders to send in research reports at the end of each funding phase, which turned out to be a helpful exercise. Apart from institutional funding, I greatly benefitted from free accommodation and good entertainment provided by friends (and friends of friends) while on research trips in Berlin, Boston, Geneva, London, New York, Paris, Washington, and Vienna. They never asked for written reports, but their hospitality was truly outstanding.

While revising the manuscript, I held a research fellowship at International Security Studies, Yale University. I am especially grateful to Paul Kennedy, the late Nuno Monteiro, and Evan Wilson for welcoming me into their academic home and to Fritz Bartel for sharing thoughts and meals, and advice on anything I asked. During the following year, I was able to write an additional chapter and revise the entire manuscript while holding a Wiener-Anspach postdoctoral fellowship at the Université libre de Bruxelles (ULB) where I was kindly welcomed by Véronique Dimier and Pieter Lagrou. Finally, in the autumn of 2019, I moved to Hamburg to join Marcus Payk and his team at Helmut-Schmidt-Universität – many thanks to all of them.

I have greatly benefitted from conversations with colleagues on various occasions. Special thanks are due to Susan Pedersen who first pointed me to the archival treasures that inspired this project. I also want to thank Michele Alacevich, Matthew Connelly, Victoria de Grazia, Tanya Harmer, Line Lillevik, Sönke Neitzel, Peter Romijn, and Vladimir Unkovski-Korica who offered helpful comments and support during the early stages. At Oxford, I am particularly grateful to Paul Betts, Tom Buchanan, Martin Ceadel, Gabriela Frei, David Priestland, and Nick Stargardt. I have also had helpful exchanges with Thomas Bottelier, Lukas Cladders, Sebastian Conrad, Patrick Finney, Robert Fox, Sakiko Kaiga, Daniel Laqua, Gabriele Metzler, Samuel Moyn, Nicholas Mulder, Jessica Reinisch, Katharina Rietzler, Davide Rodogno, Ilaria Scaglia, Matthew Stibbe, and Peter Wilson.

Many thanks to the organisers of various seminars, workshops, and conferences that have helped me to improve the arguments in this book. In particular, I am thinking of the (Un)Making the Nation Conference at Cambridge (September 2015), organised by Alastair McClure, Sophie Jung-Kim, Seung Woo Kim, and Joseph Mcquade; the Political History Network at Leiden (October 2015), organised by Anne Petterson, Anne Heyer, and Elisabeth Dieterman; the International History Seminar at Columbia (September 2016), convened by Lotte Francoise Maria Houwink ten Cate and Roy Bar Sadeh; the Gendering Peace in Europe Conference (January 2017), organised by Julie V. Gottlieb at Sheffield; and the International Doctoral Workshop in Geneva (June 2017), put together by Robert Gildea and Sandrine Kott. I also want to thank Kristoffer Liden for inviting me to become a member of the Research School on Peace and Conflict based at the Peace Research Institute, Oslo.

I am very grateful to all librarians and archivists who have allowed my research to go so smoothly, especially to Adele Torrance and Jens Boel at UNESCO in Paris, Isabelle Cramer at the Graduate Institute in Geneva, Julie Archer at Aberystwyth, Anne Woodman at Churchill Archives, Cambridge, Colin Wells and Jacques Oberson at the League of Nations Archives in Geneva, as well as Tom Rosenbaum, Bethany

J. Antos, and Patricia Rosenfield at the Rockefeller Archive Center in Sleepy Hollow, New York. I would also like to thank Jean Toynbee for her permission to use material from a restricted part of the Arnold J. Toynbee Papers. Finally, I would like to thank Michael Watson and John Haslam at Cambridge University Press as well as the peer reviewers for their useful comments.

On a personal level, I would like to thank my friends who have been an unfailing source of intellectual and emotional encouragement: Damian Boeselager, Jasper Bothe, Bernhard Clemm, Edouard Gottlieb, Fabian Hasse, Moritz Kraemer, Max Krahé, Vincent Krieger, Charlotte Lenthe, Caro Leclerc, Felix-Anselm van Lier, Eugenia Marchetti, Patty McCabe, Viktor Schulte, Max Schwefer, Philipp Stackelberg, Max Rowles, Alexis Wegerich, and Charlie Woodward. Special thanks are due to David Gössler for offering technical assistance and much-needed distraction, and to Emilia for her analytical wit and warm-hearted support during the final stage.

I am extremely grateful to my parents who have invested their time and money in a son whose geographical and professional whereabouts must have often seemed unclear to them. Their support has been an immense privilege and a source of stability to me. Finally, I would like to thank my grandparents, Ingrid and Dieter Stöckmann, both born in 1937, at a time when the story of this book was in full swing. They never went to university and we hardly ever speak about foreign affairs in our conversations. But, over the past thirty years, they have given me much more than academic guidance can.

Archival Sources

Personal Papers

Jane Addams, The Jane Addams Papers [microform], New York Public Library, New York

Fannie Fern Andrews Papers, Schlesinger Library, Harvard University, Cambridge, MA

Stanley Hartnoll Bailey Papers, LSE Archives, London

William Beveridge Papers, LSE Archives, London

John Burgess Papers, Rare Book & Manuscript Library, Columbia University, New York

James Bryce Papers, Bodleian Library, Oxford

Charles Roden Buxton Papers, Bodleian Library, Oxford

Robert Cecil, Cecil of Chelwood Papers, British Library: Manuscripts Collections, London

Lionel Curtis Papers, Bodleian Library, Oxford

David Davies, Lord Davies of Llandinam Papers, University College Wales, Aberystwyth

Anna B. Eckstein Papers, Collection: CDG-B Germany, Peace Collection, Swarthmore College, Swarthmore, PA

Agnes Headlam-Morley Papers, St Hugh's College, Oxford

Hajo Holborn Papers, Yale University Archives, New Haven, CT

Ernst Jäckh Papers, Rare Book & Manuscript Library, Columbia University, New York

Thomas Jones Papers, National Library of Wales, Aberystwyth

Albrecht Mendelssohn Bartholdy Papers, Staatsbibliothek zu Berlin, Preußischer Kulturbesitz, Mendelssohn-Archiv (SPK MA Nachl. AMB), Berlin

E. D. Morel Papers, LSE Archives, London

Gilbert Murray Papers, Bodleian Library, Oxford

Philip Noel-Baker Papers, Churchill Archives Centre, Cambridge

Margery Perham Papers, Bodleian Library, Oxford

James T. Shotwell Papers, Rare Book & Manuscript Library, Columbia University, New York

Arnold Toynbee Papers, Bodleian Library, Oxford

Arnold O. Wolfers Papers, Yale University Library, New Haven, CT

Alfred Zimmern Papers, Bodleian Library, Oxford

Institutional Archives

Carnegie Endowment for International Peace (CEIP Records), Centre Européen Records, Rare Book & Manuscript Library, Columbia University, New York

Central Organisation for a Durable Peace Collected Records (CODP), Peace Collection, Swarthmore College, Swarthmore, PA

Graduate Institute Archives, Archives institutionnelles (HEI), Graduate Institute of International and Development Studies, Geneva

Fletcher School of Law and Diplomacy Records, Tufts University, Somerville, MA

Institute of Higher International Studies (Institut des Hautes Etudes Internationales; IHEI), Panthéon-Assas University (Université Panthéon-Assas), Paris

Institute of International Studies Records, Yale University, New Haven, CT

Laura Spelman Rockefeller Memorial (LSRM), Rockefeller Archive Center, Sleepy Hollow, NY

London School of Economics and Political Science, School Archive, Central Filing Registry, London

Peace and Disarmament Committee of the Women's International Organisations Collected Records, Peace Collection, Swarthmore College, PA

Oxford University Archives, Bodleian Library, Oxford

Rockefeller Foundation (RF), RG 1, 3, 10, Rockefeller Archive Center, Sleepy Hollow, NY

Society for the Protection of Science and Learning (SPSL), Bodleian Library, Oxford

University College Wales, Council & Court of Governors Minutes, Aberystwyth

Women's International League for Peace and Freedom, British Section, LSE Archives, London
Women's International League for Peace and Freedom, United States Section, Peace Collection, Swarthmore College, Swarthmore, PA

State and Official Archives

British National Archives, Public Record Office Class FO 262, Kew
Prussian Privy State Archives (Geheimes Staatsarchiv Preußischer Kulturbesitz; GStA PK), I. HA Rep. 303 Deutsche Hochschule für Politik, Berlin
German Federal Archives, R 4901 (Reichsministerium für Wissenschaft, Erziehung und Volksbildung), Berlin
German Federal Foreign Office, Political Archive (PA AA), RZ507, R64152, R61221, Berlin
International Institute of Intellectual Cooperation (IIIC Records), Archive Group 1, UNESCO Archives, Paris
League of Nations Archives, Secretariat funds (Fonds du secrétariat), Section of international offices and intellectual cooperation (Section des bureaux internationaux et de la coopération intellectuelle), Geneva
The National Archives of Austria (Österreichisches Staatsarchiv), House, Court and State archives (Haus-, Hof- und Staatsarchiv, Sonderbestände K), Archives of the Consular Academy (Archiv der Konsularakademie), Files (Akten), Vienna
Hamburg State Archives (Staatsarchiv Hamburg; StA HH), Higher Education II (Hochschulwesen II), Hamburg
United States National Archives, RG 59, 711.5112 France, College Park, MD

Abbreviations

CODP	Central Organisation for a Durable Peace
CSIR	Council for the Study of International Relations
DHfP	Deutsche Hochschule für Politik (Berlin)
FPA	Foreign Policy Association
IAP	Institut für Auswärtige Politik (Hamburg)
ICIC	International Committee on Intellectual Cooperation
ICW	International Council of Women
IHEI	Institut des Hautes Etudes Internationales (Paris)
IIIC	International Institute of Intellectual Cooperation
IPR	Institute of Pacific Relations
IR	International Relations
ISC	International Studies Conference
IWSA	International Woman Suffrage Alliance
LNU	League of Nations Union
LSE	London School of Economics and Political Science
UDC	Union of Democratic Control
UNESCO	United Nations Educational, Scientific, and Cultural Organization
WILPF	Women's International League for Peace and Freedom

Introduction

Is there any way of delivering mankind from the menace of war?

Albert Einstein (1932)[1]

In the spring of 1915, the American educator Fannie Fern Andrews embarked on a trip to The Hague to attend a meeting of international scholars and political activists to draft a programme for peace. The meeting, although "almost within hearing distance of the guns in Belgium", was attended by thirty delegates, both men and women, from ten belligerent and neutral countries.[2] Among the participants were well-known figures, such as Norwegian internationalist Christian Lous Lange, British feminist Chrystal Macmillan, and German pacifist lawyer Walther Schücking. Over the course of three days, they hammered out a set of policies which they called the 'minimum-programme' – envisioning a liberal international order on the basis of inter-governmental institutions, free trade, and self-determination.[3]

The group became known as the Central Organisation for a Durable Peace (CODP) and soon counted hundreds of members from more than two dozen countries.[4] Andrews was elected their corresponding secretary. Her job was to edit a series of studies, a "scientific basis for the principles of the minimum programme", written by an

---

[1] Albert Einstein to Sigmund Freud, 30 July 1932, in International Institute of Intellectual Cooperation (ed.), *Why War?* (Paris, 1932).

[2] Fannie Fern Andrews, *Memory Pages of My Life* (Boston, 1948), p. 112.

[3] Manifesto, Central Organisation for a Durable Peace April 1915, CODP Collected Records, Box 1.

[4] Among the CODP members were professors, such as British political scientist Goldsworthy Lowes Dickinson and Swiss jurist André Mercier, politicians, such as former Dutch prime minister Theo Heemskerk and German social democrat Eduard Bernstein, and a range of internationalist authors and activists, including Jane Addams, Albert Einstein, Henri La Fontaine, and Elisabeth Rotten. Liste des Membres, 7–10 April 1915, CODP Collected Records, Box 1.

international group of academics and policy experts.[5] Within little more than a year, members of the CODP were working on thirty-five research projects on subjects such as disarmament, secret treaties, colonial reform, free trade, and the democratic control of foreign policy.[6] Andrews herself wrote a study on the freedom of the seas which was subsequently published as a book.[7] These publications rapidly formed a body of literature distinct from law, history, and economics. By 1919, Andrews had prepared a "course in foreign relations", one of the first introductions to the new field.[8]

Andrews did not, of course, single-handedly create International Relations (IR) as an academic discipline. Yet her case reflects a number of important characteristics of this history. Educated at Radcliffe and Harvard, she became a school reformer and a leading advocate of international education in the years leading up to the First World War.[9] She travelled widely and built an extensive network of scholars, politicians, and philanthropists. Her publications included teaching guides for schools as well as articles in government bulletins. During the 1919 Peace Conference, she was part of Woodrow Wilson's delegation to Paris as one of only a few women.[10] In 1923, her fieldwork on the League of Nations mandate system earned her a doctorate from Harvard. A few years later, she published an acclaimed book called *The Holy Land under Mandate* (1931).[11] Meanwhile, she lobbied for an international education bureau, essentially an early version of UNESCO, which became a lifelong occupation. In short, her goal was peace by education.

---

[5] 'Liste Provisoire Des Rapporteurs Du Congres International D'études A Berne', 14–18 December 1915, Fannie Fern Andrews Papers, Box 112; CODP to Arthur Watts, 30 September 1915, CODP Collected Records, Box 1.

[6] Fannie Fern Andrews, 'The Central Organisation for a Durable Peace', *The Annals of the American Academy of Political and Social Science* 66 (1916), p. 20.

[7] Fannie Fern Andrews, *The Freedom of the Seas: The Immunity of Private Property at Sea in Time of War* (The Hague, 1917).

[8] Fannie Fern Andrews, *A Course in Foreign Relations: Prepared for the Army Educational Committee* (Paris, 1919).

[9] Valeska Huber, Tamson Pietsch, and Katharina Rietzler, 'Women's International Thought and the New Professions, 1900–1940', *Modern Intellectual History* 18:1 (2021), pp. 121–45.

[10] 'Activities of Members', *Leadership in a Democracy: Journal of the National Institute of the Social Sciences* 6 (1920), pp. 112–13.

[11] Fannie Fern Andrews, *The Holy Land under Mandate*, 2 vols. (New York, 1931). See Fannie Fern Andrews Papers, Box 163, Volume 56.

This dual motive, in education and in politics, became a key factor in the formation of IR during the first half of the twentieth century. The founders of the discipline took on a range of non-academic jobs alongside their role as teachers and researchers. They advised governments, drafted treaties, ran for parliament, managed international organisations, and campaigned outside official political institutions as pacifists and feminists. Andrews assisted the US government in preparing the peace terms at the end of the First World War.[12] Alfred Zimmern, one of the first professors of IR, was voted "the ideal Prime Minister" by a British magazine in 1921.[13] The founder of Germany's first IR research institute, Albrecht Mendelssohn Bartholdy, represented his government at the Permanent Court of International Justice in The Hague and at the League of Nations Assembly in Geneva.[14] The French jurist René Cassin tried to "instruct the governments" in pursuit of a just world order.[15] By assuming the job and the rhetoric of statesmen, IR scholars blurred the boundaries between academia and diplomacy. On the one hand, they were committed to the "disinterested pursuit of objective truth", while, on the other hand, mingling with politicians or running for office themselves.[16] They were "scholarly partisans", as Andrews put it.[17]

To understand the formation of IR as an academic discipline, this book traces a range of international actors – professors, politicians, diplomats, journalists, activists, and philanthropists – who promoted the study of war and peace within the context of a dramatically changing international order. They were the architects of IR, both as founders of academic institutions and as designers of new foreign policy instruments. Their history began immediately after the outbreak of the First World War when experts such as Andrews started to write and to teach on international affairs. By the end of the war, the

---

[12] Colonel House to Fannie Fern Andrews, 17 January 1918, and response, 23 January 1918, Fannie Fern Andrews Papers, Box 113.

[13] Newspaper clipping, *The London Magazine*, reprinted in *The Times*, 19 February 1921, Alfred Zimmern Papers, Box 179.

[14] Rainer Nicolaysen, 'Albrecht Mendelssohn Bartholdy (1874–1936): Jurist – Friedensforscher – Künstler', *Rabels Zeitschrift* 75 (2011), p. 24.

[15] Jean-Michel Guieu, *Le rameau et le glaive: Les militants français pour la Société des Nations* (Paris, 2008), p. 16.

[16] International Institute of Intellectual Cooperation (IIIC), *The State and Economic Life* (Paris, 1934), p. xiii.

[17] Andrews, *The Holy Land under Mandate*, p. vi.

pioneers of IR had sketched out most of the topics that would shape interwar IR scholarship. But it was from 1919 that the discipline took shape in an institutional form, both at universities and at non-academic venues. Supported by government and private funds from across Europe and the United States, these institutions provided a transnational platform for teaching, research, and policy work. By the end of the 1920s, IR scholars had established university degrees, academic journals, and conferences. At the same time, they tried to influence foreign policy by drafting and circulating documents that fed into international treaties. As quasi-diplomats, they continued to comment on and interact with major political events during the 1930s, and shaped the debates about 'collective security' and 'peaceful change'. Eventually, their project was undermined by the spread of violent nationalism and aggressive foreign policy during the second half of the 1930s, as well as by the repression of liberal scholarship. The first era of IR came to an end in June 1940 when German troops seized Paris, one of the centres of the IR community, and forced any remaining scholars into exile.

Did the architects of IR fail? Or, put more generally, was an academic discipline able to solve the problem of war? Andrews and her colleagues were convinced that their work improved international understanding and, as a result, led to peace. They believed that international affairs could (and should) be subject to scientific examination and to public discourse. In this respect, their approach broke with nineteenth-century 'old diplomacy' which limited foreign policy to a small, male elite. Their hopes to open up the domain of international affairs coincided with a more general spread of democracy in the wake of the First World War. Some therefore saw IR as a "child of democracy".[18] If international affairs were put in the hands of the people, so they argued, education and public debate would be essential. In Alfred Zimmern's words, the idea was to apply the "scientific method ... to the art of government".[19] Evidently, the first half of the twentieth century was not the most hospitable environment for this exercise, as

---

[18] "[*ein Kind der Demokratie*]", Hans Simons and Paul Marc, 'Vorwort', in Albrecht Mendelssohn Bartholdy (ed.), *Diplomatie* (Berlin, 1927), p. v.

[19] Alfred Zimmern, *Learning and Leadership: A Study of the Needs and Possibilities of International Intellectual Cooperation* (Oxford, 1928), p. 62.

historians have amply shown.[20] Whether it was *a priori* doomed, however, is a different question.

What, then, inspired the development of IR as an academic discipline? And how do its origins inform current debates in the field? The short, and perhaps obvious, answer is that the subject has always been underpinned by political opinion, and thus clashed with the standards of scientific objectivity. The longer answer emerges by examining the archival record of historical actors – their correspondence, lecture notes, diaries, memoranda, government reports, budget tables, university syllabi, conference proceedings, propaganda leaflets, speeches, and newspaper articles. The primary sources considered in this book provide a new perspective on the underlying motivations and the intellectual programme of the emerging discipline. They offer raw, unfiltered insights into the minds of IR scholars that defy sweeping generalisations. They also demonstrate the personal and financial effort that went into this experiment and, ultimately, indicate reasons for its failures. Most importantly, these documents reflect a sense of the intellectual struggle and the political uncertainty that shaped the interwar period. Perhaps they raise more questions than they can answer, but one conclusion seems clear enough: The architects of IR did not only interpret the world at an academic level, they wanted to change it in practice.

Writing the History of a Discipline

There is a simple story about the origins of IR as an academic discipline. In the aftermath of the First World War, so that story goes, a group of so-called 'idealist' thinkers founded a number of professorships and research centres in Britain and the United States. Among the most famous were the Woodrow Wilson Chair of International Politics

---

[20] Patrick O. Cohrs, *The Unfinished Peace after World War I: America, Britain and the Stabilisation of Europe, 1919–1932* (Cambridge, 2006); Robert Gerwarth (ed.), *Twisted Paths: Europe 1914–1945* (Oxford, 2007); Sally Marks, *The Illusion of Peace: International Relations in Europe, 1918–1933*, 2nd ed. (Basingstoke, 2003); Richard Overy, *The Origins of the Second World War*, 4th ed. (London, 2014); Adam Tooze, *The Deluge: The Great War and the Remaking of Global Order* (New York, 2014); Zara Steiner, *The Lights that Failed: European International History, 1919–1933* (Oxford, 2005); and Zara Steiner, *The Triumph of the Dark: European International History, 1933–1939* (Oxford, 2011).

at Aberystwyth, Wales, the British (later Royal) Institute of International Affairs at Chatham House, London, and the Council on Foreign Relations in New York. Their idea was to underpin the newly established League of Nations with an intellectual programme based on international law and cooperation. The 'idealists' believed that morality came before power and that the League of Nations would preserve peace. When the project of peaceful cooperation failed in the 1930s, a generation of self-described 'realist' scholars argued that the founders of IR had erred, and that the global order was actually shaped by military power and national self-interest. This story, popularised by E. H. Carr and other 'realists', has continued to dominate disciplinary memory for most of the twentieth century and it is still standard textbook material today.[21]

The alleged dichotomy between two schools of thought – often called the 'first great debate'[22] – had a profound impact on the field. It allowed post-war scholars to denounce (or forget) an entire generation of their predecessors, the "metaphysicians of Geneva", as Carr called them.[23] By simplifying previous scholarship, the 'realists' downplayed the diversity of interwar IR, its intellectual nuances, and its range of actors, including women and authors outside the anglophone world. The Second World War apparently disqualified anyone associated with interwar centres for IR research. Authors such as Ernst Jäckh, Philip Noel-Baker, and William Rappard disappeared from the scene. This coincided with a continental shift from Europe to the United States. By the 1950s, IR theory was firmly in the hands of US-based scholars, such as John H. Herz, George F. Kennan, Hans Morgenthau, and Reinhold Niebuhr. They re-invented their field in opposition to what they perceived as a utopian mix of science and democracy.[24] That perception was not entirely flawed but was simplified enough to reject a whole group of scholars.

---

[21] Robert Jackson and Georg Sørensen, *Introduction to International Relations: Theories and Approaches*, 6th ed. (Oxford, 2016); Milja Kurki and Colin Wight, 'International Relations and Social Science', in Tim Dunne et al. (eds.), *International Relations Theories*, 3rd ed. (Oxford, 2013), pp. 14–35.

[22] Rainer Baumann et al. (eds.), *International Relations: The Great Debates* (Cheltenham, 2011), esp. Vol. 1. For a critical evaluation, see Brian C. Schmidt, *International Relations and the First Great Debate* (London, 2012).

[23] E. H. Carr, *The Twenty Years' Crisis, 1919–1939* (London, 1939), p. 30.

[24] Nicolas Guilhot, *After the Enlightenment: Political Realism and International Relations in the Mid-Twentieth Century* (Cambridge, 2017), pp. 12–14.

With few exceptions, subsequent generations of IR scholars reiterated this story.[25] If concerned with disciplinary history at all, they briskly discarded earlier works as "blind and sentimental".[26] This turned into a habit of renunciation, allowing young theoreticians to conveniently sideline their old rivals. As new theoretical trends gained attention over the following decades, the discipline came to be divided into schools of thought – liberalism, realism, constructivism, Marxism, functionalism, and their various offshoots. By the end of the Cold War, the image of IR as a succession of theories or 'great debates' had been deeply engrained in disciplinary identity. What is more, this self-image suggested that IR was an Anglo-American enterprise pioneered by white men.[27] Textbooks have continued to spread clichés about the early study of IR, especially that it was dominated by 'utopian liberalism', and that the essential ideas were formulated by Anglo-American men, notably by Woodrow Wilson himself.[28] They have also ignored

[25] See, for example, Frederick S. Dunn, 'The Scope of International Relations', *World Politics* 1:1 (1948), pp. 142–6; John H. Herz, 'Idealist Internationalism and the Security Dilemma', *World Politics* 2:2 (1950), pp. 157–80; Ernst B. Haas, 'Types of Collective Security: An Analysis of Operational Concepts', *American Political Science Review* 49:1 (1955), pp. 40–62; P. A. Reynolds, *An Introduction to International Relations* (New York, 1971), pp. 4–5; Hedley Bull, 'The Theory of International Politics, 1919–1969', in Brian Porter (ed.), *The Aberystwyth Papers: International Politics 1919–1969* (Oxford, 1972), p. 31; Alan Sked, 'The Study of International Relations: A Historian's View', *Millennium* 16:2 (1987), pp. 251–62. For an exception, see Kenneth W. Thompson, 'Idealism and Realism: Beyond the Great Debate', *British Journal of International Studies* 3 (1977), pp. 199–209.
[26] Herz, 'Idealist Internationalism and the Security Dilemma', p. 159.
[27] Stanley Hoffmann, 'An American Social Science: International Relations', *Daedalus* 106:3 (1977), pp. 41–60; Ekkehart Krippendorf, 'The Dominance of American Approaches in International Relations', *Millennium* 16:2 (1987), pp. 207–14; Christopher Hill, 'The Study of International Relations in the United Kingdom', *Millennium* 16:2 (1987), pp. 301–8; Hugh C. Dyer and Leon Mangasarian (eds.), *The Study of International Relations: The State of the Art* (London, 1989); Helen Louise Turton, *International Relations and American Dominance: A Diverse Discipline* (Abingdon, 2017); Ole Wæver, 'The Sociology of a Not So International Discipline: American and European Developments in International Relations', *International Organization* 52:4 (1998), pp. 687–727.
[28] Jackson and Sørensen, *Introduction to International Relations*, pp. 32–4; Kurki and Wight, 'International Relations and Social Science', pp. 16–17. For a critique, see Benjamin de Carvalho, Halvard Leira, and John M. Hobson, 'The Big Bangs of IR: The Myths That Your Teachers Still Tell You about 1648 and 1919', *Millennium* 39:3 (2011), pp. 735–58.

the origins of IR before 1919 by claiming that the field came about "after the end of the First World War" or even later.[29]

It was not until the second half of the 1980s that IR scholars began to reconsider the history of their field.[30] The revisionist turn was inspired by a feeling that the 'realists' had constructed a disciplinary identity that suited their own approach, especially in the context of Cold War power politics, and that they had wrongly portrayed inter-war scholars as naïve believers in the League of Nations. By re-reading the original publications, the revisionists argued that Carr had grossly overstated the alleged dichotomy between 'idealism' and 'realism'.[31] Did the 'first great debate' really happen? Did IR evolve in the form of waves or 'great debates'? By raising these questions, revisionists such as Lucian M. Ashworth have shaken up the basis of their own discipline.[32]

---

[29] William A. Callahan, 'International Relations: An Introduction', *YouTube Channel of the London School of Economics and Political Science (LSE)*, (20 October 2014) [accessed 21 March 2017]. See also Lucian M. Ashworth, 'A Historiographer's View: Rewriting the History of International Thought', in Andreas Gofas et al. (eds.), *The SAGE Handbook of the History, Philosophy and Sociology of International Relations* (London, 2018), p. 531; Steve Smith, Patricia Owens, and John Baylis, 'Introduction', in Smith et al. (eds.), *The Globalization of World Politics*, 6th ed. (Oxford, 2014), p. 3; Peter Wilson, 'The Myth of the "First Great Debate"', *Review of International Studies* 24:5 (1998), p. 8.

[30] William C. Olson and A. J. R. Groom, *International Relations Then and Now: Origins and Trends in Interpretation* (London, 1991); Steve Smith, 'The Forty Years' Detour: The Resurgence of Normative Theory in International Relations', *Millennium* 21:3 (1992), pp. 489–506; David Long and Peter Wilson (eds.), *Thinkers of the Twenty Years "Crisis: Inter-War Idealism Reassessed* (Oxford, 1995); Brian C. Schmidt, *The Political Discourse of Anarchy: A Disciplinary History of International Relations* (New York, 1998); Lucian M. Ashworth, *A History of International Thought: From the Origins of the Modern State to Academic International Relations* (New York, 2014); Andreas Gofas, Inanna Hamati-Ataya, and Nicholas Onuf (eds.), *The SAGE Handbook of the History, Philosophy and Sociology of International Relations* (London, 2018).

[31] Lucian M. Ashworth, 'Where Are the Idealists in Inter-war IR?', *Review of International Studies* 32:2 (2006), pp. 291–308.

[32] Lucian M. Ashworth, 'Did the Realist-Idealist Great Debate Really Happen? A Revisionist History of International Relations', *International Relations* 16:1 (2002), pp. 33–51; Aysen Dilek Lekon, *The Interplay of Realism and Idealism in the Thought of Lionel Curtis: A Critique of the Conception of the "First Debate" in International Relations*, PhD thesis (LSE, London, 2003); Wilson, 'The Myth of the "First Great Debate"', pp. 1–16; Roger Coate and Craig Murphy, 'A Critical Science of Global Relations', *International Interactions* 12:2 (1985), p. 111; Steve Smith, 'Paradigm Dominance in International

Recent literature has paid ever more attention to disciplinary history, resulting in a range of alternative accounts. David Long and Brian C. Schmidt have argued that the "dual themes of imperialism and internationalism" shaped the beginnings of the discipline during the early twentieth century.[33] Robert Vitalis has provided a similar argument about the origins of IR in the United States in the form of 'imperial relations' and 'race development'.[34] It is true, as archival records show, that university courses on the "relation of race ... to social, political and economic conditions" were not uncommon during the 1910s and 1920s.[35] But there was more to it. To reflect the disciplinary diversity Cameron G. Thies has proposed to organise IR history in terms of a "multiplicity of discourses" running alongside each other.[36] Andreas Osiander has claimed that the alleged 'idealist–realist' divide was actually a disagreement about the philosophy of history and the notion of "directional historical process".[37] Peter Wilson has shown that, given the diversity within the respective schools, there were also internal 'utopian–utopian' and 'realist–realist' debates.[38] Most recently, Jo-Anne Pemberton has presented a

Relations: The Development of International Relations as a Social Science', *Millennium* 16:2 (1987), pp. 189–206.

[33] David Long and Brian C. Schmidt, 'Introduction', in Long and Schmidt (eds.), *Imperialism and Internationalism in the Discipline of International Relations* (New York, 2005), p. 1. Imperialism and the reform of empire had an influence on IR via the *Round Table* movement and its leading figures Lionel Curtis and Philip Kerr. See Alexander C. May, *The Round Table 1910–66*, DPhil thesis (Oxford, 1995).

[34] Robert Vitalis, *White World Order, Black Power Politics: The Birth of American International Relations* (Ithaca, 2015); Robert Vitalis, 'The Noble American Science of Imperial Relations and Its Laws of Race Development', *Comparative Studies in Society and History* 52:4 (2010), 909–38. See also John M. Hobson, *The Eurocentric Conception of World Politics: Western International Theory, 1760–2010* (Cambridge, 2012); Mark Mazower, 'An International Civilization? Empire, Internationalism and the Crisis of the Mid-twentieth Century', *International Affairs* 82:3 (2006), pp. 553–66; Vineet Thakur and Peter Vale, *South Africa, Race and the Making of International Relations* (London, 2020).

[35] W. G. Wilson (Harvard and Radcliffe: Bureau of International Research) to David J. Thompson, 7 June 1926, James T. Shotwell Papers, Box 136 (a), (b).

[36] Cameron G. Thies, 'Progress, History and Identity in International Relations Theory: The Case of the Idealist-Realist Debate', *European Journal of International Relations* 8:2 (2002), p. 147.

[37] Andreas Osiander, 'Rereading Early Twentieth-Century IR Theory: Idealism Revisited', *International Studies Quarterly* 42 (1998), p. 418.

[38] Wilson, 'The Myth of the "First Great Debate"', p. 7.

staggering three-volume history of IR which meanders through the world of the League but does little to identify any substantial patterns or arguments.[39] The list of re-examinations goes on, and so does the debate over 'canonical' thinkers.[40] Never has IR history been more popular, Nicolas Guilhot noted in 2019.[41] In fact, there have been so many revisions over the last three decades that the revisionists themselves are in need of orientation.[42] Even the exercise of writing IR history in itself has become subject to debate.[43]

Regardless of their respective interpretations, most authors maintain that the founders of IR were primarily concerned with theory, not with the practice of international politics. Schmidt, for example, has cautioned against 'contextualism', the idea that current affairs shape IR scholarship.[44] Instead, he insists, disciplinary history should seek to reconstruct conversations among scholars in academic environments.[45] This focus on theoretical reconstructions is not surprising, given that the vast majority of the revisionist literature has come from

[39] Jo-Anne Pemberton, *The Story of International Relations: Cold-Blooded Idealists* (Cham, 2020).

[40] David Armitage, 'The Fifty Years' Rift: Intellectual History and International Relations', *Modern Intellectual History* 1:1 (2004), pp. 97–109; William Bain and Terry Nardin, 'International Relations and Intellectual History', *International Relations* 31:3 (2017); Duncan Bell, *Political Thought and International Relations: Variations on a Realist Theme* (Oxford, 2008); Robert M. A. Crawford, *Idealism and Realism in International Relations: Beyond the Discipline* (London, 2000); Jo-Anne Pemberton, *The Story of International Relations, Part One* (Cham, 2020); Or Rosenboim, 'Threads and Boundaries: Rethinking the Intellectual History of International Relations', in Brian C. Schmidt and Nicolas Guilhot (eds.), *Historiographical Investigations in International Relations* (Cham, 2019), pp. 97–125.

[41] Nicolas Guilhot, 'Introduction', in Brian C. Schmidt and Nicolas Guilhot (eds.), *Historiographical Investigations in International Relations* (Cham, 2019), p. 2.

[42] Peter Wilson, 'Where Are We Now in the Debate about the First Great Debate?', in Brian C. Schmidt (ed.), *International Relations and the First Great Debate* (New York, 2012).

[43] Peter Marcus Kristensen, 'Discipline Admonished: On International Relations Fragmentation and the Disciplinary Politics of Stocktaking', *European Journal of International Relations* 22:2 (2016), pp. 243–67.

[44] Brian C. Schmidt, 'On the History and Historiography of IR', in Walter Carlsnaes, et al. (eds.), *Handbook of International Relations* (London, 2002), pp. 11–13.

[45] Brian C. Schmidt, 'Internalism versus Externalism in the Disciplinary History of International Relations', in Brian C. Schmidt and Nicolas Guilhot (eds.), *Historiographical Investigations in International Relations* (Cham, 2019), p. 129.

political scientists and IR specialists who have relied on published English-language sources.[46] Self-reflective accounts of this kind, however, run the risk of making history fit the authors' own theory, rather than testing their claims against the historical evidence.[47] As outsiders to the ongoing rivalries in IR, historians can be more neutral about the uncomfortable and fuzzy origins of the discipline.

When broadening the historiographical focus, it becomes obvious that IR was not the product of isolated ideas but of human beings, driven by personal and political motives, fallible and inconsistent. Archival sources help to restore a sense of the eventful lives that the architects of IR lived. As biographical accounts of leading professors show, their political ambitions were often just as pronounced as their academic ones, perhaps most obviously in the cases of Albrecht Mendelssohn Bartholdy, William Rappard, James T. Shotwell, and Arnold J. Toynbee.[48] They were 'activist-intellectuals', as one

---

[46] Peter Marcus Kristensen and Ole Wæver, 'Peaceful Change as the First Great Debate: Interwar IR and Historical Revisionism Revisited', available at http://web.isanet.org/Web/Conferences/HKU2017-s/Archive/ede49dda-72fe-4cef-837d-d6f0b78f7a7a.pdf [accessed 7 March 2019], p. 3.

[47] See Richard Neb Lebow, 'Vorwort', in Jens Steffek and Leonie Holthaus (eds.), *Jenseits der Anarchie: Weltordnungsentwürfe im frühen 20. Jahrhundert* (Frankfurt, 2014), p. 10.

[48] Nicolaysen, 'Albrecht Mendelssohn Bartholdy (1874–1936)', pp. 1–31; Katharina Rietzler, 'Counter-Imperial Orientalism: Friedrich Berber and the Politics of International Law in Germany and India, 1920s–1960s', *Journal of Global History* 11 (2016), pp. 113–34; Martin Ceadel, *Living the Great Illusion: Sir Norman Angell, 1872–1967* (Oxford, 2009); Michael Cox (ed.), *E. H. Carr: A Critical Appraisal* (London, 2000); Lorna Lloyd, 'Philip Noel-Baker and Peace through Law', in David Long and Peter Wilson (eds.), *Thinkers of the Twenty Years' Crisis: Inter-war Idealism Reassessed* (Oxford, 1995), pp. 25–57; Daniel Bourgeois, 'Entre l'engagement et le réalisme: William Rappard et l'association suisse pour la société des nations face à la crise de 1940', in Saul Friedländer et al. (eds.), *L'historien et les relations internationales* (Geneva, 1981), pp. 215–36; Harold Josephson, *James T. Shotwell and the Rise of Internationalism in America* (London, 1975); Christopher Brewin, 'Arnold Toynbee, Chatham House, and Research in a Global Context', in Long and Wilson (eds.), *Thinkers of the Twenty Years' Crisis: Inter-war Idealism Reassessed* (Oxford, 1995), pp. 277–301; Peter Wilson, 'Leonard Woolf, the League of Nations and Peace between the Wars', *The Political Quarterly* 86:4 (2015), pp. 532–9; Paul Rich, 'Alfred Zimmern's Cautious Idealism: The League of Nations, International Education and the Commonwealth', in Long and Wilson (eds.), *Thinkers of the Twenty Years' Crisis: Inter-war Idealism Reassessed* (Oxford, 1995), pp. 79–99.

biographer put it.[49] The mélange of academic and political interests is also reflected in the memoirs of IR pioneers such as Ernst Jäckh, Helena Swanwick, and US historian William L. Langer who summarised his life under the title *In and Out of the Ivory Tower*.[50] Recent retrospectives have rightly covered a broader range of individuals and their motivations.[51]

Women in particular need to be brought back into this history. Too often their contributions remained 'anonymous', as the economist Emily Greene Balch complained in 1916.[52] Having been neglected for decades, their role in the formation of IR is now beginning to be recognised among historians, most recently in a volume edited by Patricia Owens and Katharina Rietzler.[53] Contrary to textbook knowledge – which holds that feminism in IR only appeared in the late 1980s[54] – women (and men) advocated feminist perspectives on

[49] Josephson, *James T. Shotwell and the Rise of Internationalism in America*, p. 9.

[50] Ernst Jäckh, *Der goldene Pflug. Lebensernte eines Weltbürgers* (Stuttgart, 1954); William L. Langer, *In and Out of the Ivory Tower: The Autobiography of William L. Langer* (New York, 1977); Helena Swanwick, *I Have Been Young* (London, 1935).

[51] Torbjørn L. Knutsen, 'The Origins of International Relations: Idealists, Administrators and the Institutionalization of a New Science', in Andreas Gofas et al. (eds.), *The SAGE Handbook of the History, Philosophy and Sociology of International Relations* (London, 2018), pp. 193–207.

[52] Emily G. Balch, '"The Wisconsin Plan": A Conference of Neutrals for Continuous Mediation', in George H. Blakeslee (ed.), *The Problems and Lessons of the War* (New York, 1916), p. 244.

[53] Patricia Owens and Katharina Rietzler (eds.), *Women's International Though: A New History* (Cambridge, 2021). See also Lucian M. Ashworth, 'Feminism, War and the Prospect of International Government: Helena Swanwick and the Lost Feminists of Interwar International Relations', *Limerick Papers in Politics and Public Administration* 2 (2008), pp. 1–16; Catia Cecilia Confortini, *Intelligent Compassion: Feminist Critical Methodology in the Women's International League for Peace and Freedom* (Oxford, 2012); Sarah Hellawell, *Feminism, Pacifism and Internationalism: The Women's International League, 1915–1935*, PhD thesis (Newcastle, 2017); Huber et al., 'Women's International Thought and the New Professions, 1900–1940', pp. 121–45; Patricia Owens, 'Women and the History of International Thought', *International Studies Quarterly* 62:3 (2018), pp. 467–81; J. Ann Tickner and Jacqui True, 'A Century of International Relations Feminism: From World War I Women's Peace Pragmatism to the Women, Peace and Security Agenda', *International Studies Quarterly* 62:2 (2018), pp. 221–33.

[54] See, for example, J. Ann Tickner, 'Gender in World Politics', in Steve Smith, Patricia Owens, and John Baylis (eds.), *The Globalization of World Politics*, 6th ed. (Oxford, 2014), p. 259; J. Ann Tickner and Laura Sjoberg, 'Introduction', in Tickner and Sjoberg (eds.), *Feminism and International Relations:*

international affairs since at least the 1910s.[55] Most women worked as journalists, teachers, or social workers, though some also held academic posts, such as Balch at Wellesley College or the social anthropologist Lucy Mair at the London School of Economics. While their political activism has been covered well in recent literature, historians have tended to ignore female contributions to IR as an academic discipline.[56] However, as the editor of *Jus Suffragii* Mary Sheepshanks knew as early as 1914, women did not only use "their hands ... but their brains" to understand the causes of war and peace.[57]

Conversations about the Past, Present and Future (New York, 2011), pp. 1–21; Brooke A. Ackerly, Maria Stern, and Jacqui True, 'Feminist Methodologies for International Relations', in Ackerly, Stern, and True (eds.), *Feminist Methodologies for International Relations* (Cambridge, 2006), pp. 1–16; Vivienne Jabri and Eleanor O'Gorman (eds.), *Women, Culture, and International Relations* (London, 1999); Betty A. Reardon, *Women and Peace: Feminist Visions of Global Security* (New York, 1993). For an exception, see Jill Steans, *Gender and International Relations*, 3rd ed. (Cambridge, 2013).

[55] Jan Stöckmann, 'Women, Wars, and World Affairs: Recovering Feminist International Relations, 1915–39', *Review of International Studies* 44:2 (2018), pp. 215–35.

[56] Laura Beers, 'Advocating for a Feminist Internationalism between the Wars', in Glenda Sluga and Carolyn James (eds.), *Women, Diplomacy and International Politics since 1500* (New York, 2016); Catia Cecilia Confortini, 'Links between Women, Peace, and Disarmament: Snapshots from the WILPF', in Laura Sjoberg and Sandra Via (eds.), *Gender, War, and Militarism: Feminist Perspectives* (Santa Barbara, 2010), pp. 157–68; Lela B. Costin, 'Feminism, Pacifism, Internationalism and the 1915 International Congress of Women', *Women's Studies International Forum* 5:3/4 (1982), pp. 301–15; Madeleine Herren, 'Gender and International Relations through the Lens of the League of Nations, 1919–1945', in Glenda Sluga and Carolyn James (eds.), *Women, Diplomacy and International Politics since 1500* (New York, 2016), pp. 182–201; Helen McCarthy, 'Gendering Diplomatic History: Women in the British Diplomatic Service, circa 1919–1972', in Glenda Sluga and Carolyn James (eds.), *Women, Diplomacy and International Politics since 1500* (New York, 2016), pp. 167–81; Leila J. Rupp, *Worlds of Women: The Making of an International Women's Movement* (Princeton, 1997); Ingrid Sharp and Matthew Stibbe, 'Women's International Activism during the Inter-War Period, 1919–1939', *Women's History* 26:2 (2017), pp. 163–72; Ingrid Sharp and Matthew Stibbe (eds.), *Aftermaths of War: Women's Movements and Female Activists, 1918–1923* (Leiden, 2011); Jo Vellacott, 'A Place for Pacifism and Transnationalism in Feminist Theory: The Early Work of the Women's International League for Peace and Freedom', *Women's History* 2:1 (1993), pp. 23–56.

[57] Mary Sheepshanks, 'Patriotism or Internationalism', *Jus Suffragii* 9:2 (1915), p. 184.

Institutions have received even less attention than people.[58] Yet, of course, they provided a crucial context for the formation of IR, both as intellectual environments and by providing an operational framework. Apart from the well-known think tanks in London and New York, the discipline took shape at a range of universities and non-academic institutions across Europe, the United States, and beyond. Important professorships, schools, and centres were founded in Aberystwyth (1919), Paris (1920), Berlin (1920), Hamburg (1923), London (1924), Vienna (1754 and 1920), Warsaw (1926), Geneva (1927), Rome (1928), Oxford (1930) as well as at Georgetown (1919), Princeton (1930), Tufts (1933), and Yale (1935).[59] Not to mention various non-university organisations and events, such as the Geneva summer schools, the Women's International League for Peace and Freedom, and the League of Nations associations, as well as political groups, especially socialist and liberal parties.[60] Some institutions, such

[58] "[V]ery little research has been done on the actual institutional history of this field [IR]". See David Long and Brian C. Schmidt, 'Introduction', in Long and Schmidt (eds.), *Imperialism and Internationalism in the Discipline of International Relations* (New York, 2005), p. 6. "[W]e do not possess an adequate understanding of how the field has developed". See Schmidt, 'On the History and Historiography of International Relations', p. 4.

[59] E. L. Ellis, *The University College of Wales, Aberystwyth, 1872–1972* (Cardiff, 1972); H. Bauer and E. Brighi, *International Relations at LSE: A History of 75 Years* (London, 2003); Martin Ceadel, 'The Academic Normalization of International Relations at Oxford, 1920–2012: Structures Transcended', in Christopher Hood et al. (eds.), *Forging a Discipline: A Critical Assessment of Oxford's Development of the Study of Politics and International Relations in Comparative Perspective* (Oxford, 2014), pp. 184–203; Institut des Hautes Études Internationales, *[Booklet]: Institut des Hautes Études Internationales* (Paris, 1946); Étienne Dennery, 'The Publications of the Centre d'Études de Politique Étrangère, Paris', *International Affairs* 18:1 (1939), pp. 103–5; Steven D. Korenblat, 'A School for the Republic? Cosmopolitans and Their Enemies at the Deutsche Hochschule Für Politik, 1920–1933', *Central European History* 39:3 (2006), pp. 394–430; Antonio Missiroli, *Die Deutsche Hochschule für Politik* (Sankt-Augustin, 1988); Katharina Rietzler, 'Philanthropy, Peace Research, and Revisionist Politics: Rockefeller and Carnegie Support for the Study of International Relations in Weimar Germany', *GHI Bulletin Supplement* 5 (2008), pp. 61–79; M. K. Grindrod, 'The Institut für Auswärtige Politik, Poststrasse 19, Hamburg', *International Affairs* 10:2 (1931), pp. 223–9; Pitman B. Potter, 'The Graduate Institute of International Studies, Geneva', *The American Journal of International Law* 62:3 (1968), pp. 740–2; Heinrich Pfusterschmid-Hardtenstein, *A Short History of the Diplomatic Academy of Vienna* (Vienna, 2008).

[60] Daniel Laqua, 'Activism in the "Students' League of Nations": International Student Politics and the Confédération Internationale des Étudiants,

as the Inter-Parliamentary Union or the International Arbitration League, preceded the advent of IR scholarship but provided valuable references and personal contacts beyond national and professional boundaries. The most important platform for exchange between IR thinkers and practitioners was the International Studies Conference, founded in 1928 as a joint venture of Austrian, British, French, German, Italian, and American researchers with logistical support from the League of Nations and its bodies for intellectual cooperation.[61]

The League of Nations did not only provide an infrastructure for collaborative research, it became a playground for the architects of IR. Several scholars worked for the League and its agencies, including Zimmern who served as deputy director of the Paris-based International Institute of Intellectual Cooperation, a predecessor of UNESCO, from 1926 to 1930.[62] Shotwell, himself a supporter of intellectual cooperation, used his network at the League to submit several draft treaties during the mid-1920s.[63] The League offered an ideal stage for these quasi-diplomats. Ideologically speaking, the work of the League reflected the universalist and rationalist beliefs underpinning early IR scholarship – the idea that the principles of international politics could be studied objectively.[64] Practically speaking, these

1919–1939', *The English Historical Review* 132:556 (2017), pp. 605–37; Daniel Laqua, 'Democratic Politics and the League of Nations: The Labour and Socialist International as a Protagonist of Interwar Internationalism', *Contemporary European History* 24:2 (2015), pp. 175–92; Harriet Hyman Alonso (ed.), *Women at The Hague: The International Congress of Women and Its Results* (Chicago, 2013); Helen McCarthy, *The British People and the League of Nations: Democracy, Citizenship and Internationalism, c.1918–1945* (Manchester, 2011).

[61] David Long, 'Who Killed the International Studies Conference?', *Review of International Studies* 32:4 (2006), pp. 603–22; Rietzler, 'Philanthropy, Peace Research, and Revisionist Politics'; Michael Riemens, 'International Academic Cooperation on International Relations in the Interwar Period: The International Studies Conference', *Review of International Studies* 37:2 (2011), pp. 911–28.

[62] League of Nations, 'The International Institute of Intellectual Cooperation, 1927', in League of Nations (ed.), *Brochures de Propagande, 1926–1927* (Paris, 1927), pp. 1–14.

[63] James T. Shotwell et al., 'Text of the Draft Treaty of Disarmament and Security', Foreign Policy Association Pamphlet No. 28 (New York, 1924). See Josephson, *James T. Shotwell and the Rise of Internationalism in America*, pp. 121–8.

[64] F. S. Northedge, *The League of Nations: Its Life and Times, 1920–1946* (Leicester, 1986); and F. S. Northedge, *International Intellectual Co-operation*

institutions substantiated early twentieth-century internationalism –
the growing cluster of societies, pressure groups, and organisations
that made up international society. Even before the First World War,
there were more than 600 international organisations devoted to the
sciences and humanities alone.[65] Throughout the interwar period,
these bodies continued to shape academic, social, and political life.[66]
As part of this environment, the history of IR feeds into the broader
historiography of internationalism.[67]

None of these endeavours would have been feasible without the commitment of wealthy philanthropists. The fortunes of the Rockefeller
Foundation and the Carnegie Endowment for International Peace played
a pivotal role in the spread of IR institutions across Europe and the United
States.[68] They sponsored professorships, libraries, conferences, and

within the League of Nations: Its Conceptual Basis and Lessons for the Present,
PhD thesis (LSE, London, 1953).

[65] P. H. Eijkman, *L'Internationalisme Scientifique* (The Hague, 1911); Madeleine
Herren, *Hintertüren zur Macht: Internationalismus und
modernisierungsorientierte Außenpolitik in Belgien, der Schweiz und den USA
1865–1914* (München, 2000).

[66] Christian Birebent, *Les relations internationales 1919–1939: La paix
impossible?* (Paris, 2009); Daniel Gorman, *The Emergence of International
Society in the 1920s* (Cambridge, 2012); Daniel Laqua (ed.), *Internationalism
Reconfigured: Transnational Ideas and Movements between the World Wars*
(New York, 2011).

[67] Glenda Sluga and Patricia Clavin, 'Introduction: Rethinking the History of
Internationalism', in Sluga and Clavin (eds.), *Internationalisms: A Twentieth-
Century History* (Cambridge, 2016), pp. 3–16; Glenda Sluga, *Internationalism
in the Age of Nationalism* (Philadelphia, 2013); Akira Iriye, *Cultural
Internationalism and World Order* (Baltimore, 1997); Akira Iriye, *Global
Community: The Role of International Organizations in the Making of the
Contemporary World* (Berkeley, 2004); Mark Mazower, *Governing the World:
The History of an Idea* (New York, 2012); Susan Pedersen, 'Back to the League
of Nations', *The American Historical Review* 112:4 (2007), pp. 1091–117;
Davide Rodogno et al. (eds.), *The League of Nations' Work on Social Issues:
Visions, Endeavours and Experiments* (New York, 2016); Oona A. Hathaway
and Scott J. Shapiro, *The Internationalists: How a Radical Plan to Outlaw War
Remade the World* (New York, 2017).

[68] Katharina Rietzler, 'Before the Cultural Cold Wars: American Philanthropy and
Cultural Diplomacy in the Interwar Years', *Historical Research*, 84:223 (2011),
pp. 148–64; Katharina Rietzler, 'Experts for Peace: Structures and Motivations
for Philanthropic Internationalism in the Interwar Years', in Daniel Laqua (ed.),
*Internationalism Reconfigured: Transnational Ideas and Movements between
the World Wars* (London, 2011), pp. 45–66; Katharina Rietzler, *American
Foundations and the 'Scientific Study' of International Relations in Europe,
1910–1940*, PhD thesis (UCL, London, 2009); Jens Wegener, *Creating an*

exchange programmes to the extent that one Rockefeller official commented on the margins of a 1936 memo: "I feel as though we had taken the whole world on our backs".[69] Support also came from religious internationalists, notably the Society of Friends (Quakers).[70] Most of the donors remained fairly withdrawn from actual research, but some openly pursued political goals with their endowments, such as the industrialist heir David Davies, the benefactor of the Aberystwyth chair, who wanted the professor to spread the spirit of the League of Nations.[71] By and large, however, the influence of wealthy philanthropists was more abstract and, in any event, their main impact was that the discipline existed tout court.

All of these factors made the formation of IR an exceedingly convoluted process and, as a result, make it a complicated history to write. There was not even agreement on what to call the new discipline – it went by labels such as 'International Affairs', 'International Studies', 'International Politics', 'Foreign Relations', 'Diplomacy' or, more openly partisan, 'Peace Studies' and 'League of Nations Studies'. Intellectual influences came from international law, history, economics, geography, and political theory, but also from anthropology, psychology, philosophy, sociology, and what was known as 'race studies'.[72] Locating IR among these disciplines is difficult since the

---

'*International Mind*'? *The Carnegie Endowment for International Peace in Europe, 1911–1940*, PhD thesis (EUI, Florence, 2015).

[69] Sydnor H. Walker on a memo by Tracy B. Kittredge, 15 February 1936, Folder 1009, Box 111, Series 100.S, RG 1.1, RR, Rockefeller Archive Center. Recipients included individuals and institutions in Austria, Britain, France, Germany, Hungary, Japan, the Netherlands, Norway, Poland, Sweden, Switzerland, the US, and Yugoslavia. The Rockefeller Foundation, *The Rockefeller Foundation Annual Report for 1933* (New York, 1933), pp. 6–13.

[70] For instance, the American Friends Service Committee funded the New England Institute of International Relations at Wellesley College, 22 June to 1 July 1933, Box 1, Folder 5, Russell Miller Subject Files, Fletcher School of Law and Diplomacy Records. See also, Cormac Shine, 'Papal Diplomacy by Proxy? Catholic Internationalism at the League of Nations' International Committee on Intellectual Cooperation, 1922–1939', *Journal of Ecclesiastical History* 69:4 (2018), pp. 785–805.

[71] David Davies to Sir John Williams, 5 December 1918, Lord Davies of Llandinam Papers, D4/1, U.C.W.

[72] On the relationship between International Law and IR, for example, see Martti Koskenniemi, *The Gentle Civilizer of Nations: The Rise and Fall of International Law 1870–1960* (Cambridge, 2001), pp. 440–5. On history, see Joe Maiolo, 'Systems and Boundaries in International History', *The International History Review* 40:3 (2018), pp. 576–91.

concept of 'social sciences' was itself still in the making.[73] IR also drew on nineteenth-century pacifism and non-academic work.[74] Ultimately, as one professor summarised, IR concerned "almost every sphere of human activity, material, intellectual, political".[75] National contexts, too, shaped the nature of IR, such as the legalism (or *juridisme*) in French internationalism, British imperial politics, or the educational reforms in Weimar Germany.[76] What united the architects of IR, however, was the relationship between the study and the practice of international politics. Unlike colleagues in neighbouring disciplines, the architects of IR were less interested in describing social phenomena from an outside perspective, but committed to changing the parameters of the international order. That relationship is the subject of this book.

A New History of International Relations

This book shows how a group of international thinkers built an academic discipline while simultaneously pursuing practical goals in politics and diplomacy. They came from a range of intellectual backgrounds and professions, including anything from French lawyers to British anthropologists, American journalists, and German diplomats. To capture this diverse group of individuals, the book refers to them as

---

[73] Roger E. Backhouse et al. (eds.), *A Historiography of the Modern Social Sciences* (Cambridge, 2014); Peter Wagner, *A History and Theory of the Social Sciences: Not All That Is Solid Melts into Air* (London, 2001).

[74] Carl Bouchard, *Le citoyen et l'ordre mondial (1914–1919): Le rêve d'une paix durable au lendemain de la Grande Guerre* (Paris, 2008); Martin Ceadel, *The Origins of War Prevention: The British Peace Movement and International Relations 1730–1854* (Oxford, 1996); Norman Ingram, *The Politics of Dissent: Pacifism in France 1919–1939* (Oxford, 1991).

[75] Philip Noel-Baker, 'Lecture Notes on International Relations', 1927–8 and 1928–9, Philip Noel-Baker Papers, NBKR 8/12/3.

[76] See, for example, James Cotton, 'Early International Relations Teaching and Teachers in Australia: Institutional and Disciplinary Origins', *Australian Journal of International Affairs* 67:1 (2013), pp. 71–97; Jacek Czaputowicz and Anna Wojciuk (eds.), *International Relations in Poland: 25 Years after the Transition to Democracy* (Cham, 2017); Gilles Le Béguec, *La république des avocats* (Paris, 2003); Jan Stöckmann, 'Studying the International, Serving the Nation: The Origins of International Relations (IR) Scholarship in Germany, 1912–33', *The International History Review* 38:5 (2016), pp. 1050–80; Marie-Claude Smouts, 'The Study of International Relations in France', *Millennium* 16:2 (1987), pp. 281–6; Vineet Thakur, Alexander E. Davis, and Peter Vale, 'Imperial Mission, "Scientific" Method: An Alternative Account of the Origins of IR', *Millennium: Journal of International Studies* 46:1 (2017), pp. 3–23.

the 'architects of IR' – a term deliberately fuzzy and open-ended to appreciate thinkers who operated across traditional professions and to acknowledge the fact that the first generation of IR scholars had of course not been trained in IR. Like architects, they *built* a set of institutions (departments, journals, libraries, etc.) and they *designed* plans for a new world order (draft treaties, petitions, political commentary, etc.). The metaphor also underlines the dynamic nature of IR as a discipline, which was anything but settled and well-defined during the first half of the twentieth century. Limiting the term IR to a small body of formalised scholarship neglects the various activities and publications on the margins of the new university discipline. In fact, it was the very search for a disciplinary purpose that characterised IR. To avoid overly narrow definitions, it is perhaps best described as a burgeoning academic field concerned with political questions of international life and their solutions.

Contrary to traditional historiography, this book emphasises their lives and careers, their political ambitions, and intellectual imperfections. It does not attempt to retrospectively fit their work into artificially coherent schools of thought or theories, notably the perennial camps of 'idealism' and 'realism', which turn out to be rather clumsy simplifications when held against the archival evidence. Nor does it claim that they succeeded in influencing the course of international politics. Instead, it portrays the formation of IR as a social process.[77] It shows how the architects of IR were driven by partisan and fluctuating interests, and sometimes by personal prestige, at the expense of a more consistent research agenda. Andrews, for example, claimed that the work she coordinated had a general character, but then specified that the goal was "meeting the practical situation after the war".[78] By re-integrating forgotten actors such as Andrews into the history of IR, this book challenges several long-standing assumptions in the field and offers a new account of the political constructions that continue to shape our world today.[79]

---

[77] On the "social formation" of IR, see David M. McCourt, 'The Inquiry and the Birth of International Relations, 1917–19', *Australian Journal of Politics and History* 63:3 (2017), pp. 394–405.

[78] Andrews, 'The Central Organisation for a Durable Peace', p. 17.

[79] On the long-term effects of inter-war work, see Stephen Wertheim, Ludovic Tournès, and Inderjeet Parmar, 'The Birth of Global Knowledge: Intellectual Networks in the World Crisis, 1919–1939', *International Politics* 55:6 (2018), pp. 727–33.

First, it traces the origins of the discipline from the start of the First World War, rather than 1919. The European conflict was the crucial impulse for IR pioneers to argue that foreign policy should be subject to democratic control and, consequently, to academic investigation.[80] This idea gave rise to a range of studies, such as Andrews' research series for the CODP. The resulting pamphlets, teaching guides, and books constituted the first coherent body of IR scholarship and disciplinary self-awareness. This body of work already covered most of the themes that would dominate interwar political thought, such as disarmament, sanctions, arbitration, tariffs, international governance, and colonial reform. By 1916, the London-based Council for the Study of International Relations had published the first textbook, intended "to encourage and assist the study of international relations".[81]

Second, the book extends beyond the Anglo-American world and takes into account a range of international authors and institutions who have been forgotten. The discipline was shaped by an eclectic group of professors, politicians, diplomats, journalists, and philanthropists from more than forty countries. Important research centres and university departments were located in Berlin, Geneva, Hamburg, London, New York, Oxford, Paris, and Vienna. Rather than operating in national silos, they collaborated extensively and built a transnational infrastructure through student exchanges, conferences, and professional associations. Although they used governmental institutions, particularly the League of Nations' bodies for intellectual cooperation, they did not act as national representatives but transcended official bureaucracies. These networks were not only instrumental in popularising the discipline, but they embodied the universalist idea that international politics could be studied from a global perspective.

Third, it recovers women and feminist political thought in early IR. Contrary to conventional disciplinary memory – that IR was created by a set of "founding fathers"[82] – female authors, educators, and

---

[80] Vernon Lee, 'The Democratic Principle and International Relations', in Charles Roden Buxton (ed.), *Towards a Lasting Settlement* (London, 1916), p. 209.

[81] It covered many of the constituent elements of IR, including historical, legal, economic, and imperial perspectives. A. L. Grant et al., *An Introduction to the Study of International Relations* (London, 1916), p. v.

[82] The Authors, 'Editors' Introduction', *Millennium* 38:3 (2010), p. 499. See also, Dennis Kavanagh, 'British Political Science in the Inter-War Years: The

politicians contributed to the formation of the discipline. Despite their marginalisation they began to enter male-dominated professions, such as Hungarian diplomat Rosika Schwimmer or the British journalist Helena Swanwick. An important platform for exchange was the Women's International League for Peace and Freedom, the nucleus of which was founded in 1915. Some of their work suggested a distinctly feminist approach to IR. For example, they argued that peace required democratic control of foreign policy which, in turn, required the inclusion of women in politics.[83] Others defended the essentialist claim that women were by nature more peaceful than men.[84] In any event, they contributed more substantially to the formation of IR than their professional ranks suggested.

Fourth, this book shows how IR pioneers combined the study and practice of international politics. They worked as governmental advisors, official delegates, and politicians, alongside their roles as teachers and researchers. For example, Alfred Zimmern advised the British delegation at the Paris Peace Conference. James Shotwell drafted parts of what became the Kellogg-Briand Pact. Philip Noel-Baker ran for parliament the same year that he assumed his professorship at the London School of Economics. This blend of academia and practice was not accidental. At a 1937 conference, the Austrian lawyer and diplomat Alfred Verdross proposed to form *ad hoc* committees of IR scholars in order to "exert an influence on the governments".[85] It was often hard to distinguish an author's academic claim from their political opinion since their roles usually blurred or even contradicted each other. IR was a mix of "science, pacifism, and politics", as the founder of the Deutsche Hochschule für Politik in

Emergence of the Founding Fathers', *The British Journal of Politics and International Relations* 5:4 (2003), pp. 594–613. For recent commentary, see Cai Wilkinson, *Continuing the 'all-male' theme at EISA*, 13 September 2015, available at http://duckofminerva.com/2015/09/continuing-the-all-male-theme-at-eisa.html#more-27819 [accessed 26 January 2017].

83 Margaret Hills, *Foreign Policy and the People* (London, 1917).
84 Agnes Maude Royden, 'War and the Women's Movement', in Goldsworthy Lowes Dickinson and Charles Roden Buxton (ed.), *Towards a Lasting Settlement* (London, 1915), pp. 133–45.
85 Alfred Verdross, in International Institute of Intellectual Cooperation (IIIC) (ed.), *Peaceful Change* (1938), p. 562; see also Victor Bulwer-Lytton, in International Institute of Intellectual Cooperation (IIIC) (ed.), *Peaceful Change* (1938), p. 580.

Berlin put it.[86] This blend was specific to the interwar generation. On occasion, professors have since advised (or become) politicians, with Henry Kissinger as the most prominent example, but the interwar symbiosis between academia and diplomacy was never achieved again.

Finally, it shows that early IR scholarship was inspired by practical motives rather than theoretical debate. The vast majority of early IR scholarship focused on issues of immediate political significance which were rarely approached with any analytical rigour, let alone a consistent methodological apparatus. This style of research often resulted in ambiguous and inconsistent positions. Helena Swanwick, for example, acknowledged that her work was derived "from experience, not from abstract theory".[87] Alfred Zimmern declared himself a supporter of the League of Nations, only to admit in the next sentence that this could "mean almost anything".[88] Such statements not only refute the long-standing myth of a 'great debate' between so-called 'idealist' and 'realist' theoreticians. They beg the question whether there was any serious attempt at devising theory at all.

Rather than in the minds of male Anglo-American 'idealists', the book concludes, the formation of IR took shape at the intersection of academia and diplomacy, involving a range of international men and women who worked for peace both in education and in practice. Growing out of wartime networks, the discipline was formally established at universities and research centres during the 1920s. New professorships, departments, and conferences continued to flourish during the interwar period, benefitting significantly from the support of wealthy philanthropists. The discipline rapidly gained attention among both the public and private sectors. By the 1930s, IR had become "the master-problem" of the time, as Toynbee put it.[89] Over the next years, however, the crises in Manchuria, Abyssinia, and Czechoslovakia began to complicate the hopes for a world based on peaceful cooperation, before eventually, the aggressive expansionism of Nazi Germany wrecked the interwar study of IR. What had gone wrong? Why did students of IR not have answers to recurring conflict,

---

[86] Ernst Jäckh, *Die Politik Deutschlands im Völkerbund* (Geneva, 1932), p. 18.

[87] Helena Swanwick, *Pooled Security: What Does It Mean?* (London, 1934), p. 5.

[88] Alfred Zimmern, 'British Foreign Policy since the War', 1933[?], Alfred Zimmern Papers, Box 140.

[89] Arnold Toynbee to G. G. Kullmann, 3 May 1934, Arnold Toynbee Papers, Box 117.

let alone effective policies against it? What, if anything, did the architects of IR contribute to the intellectual and practical struggle for peace?

To answer these questions, the book is arranged in six chapters, which follow a chronological order, while also addressing different themes. The first chapter traces the origins of IR during the First World War through the lens of educators, politicians, and pressure groups who argued that foreign policy should be subject to democratic control and scientific investigation. The second chapter surveys the genesis of the discipline during the 1920s at a range of universities as well as non-academic institutions in Europe and the United States. The third chapter shows how IR benefitted from international cooperation, particularly from the League of Nations' bodies for intellectual cooperation, and how the ethos of a universal scientific community inspired the study of IR. The fourth chapter illustrates how IR professors tried to act as diplomats and politicians, notably in the making of 1920s security treaties. The fifth chapter zooms in on one of the most important policy debates of the 1930s – the concept of international sanctions known as 'collective security' – and it reveals how ambiguously many IR scholars treated the topic in and outside the classroom. Finally, the sixth chapter examines how Nazi Germany impacted IR scholarship at home and abroad, and how research in the field came to a halt within the first year of the Second World War. The conclusion contextualises the architects of IR within the broader disciplinary history, and critiques the analytical categories employed by IR scholars more generally.

This study is based on a wide range of primary sources. The architects of IR left an enormous amount of published material, both in academic books and journals as well as in popular pamphlets and newspapers that circulated in Europe and the United States. Their published record is complemented by a wealth of correspondence, diaries, and memoranda, now stored in collections of private papers, such as those of Fannie Fern Andrews at Harvard, Albrecht Mendelssohn Bartholdy in Berlin, or Alfred Zimmern at Oxford. Many universities have kept records of their departments and chairs, including the Graduate Institute in Geneva and the Konsularakademie in Vienna. Further evidence on the institutional setting of early IR is recorded in the archives of non-governmental institutions, such as the Rockefeller Foundation in New York or the Women's League of

International Peace and Freedom in London. Finally, governmental archives, such as the Political Archive of the German Foreign Office in Berlin or the records of the League of Nations in Geneva, demonstrate the links between academia and official policy.

Consequently, this is primarily a work of transnational and intellectual history, but it draws on traditional political history, too, and it intervenes in debates shaped by political scientists and IR specialists. To accommodate these diverse connections, the methodological approach of this study is fairly inclusive and based on well-established historiographical practice.[90] The plan is, basically, to examine individuals and institutions from within and beyond the familiar IR canon and to contrast their activities with the perceived wisdom in disciplinary historiography. Working with archival sources helps to gain a more immediate understanding of contemporary life, but it bears the risk of taking actors at face value and of replicating contemporary biases (Eurocentrism, elitism, etc.). Whenever there are doubts about the intentions of historical actors, the book exposes their ambiguity and vagueness rather than retrofitting them into anachronistic categories. It is significant, for example, that, contrary to recent claims, interwar IR scholars did have a notion of the term 'idealism' and that they mostly rejected it. That does not imply, however, that 'idealism' is necessarily a useful category to refer to entire groups of individuals. Things were more complicated.

No book can tell the entire story. There were significant contributions to the formation of IR that are outside the scope of this study, either chronologically, geographically, or thematically. It is true, for example, that there were pathbreaking publications prior to 1914, such as Paul Reinsch's *World Politics at the End of the Nineteenth Century* (1900) or William Archer's *The Great Analysis: A Plea for a Rational World Order* (1912). But they were not integrated into the main body of early IR scholarship. It is also true that non-Western authors wrote on international affairs, such as the Chinese foreign

---

[90] C. A. Bayly et al., '*AHR* Conversation: On Transnational History', *American Historical Review* 111:5 (2006), pp. 1441–64; Patricia Clavin, 'Time, Manner, Place: Writing Modern European History in Global, Transnational and International Contexts', *European History Quarterly* 40:4 (2010), pp. 624–40; Zara Steiner, 'On Writing International History: Chaps, Maps and Much More', *International Affairs* 73:3 (1997), pp. 531–46.

Woodrow Wilson Chair at Aberystwyth, Wales.[9] By regarding university professorships as definite indicators of disciplinary formation, however,
these accounts underestimate the intellectual and practical traditions that
gave rise to the study of IR. In particular, the conventional story erroneously
portrays IR scholars as followers of the League of Nations, whereas their
plans actually preceded its creation. Dating the origins of IR to 1919 also
ignores the extensive network of scholars, politicians, and philanthropists
who enabled the rapid institutional development at the end of the war.
Finally, the traditional narrative mistakenly frames the origins of IR as an
interwar school of 'idealism' and accuses the founders of naïve trust in
international cooperation, whereas in fact the architects of IR were influ-
enced first and foremost by the origins of war, not by the ideals of peace.

The first efforts at studying war and peace, in a reasonably coherent
and academic manner, emerged from an international network of liberal
intellectuals and pressure groups in 1914. Many of them were not formally academics, such as British author Leonard Woolf or the members
of the Central Organisation for a Durable Peace, an alliance of war critics
formed in 1915 in The Hague. In a survey of wartime writings on peace,
Carl Bouchard found that only 34 out of 139 authors held academic
positions, while the majority worked as journalists, bankers, lawyers, or
in other professions.[10] Women in particular used non-academic platforms since they were largely excluded from senior university positions.
Nonetheless they emphasised the importance of education for preventing
war because "educated persons [would not] kill each other", as German
feminist-pacifist Lida Gustava Heymann put it.[11] Many of these actors
pursued both academic research and political goals, though some were
explicitly devoted to education, such as the Council for the Study of
International Relations, founded in 1915 in London. In a few cases,
universities showed interest in the study of IR more concretely, although
wartime restrictions prevented them from installing new professorships
or departments. As early as September 1914, the Master of Balliol
College, Arthur Lionel Smith, recognised the debate about the First
World War as "a splendid educational opportunity".[12]

[9] P. A. Reynolds, *An Introduction to International Relations* (London, 1971), p. v.
[10] Carl Bouchard, *Le citoyen et l'ordre mondial (1914–1919): Le rêve d'une paix durable au lendemain de la Grande Guerre* (Paris, 2008).
[11] Heymann, 'What Women Say about the War', p. 207.
[12] Arthur L. Smith to E. D. Morel, 5 September 1914, E. D. Morel Papers, MOREL/F6/2.

What, then, inspired people such as Toynbee to start working on international relations? There were multiple motives, often overlapping, but three main themes stand out. The first idea, pioneered by Norman Angell in his 1910 book *The Great Illusion*, was that the world had become so economically intertwined that it was no longer profitable to wage war, even for the victorious side.[13] To understand this new world in all its complexities, the British economist and 'Angellite' J. A. Hobson argued, one would have to study international relations.[14] A second argument was that the Great War had been caused by a flawed system of diplomacy and that foreign policy should be subject to democratic control rather than the secretive dealings of a small elite. This strand of thought was vocally advocated by a transnational campaign of politicians and scholars, including German socialist Eduard Bernstein and British historian Alfred Zimmern.[15] Finally, the war inspired debates on a permanent intergovernmental organisation, an idea that attracted countless studies and pamphlets, and which fed into the creation of the League of Nations. In short, early IR was inspired by globalisation, democracy, and international order. All three motives were based on questions about how the political world worked, but also, crucially, about how it should work.

This chapter traces the origins of IR scholarship from the outbreak of the First World War to the making of the peace. It follows a set of pioneering thinkers and pressure groups across Europe and the United States to demonstrate both the intellectual roots and the practical infrastructure of the emerging discipline. The chapter begins by reviewing the state of international affairs on the eve of the war which inspired a set of writings on economic interdependence and world order. The second section shows how the conflict itself prompted authors to reflect on the causes of war and the conditions for peace. The third section examines the intellectual preparation of the post-war order within an emerging community of IR experts. The final section

---

[13] Norman Angell, *The Great Illusion: A Study of the Relation of Military Power in Nations to Their Economic and Social Advantage* (London, 1910).

[14] J. A. Hobson, 'The Open Door', in G. Lowes Dickinson (ed.), *Towards a Lasting Settlement* (London, 1915); David Long, *J. A. Hobson's Approach to International Relations: An Exposition and Critique*, PhD thesis, LSE (London, 1991), p. 240.

[15] Jan Stöckmann, 'The First World War and the Democratic Control of Foreign Policy', *Past & Present* 249:1 (2020), pp. 121–66.

reveals how the founders of IR contributed as government advisors to the Paris Peace Conference and, simultaneously, laid the institutional foundations of the discipline. As a result, this chapter concludes, the origins of IR were deeply intertwined with wartime events and inspired by the making, not just interpreting, of international politics.

The World in July 1914

Writings on international affairs existed, there is no doubt, long before the twentieth century.[16] But there is little value in citing Thucydides, Machiavelli, the Abbé de Saint-Pierre, Immanuel Kant, or other 'great' thinkers, if their works share no characteristics with what we now call IR. Most philosophers, historians, and geographers who wrote on international affairs before the twentieth century did so from their own isolated perspectives. They were not integrated into a coherent academic community devoted to a common set of questions. Nor did they establish the institutional framework necessary to organise an academic discipline. This does not imply, of course, that their work was not influential. On the contrary, there were important forerunners to modern IR scholarship, both intellectual pioneers, such as the political scientist John. W. Burgess, and institutional models, such as the pacifist movement or the Inter-Parliamentary Union.[17] But pre-twentieth-century authors explored only patches of the terrain that IR scholarship covered during the interwar period. They barely constituted a

---

[16] Gilberte Derocque, *Le Projet de Paix Perpétuelle de l'Abbé de Saint-Pierre comparé au Pacte de la Société des Nations* (Paris, 1929); Lucian M. Ashworth, *A History of International Thought* (New York, 2014); Edward Keene, *International Political Thought: An Historical Introduction* (Cambridge, 2005); Torbjøn L. Knutsen, *A History of International Relations Theory* (Manchester, 2020).

[17] Burgess was the key figure in setting up the Faculty of Political Science at Columbia University. Like later IR pioneers, Burgess worked across the fields of history, political science, and law, and he drew on a network of "men of affairs from the world at large". John Burgess, 'Founding of the Faculty of Political Science' [on the occasion of the 50th anniversary], 1930, Box 13, John Burgess Papers. On the pacifist movement, see Martin Ceadel, *The Origins of War Prevention: The British Peace Movement and International Relations 1730–1854* (Oxford, 1996); Sandi E. Cooper, 'Pacifism in France, 1889–1914: International Peace as a Human Right', *French Historical Studies* 17:2 (1991), pp. 359–86.

scholarly community and they established none of the institutional
pillars of an academic discipline.

What we are really looking for in determining the origins of IR as an
academic discipline, then, is a minimum level of academic style and
coherent scholarship, fostered by transnational exchange and notice-
ably distinct from other fields. This moment occurred at some point
during the first two decades of the twentieth century, but it can most
plausibly be pinned down to 1914, just after the outbreak of the Great
War. It was at this point that authors, politicians, and activists began
to perceive their work on international politics as a common field.
They now collaborated internationally, published in academic style,
gathered at conferences and, perhaps most obviously, suggested that
the subject should be taught at schools and universities. This was the
moment when they began to regard their work as a new field, as
contemporary documents show.[18]

In order to understand the effect of the First World War on international political thought, it is important to remember the state of affairs
in July 1914 – a moment that economic historians have described as the
first peak of globalisation.[19] It was a time of unprecedented levels of
international trade and cultural exchange, propelled by nineteenth-
century industrialism, imperialism, and technological change.
Platforms for political conversation, such as the Inter-Parliamentary
Union or the Anglo-German Understanding Conference, were flourish-
ing.[20] July 1914 was the closest the world had ever been to a global
society. At the same time, this meant that local shocks could have wide-
ranging consequences, not just through military alliances but because
national economies were increasingly dependent on each other.

---

[18] Social Science Research Council, 'Report of the Director of the Program of
Research in International Relations for the Year 1931', 'confidential', 2 January
1932, James T. Shotwell Papers, Box 136.
[19] See, for example, Kevin H. O'Rourke and Jeffrey G. Williamson, 'When Did
Globalisation Begin? ', *European Review of Economic History* 6 (2002),
pp. 23–50.
[20] Arthur Deerin Call, 'Parliament of Man? A Sketch of the Interparliamentary
Union', *World Affairs* 99:4 (1936), pp. 214–20; Martin Albers, 'Between the
Crisis of Democracy and World Parliament: The Development of the Inter-
Parliamentary Union in the 1920s', *Journal of Global History* 7 (2012),
pp. 189–209; British Joint Committee, *Report of the Proceedings of the
Anglo-German Understanding Conference, London, 1912* (London, 1913).

The most prominent analyst of economic interdependence was the British journalist Norman Angell, best known for his influential book *The Great Illusion* (1910). Having lived abroad from a young age, Angell became Paris editor of the *Daily Mail* in 1905 and began to form his ideas, leading to a small book that was first published in 1909 under the title *Europe's Optical Illusion*. Angell argued that the web of international economic activity had made it impossible for any government to gain a material advantage by waging war. Conquering a foreign country would harm the opponent's economic output, trade, and ability to pay creditors. Ultimately, Angell argued, the victorious country would suffer from the weakening of the foreign economy. That insight was fundamentally at odds with the orthodox view – the 'great illusion' – that military conquest brought material advantage.[21] Angell therefore suggested that the old warlike approach be replaced by "a policy of some kind" to regulate the use of force, if not to rule it out entirely.[22]

His idea rapidly gained influence with politicians and intellectuals but also spread among the general public via so-called Norman Angell societies. In 1912, Angell's work caught the attention of the industrialist Richard Garton who set up a foundation "to promote the study of International Polity", and helped to publish the journal *War and Peace*.[23] The journal featured articles on current diplomatic affairs by prominent international authors, such as German economist Lujo Brentano and British sociologist Leonard Hobhouse. The intention of *War and Peace* was, according to the editors, to discuss international relations from a "strictly non-party" point of view.[24] And indeed the journal even ran critical articles, such as 'The Fallacy of Norman Angellism'.[25]

The authors publishing in *War and Peace* soon formed a nucleus of experts on international relations, including the journalist H. N. Brailsford,

---

[21] Angell, *The Great Illusion*, p. vii.

[22] Norman Angell, 'Problems and Lessons of the War', in George H. Blakeslee (ed.), *The Problems and Lessons of the War* (New York, 1916), p. 8.

[23] See notes on the cover of *War and Peace* 1:1 (1913). It was later known as *The International Review* and, from 1917, as *Nation Supplement: A Journal of International Politics and a League of Nations*. M. Manus to Fannie Fern Andrews, 24 April 1917, Fannie Fern Andrews Papers, Box 43, Folder 475.

[24] See notes on the cover of *War and Peace* 1:1 (1913).

[25] A. Rifleman, 'The Fallacy of Norman Angellism', *War and Peace* 1:4 (1914), p. 103.

the Liberal politician Arthur Ponsonby, and the political theorist Goldsworthy Lowes Dickinson. The group also maintained relationships with international authors, such as the German socialist politician Eduard Bernstein or the French law professor Pierre Aubry. Not all of them were 'Angellites', as enthusiasts of *The Great Illusion* became known. Nor were 'Angellites' the only authors writing in the field. Many future IR experts were still working in related disciplines, or simply trying to survive the war, such as the German economist Moritz Julius Bonn who had embarked on a research visit to the United States just before the outbreak of hostilities in July 1914.[26] Gradually, over the course of the war, their publications and correspondence gave rise to a coherent discourse.

One of the groups associated with *War and Peace* was the Association (later renamed the Civil Union) for the Right Understanding of International Interests. Its director, the businesswoman M. Talmadge, offered study circles to discuss problems raised by Angell's work.[27] The Universities of Cambridge and Manchester had "War and Peace Societies". There were "International Polity Clubs" in Glasgow, Leeds, and York.[28] Reading circles and study groups mushroomed across Britain. All of these projects implied that it was possible to talk about international politics from a rational point of view, and that ordinary people could study a subject traditionally reserved for aristocratic diplomats. In short, they saw international relations as a science rather than an art. Despite the increasing complexity of the world – or precisely because of it – people now argued that it was important to really understand what was going on.

Against the odds of contemporary gender stereotypes, women worked on international politics from the outset.[29] One of the most ambitious female pioneers of IR was the German teacher and peace activist Anna B. Eckstein who toured Europe and the United States to

---

[26] Moritz Julius Bonn, *Musste es sein?* (Munich, 1919); Patricia Clavin, 'A "Wandering Scholar" in Britain and the USA, 1933–1945: The Life and Work of Moritz Bonn', in Anthony Grenville (ed.), *Refugees from the Third Reich in Britain* (New York, 2003), pp. 27–42.

[27] Advertisement by The Association for the Right Understanding of International Interests in *War and Peace* 1:3 (1913), p. 83.

[28] 'The International Polity Movement', *War and Peace* 1:3 (1913), p. 84.

[29] Emily G. Balch, '"The Wisconsin Plan": A Conference of Neutrals for Continuous Mediation', in George H. Blakeslee (ed.), *The Problems and Lessons of the War* (New York, 1916), p. 244.

lecture on arbitration since the early 1910s.[30] Inspired by Kantian philosophy and her family's experience of the Franco-Prussian war, Eckstein became one of the most persevering peace activists during the first half of the twentieth century. After moving to Boston in the 1890s, Eckstein began to write on international affairs and from 1902 she published in journals such as *Die Friedens-Warte*. She was well connected among the burgeoning American pacifist movement as well as religious internationalists, such as the British Quaker Joseph Allen Baker.[31] Having devised the first version of her manifesto in 1907, she then collaborated with Fannie Fern Andrews to turn the document into an international treaty for security and arbitration, which they called 'world petition' (*Weltpetition*).[32] It specified that territorial changes required the consent of the local population and that disputes were to be submitted to an arbitration court.[33] Eckstein built an impressive transnational network and in 1913 she was nominated for the Nobel Peace Prize.[34] At the end of the First World War, her world petition was re-published along with a preface by the international lawyer Theodor Niemeyer who praised it as a commendable way to promote the ideals of the League of Nations.[35] Niemeyer was not the only man to acknowledge the work of women in the field. In September 1914, the British author and politician E. D. Morel told the feminist-pacifist preacher Agnes Maude Royden that "[t]here is no reason why the intelligence of women should be less able to cope with questions of foreign policy than the intelligence of men".[36]

Early twentieth-century experiences of international life raised questions about the political and economic forces that decided over war and peace. These questions, in turn, inspired more detailed writings on international governance, such as Angell's *Foundations of*

[30] For instance, Lecture 'Pour l'Arbitrage Internationale', 18 April 1912, Anna B. Eckstein Papers, Box 2.

[31] Karl Eberhard Sperl, *Miss Eckstein und ihr Peace on Earth* (Meeder, 2018).

[32] Rüdiger Spenlen, *Anna B. Eckstein: Coburger Pazifistin und Vordernkerin für den Völkerbund* (Coburg, 1985).

[33] Anna B. Eckstein, *Weltpetition zur Verhütung des Krieges zwischen den Staaten*, 28 April 1911, Anna B. Eckstein Papers, Box 2.

[34] 'Nomination Database', available at www.nobelprize.org/nomination/archive/list.php [accessed 25 July 2018].

[35] Anna B. Eckstein, *Staatenschutzvertrag zur Sicherung des Weltfriedens* (Munich, 1919).

[36] E. D. Morel to Agnes Maude Royden, 9 September 1914, E. D. Morel Papers, MOREL/F6/2.

International Polity (1914). In response to the same question, the Scottish writer William Archer offered an optimistic view in his 1912 book *The Great Analysis*, published anonymously but accompanied by a powerful preface by Gilbert Murray. Archer proposed a thought experiment to show that governing the world did not have to be a utopian dream: He described how social life could be organised on an imaginary globule of the size of Yorkshire. Governing the actual globe, he then argued, was essentially the same challenge, just on a different scale. By using people's combined intellectual power in a 'great analysis', they could master the problem of world order.[37] Archer's book was a manifesto for using reason in politics. Its goal was, as Murray summarised, "to find out by organised knowledge what is good for society as a whole".[38]

It is important at this stage to emphasise the normative component in those works. Authors such as Angell and Archer were interested in how the world *ought* to be organised, not just how it *was* organised. They acknowledged the potential conflict between those two modes of inquiry but denied that they were incompatible. In a chapter on 'moral factors', Angell criticised the widespread assumption that reason had no effect on the course of international affairs.[39] He called this the "imaginary gulf between … idealism and reason".[40] These two motives, the pursuit of the good and the search for a more rational world order, became core features of the emerging discipline of IR. Later, in the 1930s, so-called 'realist' IR scholars claimed that the founders of IR had been entirely unaware and naïve about the relationship between morality and power. A closer look at the original documents, however, reveals that many authors were torn between their "moral sense" and "objective standards", rather than being in denial of either.[41]

The outbreak of war in July 1914 dramatically changed the picture. It undermined the Angellian logic that warfare would become

[37] William Archer, *The Great Analysis* (New York, 1912), pp. 37–41.
[38] Gilbert Murray, 'Preface', in William Archer, *The Great Analysis* (New York, 1912), p. vii.
[39] Norman Angell, *The Foundations of International Polity* (London, 1914), p. 49.
[40] Ibid., p. xii.
[41] UDC, 'Why Should Democracy Control Foreign Policy?', *Union of Democratic Control Leaflet* No. 1 (London, 1914); and Henry N. Brailsford, 'The Organisation of Peace', in G. Lowes Dickinson (ed.), *Towards a Lasting Settlement* (London, 1915), p. 159.

unattractive because of economic interdependence.[42] The British government did not share Toynbee's concern that "[i]f we beat Germany our own mills and factories will have been at a standstill".[43] Military strategy was more urgent than long-term economic performance or the concerns of dissenting political commentators, many of whom saw the war as both immoral *and* unreasonable.[44] Within a few weeks, the old continent plunged into barbaric warfare which cost millions of lives, wiped out four empires, and reshuffled the international order. Citizens across the globe witnessed unprecedented levels of violence and destruction. International trade collapsed, national borders were redrawn, and political regimes were replaced. The Great War, as it was known then, was a watershed moment in the way foreign affairs were handled, and thought about. It was a "deluge", to quote Adam Tooze.[45] For the architects of IR, the war was a crucial experience, as Alfred Zimmern reflected:

The reason for this remarkable change of outlook, this rapid stride forward in political thinking, this revolution in the estimate of what was both practicable and desirable, is to be found in the war.[46]

Above all, the war revealed the inability of 'old diplomacy' to preserve peace. It put an end to the Concert of Europe logic, which had shaped international relations for almost a century since the Congress of Vienna. The congress system had been based on a complex network of bi-lateral and multi-lateral treaties, some open and others secret, which were supposed to maintain a European 'balance of power', interpreted in terms of military and territorial strength.[47] Although the congress system had kept nineteenth-century Europe relatively peaceful, war had still been a normal mode of diplomacy. As Prussian military theorist Carl von Clausewitz famously put it, war

---

[42] For an alternative interpretation see Erik Gartzke and Yonatan Lupu, 'Trading on Preconceptions: Why World War I Was Not a Failure of Economic Interdependence', *International Security* 36:4 (2012), pp. 115–50.
[43] Toynbee, *Nationality and the War*, p. 4.   [44] See, for instance, ibid., p. 7.
[45] Adam Tooze, *The Deluge: The Great War and the Remaking of Global Order* (New York, 2014).
[46] Alfred Zimmern, *The League of Nations and the Rule of Law, 1918–1935* (London, 1936), p. 137.
[47] Beatrice de Graaf, Ido de Haan, and Brian Vick (eds.), *Securing Europe after Napoleon: 1815 and the New European Security Culture* (Cambridge, 2019).

was just the "continuation of politics by other means".[48] The First
World War, with casualties rapidly in the hundreds of thousands on
the Western front alone, dramatically questioned that approach.

The war was essential to the formation of IR because its effects were
more wide-ranging than in previous conflicts. Trench warfare in
Western Europe was only the most spectacular pinnacle of the global
experience of war.[49] The consequences were felt by soldiers, families,
and businesses, whether they were politically interested or not. Many
academics, too, were drawn into the war effort and experienced the
war first-hand, such as Philip Noel-Baker who served with ambulance
units in France or Charles Webster who was in the Army Service
Corps.[50] For David Mitrany, who himself enlisted with the British
armed forces, the war was a great shock to the international system
and it motivated him to become engaged in foreign policy instead of
pursuing a career in social work.[51] Several institutions for the study of
IR were dedicated to the victims of the Great War. David Davies, the
benefactor of the IR chair in Aberystwyth, made his endowment in
memory of students killed in the war.[52] Similarly, the co-founder and
president of the Deutsche Hochschule für Politik (DHfP) in Berlin,
Ernst Jäckh, declared that he "founded the Hochschule in memory of
his only son who fell in France as a young boy".[53] It is hard to
overestimate the impact of the Great War on contemporary political
thinkers. In addition to that, its disastrous consequences for the population generated an audience for the study of IR. Citizens no longer
took governmental foreign policy for granted.

Women in particular referenced the universal experience of human
suffering as a reason to study the problems of war and peace.
Swanwick's critique of 'Prussianism' was based precisely on that

---

[48] Carl von Clausewitz, *On War*, transl. and ed. by Michael Howard and Peter
   Paret (Princeton, 1987 [1832]) p. 87.
[49] Jay Winter, *The Experience of World War I* (London, 1988).
[50] David Howell, 'Baker, Philip John Noel-, Baron Noel-Baker', in *Oxford
   Dictionary of National Biography* (Oxford, 2004); G. N. Clark, 'Webster, Sir
   Charles Kingsley', in *Oxford Dictionary of National Biography* (Oxford, 2004).
[51] David Mitrany, *The Functional Theory of Politics* (London, 1975), pp. 4–5.
[52] E. L. Ellis, *The University College Wales, Aberystwyth, 1872–1972*
   (Aberystwyth, 1972), p. 188.
[53] Speech by Ernst Jäckh, delivered at the International Studies Conference,
   London, 1 June 1933, IIIC Records, Box 317, Folder 3.

conviction.[54] Women looked after widows and orphans, treated the wounded, cared for refugees and POWs, all the while replacing men in their regular jobs to earn a sufficient income for the household. In short, British suffragist-pacifist Agnes Maude Royden summarised, "women know the sufferings of war without its glory".[55] In order to address their concerns, they formed international groups of likeminded women who taught and wrote on international affairs. The most influential one of these groups, the Women's International League for Peace and Freedom (WILFP), was founded on the demand to stop the war and to work for a negotiated peace.[56] Their work was largely overlooked by men in positions of power, but it did resonate with a few male scholars. For example, the French economist Edgard Milhaud cited a woman who had lost four of her five sons in the war as a reason to study the organisation of peace.[57] Whether taking gender roles into account or not, there is no doubt that the First World War had an enormous influence on the origins of IR.

Understanding the Causes of War

Why did war break out in July 1914? This was the most immediate question for the architects of IR, who like the general public, were shocked by the horrors of the conflict as well as by the inability of their governments to return to peaceful negotiations. Unsurprisingly, most authors devoted at least some time to this question. One of the first studies was H. N. Brailsford's *The Origins of the Great War* (1914) in which the British journalist criticised the system of secret treaties and military rivalry.[58] He also outlined a set of peace terms, including general disarmament and the use of plebiscites to settle border disputes. Other notable works included Paul Fauchille's document collection *La guerre de 1914* (1916), Otto Hoetzsch's collection of

---

[54] Helena Swanwick, *Women and the War* (London, 1915), p. 5.

[55] Agnes Maude Royden, 'War and the Woman's Movement', in G. L. Dickinson and C. R. Buxton (eds.), *Towards a Lasting Settlement* (London, 1915), p. 134.

[56] WILPF, *Women's International League for Peace and Freedom, 1915–1938: A Venture in Internationalism* (Geneva, 1938), p. 6. See David S. Patterson, *The Search for a Negotiated Peace: Women's Activism and Citizen Diplomacy in World War I* (New York, 2008).

[57] Edgard Milhaud, *Plus jamais! L'organisation de la paix, le pacte de la Société des nations, les amendements nécessaires* (Geneva, 1919), p. i.

[58] H. N. Brailsford, *The Origins of the Great War* (London, 1914).

newspaper articles in *Der Krieg und die Große Politik* (1917), and
Helena Swanwick's essay *Women and War* (1915). They wrote from
different angles and employed different styles but essentially pursued
the same research goal – to understand, by rational inquiry, the causes
and patterns of the current war. In doing so, they associated themselves
with an emerging network of scholars, politicians, journalists, activists,
and philanthropists who subsequently set up the first IR institutions. In
other words, the war jump-started the development of IR as a new
academic field.

The most striking argument in this emerging literature was that the
war had been caused by a flawed system of international politics. Until
1914, the critics argued, foreign policy had been in the hands of governments unaccountable to parliamentary control. International treaties
had been kept secret and diplomatic services had recruited their officials
from a small elite. Virtually all decision-makers were white men. The
ruling class regarded war as a "pleasure party" (*Lustpartie*), to use
Immanuel Kant's words.[59] While the lack of democratic control was
obvious in the case of Germany, none of the belligerent governments
was particularly open for dissent either. Nor did the dissenters stand
much of a chance. The British, for example, imprisoned E. D. Morel for
sending pamphlets to French writer Romain Rolland in neutral
Switzerland. By loosely referring to France and Britain as "the democracies", historians have neglected the effects of female disenfranchise-
ment, censorship, and the intimidation of the opposition.[60]

If decisions on war and peace were subject to democratic control, so
contemporary IR scholars argued, governments would not enter into
violent conflict as easily as they did in July 1914. Instead of putting the
blame on any particular government, the advocates of democratic
control condemned the "manner in which foreign affairs are conducted".[61] They criticised the lack of parliamentary oversight, the
secrecy of treaties and agreements, the elitist composition of foreign
services, and, crucially, the lack of public education in foreign affairs.
Their programme was related to, but not identical with the Wilsonian

[59] Immanuel Kant, *Zum ewigen Frieden. Ein philosophischer Entwurf* (Leipzig, 1795), p. 206.
[60] Dan Reiter and Allan C. Stam, *Democracies at War* (Princeton, 2002), 124; Bouchard, *Le citoyen et l'ordre mondial (1914–1919)*, p. 11.
[61] Arthur Ponsonby, 'Parliament and Foreign Policy', UDC Pamphlet No. 5 (1915), p. 1.

demand for 'open covenants, openly arrived at'. Openness was a necessary requirement, but even if government documents were available to the public, people needed to be able to understand them and exercise control over foreign policy decisions. "Ignorance, that is the origin of wars", as Dickinson put it.[62] The goal therefore was to study international relations as comprehensively as possible.

Members of this campaign came from a variety of backgrounds, including socialist and liberal politicians, pacifists, suffragists, as well as professors of international law and related disciplines. Among the supporters were Fannie Fern Andrews, Eduard Bernstein, French lawyer Lucien Le Foyer, Norwegian internationalist Christian Lous Lange, British liberal politician Arthur Ponsonby, as well as academics such as Dickinson, Walther Schücking, and Alfred Zimmern. Gilbert Murray was sympathetic, too, and signed a petition against entering the war (although he later regretted it).[63] The campaigners were organised in numerous national and international pressure groups, including socialist parties as well as pacifist and feminist organisations. It is important, however, not to buy too much into these labels. To Belgian lawyer Henri La Fontaine, for example, pacifism did not mean to necessarily reject the use of force but merely to submit it to international law.[64] Unlike bureaucratic elites or national representatives, they tended to adopt policies independent of their own national background.[65] Although there was no formal hierarchy, many were associated with the Central Organisation for a Durable Peace (CODP) which served as a kind of umbrella institution.[66]

In April 1915, the CODP held an international conference in The Hague with delegates from ten countries, both neutral and belligerent.[67] It was hosted by the Dutch liberal politician Hendrik Coenraad Dresselhuijs and the pacifist lawyer Benjamin de Jong van Beek en Donk. Among the participants were Dickinson and Andrews as well as

---

[62] G. Lowes Dickinson, *After the War* (London, 1915), p. 5.
[63] Gilbert Murray, *The League of Nations Movement: Some Recollections of the Early Days* (London, 1955), p. 3.
[64] Henri La Fontaine, 'On What Principles Is the Society of States to Be Founded?', *The Annals of the American Academy of Political and Social Science* 72 (1917), p. 89.
[65] Carl Bouchard, 'Des citoyens français à la recherche de la paix durable (1914–1919)', *Guerres mondiales et conflits contemporaines* 222:2 (2006), p. 71.
[66] Manifesto, 1915, CODP Records, Box 1.
[67] CODP, *A Durable Peace: Official Commentary on the Minimum-Program* (The Hague, 1915).

the German pacifists Ludwig Quidde and Walther Schücking. By March 1916, the CODP had close to 200 members, including eminent scholars and pacifists, such as Jane Addams, Emily Greene Balch, Albert Einstein, Henri La Fontaine, J. A. Hobson, Christian Lous Lange, Paul Otlet, Charles M. Trevelyan, and Hans Wehberg.[68] Several pioneers of IR scholarship, such as Albrecht Mendelssohn Bartholdy, were associated with the CODP.

Over the course of the conference, the delegates discussed the causes of war and the conditions for peace, and drafted what they called the "minimum programme" for the post-war order.[69] According to the CODP, the principal causes of the war were secret diplomacy, inflated nationalism, imperialism, an overly sensational press, and the private arms industry. In response to these problems, they formulated five key demands as part of the minimum programme: (i) no transfer of territories against the will of the people, (ii) equal access to colonial raw materials, (iii) further development of arbitration and international governance, (iv) disarmament and freedom of the seas, and (v) democratic control of foreign policy.[70] These themes were further elaborated at subsequent meetings in Switzerland and by 1916, the CODP had set up several "permanent committees of research".[71] The primary goal of the CODP was to gather likeminded voices and to discuss their solutions to international conflict. While the CODP never provided any formal education, it sought to "enlighten public opinion" through events and publications.[72] In addition to that, like other early IR institutions, its members were also keen to influence official policy. A November 1917 memo by the American section of the CODP reflected on how they could "assist the government".[73]

More broadly, their goal was to generate public discourse on foreign affairs. They rejected the idea that international relations were too "difficult to understand", and launched a campaign to popularise the study and practice of foreign affairs.[74] This underlined the relationship

---

[68] Liste des Members, 1 March 1916, CODP Records, Box 1.
[69] CODP, A Durable Peace.   [70] Manifesto, 1915, CODP Records, Box 1.
[71] See Halvden Koht and Mikael H. Lie, *Parliamentary Control of Foreign Politics* (The Hague, 1916); Carl Lindhagen, *Der Parlamentarismus: seine Kontrolle der Auslandspolitik und über sich selbst* (The Hague, 1917).
[72] CODP, circular, 30 September 1915, Box 1, CODP Records.
[73] Memo, November 1917, CODP Records, Box 3.
[74] G. Lowes Dickinson, 'Democratic Control of Foreign Policy', *The Atlantic* (August, 1916).

between democracy and education in foreign affairs, a link that continued to shape the field, as David Allen has shown in his study of the Foreign Policy Association.[75] "If the people are to exercise an effective control of foreign affairs", Leonard Woolf argued in a 1918 letter to Gilbert Murray, "we must have an educated and informed public opinion on these subjects".[76] In other words, the study of IR was a necessary prerequisite for democratic governance and, in turn, international peace. Or, as Arthur Ponsonby, one of the principal advocates of this argument, put it in his book *Democracy and Diplomacy* (1915):

When a small number of statesmen, conducting the intercourse of nations in secrecy, have to confess their inability to preserve good relations, it is not an extravagant proposal to suggest that their isolated action should be supplemented and reinforced by the intelligent and well-informed assistance of the people themselves.[77]

Ponsonby was a leading member of the Union of Democratic Control (UDC), a progressive, anti-militarist pressure group that opposed the British war policy. Specifically, the UDC demanded that no treaty or international arrangement should enter into force without the consent of parliament.[78] The UDC published a journal called *Foreign Affairs: A Journal of International Understanding* from June 1919, three years before the Council on Foreign Relations launched the now-famous journal under the same name.[79] The UDC's objectives were shared by likeminded groups abroad, including the Dutch Anti-War Council, the Swiss Committee for the Study of the Foundations of Durable Peace as well as the German and Austro-Hungarian Socialists.[80] Despite the war, they collaborated across borders and met at international conferences, such as the 1915 CODP meeting in The Hague

---

[75] David Allen, *Every Citizen a Statesman: Building a Democracy for Foreign Policy in the American Century*, PhD thesis (New York, 2019).
[76] Leonard Wolf to Gilbert Murray, 28 September 1918, Gilbert Murray Papers, Box 178.
[77] Arthur Ponsonby, *Democracy and Diplomacy: A Plea for Popular Control of Foreign Policy* (London, 1915), p. 7.
[78] Mission Statement of the Union of Democratic Control, 10 June 1918, Gilbert Murray Papers, Box 178.
[79] E. D. Morel to Gilbert Murray, 26 June 1919, Gilbert Murray Papers, Box 39. From 1925 to 1928, *Foreign Affairs* was edited by Helena Swanwick.
[80] Neutral Conference for Continuous Mediation, *Twenty-Two Constructive Programs for Peace and World Organisation* (Stockholm, 1916).

and the Neutral Conference for Continuous Mediation in Stockholm in 1916.[81]

An important venue for this cause was the Inter-Parliamentary Union, a long-time champion of international arbitration and parliamentary cooperation. Founded in 1899 by the Franco-British pacifist politicians Frédéric Passy and Randal Cremer, the Inter-Parliamentary Union offered a forum for parliamentarians and circulated their work, such as that of French diplomat Paul d'Estournelles de Constant who directed the French section on arbitration.[82] By the eve of the Great War, the Union brought together hundreds of likeminded representatives from across the globe, including non-European countries such as Japan and Russia. In their 1915 report, the members of the Inter-Parliamentary Union adopted, for the first time, the control of foreign policy as a particular field of parliamentary practice, arguing that public supervision was the only guarantee against the mistakes of the governments.[83]

Women were among the first and most outspoken advocates of democratic control. To them the war seemed particularly unjust since none of the European powers had introduced the female suffrage by 1914. In the August edition of the International Woman Suffrage Alliance's (IWSA) magazine *Jus Suffragii*, the Hungarian feminist Rosika Schwimmer described the Great War as the "bankruptcy of the man-made world", invoking Bertha von Suttner's argument that without political rights women were unable to change the laws and conditions that led to violent conflict.[84] By September 1914, women from belligerent and neutral countries were collaborating on a programme for peace.[85] Helena Swanwick, for example, demanded gradual disarmament, open diplomacy, democratic control of foreign policy, respect for national minorities, and the liberation and education

---

[81] On the latter, see Louis Lochner, 'The Neutral Conference for Continuous Mediation at Stockholm', *Advocate of Peace* 78:8 (1916), pp. 238–41.

[82] Stéphane Tison (ed.), *Paul d'Estournelles de Constant: Concilier les nations pour éviter la guerre* (Rennes, 2015), pp. 47–8.

[83] Union Interparlementaire, *Rapport du Secrétaire Général au Conseil Interparlementaire pour 1915* (Christiania, 1915), p. 59.

[84] Rosika Schwimmer, 'The Bankruptcy of the Man-Made World-War', *Jus Suffragii* 8:12 (August, 1914), p. 148.

[85] Millicent Fawcett and Chrystal Macmillan, 'International Manifesto of Women', *Jus Suffragii* 8:13 (September, 1914), p. 159.

of women.[86] The British educationalist and suffragist Millicent Fawcett wrote on what would now be called democratic peace theory, citing thinkers from Grotius to Rousseau and Kant, as well as on the need for an international congress at the end of the war.[87]

In the spring of 1915, several hundred women from a dozen countries met in The Hague to discuss problems of war and peace. They formed what became known as the Women's International League for Peace and Freedom (WILPF).[88] Organised by the Dutch physician and suffragist Aletta Jacobs, the 1915 meeting gathered prominent feminist-pacifists, including Helena Swanwick, Jane Addams, and Rosika Schwimmer. Observing the war from the perspective of women, they adopted a distinctly feminist approach to the problem of peace, emphasising the rights of women and children in war, humanitarian concerns, the value of education, and the democratic control of foreign policy. Some argued that women were inherently more peaceful than men and that, had they been included in foreign policy decisions, the war would never have broken out.[89] The American economist Emily Greene Balch, herself a WILPF member, criticised the practice of secret diplomacy by "gentlemen's agreement".[90]

Building on these considerations, WILPF compiled a peace programme, not dissimilar from the CODP, including both feminist points as well as general ones: (i) no transfer of territory without approval by the men and women concerned, (ii) governments to settle disputes by arbitration and imposition of social, moral, and economic sanctions if necessary, (iii) democratic control of foreign policy, (iv) equal political rights for women, (v) disarmament and control of arms traffic, (vi) free

---

[86] Helena Swanwick, 'The Basis of Enduring Peace', *Jus Suffragii* 9:4 (January, 1915), p. 217.

[87] Millicent Fawcett, 'Women's Suffrage and a European Congress after the War', *Jus Suffragii* 9:7 (April, 1915), p. 262.

[88] Ingrid Sharp, 'The Women's Peace Congress of 1915 and the Envisioning of Women's Rights as Human Rights', in Helen McCarthy et al., *Women, Peace and Transnational Activism, a Century on History & Policy*, 30 March 2015, available at www.historyandpolicy.org/dialogues/discussions/women-peace-and-transnational-activism-a-century-on [accessed 28 February 2016].

[89] Agnes Maude Royden, 'War and the Women's Movement', in Charles Roden Buxton (ed.), *Towards a Lasting Settlement* (London, 1915), p. 134; Olive Schreiner, quoted in C. K. Ogden, *Militarism versus Feminism* (London, 1915), p. 59.

[90] Emily Greene Balch, 'The War in Its Relation to Democracy and World Order', *The Annals of the American Academy of Political and Social Science* 72 (1917), p. 29.

and equal trade, and (vii) abolishment of secret treaties.[91] The women who assembled in The Hague in the spring of 1915 stressed that they did not demand an immediate peace but wanted to study the conditions for permanent peace to be considered when hostilities had ended.[92]

Women were also involved in educational activities in the field of IR. The British section of WILPF argued in 1916 that "teaching and liberating" the minds of the new generations was key to the goal of international peace.[93] The social worker Mary Sheepshanks called upon fellow feminist-pacifists to "use their brains", not just their hands, in the struggle for peace.[94] In 1917, WILPF demanded that education programmes be adapted to the "higher ideals that are necessary for successful reconstruction after the war".[95] While devising these programmes, women stressed that international politics had to be taught to a wide audience, such as Margaret Hills argued in *Foreign Policy and the People* (1917).[96] Wartime membership of WILPF increased to several thousand women from 23 countries – by 1918, the British section alone counted 3,687 members.[97] The collaboration of women on questions of IR during the Great War was a significant contribution to the formation of the discipline, soon complemented by more formal projects, including summer schools, lectures, and publications.[98]

Perhaps the most obvious indicator of the 'birth' of IR during the mid-1910s was the creation of the Council for the Study of International Relations (CSIR) in London. It was founded in 1915 by

---

[91] WILPF, *Women's International League for Peace and Freedom*, LSE Archives, WILPF/20/5, folder 1.

[92] 'The International Congress of Women at The Hague', *Jus Suffragii* 9:7 (April, 1915), p. 261; and 'International Congress of Women', *Jus Suffragii* 9:9 (June, 1915), pp. 301–2.

[93] WILPF (British Section), *First Yearly Report: October 1915–October 1916* (London, 1916), p. 3.

[94] Mary Sheepshanks, 'Patriotism or Internationalism', *Jus Suffragii* 9:2 (1915), p. 184.

[95] WILPF (British Section), *Second Yearly Report: October 1916–October 1917* (London, 1917), p. 10.

[96] Margaret Hills, *Foreign Policy and the People* (London, 1917), p. 5.

[97] Women's International League (British Section), *Second Yearly Report: October 1916–October 1917* (1917), LSE Archives, WILPF/2/1.

[98] The first summer schools were held in 1922 at Geneva, Burg Lauenstein (Frankenwald), Lugano, and Varese. WILPF, *Bulletin of the Women's International League for Peace and Freedom* (Geneva, 1922), LSE Archives, WILPF/5/9.

the historian A. J. Grant, the economist and Labour politician Arthur Greenwood, the lawyer J. D. I. Hughes, the Balliol historian F. F. Urquhart, and the *Round Table* editor Philip Kerr.[99] James Bryce, the lawyer, diplomat, and Liberal politician, acted as president. The goal of the CSIR was "to encourage and assist the study of international relations from all points of view".[100] In doing so the CSIR responded to the increasing demand by "men and women" to study IR.[101] CSIR associates published a series of foreign policy articles as well as so-called 'aids to study'. They also helped to form study circles using CSIR material – including pamphlets titled *International Relations: A Scheme of Study, Outline Syllabuses of Some Problems of the War*, and *The Causes of the War: What to Read*. In 1916 the CSIR published the discipline's first textbook named *An Introduction to the Study of International Relations* which was complemented by an *Introductory Atlas of International Relations*, covering contemporary IR issues such as economic relations, international law, imperialism, and European unity.[102]

The CSIR's mission was echoed by a wide range of interest groups, including the League of Nations Societies in various countries; women's societies, such as WILPF or the International Council of Women (ICW); pacifist societies, such as the Bureau international de la paix or the World Peace Foundation; religious groups, especially the Society of Friends (Quakers); legal associations, such as the Institut de Droit International; philanthropists, such as the Carnegie Endowment for International Peace (CEIP); as well as groups devoted to the study of a new international order, notably the CODP.[103] In Britain, many of the key figures were associated with the Round Table Movement, a group of imperial reformers organised by Lionel Curtis and Philip

[99] Martel, 'From Round Table to New Europe', p. 30.
[100] R. W. Seton-Watson et al., *Foreign Series: The Council for the Study of International Relations* (London, 1915).
[101] Percy Alden and George Peverett, 'Council for the Study of International Relations, Letter to the Editor', *The Spectator*, 6 March 1915 (London, 1915).
[102] A. L. Grant et al., *An Introduction to the Study of International Relations* (London, 1916).
[103] On the role of interest groups, see, for example, Helen McCarthy, *The British People and the League of Nations: Democracy, Citizenship and Internationalism c.1918–45* (Manchester, 2011).

Kerr, and inspired by Alfred Milner.[104] These bodies did not work in national isolation but collaborated, from the outset, across borders and often across political or religious groups. The British League of Nations Union, for example, sought to make their campaign more effective by drawing on "a body of enlightened opinion in all countries", and collaborated with likeminded actors in France, Belgium, Holland, Switzerland, Italy, Denmark, and Germany.[105] But international political thought was not just exported from Anglo-American actors to the rest of the world. French pacifists were considering Wilsonian policies long before the American president arrived in Paris.[106] The former prime minister of France, Léon Bourgeois, chaired a research committee on a future league of nations in 1917.[107] German lawyers, too, were working on the legal fundament of the League of Nations even though they were not asked to participate.[108] The mutual transnational exchange between these actors underscored the ethos of early IR scholarship – that people from any background could engage in the study of international politics.

In the United States, interest in the war increased considerably in 1917 when President Wilson decided to join the Entente powers. That spring, the American Academy of Political and Social Science held a special meeting devoted to questions of war and peace. The president of the Academy L. S. Rose thought that the war "made the obligation all the more clear to consider in a scientific and non-partisan spirit" the problems arising from the war.[109] Contributions came from well-known professors and politicians, including Balch, Franklin Henry Giddings, and Walter L. Fisher. Their papers covered all of the familiar problems from self-determination to a future intergovernmental organisation. Most notably, perhaps, they regarded the war as a

---

[104] Deborah Lavin, *From Empire to International Commonwealth: A Biography of Lionel Curtis* (Oxford, 1995).

[105] Memorandum by the Education Committee of the League of Nations Union and List of Foreign Scholars, December 1918[?], Gilbert Murray Papers, Box 179.

[106] Sandi Cooper, *Patriotic Pacifism: Waging War on War in Europe, 1815–1914* (Oxford, 1991).

[107] Léon Bourgeois, *Le Pacte du 1919 et la Société des Nations* (Paris, 1919).

[108] 'Der neue Völkerbundentwurf der Entente, mit kritischer Einleitung von A. Mendelssohn-Bartholdy', *Deutsche Liga für Völkerbund*, 8. Flugschrift, 1919, Berlin.

[109] L. S. Rose, 'Foreword', *The Annals of the American Academy of Political and Social Science* 72 (1917), p. vii.

civilisational catastrophe that required countries of a similar kind, political as well as cultural (and sometimes racial), to cooperate in a league of democracies, rather than to build a universal alliance. But, as with most other conferences of this kind, it was mostly a venue to exchange ideas.

The war helped to organise these ideas, and gave rise to the first coherent body of IR literature. It challenged Angell's logic of economic interdependence, it delegitimised authoritarian foreign policy, and it initiated a debate on the principles of international governance. As Zimmern noted in 1916, "the war is being waged about ideas, and the settlement at its close will be determined by ideas".[110] The architects of IR shaped these debates and built institutional homes for them. They were convinced that international politics should, once and for all, become part of the public realm, open for investigation, public debate, and academic investigation. Toynbee's goal was "converting public opinion".[111] Studying the causes of war presupposed that there were causal mechanisms or patterns in international conflicts that could be rationally understood. At the same time, the architects of IR believed strongly in the political and moral value of their research. They pursued both academic and political goals, a delicate combination that continued to shape the emerging discipline as scholars turned from the causes of war to the conditions for peace.

Towards a New International Order

Soon after the outbreak of the war, the focus shifted from trying to understand its causes to finding solutions for peace. The goal was to normalise international relations in a web of new institutions. One of the first proposals for "an organisation to secure peace" was worked out by Goldsworthy Lowes Dickinson and his entourage of liberal political thinkers.[112] In his manifesto *After the War* (1915) he described how a future "league of peace" would require governments to settle their dispute by peaceful means. The league would operate an arbitration court as well as a conciliatory council. It would impose

---

[110] Alfred Zimmern, 'Nationality and Government', *Sociological Review* a8:4 (1916), p. 213.

[111] Arnold Toynbee, *Nationality and the War* (London, 1915), p. 10.

[112] Sakiko Kaiga, *Britain and the Intellectual Origins of the League of Nations, 1914–1919* (Cambridge, 2021).

sanctions and exercise economic pressure where necessary. Staffed with temporary clerks from the various member states, the league would represent an independent, truly international authority. By organising international trade, tourism, cultural affairs, and scientific cooperation, the league would foster the sense of an international community, Dickinson envisioned. He explicitly invited the United States to form part of the league, and he warned against humiliating Germany. Crucially, he incorporated the idea of democratic control into his vision for the league. "The improbability of war", he argued, "would be increased in proportion as the issues of foreign policy should be known to and controlled by public opinion".[113]

The ideas put forward in *After the War* were shared by a range of individuals and organisations, from scholars and journalists to independent writers and pacifist activists. It is hard to categorise them in retrospect because they often changed opinions themselves or simply refused to be associated with any particular camp. Perhaps it was in their very nature as dissenters to defy harmonious organisation.[114] Yet as internationalists they agreed that there were important problems best solved beyond the level of national polities. It was from this pool of thinkers that some of the most important contributions to early IR scholarship emerged. The British Liberal politician Charles Roden Buxton edited a 1915 volume called *Towards a Lasting Settlement* with contributions on nationalism, trade, the women's movement, democratic control, and the peace settlement by a range of prominent authors, including H. N. Brailsford, Dickinson, J. A. Hobson, and Agnes Maude Royden.[115] In 1916, the American writer Randolph Bourne edited a compilation of peace proposals called *Towards an Enduring Peace* which featured works by a range of international intellectuals, including Jane Addams, Norman Angell, Eduard Bernstein, Brailsford, Nicholas Murray Butler, Buxton, John Bates Clark, Dickinson, Hobson, Walter Lippmann, Romain Rolland, Ludwig Quidde, Toynbee, and Zimmern.[116] The compendium also listed groups and institutions working on a new international order,

---

[113] Dickinson, *After the War*, p. 34.
[114] A. J. P. Taylor, *The Trouble Makers: Dissent Over Foreign Policy, 1792–1939* (London, 1957); Norman Ingram, *The Politics of Dissent: Pacifism in France 1919–1939* (Oxford, 1991).
[115] Charles Roden Buxton, *Towards a Lasting Settlement* (London, 1915).
[116] Randolph S. Bourne, *Towards an Enduring Peace: A Symposium of Peace Proposals and Programs, 1914–1916* (New York, 1916).

such as the CODP and the International Congress of Women. But the idea of the League of Nations also developed in private conversations, such as those of Theodore Marburg, secretary of the League to Enforce Peace, who corresponded with leading politicians throughout the war.[117]

In France, the idea of the League of Nations was promoted by a set of lawyers, pacifists, and socialist politicians, including Léon Bourgeois, Gustave-Adolphe Hubbard, and Pierre Laval, who expanded on the work of Théodore Ruyssen and his Association de la paix par le droit.[118] Despite government censorship, they were able to build a network of sympathisers and established a series of internationalist pressure groups, beginning with the Ligue du droit des peuples pour la constituante mondiale in December 1916. With the support of Belgian peace activist Paul Otlet, they put up a series of meetings at the École des hautes études sociales in the spring of 1917, attended by up to 400 interested citizens. Among the speakers were the politician Jean Hennessy and the feminist-pacifist writer Marcelle Capy.[119] The Ligue and its successor organisations maintained the dual function of political propaganda and scientific inquiry, although they were not solely comprised of members of the intellectual elite.[120] Like their Anglo-American counterparts, although somewhat more hesitantly, they entertained transnational contacts during the war.

One notable figure was Edgard Milhaud, a French socialist and economics professor.[121] Educated widely in philosophy, sociology, and economics, Milhaud spent several years in Germany to conduct research for a book on socialist democracy. He then served as an economic advisor in the French ministry of commerce and eventually, in 1902, was appointed professor of political economy in Geneva. During the First World War, he wrote several books on the

---

[117] John H. Latané (ed.), *Development of the League of Nations Idea: Documents and Correspondence of Theodore Marburg* (New York, 1932).

[118] Jean-Michel Guieu, "Pour la paix par la Société Des Nations': La laborieuse organisation d'un mouvement français de soutien à la Société Des Nations (1915–1920)', *Guerres mondiales et conflits contemporaines* 222:2 (2006), pp. 89–102.

[119] Jean-Michel Guieu, *Le rameau et le glaive: Les militants français pour la Société des Nations* (Paris, 2008), p. 37.

[120] Bouchard, 'Des citoyens français à la recherche de la paix durable (1914–1919)', p. 69.

[121] Bouchard, *Le citoyen et l'ordre mondial (1914–1919)*, pp. 72–4.

organisation of peace and the future League of Nations.[122] Once the
governments had settled the peace terms, Milhaud argued, the power
had to return to the parliaments and, eventually, to the people themselves. He also pressed for a strong interpretation of international
sanctions to give the new organisation enough authority.[123] From the
vantage point of Geneva, he was able to build a network of likeminded
authors, including the socialists Léon Blum, Hubert Bourgin, and
Albert Thomas who became the first director of the International
Labour Office in 1919 and who invited Milhaud to do further work
on social and economic problems in the 1920s.

The work of these individuals and various international groups
covered essentially all major questions of early IR scholarship from
collective security to economic cooperation, from imperial reform to
international organisations. Notable works included George
H. Blakeslee's *The Problems and Lessons of the War* (1916), Charles
W. Eliot's, *The Road Toward Peace* (1915), C. Ernest Fayle's *The
Great Settlement* (1915), Alfred Hermann Fried's, *Europäische
Wiederherstellung* [European Reconstruction] (1915), J. A. Hobson's
Towards International Government (1915), Oliver Lodge's *The War
and After* (1915), A. Lawrence Lowell's *League to Enforce Peace*
(1915), Henri La Fontaine's *The Great Solution: Magnissima Charta*
(1916), E. D. Morel's *Truth and the War* (1916), Raymond Unwin's,
The War and What After (1915), J. J. Ruedorffer's *Grundzüge der
Weltpolitik in der Gegenwart* [Basics of Contemporary World Politics]
(1914), Leonard Woolf's *International Government* (1916), F. von
Wrangel's *Internationale Anarchie oder Verfassung?* [International
Anarchy or Constitution?] (1915), and Alfred Zimmern's *Nationality
& Government* (1918).

These were no longer isolated publications but formed a distinct
body of scholarship. Authors referenced each other's publications and
often shared drafts for comments, thus creating a sense of disciplinary
unity.[124] Despite the ongoing conflict, they collaborated across borders

---

[122] Edgard Milhaud, *Du droit de la force à la force du droit* (Geneva, 1915); Edgar
Milhaud, *La société des nations* (Paris, 1917); Milhaud, *Plus jamais!*.
[123] Milhaud, *Plus jamais!*, pp. 339–41.
[124] See, for example, Alfred Zimmern to Philip Kerr, 4 October 1915, Lionel Curtis
Papers, c.817. Charles Roden Buxton's 1916 *A Practical, Permanent, and
Honourable Settlement of the War* referenced G. Lowes Dickinson, J. A.
Hobson, H. N. Brailsford as well as German and French sources.

by cross-publishing, forming alliances, and meeting up where possible.[125] While the war prohibited the establishment of any formal, university-based institutions, the architects of IR saw the need for political education and called for reforms. In 1917, the German orientalist and politician Carl Heinrich Becker argued that the study of IR (*Auslandsstudien*) was "a practical requirement of the state".[126] Becker saw the need for well-trained state officials but also wanted to educate the population at large. After the war, Becker's plans inspired the creation of several institutions for the study of IR as well as the new school subject 'citizen education' (*Staatsbürgerkunde*).

Although the authors varied widely in professional background and style of writing, they agreed on their role in reforming the international order as a whole. They unequivocally rejected the system of foreign relations that had, so they argued, brought about the First World War – in the words of James Bryce, "getting rid of what is called the Old Diplomacy".[127] That system, the critics claimed, rested on secret treaties, militarist societies, and authoritarian governments. It was operated by a small elite of ministers, generals, and diplomats at the cost of soldiers, women, and the population at large. In fact, the general public was so uninformed about foreign affairs that, as Labour politician Philip Snowden once remarked, if war had broken out during the Second Moroccan Crisis in 1911 not more than 100 people would have understood why.[128]

New diplomacy, therefore, was designed to make international relations more open, democratic, and peaceful.[129] International treaties

[125] See, for instance, publications such as Ferdinand Buisson, 'France and the League of Nations: Wilson's Programme as Interpreted by the French Groups of the Left', *The International Review* 64 (1919), pp. 19–26.
[126] C. H. Becker, 'Die Denkschrift des preußischen Kultusministeriums über die Förderung der Auslandsstudien', Drucksachen des Preußischen Abgeordnetenhauses, 22. Legislaturperiode. VI. Session (1916/17.), Nr. 388, 24.1.1917. See also, Béatrice Bonniot, 'Von der politischen Bildung zur Politikwissenschaft: Der Beitrag Carl Heinrich Beckers zur Entstehung einer neuen wissenschaftlichen Disziplin', in Manfred Gangl (ed.), *Das Politische: Zur Entstehung der Politikwissenschaft während der Weimarer Republik* (Frankfurt a.M., 2008), pp. 65–76.
[127] Viscount Bryce, 'Foreign Policy and the People', *The International Review* 64 (1919), p. 9.
[128] Philip Snowden, 'Democracy and Publicity in Foreign Affairs', in Charles Roden Buxton (ed.), *Towards a Lasting Settlement* (London, 1915), p. 182.
[129] See Arno J. Mayer, *Political Origins of the New Diplomacy, 1917–1918* (New Haven, 1959).

and agreements were to be public. Armaments were to be kept at an absolute minimum. International affairs were to be governed democratically and, in cases of dispute, to be dealt with peacefully at an arbitration court. Women were to be given the vote and to participate in political life. Public offices, especially the diplomatic services, were to be made more accessible to represent more accurately the interests of society. Finally, the image of international affairs as an incomprehensible art was to be demystified and instead to be taught in schools and universities.

This programme was not just a collection of vague ideas, it was supplemented by detailed studies on every aspect of the new order. With regard to democratic control of foreign policy, for example, the Swiss author and politician Joseph Scherrer-Füllemann proposed to install parliamentary committees as a venue for foreign policy debates.[130] Important decisions, such as declarations of war or international treaties, were to be discussed in public and sanctioned by parliament. In a 1917 essay, the Swedish socialist politician Carl Lindhagen specified that there should be two separate parliamentary committees of certain minimum sizes to avoid party coterie.[131] These reforms would encourage political parties to devote more room to foreign policy in their programmes and help to generate public debate. Scherrer-Füllemann also suggested using the Inter-Parliamentary Union as a mediator between rival governments. A similar proposal, to "bundle the powers of parliaments", was presented by Norwegian historian and internationalist Christian Lous Lange.[132] Other CODP associates went into even more detail and published in academic journals, including *The American Political Science Review*.[133]

The most obvious novelty about new diplomacy, however, was the concept of an intergovernmental organisation – the future League of Nations. Plans for such an authority had been floated for decades, perhaps as far back as Kant's *Perpetual Peace* (1795). But it was during the First World War that the debate on a permanent body regulating

[130] Joseph Scherrer-Füllemann, 'Die Kontrolle der Auswärtigen Politik', in CODP, *Berner Zusammenkunft zur Besprechung der zukünftigen Völkerbeziehungen* (The Hague, 1917), pp. 36–8.
[131] Lindhagen, *Der Parlamentarismus*.
[132] Christian Lous Lange, *The Conditions of a Lasting Peace: A Statement of the Work of the Union* (Oslo, 1917), p. 13.
[133] Denys P. Myers, 'The Control of Foreign Relations', *The American Political Science Review* 11:1 (1917), pp. 24–58.

all aspects of international life really took off. The League differed from nineteenth-century diplomacy in that it was an "organised" concert of powers, as Zimmern put it.[134] Others, such as Woolf, envisioned a more advanced "supernational authority", featuring a court, a council, and a secretariat.[135] Most experts agreed that some sort of international institution would help to prevent future conflict, but there were open questions. Who would be allowed to join? How would the League be governed? Which policy instruments would it be able to employ?

The architects of IR were at the centre of these debates.[136] They believed that a well-organised international organisation, based on reason and the rule of law, would make the world a more peaceful place. The advantage of a permanent institution over intermittent conferences was that national representatives would grow accustomed to one another, leading to "a better understanding" between the various nations, so Zimmern argued.[137] Zimmern was one of the principal advocates of this rational notion of international affairs which implied that good analysis would lead to good solutions. At the height of the war, in November 1915, Zimmern claimed there was "no more important duty ... than the close and searching analysis of political ideas".[138] However, he did not assume that a fixed legal apparatus would do the job. It would have to be an active political union, comprising as many countries as possible, and informed by recurring deliberations.[139] He was especially concerned about how it could be "reconciled with the democratic control of foreign policy".[140]

---

[134] Alfred Zimmern, 'British Foreign Policy since the War', dated 1930, Alfred Zimmern Papers, Box 140 [emphasis added].

[135] Leonard Woolf, *International Government* (New York, 1916), p. 376.

[136] The 1918 Philimore Report, commissioned by the British government, acknowledged the wartime work done by "Viscount Bryce and his friends, the British League of Nations Society, [...] the Union of Democratic Control, L'Organisation Centrale pour une Paix Durable (The Hague)". See Walter Philimore, *The Committee on the League of Nations: Final Report*, 3 July 1918, Philip Noel-Baker Papers, NBKR 4/436.

[137] Zimmern, *The League of Nations and the Rule of Law*, p. 1.

[138] Zimmern, 'Nationality and Government', paper read before the Sociological Society, 10 November 1915, printed in Alfred Zimmern, *Nationality and Government* (London, 1918), pp. 32–60.

[139] Stephen Wertheim, 'The League of Nations: A Retreat from International Law?', *Journal of Global History* 7 (2010), pp. 210–11.

[140] Alfred Zimmern to Herbert Croly, 14 October 1918, Alfred Zimmern Papers, Box Adds. 1.

For Toynbee, too, the future international order would have to be based on reason and open debate. To him, internationalism was the logical conclusion from the increasing interdependence of states and a matter of civilisational progress.[141] He called it "a co-ordination of knowledge on a large scale".[142] Toynbee's research on nations and nationality, published in *Nationality and the War* (1915), did exactly that. In encyclopaedic detail, he studied the history and geography of rivalling nations in order to develop a scheme for European reconstruction and permanent peace. While he had no illusions about the prospect of his endeavour – "in the last resort there must always be minorities that suffer" – Toynbee believed that rational investigation was the way to a more peaceful world.[143] Like Zimmern, he rejected a legalistic version of international cooperation as 'lifeless contracts', and preferred strong executive powers.[144]

Both Toynbee and Zimmern were convinced that the level of political negotiation had to be international. They agreed on the "bankruptcy of the national state" and the inadequacies of old diplomacy.[145] The nature of modern international relations had become so complex and the scope of violence so destructive that solutions had to be found on the international stage. It was no longer plausible to pursue a strategy of unilateral military preponderance or "peace by preparedness", as their American colleague George H. Blakeslee argued in 1915.[146] To prevent another war, and the enormous costs associated with it, governments had to find a mechanism of conflict resolution. It was an experiment of a new kind of diplomacy. Zimmern regarded it as an "instrument of cooperation", the effectiveness of which, he readily admitted, depended on the willingness of its members to support its mission.[147]

Their German colleague Albrecht Mendelssohn Bartholdy, an international lawyer with connections to leading politicians, agreed on the basic outlines of the League of Nations.[148] He was sympathetic to a

---

[141] Arnold Toynbee, *The New Europe* (London, 1916), pp. 64–5.
[142] Toynbee, *Nationality and the War*, p. 16.   [143] Ibid., p. 17.
[144] Ibid., p. 494.   [145] Ibid., p. 7.
[146] George H. Blakeslee, 'The War Problem and Its Proposed Solutions', in George H. Blakeslee (ed.), *The Problems and Lessons of the War* (New York, 1916), pp. xxviii–xxix.
[147] Zimmern, *The League of Nations and the Rule of Law*, pp. 282–3.
[148] Albrecht Mendelssohn Bartholdy, 'Ein Internationaler Schiedsgerichthof', *Deutsche Juristen-Zeitung*, 10 December 1918, pp. 1–2.

strong international authority for arbitration and, if necessary, sanctions. In an article for the German League of Nations Union (*Deutsche Liga für Völkerbund*), he particularly welcomed the concept of "international cooperation (*gemeinschaftliche Weltarbeit*)".[149] Although coming from a legal background, he did not advocate a court-based international order but stressed the role of active political institutions. "The alliance system has lost the war, the league system has won it", he summarised.[150] However, Mendelssohn Bartholdy also criticised certain aspects of the emerging Covenant, such as the unanimity rule in the Council or the possibility for individuals to appeal to the court. He was particularly vocal about self-determination and the protection of minorities.[151]

Mendelssohn Bartholdy did not keep those ideas to himself. He corresponded with high-ranking politicians and published in a wide range of media outlets. His drafts for the League were read, amongst others, by Prussian Finance Minister Albert Südekum and interim Chancellor Max von Baden.[152] In January 1919, the head of the legal department at the German foreign office Walter Simons asked Mendelssohn Bartholdy to study certain legal aspects of the Covenant and to accompany the German delegation to Paris.[153] Along with historian Hans Delbrück and sociologist Max Weber, Mendelssohn Bartholdy advised the German government on the peace treaty. There is no evidence that he had any influence on German policy, but his private papers are testimony to his ambitions.

Mendelssohn Bartholdy belonged to the foreign policy group *Heidelberger Vereinigung*, which included von Baden, the banker

[149] Albrecht Mendelssohn Bartholdy, 'Der neue Völkerbundentwurf der Entente, mit kritischer Einleitung von A. Mendelssohn-Bartholdy', *Deutsche Liga für Völkerbund* 8 (1919), p. 8.
[150] '*Das Bündnis hat den Krieg verloren, der Bund hat ihn gewonnen.*' Albrecht Mendelssohn, 'Der Bund. Zur Verfassungsfrage', *Der Neue Merkur*, Sonderheft: Der Vorläufer (1919), p. 26.
[151] Albrecht Mendelssohn Bartholdy, 'Verhandlungen der am 21. September 1918 eingesetzten Studienkommission für den Völkerbund', *Mitteilungen der Deutschen Gesellschaft für Völkerrecht* 2 (1919), pp. 16–17.
[152] Albert Südekum to Albrecht Mendelssohn Bartholdy, 27 January 1919, Albrecht Mendelssohn Bartholdy Papers, MA Nachl. 2,32; and Max von Baden to Albrecht Mendelssohn Bartholdy, 19 February 1919, Albrecht Mendelssohn Bartholdy Papers, MA Nachl. 2,42.
[153] Walter Simons to Albrecht Mendelssohn Bartholdy, 12 January 1919, Albrecht Mendelssohn Bartholdy Papers, MA Nachl. 2,26.

Carl Melchior, and the army general Max Montgelas. They were critical of the peace terms and promoted research on a German-friendly settlement. On their pressure, the German foreign office commissioned an extended version of Karl Kautsky's *Die Deutschen Dokumente zum Kriegsausbruch 1914* (1921) and asked Mendelssohn Bartholdy to contribute the first volume – the second and third were covered by Walther Schücking and Mongelas, respectively.[154] After the end of the war, members of the *Heidelberger Vereinigung*, with financial support from banker Max Warburg, established the Institut für Auswärtige Politik in Hamburg – Germany's first research institute exclusively devoted to IR – and appointed Mendelssohn Bartholdy its inaugural director.

These networks between professors, politicians, and philanthropists provided an ideal environment for devising the new international institutions, and for establishing a new academic discipline. Interaction with high-ranking politicians was routine practice for the architects of IR. In August 1918, Alfred Zimmern was appointed a temporary clerk at the foreign office.[155] In October, he presented his ideas on the League to an audience of politicians, presided by the former prime minister and then leader of the opposition Herbert Asquith.[156] Shortly thereafter Zimmern was sent to Paris on behalf of the British government. Whenever not present in Paris himself, he was regularly updated by his friends in the Foreign Office, such as the diplomat and politician Eustace Percy, who assured him that their draft was in good shape against the "pretty sterile" American and "terribly legalistic" French drafts.[157] In May 1919, Zimmern resigned from his position at the foreign office and took up the Woodrow Wilson Chair at Aberystwyth, Wales, to become the first IR professor in history.[158] Zimmern's professional biography, like those of others, makes it impossible to isolate his intellectual output from his practical experiences and the general political context.

---

[154] Auswärtiges Amt to Albrecht Mendelssohn Bartholdy, 3 August 1919, Albrecht Mendelssohn Bartholdy Papers, MA Nachl. 2,127.

[155] J. G. C. Likey (?), 12 August 1918, Alfred Zimmern Papers, Box 15.

[156] 'League of Nations', *Manchester Guardian*, 31 October 1918, Alfred Zimmern Papers, Box 179.

[157] Eustace Percy to Alfred Zimmern, 16 January 1919, Alfred Zimmern Papers, Box 16.

[158] Foreign Office to Alfred Zimmern, 10 May 1919, Alfred Zimmern Papers, Box 16.

At the Peace Conference

When the governments assembled in Paris in January 1919 they were assisted by an entourage of academic advisors, many of whom were involved in the formation of IR.[159] They wrote memoranda, studied historical treaties, gathered demographic data, and prepared official negotiations. Among the advisors were Fannie Fern Andrews, E. H. Carr, Archibald Coolidge, Lionel Curtis, Albert Geouffre de Lapradelle, Ferdinand Larnaude, Paul Mantoux, Albrecht Mendelssohn Bartholdy, Philip Noel-Baker, William Rappard, Walther Schücking, James T. Shotwell, Arnold Toynbee, Charles Webster, and Alfred Zimmern. The conference gave them an ideal opportunity to exchange ideas and to partake in the making of international relations. Within the history of IR, this was a crucial moment since it manifested the relationship between scholars and practitioners of foreign policy.

The political agenda was daunting. After four years of warfare on an unprecedented scale, the leaders of Britain, France, and the United States effectively decided on the fate of people across the globe. Other governments, nationalist activists, and various interest groups were submitting their petitions to the conference. Meanwhile, it is worth remembering, some regions of the world were still at war after 1918, notably Soviet Russia, the former Ottoman Empire, and Ireland.[160] Amidst this chaotic context, the peacemakers had to decide on territorial changes, military restrictions, economic reparations, colonial revisions, humanitarian provisions, and the creation of the world's first intergovernmental organisation. How could a new international order satisfy all those interests? Who was to make the decisions? And which role did IR scholars have to play in all this?

---

[159] Tomás Irish, 'Scholarly Identities in War and Peace: The Paris Peace Conference and the Mobilization of Intellect', *Journal of Global History* 11:3 (2016), pp. 365–86; David M. McCourt, 'The Inquiry and the Birth of International Relations, 1917–19', *Australian Journal of Politics and History* 63:3 (2017), pp. 394–405; Jonathan M. Nielson, 'The Scholar as Diplomat: American Historians at the Paris Peace Conference of 1919', *The International History Review* 14:2 (1992), pp. 228–51; Marcus Payk, *Frieden durch Recht? Der Aufstieg des modernen Völkerrechts und der Friedensschluss nach dem ersten Weltkrieg* (Berlin, 2019), pp. 267–318.

[160] Robert Gerwarth, *The Vanquished: Why the First World War Failed to End* (New York, 2016).

Drawing on their wartime experiences, the architects of IR threw themselves into the work. "No method of study can equal a first hand acquaintance", as one of their reports explained.[161] Although some of them were lawyers, the majority came from other backgrounds and their conversations went beyond legal analysis. Crucially, they did not just provide expertise when asked to, but they sought to actively shape the conference outcomes. In December 1918, Dickinson urged Murray – both were members of the British League of Nations Union (LNU) – that "the Union is to get in contact with the peace conference, and try to influence it".[162] WILPF sent a delegation to Paris led by Jane Addams to convey their programme for peace and to protest the exclusion of women in the negotiations.[163] The American historian James Shotwell tried to convince British delegates of the need to publish diplomatic records for the sake of open diplomacy.[164] Their work went far beyond professorial duties. Not only did they make normative claims in written work, but they intervened in foreign policy in the most immediate way possible.

For many, the most interesting project at Paris was the drafting of the League of Nations Covenant – affectionately called the world's 'declaration of interdependence'. Scholars such as Toynbee put their hopes on a strong international institution that would overcome the problem of nationalism.[165] The League incorporated all the fundamental ideas that motivated the study of IR. Starting from the assumption that the world was growing together economically and that war was the result of a flawed system of international relations, the architects of the League argued that an intergovernmental organisation could help to control those increasingly complex relationships on the basis of law and democracy. It was the logical conclusion from the horrors of the

---

[161] The Royal Institute of International Affairs, *Chatham House Annual Report 1919–1925* (London, 1919), p. 9.

[162] G. Lowes Dickinson to Gilbert Murray, 4 December 1918, Gilbert Murray Papers, Box 179.

[163] WILPF, *Report of the International Congress of Women*, Zurich, 12–17 May 1919, p. 163. LSE Archives, WILPF/20/5, Folder 2.

[164] 'I had a good time talking to Sir Eyre Crowe of the Foreign Office but failed to convince him of the need of opening the British archives.' James T. Shotwell, *At the Paris Peace Conference* (New York, 1937), p. 357.

[165] 'I am rather hopeful about the League. It is becoming concrete, and Cecil has good devils' Arnold Toynbee to Gilbert Murray, 25 January 1919, Arnold Toynbee Papers, Box 72.

war and the course of world history. The various pro-League pressure groups, such as the LNU, helped to gather these sentiments.[166] For Philip Noel-Baker, a prominent member of the LNU, the League was a "necessary result of the development of human society".[167] It was to organise the world not just from a geopolitical point of view but as a holistic institution solving the various economic, legal, cultural, and humanitarian problems of the time.

It is difficult to trace the contributions of individual IR scholars to the final text of the Covenant, or to measure the influence that they had on the League as it took shape. But there is evidence that their efforts did not go unnoticed. Perhaps the most prominent example was Zimmern's December 1918 draft of the League Covenant which Lord Cecil took to Paris.[168] The French equivalent, a study commission directed by Léon Bourgeois (and including among others Paul d'Estournelles de Constant), was less successful in convincing their government to adopt an internationalist position and to put arbitration at the heart of the new organisation.[169] But there were other important individuals. The historian James Headlam-Morley "played a major part in the drafting of the minorities protection treaties", as Zara Steiner pointed out.[170] He also pressed for the covenant to incorporate

---

[166] Murray, *The League of Nations Movement.*
[167] Memo 'On the Meaning of the League of Nations', 1919[?], Philip Noel-Baker Papers, NBKR 4/436.
[168] Zimmern, *The League of Nations and the Rule of Law*, 2nd ed., pp. 190–6; D. J. Markwell, 'Zimmern, Sir Alfred Eckhard, 1879–1957', in *Oxford Dictionary of National Biography* (Oxford, 2004), available at http://ezproxy-prd .bodleian.ox.ac.uk:2167/view/10.1093/ref:odnb/9780198614128.001.0001/ odnb-9780198614128-e-37088?rskey=BznVtp&result=1 [accessed 31 July 2018].
[169] Guieu, '"Pour la paix par la Société Des Nations"; Vincent Laniol, 'Ferdinand Larnaude, a "Technical Delegate" at the Peace Conference of 1919: Between Expertise and "War Culture"', *Relations Internationales* 149:1 (2012), pp. 43–55; Tison, *Paul d'Estournelles de Constant*, p. 54; Andrew Williams, *Failed Imagination?: New World Orders of the Twentieth Century* (Manchester, 1998), p. 56; Marie-Adélaïde Zeyer, *Léon Bourgeois, père spirituel de la Société des Nations* (Paris, 2006).
[170] Zara Steiner, 'The Historian and the Foreign Office', in Christopher Hill and Pamela Beshoff (eds.), *Two Worlds of International Relations: Academics, Practitioners and the Trade in Ideas* (London, 1994), p. 42. See also David Kaufman, '"A House of Cards Which Would Not Stand": James Headlam-Morley, the Role of Experts, and the Danzig Question at the Paris Peace Conference', *Diplomacy & Statecraft* 30:2 (2019), pp. 228–52; Irish, 'Scholarly Identities in War and Peace'.

a mechanism for the modification of treaties.[171] Fannie Fern Andrews, the American educator, supplied Colonel House with studies on the freedom of the seas.[172] Philip Noel-Baker advised Lord Cecil on disarmament and legal questions, before taking up a position at the League of Nations Secretariat.[173] Minutes of the Peace Conference show that both Shotwell and Toynbee attended meetings of the 'big three'.[174] Whatever their actual impact on the final treaty, IR scholars were overwhelmingly supportive of the League and saw it as a chance to advance their own work.

Besides the League of Nations, IR scholars were most interested in the peace terms for Germany. Several authors voiced their concern with the Versailles Treaty, arguing that it was unfair towards Germany and that it would not serve international peace in the long run. "I think the country ought to be told in planer language", wrote Zimmern to Toynbee in August 1919, "that the break of the armistice agreement of Nov. 5 1918 is as great a crime against the Law of nations as the break of the Belgian Treaty, and far less excusable".[175] Toynbee agreed. He suggested admitting Germany to the League of Nations straight away – "I think we shall get Germany in pretty soon" – and he was willing to widen the break with Russia and Hungary for this cause.[176] Part of their reasoning was that they regarded Germany as a bulwark against Bolshevism, but their pro-German attitude also derived from their vision for an inclusive postwar system of international cooperation. This approach was related to John Maynard Keynes's critique of the peace terms as well as to the common notion that "the Allied Governments have proposed such terms as no nation would accept".[177] Many IR scholars in the allied countries believed that not the entire German people should be held

---

[171] James Headlam-Morley to Alfred Zimmern, 26 May 1919, Alfred Zimmern Papers, Box Adds. 1.

[172] Colonel House to Fannie Fern Andrews, 17 January 1918, Fannie Fern Andrews Papers, Box 113.

[173] Howell, 'Baker, Philip John Noel-, Baron Noel-Baker'.

[174] American Commission to Negotiate Peace, Secretary's Notes, 13 February 1919.

[175] Alfred Zimmern to Arnold Toynbee, 10 August 1919, Arnold Toynbee Papers, Box 86.

[176] Arnold Toynbee to Gilbert Murray, 27 July 1919, Arnold Toynbee Papers, Box 72.

[177] *The Daily News*, Saturday 24 May 1919, press clipping, Gilbert Murray Papers, Box 181.

accountable for the poor decisions made by the Kaiser and a handful of generals. Consequently, they began in August 1919 to reach out to German scholars, for example via the Oxford Society for Promoting International Understanding and Friendship.[178]

More significant for the development of IR as a discipline than the peace terms and the Covenant, however, was the atmosphere in Paris from which they emerged. President Wilson's historic decision to sail to Europe was widely received as a signal for the importance he assigned to international reconciliation, and it stimulated hope for liberal reforms of the international order in many parts of the world.[179] Wilson's own delegation was accompanied by his legendary group of advisors, 'The Inquiry', which was composed of more than one hundred professors and experts. It was a summit of "leaders of thought and action", as one report described it.[180] During the entire conference, the French, British, and American League of Nations interest groups occupied a common office located conveniently close to the plenipotentiaries at the Palais d'Orsay.[181] These encounters gave rise to an optimistic atmosphere and bolstered the conviction that international peace could be mastered.[182] The format of the conference served as a showcase for how world governance might work, but it also provided a chance for all kinds of activists, experts, and scholars to sound out potential collaborators. This impression of the peace conference is well captured in the report of a group of IR experts who met in Paris:

Here were congregated under one roof trained diplomatists, soldiers, sailors, airmen, civil administrators, jurists, financial and economic experts, captains of industry and spokesmen of labour, members of cabinets and parliaments, journalists and publicists of all sorts and kinds. … At meals, and when off

---

[178] Oxford Society for Promoting International Understanding and Friendship, 26 August 1919, Gilbert Murray Papers, Box 181.

[179] See Erez Manela, *The Wilsonian Moment: Self-determination and the International Origins of Anticolonial Nationalism* (Oxford, 2007).

[180] Draft Report on the British Branch of the Institute of International Affairs, p. 2, James T. Shotwell Papers, Box 43.

[181] Guieu, *Le rameau et le glaive*, p. 55.

[182] Arnold Toynbee was impressed by the conference and the "overwhelming sense of its own power", although he later changed his opinion. Toynbee to Murray, 26 March 1919, Arnold Toynbee Papers, Box 72. On the general atmosphere of the conference, see Margaret Macmillan, *Peacemakers: The Paris Peace Conference of 1919 and Its Attempt to End War* (London, 2001).

duty, there was no convention against 'talking shop' ... A unique opportunity was thus given to every specialist of grasping the relation of his own particular question to all the others involved[183]

It was these transnational, primarily transatlantic, encounters that gave rise to two influential think tanks – the British Institute of International Affairs in London and the Council on Foreign Relations in New York. The idea arose during several unofficial meetings dating back to February 1919 at which members of the British and US delegations, including Lionel Curtis, Philip Noel-Baker, and Alfred Zimmern, floated the idea of turning the Parisian atmosphere into a more permanent institution.[184] The decisive meeting took place on 30 May 1919.[185] It was attended by the American historians George Louis Beer and James Shotwell, the lawyer James Brown Scott, the diplomat Stanley Hornbeck, General Tasker Bliss, as well as the British statesmen and diplomats Lord Cecil, Lionel Curtis, Eyre Crowe, Eustace Percy, and the historians James Headlam-Morley and Harold Temperley.[186] Their goal was "to keep its members in touch with the international situation and enable them to study the relation between national policies and the interests of society as a whole".[187]

The Anglo-American initiative inspired a whole range of IR research institutes across Europe. Several members of the German delegation – including the sociologist Max Weber, the soon-to-be foreign minister Walter Simons, the banker Carl Melchior, and the international lawyer Albrecht Mendelssohn Bartholdy – helped to establish the Institut für Auswärtige Politik in Hamburg. French statesmen Léon Bourgeois and Raymond Poincaré became members of the honorary council of the Institut des Hautes Etudes Internationales in Paris. The founders of the Geneva Graduate Institute of International Studies, the Swiss diplomat William Rappard and the French historian Paul Mantoux, both attended the Paris Peace Conference. Having participated in active

---

[183] Draft Report on the British Branch of the Institute of International Affairs, James T. Shotwell Papers, Box 43.
[184] Albert Mansbridge to Alfred Zimmern, 1 March 1919, Alfred Zimmern Papers, Box 16.
[185] Michael Riemens, 'International Academic Cooperation on International Relations in the Interwar Period: The International Studies Conference', *Review of International Studies* 37:2 (2011), p. 913.
[186] Personal Diary, James T. Shotwell Papers, Box 41, Folder 1.
[187] Draft Report on the British Branch of the Institute of International Affairs, p. 4, James T. Shotwell Papers, Box 43.

diplomacy themselves, they shared the idea that international affairs should be subject to scholarly investigation.

Despite tireless campaigning, women were largely excluded from the conference. Since 1915, they had been insisting that "an international meeting of women shall be held in the same place and at the same time" as the Peace Conference.[188] While they were denied access to official negotiations in Paris, they met up in Zurich and worked on the various aspects of the peace settlement in parallel to their male colleagues. Their key demands were to grant membership of the League of Nations to all nations, to consistently apply the principle of self-determination, to make provisions for treaty revisions, to avoid military force when imposing blockades, to reduce armaments immediately, to internationalise colonial territories, and to allow free access to raw materials. They also demanded full equality for women, amnesty for political prisoners as well as freedom of communication and travel.[189] Finally, they called for educational reforms. Helena Swanwick, a WILPF member and prolific writer on international affairs, argued that the League had to be popularised through education and public debate. "The peoples in any country in the world want to study foreign affairs", she wrote in August 1919.[190]

Apart from these elite-level networks, the Peace Conference also attracted popular attention to the conduct of foreign affairs. "Diplomacy was coming down among the people", as David Mitrany put it.[191] President Wilson's case for open diplomacy – "open covenants of peace, openly arrived at" – suggested that it was the right of the people to be adequately informed about foreign affairs. Now there was a viable chance that people might be better informed about the causes for war and the making of peace. Zimmern actually favoured the "representation of peoples rather than governments" at the Peace Conference.[192] Female IR writers, though not invited to Paris, were the most progressive advocates of popular involvement in

---

[188] WILPF, *Extract from the Forthcoming Report of the International Congress of Women: Held at Zurich, May 12–17, 1919* (Geneva, 1919[?]), p. 46.

[189] WILPF, *Women's International League for Peace and Freedom, 1915–1938: A Venture in Internationalism* (Geneva, 1938), pp. 10–11, LSE Archives, WILPF/20/5, folder 1.

[190] Helena Swanwick, 'Democracy and the League of Nations', in WILPF, *Towards Peace and Freedom*, August 1919, LSE Archives, WILPF/2009/15/6/2.

[191] Mitrany, *The Functional Theory of Politics*, p. 7.

[192] Raymond [?] to Alfred Zimmern, 4 February 1918, Alfred Zimmern Papers, Box 15.

international affairs. In a 1919 essay entitled *Democracy and the League of Nations*, Swanwick explained the goal of WILPF was "to rouse the great mass of people in every country to take an interest in these great matters".[193] Democratic control of foreign policy required appropriate forms of information and education, motives that were propelled by the Peace Conference.

IR as a university discipline owes a lot to the Peace Conference. The negotiations showed the need for experts at the intersection of international law, history, economics, and political science. While coming from different disciplinary and national backgrounds, the architects of IR agreed on the benefits of a new, common subject, the name of which remained uncertain for the time being. The participants realised that none of their academic disciplines sufficiently covered what was now at stake, and so their work at Paris created a sense of disciplinary identity.[194] Paris also suggested that there would be plenty of professional opportunities for students of the new discipline, both at the national level and as at the League of Nations. The Peace Conference stirred the hope that international relations would become more rational, and thus more suitable for academic research.

The shortcomings of new diplomacy, however, became apparent almost immediately when the victorious governments blatantly disregarded the principles of self-determination and open diplomacy. In March, Toynbee wrote to Murray that his colleagues at the Foreign Office were beginning to feel "very depressed" about the prospects of the peace. "The Conference", Toynbee reported, "has rather suddenly passed from an overwhelming sense of its own power to a probably equally exaggerated sense of helplessness".[195] The project of the League of Nations seemed to lose its momentum before it was formally established. By July, Toynbee admitted being "more afraid of its going

---

[193] Helena Swanwick, 'Democracy and the League of Nations', in WILPF, *Towards Peace and Freedom* (August 1919), p. 15, LSE Archives, WILPF/ 2009/15/6/2.

[194] "Men [sic!] who never imagined they had anything in common began to discover how much in common they really had." Draft Report on the British Branch of the Institute of International Affairs, p. 1, James T. Shotwell Papers, Box 43.

[195] Arnold Toynbee to Gilbert Murray, 26 March 1919, Arnold Toynbee Papers, Box 72.

wrong".[196] French sociologist Célestin Bouglé, too, was disappointed about the "pale and imperfect" outcome of the negotiations.[197]

Although the conference was formally international, it largely excluded non-Western actors, women, and nationals of those countries that were politically out of favour. World politics were firmly in the hands of "white men in white men's countries".[198] In the end, most decisions were taken by the 'big three', rather than an open council of parliamentary representatives. In addition to political pressure, the conference operated under the constraints of time and resources. Only a few delegates actually possessed a detailed grasp of the final documents. So great was the disappointment among some of the IR pioneers that by May 1919, Toynbee described it as "a soul-destroying affair".[199] Zimmern, too, felt "disgusted and depressed".[200] In many respects, 1919 did not mark the 'birth of IR', as disciplinary histories usually claim, but it *concluded* the first episode of IR scholarship, a period that defined the political context and intellectual challenges ahead. Did the architects of IR fail to see the risks and problems of their endeavour?

Whatever the flaws and failures of the peace, it did raise expectations among the peoples of the world by introducing new normative principles of international politics beyond Versailles.[201] In particular, it gave rise to a new body of thought which assumed that foreign politics could be controlled by democratic institutions and studied by academics. "There is nothing that I am so anxious to devote my time to as the enlightenment of public opinion about the League", declared Conservative politician and educationalist Eustace Percy in May 1919.[202] This attitude should not be misinterpreted as 'idealism',

---

[196] Arnold Toynbee to Gilbert Murray, 27 July 1919, Arnold Toynbee Papers, Box 72.

[197] Guieu, *Le rameau et le glaive*, p. 59.

[198] Theodore Marburg, 'Sovereignty and Race as Affected by a League of Nations', *The Annals of the American Academy of Political and Social Science* 72 (1917), p. 145.

[199] Arnold Toynbee to Rob[ert] Cecil, 21 May 1919, Arnold Toynbee Papers, Box 80.

[200] Alfred Zimmern to Arnold Toynbee, 10 August 1919, Arnold Toynbee Papers, Box 86.

[201] Marcus M. Payk and Roberta Pergher, 'Introduction', in Marcus M. Payk and Roberta Pergher (eds.), *Beyond Versailles: Sovereignty, Legitimacy, and the Formation of New Polities after the Great War* (Bloomington, 2019), p. 4.

[202] Eustace Percy to Gilbert Murray, 26 May 1919, Gilbert Murray Papers, Box 181.

however. There were 'doubts' about the League as early as 1919.[203] They wanted "to speak of the League of Nations not as an ideal or a dream", Gilbert Murray declared in November 1918, "but as a piece of practical political business".[204] The pioneers of IR never believed that an institution alone could secure world peace.[205] Instead, what they underestimated was that foreign affairs remained first and foremost *political* affairs, and that partisan interests torpedoed the idea of 'objective' international conditions. There were no unbiased conclusions to be drawn, no scientific laws to be discovered, and no objective truths to be found. For IR as a social science, the Peace Conference was an instructive experience, albeit a problematic one. From a historical point of view, the conference was just as discouraging. The American withdrawal from Europe in March 1920 terminated their wartime alliance with France and Britain. US isolationism as well as the exclusion of Japan, Soviet Russia, and Germany put an end to the vision of global governance, and as such to IR as a global discipline.

Conclusion

"How many of Toynbee's tales or anecdotes start in the wartime foreign office or at the peace conference of 1919", *The Economist* remembered in 1967 looking back on the historian's career.[206] Over the course of five years, the classics tutor Arnold J. Toynbee had metamorphosed into a government advisor and an expert on international affairs. He had published articles and books, worked for the Foreign Office, and built a network of likeminded intellectuals and politicians. The resulting ideas and institutions that formed the discipline of IR were irrevocably linked to the experiences between July 1914 and June 1919 – the horrors of the war and the efforts for lasting

[203] Raymond W. Postgate, *Doubts Concerning a League of Nations* (London, 1919).
[204] Speech delivered at the Liberal Jewish Synagogue, 17 November 1918, entitled 'Problems of the League of Nations', Gilbert Murray Papers, Box 179.
[205] "As far as I can see, you believe that a League of Nations is quite impossible, at least, a League in the sense of, let us say, Mr. Wilson." Walter E. Weyl to Alfred Zimmern, 15 October 1918, Alfred Zimmern Papers, Box 15.
[206] Newspaper clipping of a review of Arnold J. Toynbee, *Acquaintances* (Oxford, 1967), in *The Economist*, 27 May 1967, Arnold Toynbee Papers, Box 25.

peace. It was this episode that inspired the study of IR and made it, as Toynbee later put it, "the master problem of the present age".[207]

The First World War was a disruptive moment for the existing world order as much as for the ideas underlying it. Empires collapsed, monarchs were dethroned, and borders were redrawn. Old diplomatic practices were put into question by the advocates of self-determination, open treaties, and democratic control of foreign policy. The architects of IR were at the forefront of these reforms. Despite ongoing hostilities, and in opposition to the political establishment, they seized a moment of turmoil to criticise the existing foreign policy system and to draw up proposals for a new world order. Specifically, they demanded a negotiated peace, the publication of secret treaties, disarmament, more parliamentary control over foreign policy, universal franchise, national self-determination, free trade, and the establishment of a league of nations. Their goal was a global order based on international law and institutions, democratic standards, and open markets which, so they claimed, would lead to a more peaceful world.

This was an ambitious agenda. Yet, as this chapter has shown, the intellectual roots of IR cannot be reduced to 'idealist' post-war planning. Devising plans for the League of Nations was not in itself 'idealist', a label that the architects of IR vehemently rejected.[208] Quite the contrary, they were well aware of the implications of military power and nationalist sentiments. Toynbee, for one, readily admitted that national identity had to be built into the foundations of an internationalist order.[209] Zimmern viewed the League of Nations as nothing but "an adaptation" of the previous system – "an organised concert of the powers".[210] Mendelssohn Bartholdy devoted an entire essay to the concept of 'power'.[211] These studies were perplexingly eclectic and by no means fit into a well-defined school of 'idealism'. It is true therefore, as Brian C. Schmidt and other disciplinary historians have argued, that early IR scholarship was by no means as trivially

---

[207] Arnold Toynbee to G. G. Kullmann, 3 May 1934, Arnold Toynbee Papers, Box 117.
[208] Dickinson, *After the War*, p. 37.
[209] Arnold Toynbee, *Nationality and the War* (London, 1915), p. 12.
[210] Alfred Zimmern, 'British Foreign Policy since the War', 1930, Alfred Zimmern Papers, Box 140.
[211] Albrecht Mendelssohn Bartholdy, 'Macht, Großmacht und Menschlichkeit', *Der Neue Merkur* (November, 1919).

'idealist' or 'utopian' as E. H. Carr later asserted.[212] Even during the formative phase of IR, the supposed seedbed of 'idealism', there were elements of 'realism' in their work. Toynbee, for example, regarded the League of Nations as an instrument to balance power relations in continental Europe.[213]

Subsequent interpretations of early IR scholarship have mistaken its normative character either for naïve 'idealism' or for manifestations of some other general theory. In fact, these works were the result of the political interests pursued by its authors. The crucial impulse for the formation of IR was not an uncritical belief in the League of Nations as a guarantor of world peace. Nor was it the rise of economic interdependence, or the need for imperial reform, which brought about the new discipline, although all of these issues played a role. The principal motivation sprang from the practical efforts to bring about a new international order. The architects of IR used this new order as an intellectual playground. They pursued political goals while claiming to apply academic standards, although they rarely acknowledged, let alone discussed the political nature of their work.

In particular, the protagonists of IR believed that issues of war and peace could and should be subject to rational investigation. They argued that education in IR was essential in order to make foreign politics more accountable and, as a result, the world more peaceful. This argument was motivated by the experience of the war and the growing public interest in foreign affairs. It was tied to the women's campaign for universal suffrage as well as to the more general wave of democratisation in the wake of the war. The study of IR was rooted in the idea of democracy and it relied on democratic practices. In order to study international affairs properly scholars needed access to diplomatic documents. In order to have meaningful debates about foreign policy choices there had to be legislative procedures to bring about change. Without those prerequisites the study of IR would be speculation at best, propaganda at worst.

The tension between academic rigour and political ambition was apparent even before IR became a formal university discipline, before the first professor was appointed, and before the first degrees were

---

[212] See, for example, Brian C. Schmidt, *International Relations and the First Great Debate* (London, 2012).

[213] Arnold Toynbee to Gilbert Murray, 27 July 1919, Arnold Toynbee Papers, Box 72.

awarded. Conflicting motivations continued to shape the institutional formation of the discipline, which the next chapter will address in more detail. Wartime conditions had made it impossible to establish IR at the university level. Yet, as this chapter has shown, the foundations of the discipline were laid *during* the First World War and the founders were intellectually inspired *by* the war. In the absence of formal institutions, the architects of IR relied on personal networks and advocacy groups, small publications, and impromptu conferences. This environment turned out to be decisive for the formation of the discipline.

2 | *Genesis of a Discipline*

The subject makes a perfectly intelligible and justifiable academic whole.

Philip Noel-Baker (1929)[1]

Introduction

In the spring of 1919, while the governments were still negotiating in Paris, the University of Aberystwyth appointed the classicist Alfred Zimmern as the inaugural Woodrow Wilson Professor of International Politics.[2] It was the first university chair of its kind, endowed by the Liberal politician and philanthropist David Davies. The idea of the Wilson professorship was, as its name suggested, to promote the academic study of international affairs in a Wilsonian spirit and to unmask the old balance-of-power logic which, as many believed, had caused the First World War.[3] When Davies announced his endowment in December 1918, he knew that he wanted a Wilsonian comrade on the chair and someone willing to work beyond the classroom.[4] Zimmern was Davies's ideal candidate – educated at Oxford, experienced in foreign policy, and committed to international cooperation. Without delay, Zimmern resigned from the British Foreign Office and moved to the Welsh coastal town, thus making International Relations (IR) a university discipline.[5]

Zimmern's appointment was just one instance of a whole range of new professorships, departments, university degrees, journals,

---

[1] Philip Noel-Baker to Gilbert Murray, 9 November 1929, Gilbert Murray Papers, Box 415.
[2] Council Meeting, 25 April 1919, Council & Court of Governors Minutes, University College Wales Archives.
[3] E. L. Ellis, *The University College Wales, Aberystwyth, 1872–1972* (Aberystwyth, 1972), p. 187.
[4] David Davies to Sir John Williams, 5 December 1918, Lord Davies of Llandinam Papers, D4/1, University College Wales, Aberystwyth.
[5] Resignation Confirmation, 10 May 1919, Alfred Zimmern Papers, Box 16.

conferences, and professional associations which emerged during the decade after the First World War. Across Europe and the United States, the study of IR became a respected academic field and a popular subject among students – men and women – who aspired to shape the new international order. Among the most important centres of scholarship were the Institut des Hautes Etudes Internationales in Paris, founded in 1921; the Deutsche Hochschule für Politik in Berlin, founded in 1920; the Konsularakademie in Vienna, restored in 1920; the School of Foreign Service at Georgetown University, Washington, DC, founded in 1919; and the Graduate Institute of International Studies in Geneva, founded in 1927. Besides university programmes, IR was taken up by private research institutes, most prominently the Council on Foreign Relations in New York, founded in 1921, and the British (later Royal) Institute of International Affairs at Chatham House in London, founded in 1920. Perhaps most importantly, the architects of IR established platforms of international exchange, such as the Institute of Pacific Relations, the Williamstown lectures, or the summer schools organised by the Women's International League for Peace and Freedom (WILPF). By building these institutions and shaping their practices, the founders acted as 'architects' in much the same sense as the term is commonly used to describe pioneers of political systems.[6] By the end of the 1920s, there were more than forty IR institutions in a dozen countries, a handbook listed.[7]

Intellectual influences came from a range of fields, primarily from history, law, political science, and economics but also from anthropology, sociology, and philosophy. While drawing on their respective backgrounds, the first generation of IR scholars gradually developed a distinct disciplinary identity by deliberately moving beyond established approaches and institutions. Their research covered international issues "of law and politics in their broadest sense and of ethics and economics".[8] They wrote university curricula and drew up

---

[6] See, for example, G. John Ikenberry, 'The End of Liberal International Order?', *International Affairs* 94:1 (2018), pp. 15–16.
[7] International Institute of Intellectual Cooperation, *Handbook of Institutions for the Scientific Study of International Relations* (Paris, 1929).
[8] Draft deed of the Woodrow Wilson Chair, Aberystwyth, 1919[?], Dr Thomas Jones CH Papers, Vol. 12.

bibliographies, such as Albrecht Mendelssohn Bartholdy's compendium in the journal *Europäische Gespräche* (1924–33) or Parker
Thomas Moon's *Syllabus on International Relations* (1925). In the
wake of this trend, the University of Oxford established a chair in IR
and affirmed that "teaching of the subject will be a permanent
requirement ... not only a valuable but an essential factor in the work
of the University".[9]

The genesis of IR as an academic discipline enjoyed a favourable
political climate. As the world recovered from its most sweeping war
yet, the victorious governments decided to entirely rethink the system
of international politics. Some of this new thinking was written into the
peace treaties, but the terms left plenty of room for interpretation and
for renegotiating what Patrick Cohrs has called "the unfinished
peace".[10] The central site of this debate was the League of Nations
which was supposed to mediate disputes and organise international
life. The League provided a framework for the architects of IR to
operate in, both intellectually and socially.[11] On the one hand, it
reflected the ethos of the new discipline to make international politics
more accessible to scholars, journalists, and the public at large. On the
other hand, the League required trained personnel. To fulfil this need,
IR departments began to offer professional education, sometimes in
collaboration with foreign offices, in order to educate the next generation of diplomatic officials.

Although governments were interested in, and relied on, the educa-
tion of foreign policy experts, most institutions were financed by
private donors and endowments, notably by the Rockefeller
Foundation and the Carnegie Endowment for International Peace.
American philanthropists sponsored IR research in London, Berlin,
Paris, Geneva as well as at Harvard, Columbia, Chicago, and Yale
Universities, and the Brookings Institution.[12] Private sponsors also
supported conferences, publications, and lecture series. Their goal

---

[9] Report by the Board of the Faculty of Social Sciences, 5 May 1934, Gilbert
   Murray Papers, Box 415.
[10] Patrick O. Cohrs, *The Unfinished Peace after World War I: America, Britain
   and the Stabilisation of Europe, 1919–1932* (Cambridge, 2006).
[11] See, for instance, Raymond Fosdick et al. (eds.), *The League of Nations Starts:
   An Outline by Its Organisers* (London, 1920).
[12] Memo, 13 November 1929, Folder 915, Box 101, Series 100.S, RG 1.1, RF,
   Rockefeller Archive Center.

was to support international cooperation by "educational and practical" means – an ambitious programme that amounted to a type of cultural diplomacy, as Katharina Rietzler has argued.[13] Political pressure groups, League of Nations societies, and religious internationalists were important sponsors, too. It is difficult to assess in retrospect to what extent these efforts were guided by an ideological agenda. Was it 'idealism' – to use the common label – that shaped the genesis of IR?

As the records of IR institutions and individuals show, their principal motive was to explore new diplomatic instruments to establish a peaceful international order. Diplomacy was no longer the domain of inherited titles and natural law. The architects of IR sought to open up this new world to researchers, students, and the general public. It is difficult, however, to identify a consistent approach underpinning their work, let alone a school of 'idealists'. If anything, they saw their discipline as an applied science of democracy, a symbiosis of "expert knowledge and popular control".[14] To advance this project, they needed an institutional framework, academic credibility, and financial support. That also explains why many professors and educators were associated with non-university groups, such as the Peace Through Law Association (Association de la paix par le droit), which Norman Ingram aptly labelled "pacifism of the pedagogues".[15] It was this composition that gave rise to the university discipline IR as we know it today.

Histories of IR have paid little attention to the institutional environment of early IR scholarship and focused instead on re-interpreting the published works of well-known authors.[16] This chapter draws on archival sources from across Europe and the United States to uncover the motives behind these institutions and to contextualise the intellectual output they produced over the following decades. It begins in

---

[13] Memo by Tracy Kittredge for S. H. Walker on Geneva Summer Schools (since 1924), 15 February 1935, Folder 60, Box 7, RG 3, RF, Rockefeller Archive Center; Katharina Rietzler, 'Before the Cultural Cold Wars: American Philanthropy and Cultural Diplomacy in the Interwar Years', *Historical Research* 84:223 (2011), pp. 148–64.

[14] Alfred Zimmern, *Learning and Leadership: A Study of the Needs and Possibilities of International Intellectual Cooperation* (Oxford, 1928), p. 62.

[15] Norman Ingram, *The Politics of Dissent: Pacifism in France 1919–1939* (Oxford, 1991), p. 17.

[16] Lucian M. Ashworth, *A History of International Thought: From the Origins of the Modern State to Academic International Relations* (New York, 2014), p. 7.

Aberystwyth and covers the famous IR chairs at the London School of Economics and Oxford as well as Chatham House, the most important British non-university institution in the field. The second section looks at university departments in continental Europe that played important roles during the interwar period but have since been largely forgotten, including those in Berlin, Hamburg, Paris, Vienna, and Geneva. As the next section shows, American universities adopted IR from a somewhat remote perspective, given the temporary American withdrawal from the international stage. Yet the subject soon flourished on university campuses such as Georgetown, Chicago, Princeton, and Yale as well as among the political and financial establishment in Washington and New York. Finally, the last section presents a few examples of the global spread of IR while acknowledging that the discipline remained heavily Eurocentric throughout the interwar period.

By 1930, when Zimmern took up the Montague Burton Chair at Oxford, he triumphantly concluded that "the study of international relations ha[d] been lifted from the sphere of propaganda" and found "its rightful place among the other university studies".[17] That observation, although partly true, hints at the contentious reputation of the emerging discipline. Zimmern's critics were "getting a little tired of ten years of [League of Nations] propaganda".[18] The reasons for the controversial nature of early IR scholarship, this chapter argues, are to be found in its institutional history as much as in its intellectual origins.

The Cradle of International Relations

Aberystwyth was a somewhat arbitrary location for the birth of IR. David Davies's original idea was to install two professorships, one in Oxford and one in Strasbourg. But Thomas Jones, an influential civil servant better known as T. J., convinced Davies to have it based in Wales, where they both came from.[19] Born into a wealthy industrialist family, Davies was a Liberal member of parliament and an avid

---

[17] Inaugural Lecture, 1930, Alfred Zimmern Papers, Box 140.
[18] Hugh Richardson to Gilbert Murray, 27 May 1930, Gilbert Murray Papers, Box 415.
[19] "DD. had suddenly got [an idea] of founding a Wilson Chair of International Politics at Oxford and another at Strasbourg, to be called the Grey Chair [...] I fought with all my might for putting the former at Aberystwyth and was well

supporter of the League of Nations. Among other causes, he financed the British League of Nations Union, where he sat on the executive committee alongside Lord Robert Cecil and Gilbert Murray.[20] His circle also included Walter Phillimore, chairman of the committee who prepared the Phillimore report on the League of Nations.[21] In November 1918, Davies sent a letter to some of his friends, later published in *The Times*, in which he outlined the idea of a professorship, to be endowed by himself and his sisters:

for the study of those related problems of law and politics, of ethics and economics, which are raised by the project of a League of Nations, and for the encouragement of a truer understanding of civilisations other than our own. We are prepared to contribute for this object the sum of £20,000, and we should be glad, if our proposal is accepted, that the Chair should be associated with the illustrious name of President Wilson.[22]

A committed philanthropist, Davies had previously donated to the National Library of Wales and the fight against tuberculosis. Now, in the wake of what he considered a civilisational catastrophe, he turned to international affairs and dedicated the Wilson Chair to the memory of students who had fallen in the Great War. A 1918 newspaper article called it the "brain of the League of Nations".[23] Davies strongly believed in international cooperation, and he considered it a service to humanity to support academic research in this field.[24] It was the responsibility of universities, he argued, to educate a new generation of diplomats, politicians, and civil servants who were committed to the cause of the League. He also decreed a representative of the League to sit on the board of trustees.[25] Ultimately, Davies's intention was to spread "knowledge and enlightened public opinion in all countries".[26]

---

backed by Miss Davies and ultimately I succeeded". Thomas Jones to Watkins, 30 November 1918, Thomas Jones Papers, Vol. 12.

[20] Memo by Gilbert Murray, 25 April 1919, Gilbert Murray Papers, Box 181.

[21] Minutes of a meeting of Lord Cecil's advisory committee at the Foreign Office, 22 January 1919, Gilbert Murray Papers, Box 180.

[22] *The Times*, 7 December 1918, Press clipping, Thomas Jones Papers, Vol. 12.

[23] William Archer, 'A New Science', December 1918, Newspaper clipping, Thomas Jones Papers, Vol. 12.

[24] Ellis, *The University College Wales*, p. 187.

[25] Copy of Trust Deed, David Davies endowment to Aberystwyth, 1922, Fletcher School of Law and Diplomacy Records, Box 1, Folder 2.

[26] *The Times*, 7 December 1918, Press clipping, Thomas Jones Papers, Vol. 12.

While his motives were clear, the appointment procedure for the chair
was somewhat obscure. Neither the official endowment letter nor the
university council minutes specified any academic requirements for the
position. There was not even a list of applicants. Davies wanted no less
than "the best international scholar the world possesses".[27] T. J. con-
tacted Zimmern in November 1918 to find out whether he might be
interested in the position.[28] A few days later, on 8 December, Zimmern
responded favourably.[29] Without any formal election, he was appointed
inaugural Woodrow Wilson Professor in the spring of 1919.[30]

Zimmern was Davies's ideal candidate. Educated at New College,
Oxford, Zimmern became a classics tutor in 1904 and served as an
inspector at the Board of Education from 1912 to 1915.[31] During this
time, he developed an interest in international affairs and popular
education, and began to publish in journals such as *The Economic
Review*, *The Sociological Review*, and *The New Republic*.[32] After the
outbreak of the war, he became involved at the League of Nations
Society (later Union) and drafted foreign policy documents for the
government. From August 1918 until May 1919, Zimmern served as
an advisor to the intelligence department at the British Foreign Office
and participated in the negotiations in Paris.[33] While there, he was
involved in the formation of the British Institute of International
Affairs and established relationships with colleagues from the United
States and Europe. Zimmern's biography, even prior to his appointment at Aberystwyth, was characteristic for many IR pioneers in the
way he transcended professional and national boundaries.

[27] David Davies to John Williams, 5 December 1918, quoted in Ellis,
The University College Wales, p. 188.
[28] Thomas Jones to Watkins, 30 November 1918, Thomas Jones Papers, Vol. 12.
[29] Alfred Zimmern to Thomas Jones, 8 December 1918, Thomas Jones Papers,
Vol. 12.
[30] Davies later admitted that he had "practically nominated" him to the Wilson
Chair. Ellis, *The University College Wales*, p. 221.
[31] D. J. Markwell, 'Zimmern, Sir Alfred Eckhard (1879–1957)', *Oxford
Dictionary of National Biography* (Oxford, 2004), available at http://ezproxy-
prd.bodleian.ox.ac.uk:2167/view/article/37088 [accessed 1 February 2017];
Tomohito Baji, *The International Thought of Alfred Zimmern: Classicism,
Zionism and the Shadow of Commonwealth* (Cham, 2021).
[32] Alfred Zimmern, 'The Alien's Act: A Challenge', *The Economic Review* 21:2
(1911), pp. 187–97; Alfred Zimmern, 'Nationality and Government',
Sociological Review a8:4 (1916), pp. 213–33.
[33] Appointment notification, 12 August 1918, Alfred Zimmern Papers, Box 15.

After accepting the appointment, Zimmern drew up a curriculum for the newborn subject and defined the lifestyle of an IR professor. He interpreted his role as a general public service involving extensive travel and non-academic stints. The university granted him one term of absence per year as well as an academic assistant – a position designed for Sydney Herbert.[34] Zimmern wanted:

to act as exchange professor in a foreign country for a term, or to sit on Commissions dealing with international questions, apart from the paramount necessity of travel: for, while the chemist can work in a laboratory on the spot, his laboratory is like the ever changing water.[35]

He also wanted to attract foreign students and establish an international library network.[36] Zimmern's successors in the Wilson Chair, Charles Webster and Jerome D. Greene, continued this tradition and compiled detailed annual reports, imitating the style of diplomatic despatches and taking pride in their semi-political missions to Europe, the United States, Japan, India, and elsewhere.[37] As a result of their non-academic preoccupations and the lack of a formal degree in International Politics, student numbers at Aberystwyth never exceeded a dozen during the interwar period.[38]

The establishment of the Aberystwyth chair was widely celebrated by academics and the press. Oxford classicist Gilbert Murray welcomed Davies's endowment as the culmination of their common work at the League of Nations Union, "trying to get the best brains in the country to cooperate in studying these problems", and he saw the Wilson Chair as part of an emerging field spanning neighbouring disciplines.[39] Like Murray, the writer and critic William Archer saw the implications of Aberystwyth in building "a new science".[40] He described it as a response to the theory of nationalism and as an

---

[34] Alfred Zimmern to Thomas Jones, 8 December 1918; and Draft Contract for the Wilson Chair, Thomas Jones Papers, Vol. 12.
[35] Ibid.
[36] Alfred Zimmern to David Davies, 24 March 1919, Thomas Jones Papers, Vol. 12.
[37] "I saw a number of members of the Government and other public men. In these three tours I travelled about seven thousand miles". See Report for Year 1925–6 by Charles Webster, David Davies of Llandinam Papers, D4/1 (Wilson Chair).
[38] Departmental Report, 23 November 1942, Thomas Jones Papers, Vol. 12.
[39] *The Observer*, 15 December 1918, Newspaper clipping, Thomas Jones Papers, Vol. 12.
[40] William Archer, 'A New Science', December 1918, Newspaper clipping, Thomas Jones Papers, Vol. 12.

intellectual exercise for international organisations, an emerging
field for which he credited Leonard Woolf's book *International
Government* (1916). The Wilson Chair was undoubtedly an important
milestone in the formation of IR, though Zimmern's tenure was cut
short in June 1921 following a private affair.[41]

More important than a single academic appointment, however, was
the surging interest in international affairs in Britain, manifested in
student societies, reading circles, and a flood of educational and political pamphlets. Besides university-based organisations, the study of IR
was promoted by pressure groups, such as the League of Nations
Union and the Fabian Society. Public discourse was no longer limited
to the parliament and a few influential newspapers. The League of
Nations and its associated bodies inspired a new culture of political
participation, as Helen McCarthy has shown.[42] What is more, the
female franchise now allowed women to formalise their long-standing
interest in international affairs and compete for political offices which,
in turn, inspired a new generation of women to pursue education and
research in the field.[43] Advocacy groups, such as WILPF, demanded
more female representation at international organisations.[44]

The new interest in international affairs was perhaps best reflected
by the British Institute of International Affairs. It was founded on
5 July 1920 by a set of politicians and foreign policy experts, led by
Lionel Curtis and Philip Kerr who had previously organised the Round
Table Movement. Original members of the British Institute of
International Affairs included the politicians Robert Cecil, Eustace
Percy, and Arthur Ponsonby as well as the historians Arnold
Toynbee and Alfred Zimmern.[45] Growing out of the informal meetings
of Anglo-American experts at the Paris Peace Conference, the Institute

---

[41] Ellis, *The University College Wales*, p. 217.
[42] Helen McCarthy, *The British People and the League of Nations: Democracy,
Citizenship and Internationalism, c. 1918–1945* (Manchester, 2011), p. 1.
[43] Valeska Huber, Tamson Pietsch, and Katharina Rietzler, 'Women's
International Thought and the New Professions, 1900–1940', *Modern
Intellectual History* 18:1 (2021), pp. 121–45.
[44] Jan Stöckmann, 'Women, Wars, and World Affairs: Recovering Feminist
International Relations, 1915–39', *Review of International Studies* 44:2 (2018),
pp. 232–3.
[45] 'Original Members of the British Institute of International Affairs', 1920,
Chatham House Online Archive.

was supposed to be a permanent platform for research and debate on international affairs – the American counterpart being the Council on Foreign Relations. In 1923, the Institute moved into its premises at Chatham House, a gift from colonel Reuben Wells Leonard. Financial support came from the newspaper tycoon William Waldorf Astor and from Robert Brand, the founder of the Imperial Munitions Board and a former civil servant.[46]

The British Institute of International Affairs hosted regular debates and social events, gathering prominent politicians, professors, and business people. Women were admitted from the outset. The writers Ray Strachey and Edith Balfour Lyttelton served on the executive committee and Eleanor Cargin as secretary. Helena Swanwick was a member, too.[47] The Institute published a journal as well as reports on current affairs and official documents. From 1925, Toynbee (the director of studies) edited the *Survey of International Affairs*, an annual summary of current events. In 1926, the Institute received its Royal Charter and became the Royal Institute of International Affairs. On this occasion, it reaffirmed its mission "to encourage the scientific study of international politics, economics, and jurisprudence".[48]

The idea of Chatham House was to create a space at the intersection of research and politics, leaving its relationship with the government deliberately ambiguous.[49] Its members came from various professional and political backgrounds but they agreed that studying IR in a non-official environment would produce fruitful research and policy recommendations. They were convinced that informed debates would benefit the quality of foreign policy. By serving the dual purposes of research and political consultancy, however, Chatham House assumed a tricky role. It was neither an impartial observer of international affairs nor a sponsor of a specific political agenda.

There was an obvious tension, too, between the claim to inform the general public and the exclusive events held at St. James' Square. On the one hand, the founders of the Institute committed to "widespread and accurate knowledge".[50] They understood themselves as

---

[46] Andrea Bosco, 'Introduction', in Andrea Bosco and Cornelia Navari (eds.), *Chatham House and British Foreign Policy, 1919–1945* (London, 1994), p. 6.
[47] 'Rules and List of Members 1922', July 1922, Chatham House Online Archive.
[48] '30th Anniversary Banquet', 7 July 1949, Chatham House Online Archive.
[49] Bosco, 'Introduction', p. 8.
[50] '30th Anniversary Banquet', 7 July 1949, Chatham House Online Archive.

champions of political enlightenment and some members, such as
Zimmern, had actually worked in popular education. On the other
hand, they often withdrew to closed seminar rooms and tried to influence policy through the very kind of backdoor diplomacy which they
condemned as having caused the recent war. Chatham House was an
"unashamedly elitist institution" embedded in London's social clubs.[51]
As such it reflected the more general dilemma of early IR scholarship –
to democratise a domain of government that was notoriously
undemocratic.

Five years after Aberystwyth, in December 1923, the banker and
philanthropist Ernest Cassel made an endowment to the London
School of Economics and Political Science (LSE) for a professorship
in "International Affairs".[52] The LSE, then directed by economist and
social reformer William Beveridge, thought that the subject nicely
complemented the spectrum of social sciences already taught at the
school, including economics, political science, sociology, and anthropology.[53] Founded just over thirty years earlier by a group of Fabians,
the LSE was a progressive institution committed to educating a new
generation of students for public service. As such it was an obvious
home for a new academic subject with ambitious goals. Beveridge
welcomed the offer and thought the professor should cover "methods
of diplomacy, treaties, League of Nations, arbitration, and racial
problems ...".[54] Initially, there was no distinct department, and so
the Cassel Chair was adopted by the history faculty for the time being.

Most LSE professors acknowledged the increasing importance of
international politics, especially with regard to the recent war and the
new role played by the League of Nations.[55] At the same time, however, the history faculty warned that "special care must be taken to
prevent the Chair from becoming identified with propaganda for or

[51] Donald Cameron Watt, 'Foreword', in Andrea Bosco and Cornelia Navari (eds.),
Chatham House and British Foreign Policy, 1919–1945 (London, 1994), p. i.
[52] Edwin Deller to William Beveridge, 21 December 1923, LSE Archives, Central
Filing Registry, Box 252: 134/8/A,B.
[53] Ralf Dahrendorf, *A History of the London School of Economics and Political
Science, 1895–1995* (Oxford, 1995), p. 199.
[54] William Beveridge to Twentyman, 11 December 1923, LSE Archives, Central
Filing Registry, Box 252: 134/8/A,B.
[55] F. S. Northedge, *Department of International History: A Brief History,
1924–1971*, LSE Archives, School History, Box 12.

against the League".[56] The LSE was wary to give the new chair an ideological branding like the Wilson Chair at Aberystwyth, and warned against confusing scientific investigation with political propaganda. Yet, it was widely understood that the Cassel Professor would not simply observe and explain international politics, but make normative claims about it. Like most early IR professorships, the Cassel Chair was established with the aim of preventing future conflicts by teaching a certain type of diplomacy.

Half a dozen candidates applied for the LSE professorship, including Zimmern who had stepped down from the Aberystwyth chair. The successful candidate was Philip Noel-Baker, a gifted young scholar and politician who had previously worked at the British Foreign Office, served as Cecil's assistant during the Paris Peace Conference, and then worked for the first secretary-general of the League of Nations, Sir Eric Drummond, in Geneva.[57] Besides, Noel-Baker was a successful middle-distance runner and winner of an Olympic silver medal in 1920. His public profile appealed to the committee and he was elected to start in the 1924–5 academic year.[58] Noel-Baker's lectures dealt with global interdependence and the new forms of international organisation, focusing especially on the League of Nations and disarmament.[59] LSE historian F. S. Northedge described Noel-Baker's portfolio as biased towards questions of "peaceful settlement of international disputes", but considered his appointment a breakthrough for the study of IR.[60]

Thanks to the popularity of Noel-Baker's classes the subject became a fully fledged university discipline in 1927, when the LSE received a Rockefeller grant and opened a department of International Relations.[61] To unfold its potential and spread its influence, the

---

[56] Reports of Boards of Studies in History and Economics, 6 February 1924, LSE Archives, Central Filing Registry, Box 252: 134/8/A,B.

[57] Noel-Baker's application included letters of reference from Cecil, Drummond, Arthur Pigou, and Fridtjof Nansen. See application letter, 23 April 1924, Philip Noel-Baker Papers, NBKR 8/8/1.

[58] Edwin Deller to William Beveridge, 5 May 1924, Central Filing Registry, Box 252: 134/8/A,B, LSE Archives, London.

[59] Lecture notes, 1927–8 and 1928–9, Philip Noel-Baker Papers, NBKR 8/ 12/3.

[60] F. S. Northedge, *Department of International History: A Brief History, 1924–1971*, LSE Archives, School History, Box 12.

[61] Nicholas Sims, *Foundation and History of the International Relations Department* (London, 2003), available at www.lse.ac.uk/internationalRelations/aboutthedepartment/historyofdept.aspx [accessed 12 December 2014].

department set up collaborative programmes with other institutions for the study of IR, including the Royal Institute of International Affairs in London and the Graduate Institute of International Studies in Geneva. In 1928, LSE director Beveridge offered a prize for the best student in the Department to visit Geneva.[62] Just as important were the encounters "outside the classroom", as a 1929 brochure put it.[63] Arnold Toynbee was a crucial asset in this respect, as he simultaneously served as professor of International History at LSE and as director of studies at Chatham House. Toynbee kept a high profile in London's foreign policy circles and was convinced that any student of IR should be acquainted with its practice.[64]

Given the political ambitions of early IR scholars, it comes as no surprise that Noel-Baker held his professorship no longer than five years before re-entering the world of politics. In 1929, he took up a seat in the House of Commons as a Labour MP and became private secretary to Foreign Secretary Arthur Henderson.[65] Noel-Baker's successor had big shoes to fill and academic credentials were not enough for this position. James Shotwell recommended David Mitrany on the grounds of Mitrany's work for the Carnegie Endowment for International Peace and his accolades in "furthering the policies for which it stands".[66] Eventually, the chair went to the legal expert Charles Manning who himself had experience at the League of Nations and, like almost every one of his British colleagues, was educated at Oxford. Not that these career patterns would have prevented them from independent thinking, but it raised questions about the social barriers to entering the field.

At the end of the 1920s, the University of Oxford decided to establish a chair in International Relations, too. The reason for this delay, Martin Ceadel has speculated, lay in the "historic peculiarities" of the medieval university with its collegiate system and conservative curriculum.[67] The papers of Thomas Jones (T. J.), however, reveal that it was

---

[62] Ibid.   [63] LSE Brochure, Session 1928–9, Gilbert Murray Papers, Box 415.
[64] Arnold Toynbee to Gilbert Murray, 9 May 1929, Gilbert Murray Papers, Box 415.
[65] Memo on the Cassel Chair, 1929(?), LSE Archives, Central Filing Registry, Box 252: 134/8/A,B.
[66] James Shotwell to William Beveridge, 3 July 1929, LSE Archives, Central Filing Registry, Box 252: 134/8/A,B.
[67] Martin Ceadel, 'The Academic Normalisation of IR at Oxford', in Christopher Hood et al., *Forging a Discipline: A Critical Assessment of Oxford's*

only because T. J. convinced David Davies in 1918 to offer the endowment to Aberystwyth that it did not go to Oxford.[68] Nor was there a lack of academic interest at Oxford. The Master of Balliol College, Arthur Lionel Smith, called the Aberystwyth professorship in 1919 "an extraordinarily interesting and valuable new departure in our educational system".[69] Indeed, IR topics were taught at Oxford since at least the early 1920s. The Politics, Philosophy and Economics (PPE) degree was established in 1921, including an optional paper on 'The Development of International Relations since 1815'. Among the first tutors were Manning and John Redcliffe-Maud.

In November 1929, a professorship was endowed by the Lithuanian-born textile merchant Montague Burton who, like other IR philanthropists, had a clear conception of what the discipline should focus on. "His real interest is in the League of Nations and constructive peace", explained Gilbert Murray who liaised between Burton and the university authorities.[70] It was to be "a League of Nations Chair in fact", Murray transmitted.[71] When Burton approached Murray with a formal offer to donate shares of his company to the amount of a full professorship, he intended to call it "The Montague Burton Chair of International Peace".[72] Murray was positively inclined but wanted to speak to some colleagues first. His friend Noel-Baker replied that he was in principle satisfied with the idea but urged the chair to be called 'International Relations' rather than 'International Peace'.[73] Following further debate at the university council, Murray told Burton that Oxford would be honoured to accept the offer but that there were concerns about its ideological bias:

Development of the Study of Politics and International Relations in Comparative Perspective (Oxford, 2014), pp. 185–6.
[68] Thomas Jones to Watkins, 30 November 1918, Thomas Jones Papers, Vol. 12.
[69] Arthur Lionel Smith to Thomas Jones, 16 March 1919, Dr Thomas Jones Papers, Vol. 12, National Library of Wales.
[70] Gilbert Murray to Fisher, 4 November 1929, 7 November 1929, Gilbert Murray Papers, Box 415.
[71] Gilbert Murray to Philip Noel-Baker, 4 November 1929, Gilbert Murray Papers, Box 415.
[72] Montague Burton to Gilbert Murray, 7 November 1929, Gilbert Murray Papers, Box 415.
[73] Philip Noel-Baker to Gilbert Murray, 9 November 1929, Gilbert Murray Papers, Box 415.

They have a difficulty in the title. A Professorship of Peace might seem to suggest propaganda rather than education, and they would prefer some such title as 'The Montague Burton Chair of International Relations'.[74]

Apart from the name of the chair, there was also debate about the members of the appointment committee. Burton insisted that besides professors of the law, history, and politics faculties, Lord Cecil and Gilbert Murray should be on the panel, both of whom he was certain agreed with his agenda. To emphasise his point, he asked the committee to keep in mind that:

the under-lying motive of the Donor is the furtherance of International Peace in accordance with the deliberations and decisions of the League of Nations at Geneva.[75]

Eventually, the university's call for applications specified that the future professor would teach:

the theory of International Relations and on methods of international cooperation with particular reference to the work and aims of the League of Nations.[76]

Some thought that these conditions meant to ideologically predetermine the chair and a debate ensued in the *Manchester Guardian* about the extent to which a university could impose a political line on its appointee.[77] In the end, the selection committee adopted Noel-Baker's recommendation but complied with the donor's request and appointed Zimmern to the chair, which he accepted in August 1930. To everyone's satisfaction, Zimmern managed to generate a lot of interest in his lectures. By 1934, the social studies department reported that the chair had become "not only a valuable but an essential factor in the work of the University".[78]

The Montague Burton chair was a milestone in the history of IR as an academic discipline. The subject was now taught at the most

[74] Gilbert Murray to Montague Burton, 27 December 1929, Gilbert Murray Papers, Box 415.
[75] Montague Burton to S. Craig, 15 January 1930, Oxford University Archives, UR6/MB/1, file 1.
[76] Call for applications, dated 17 June 1930, Oxford University Archives, UR6/MB/1, file 1.
[77] Hugh Richardson to Gilbert Murray, 27 May 1930, Gilbert Murray Papers, Box 415.
[78] Ceadel, 'The Academic Normalisation of IR at Oxford', p. 189.

influential university in Britain which educated the country's political and diplomatic elite. Even though student numbers did not exceed a few dozen at first, the discipline gained significantly in publicity. While Cambridge did not have a professorship until much later, there was interest in the field, too. Arnold McNair, Whewell Professor of International Law at Cambridge, regretted the absence of an IR chair in his university and took the liberty to "stray a little across the frontier which divides law from politics".[79] By the 1930s, then, IR was firmly established in British academia, although this was by no means the only site of interwar IR scholarship.

From Berlin to Geneva

Although today the vast majority of (and certainly the most prestigious) IR departments are located in the Anglo-American world, the origins of the discipline lay in continental Europe, too. After all, the war had primarily been fought on the 'old continent'. Here were the roots of the conflict and the solutions to peace. Europe was a natural habitat for IR scholars. Indeed even those who later worked overseas often had a personal background in Europe, especially in Germany, including Hajo Holborn, Hans Morgenthau, Reinhold Niebuhr, and Arnold Wolfers. Europe accentuated the fundamental geopolitical problems studied by IR – nations, borders, minorities, economic interdependence, arms races, and the imbalance of political power. What is more, European powers exported these concepts (and problems) through their colonial empires. Perhaps unsurprisingly then, many of the early institutions were established in continental Europe.

In October 1920, the journalist and liberal politician Ernst Jäckh co-founded the Deutsche Hochschule für Politik (DHfP) in Berlin. The DHfP was a graduate school that offered short-term courses in domestic and foreign politics, sociology, as well as cultural studies.[80]

---

[79] Arnold McNair, 'Collective Security', *British Year Book of International Law* 17 (1936), p. 150.

[80] See Rainer Eisfeld, *Ausgebürgert und doch angebräunt: Deutsche Politikwissenschaft 1920–1945*, 2nd ed. (Baden-Baden, 2013); Manfred Gangl, 'Die Gründung der Deutschen Hochschule für Politik', in Manfred Gangl (ed.), *Das Politische. Zur Entstehung der Politikwissenschaft während Weimarer Republik* (Frankfurt, 2008), pp. 77–96; Steven D. Korenblat, 'A School for the Republic? Cosmopolitans and Their Enemies at the Deutsche Hochschule Für Politik, 1920–1933', *Central European History*, xxxix:3 (2006), pp. 394–430;

Jäckh was a national-liberal journalist and politician and a confidant of Friedrich Naumann, the founding president of the German Democratic Party.[81] Jäckh wanted the DHfP to educate a new generation of diplomats and public servants in the spirit of a "new Germany".[82] He founded the school in memory of his son who had been killed in action in France.[83] The DHfP was inspired by Naumann's *Staatsbürgerschule*, a 'school of citizenship' for the Weimar Republic founded in 1918. After Naumann's death in August 1919, Jäckh turned his idea into a larger institution. He received prominent support from historians Hans Delbrück, Friedrich Meinecke, and Otto Hoetzsch as well as politicians, diplomats, and industrialists, such as Richard von Kühlmann and Walter Simons.[84] The DHfP's political stance was predominantly liberal. Most of its staff welcomed the Weimar Republic and supported Germany's accession to the League of Nations, although faculty members came from a wide range of political backgrounds, including the conservative political theorist Carl Schmitt who taught at the DHfP from 1930.[85]

Like its Anglo-American counterparts, the DHfP enjoyed the support of wealthy philanthropists alongside government funds and student fees.[86] Donations came from Robert Bosch, Walther Rathenau, Carl Friedrich Siemens, Hjalmar Schacht, and Carl Melchior.[87] In 1926, the Carnegie Endowment sponsored a chair for foreign policy and history at the DHfP.[88] Among the long list of prominent lecturers were the politician Gertrud Bäumer, the economist Moritz Julius Bonn,

Erich Nickel, *Politik und Politikwissenschaft in der Weimarer Republik* (Berlin, 2004).
[81] Peter Weber, 'Ernst Jäckh and the National Internationalism of Interwar Germany', *Central European History* 52:3 (2019), pp. 406–7.
[82] Ernst Jäckh, *The New Germany: Three Lectures by Ernst Jäckh* (Oxford, 1927), p. 64.
[83] Speech by Ernst Jäckh, delivered at the International Studies Conference, London, 1 June 1933, IIIC Records, Box 317, Folder 3.
[84] 'Zur Hochschule für Politik', by E. Jäckh, *Deutsche Politik*, 12 November 1920, Heft 46, Ernst Jäckh Papers, Box 15.
[85] Joseph J. Bendersky, *Carl Schmitt: Theorist for the Reich* (Princeton, 1983), pp. 141–2.
[86] Hans Freytag to DHfP, 8 July 1929, GStA PK, I. HA Rep. 303, Nr. 2115.
[87] Roswitha Wollkopf, *Zur politischen Konzeption und Wirksamkeit der Deutschen Hochschule für Politik (1920–1933)*, PhD thesis (Berlin, 1983), p. 11.
[88] GStA PK, HA Rep. 303 (neu) Nr. 51. See also Katharina Rietzler, 'Philanthropy, Peace Research and Revisionist Politics: Rockefeller and Carnegie Support for the Study of International Relations in Weimar Germany', *Bulletin of the*

the historian Hans Delbrück, the editor and politician Theodor Heuss, the historian Hajo Holborn, and, as visiting speakers, French historian Pierre Renouvin, Columbia University president Nicholas Murray Butler and the historian James Shotwell.[89] The DHfP offered courses in domestic and foreign politics, sociology, as well as cultural and social policy, attracting several hundred students per semester, most of whom attended individual DHfP seminars rather than reading for full degrees.[90] Given its academic record, the DHfP quickly rose to international prominence and was sometimes referred to as a sister institution of the LSE or Sciences Po.[91]

The principal motivation for founding the DHfP was to reintegrate Germany into the international community. It was an attempt to rationalise the conduct of politics within a new democratic governance system, both nationally and internationally. Many of the DHfP's lecturers and governors, such as Jäckh or Bäumer, were politically active themselves and welcomed the opportunity to study issues previously undisclosed to the public. The DHfP encouraged political life on campus and modelled its curriculum according to the needs of future government officials. In fact, it offered courses specifically designed for diplomat trainees.[92] One of its lecturers, Arnold Wolfers, stylised the DHfP as a "school of democracy", a label that historians have since rejected with regard to its inglorious history after 1933, but which nonetheless captures the spirit of its original purpose.[93] The DHfP was also inspired by the orientalist and education reformer Carl Heinrich Becker who argued that Germany required institutions for the study of

---

German Historical Institute 5 (2008), pp. 61–79; Antonio Missiroli, *Die Deutsche Hochschule für Politik* (Sankt Augustin, 1988), pp. 21–3, 36.

[89] Ernst Jäckh, 'Zur Hochschule für Politik', *Deutsche Politik* Heft 46, 12 November 1920, Ernst Jäckh Papers, Box 15. In 1920–1, the DHfP had 60 lecturers. Nickel, *Politik und Politikwissenschaft in der Weimarer Republik*, p. 81.

[90] Jan Stöckmann, 'Studying the International, Serving the Nation: The Origins of International Relations (IR) Scholarship in Germany, 1912–33', *The International History Review* 38:5 (2016), pp. 1050–80.

[91] Radio documentary on Arnold Toynbee's visit to Germany in 1936, broadcast on 13 April 1967, *Bayerischer Rundfunk*, Arnold Toynbee Papers, Box 13.

[92] Korenblat, 'A School for the Republic?', p. 394.

[93] Detlef Lehnert, '"Schule der Demokratie" oder "politische Fachhochschule"?: Anspruch und Wirklichkeit einer praxisorientierten Ausbildung der Deutschen Hochschule für Politik, 1920–1933', in Gerhard Göhler and Bodo Zeuner (eds.), *Kontinuitäten und Brüche in der deutschen Politikwissenschaft* (Baden-Baden, 1991), p. 65.

IR (*Auslandsstudien*) to deal with the rising phenomenon of globalisation.[94] Becker's point reflected the twofold observation, traced in Chapter 1, that the world had become more interdependent and therefore needed new forms of international organisation. To master this new world IR seemed like an appropriate training.

Considerably smaller than the DHfP but similarly influential was the Institut für Auswärtige Politik (IAP) in Hamburg. Primarily a research centre and library, the IAP was the joint creation of a group of statesmen, intellectuals, and businessmen, including Max von Baden, Lujo Brentano, Hans Delbrück, Carl Melchior, Max Montgelas, Max Warburg, and Max Weber.[95] At the end of the war, this informal foreign-policy circle, known as the *Heidelberger Vereinigung*, set out to furnish an "independent study on the responsibility for the war" – essentially an academic justification for the German war policy.[96] A preliminary bureau was set up in February 1921 with the law professor Albrecht Mendelssohn Bartholdy as inaugural director. In January 1923, it became a research institute affiliated with the University of Hamburg.[97] Initially more of an information and archive centre, the IAP soon evolved into a fully fledged research institute with regular lectures, guest speakers, and its own periodical, suitably called *Europäische Gespräche*, published between 1924 and 1933.

---

[94] C. H. Becker, 'Die Denkschrift des preußischen Kultusministeriums über die Förderung der Auslandsstudien', *Drucksachen des Preußischen Abgeordnetenhauses*, 22. Legislaturperiode. VI. Session (1916/17.), Nr. 388, 24.1.1917. See Béatrice Bonniot, 'Von der politischen Bildung zur Politikwissenschaft: Der Beitrag Carl Heinrich Beckers zur Entstehung einer neuen wissenschaftlichen Disziplin', in Manfred Gangl (ed.), *Das Politische: Zur Entstehung der Politikwissenschaft während der Weimarer Republik* (Frankfurt a.M., 2008), pp. 65–76.

[95] Gisela Gantzel-Kress and Klaus Jürgen Gantzel, 'The Development of International Relations Studies in West Germany', in Ekkehart Krippendorff and Volker Rittberger (eds.), *The Foreign Policy of West Germany: Formation and Contents* (London, 1980), pp. 197–269; Gisela Gantzel-Kress, 'Das Institut für Auswärtige Politik im Übergang von der Weimarer Republik zum Nationalsozialismus (1933 bis 1937)', in Eckart Krause, Ludwig Huber, and Holger Fischer *Hochschulalltag im 'Dritten Reich': Die Hamburger Universität 1933–1945, Teil II: Philosophische Fakultät Rechts- und Staatswissenschaftliche Fakultät* (Berlin, 1991), pp. 913–38.

[96] Max Warburg to Albrecht Mendelssohn Bartholdy, 12 January 1920, Albrecht Mendelssohn Bartholy Papers, SPK MA Nachl. AMB, 2,27,9.

[97] Muriel K. Grindrod, 'The Institut für Auswärtige Politik, Poststrasse 19, Hamburg', *International Affairs* 10:2 (1931), pp. 223–4.

As Mendelssohn Bartholdy liked to stress, it was modelled after British and American institutions for the study of IR, and there was regular exchange with foreign colleagues since the early 1920s.[98] Although Mendelssohn Bartholdy came from a legal background himself, specialising in civil procedure and international private law, he now focused on political questions of international life. The IAP became a well-respected IR institute and featured a library that was "almost identical with that of Chatham House".[99] Among the few affiliated scholars were liberal political scientists, lawyers and historians, including Hans von Dohnányi, Theodor Haubach, Magdalene Schoch (the first female lawyer to habilitate in Germany), and Alfred Vagts. The IAP entertained relationships with the DHfP as well as international partners.[100] Its mission was in line with other centres for the study of IR, though perhaps with a stronger background in law and history.

Mendelssohn Bartholdy was a widely respected international lawyer, a descendant of an accomplished Jewish family and a prominent public intellectual.[101] He attempted a curious balancing act between intellectual independence and official German policy. He was a "conciliatory diplomat", as historians have described him, albeit with a nationalist undertone.[102] The German government recruited him for negotiations at Versailles, The Hague, and Geneva. He also helped to edit official document collections.[103] He vigorously rejected

---

[98] Memo by the Trustees of the Anglo-American University Library for Central Europe, signed by Gilbert Murray, Arnold S. Rowntree, and William Temple, 1920(?), Albrecht Mendelssohn Bartholdy Papers, SPK MA Nachl. AMB, 2,27,49.

[99] Grindrod, 'The Institut für Auswärtige Politik, Poststrasse 19, Hamburg', p. 227.

[100] Walter Simons to Werner Picht, 1 October 1927, GStA PK, I. HA Rep. 303, Nr. 2116.

[101] Rainer Nicolaysen, 'Albrecht Mendelssohn Bartholdy (1874–1936): Jurist, Friedensforscher, Künstler', *Rabels Zeitschrift* 75 (2011), pp. 1–31.

[102] Gisela Gantzel-Kress, ' Albrecht Mendelssohn Bartholdy: Ein Bürgerhumanist und Versöhnungsdiplomat im Aufbruch der Demokratie in Deutschland', *Zeitschrift des Vereins für Hamburgische Geschichte*, Bd. 71 (1985), pp. 127–43; Stöckmann, 'Studying the International, Serving the Nation', 1050–80.

[103] Hans Freytag to Albrecht Mendelssohn Bartholdy, 12 January 1920, SPK MA Nachl. AMB, 2,27,15. Mendelssohn Bartholdy was asked to revise Karl Kautsky's document collection on the causes of the war (*Die deutschen Dokumente zum Kriegsausbruch 1914*) which failed to meet the approval of the political leadership and was consequently reviewed by Walther Schücking

the Versailles Treaty and in December 1930, he suggested that Germany should leave the League of Nations.[104] On the other hand, Mendelssohn Bartholdy maintained an extensive network of influential figures abroad, he travelled and lectured widely, and he invited international authors to write for _Europäische Gespräche_, including David Mitrany, Nikolaos Politis, and James T. Shotwell. When the Nazis went about to close the IAP in 1933, they concluded that it was "the personal work of Mendelssohn Bartholdy ... a Western, pacifist, cosmopolitan propaganda institute of foreign policy" which was "exercising a bad influence abroad, especially in the English-speaking world".[105] With Mendelssohn Bartholdy in exile, the IAP went dormant in 1934.

But Germany was not the only place where IR developed. In 1920, the lawyers Paul Fauchille and Albert Geouffre de Lapradelle together with the Chilean diplomat Alejandro Álvarez founded the Institut des Hautes Etudes Internationales (IHEI) in Paris, a university centre today affiliated to the Université Panthéon-Assas (Paris II). Co-funded by government funds and student fees, the IHEI offered courses in international law and diplomacy as well as free-standing classes to non-degree readers. The curriculum included seminars on 'international morality' and 'the League of Nations'.[106] According to its statutes, the IHEI was not only supposed to educate the next generation of diplomats but also to take a stance on current affairs and promote the ideas of justice and morality in international affairs.[107] To this end, the IHEI hosted public lectures and boasted a prominently staffed advisory board, including Arthur Balfour, Edvard Beneš, Léon Bourgeois, Paul Hymans, Raymond Poincaré, and James Brown Scott.[108]

and Max Montgelas. The other publication that resulted from these efforts was the forty-volume document collection _Die Große Politik der Europäischen Kabinette 1871–1914_, edited by Mendelssohn Bartholdy, Johannes Lepsius, and Friedrich Thimme. See Nickel, _Politik und Politikwissenschaft in der Weimarer Republik_, pp. 68–73.

[104] Albrecht Mendelssohn Bartholdy, 'Soll Deutschland kündigen?', _Europäische Gespräche_, Heft 12 (1930), pp. 589–600.
[105] Report on IAP, addressed to Staatssekretär Ahrens, 19 July 1933, StA HH HW II, 361–5 II, Ad 22/1, Bd. 2, p. 9; and report on IAP by Dr. Ing. H. Grothe (Verbindungsstelle des Aussenpolitischen Amtes der NSDAP), 28 July 1933, StA HH, HW II, 361–5 II, Ad 22/1, Bd. 2, p. 18.
[106] Opening Announcement, 1921, IHEI Records, Boîte 1.
[107] Statutes, 1921[?], IHEI Records, Boîte 1.
[108] Press Statement, 1921[?], IHEI Records, Boîte 1.

Like all pioneers of IR scholarship, the IHEI was embedded in an international network of collaborators and sponsors. From the mid-1920s, the Carnegie Endowment for International Peace sponsored a chair, held by André Tibal, along with a series of public lectures.[109] The IHEI also maintained close ties with other IR research institutes abroad and employed international staff. Faculty member Louis Eisenmann helped to establish international conferences. As early as 1921, the IHEI counted forty students from Europe, Russia, and the Americas, three of whom were women.[110] Some came from as far as Bolivia, Iceland, and Syria. Internationalism was the *leitmotiv* engrained in the IHEI. On the other hand, as the dean of the law faculty stressed, the IHEI "admirably served the French cause" by educating future diplomats and lawyers.[111] Preserving traditional French diplomatic culture (including the language and the colonies) remained a priority for French IR scholars during the interwar period. Like their overseas colleagues, the IHEI was torn between various forms of internationalism and nationalism. The inception of the League of Nations, however, forced French scholars to adapt their intellectual programme to a specific institutional framework or to formulate amendments to it.[112]

Intellectually speaking, IHEI scholars drew on a long tradition of international law and political science. One strand of scholarship went back to 1872, the aftermath of the Franco-Prussian war, and the beginnings of political science at Sciences Po in Paris. The other body of thought derived from international and humanitarian law, developed inter alia by Louis Le Fur, Maurice Bourquin, and Marcel Sibert, all of whom lectured at IHEI. Their subjects ranged from the League of Nations to 'human rights'.[113] Georges Scelle, an international lawyer based in Dijon and later in Geneva, wrote pioneering legal studies on the protection of minorities, the law of the seas, and international labour law. Like others, Scelle occasionally advised the

---

[109] Poster by CEIP, 1934, IHEI Records, Boîte 1. See Pemberton, *The Story of International Relations, Part One*, pp. 93–4.
[110] List of students, February–May 1921, IHEI Records, Boîte 2.
[111] Letter by the dean of the law faculty, 11 July 1929, IHEI Records, Boîte 1.
[112] Jean-Michel Guieu, 'La paix par la Société des Nations? Les évolutions du pacifisme français dans les années 1920', in Stéphane Tison (ed.), *Paul d'Estournelles de Constant: Concilier les nations pour éviter la guerre* (Rennes, 2015), pp. 163–79.
[113] Louis Le Fur, *Philosophie du droit des gens* (Paris, 1930).

French government, worked at the foreign ministry, and eventually became director of the International Law Commission at the United Nations.[114] French politics had cultivated a habit of appointing lawyers to high-ranking government offices, especially during Raymond Poincaré's tenures.[115] In addition to that, there were several interest groups advocating 'legal pacifism' since the late nineteenth century.[116] As a result of these traditions the French origins of IR scholarship were somewhat more legalistic than their European neighbours. While essentially studying the same topic – the origins of war and peace – they approached it from the perspective of international law. And they argued that it was "on the basis of international law" that political, diplomatic, and military leaders should work for peace.[117] Meanwhile, the work of Pierre Renouvin on the origins of the First World War had a profound impact on the history of international relations in France, but it resonated less with the IR community.[118]

A few years later, in 1935, a younger generation of aspiring diplomats founded the Centre d'études de politique étrangère in Paris. One of them, Étienne Dennery, was a graduate of the Ecole Normale Supérieure with an *agrégation* in history and geography. He spent time in China and wrote an acclaimed book on Asian demographics before working for the Lytton Commission in 1931.[119] His co-founder was the diplomat and politician Louis Joxe who, like Dennery, was a trained historian and geographer, and went on to serve in senior positions at the French foreign

[114] Antonio Tanca, 'Georges Scelle (1878–1961) Biographical Note with Bibliography', *European Journal of International Law* 1:1 (1990), pp. 240–9.
[115] Gilles Le Béguec, *La République des avocats* (Paris, 2003), pp. 18–19. See also, Jean-Michel Guieu, 'State Sovereignty in Question: The French Jurists between the Reorganization of the International System and European Regionalism, 1920–1950', in Julian Wright and H. S. Jones (eds.), *Pluralism and the Idea of the Republic in France* (Basingstoke, 2012), pp. 215–30.
[116] Jean-Michel Guieu, *Le rameau et le glaive: Les militants français pour la Société des Nations* (Paris, 2008), pp. 24–5.
[117] Statutes, 1921[?], IHEI Records, Boîte 1.
[118] Laurence Badel, 'Diplomacy and the History of International Relations: Redefining a Conflictual Relationship', *Diplomatica* 1:1 (2019), pp. 33–9; Laurence Badel, 'Die französische Historiographie zu den internationalen Beziehungen: transnational oder realistisch?', in Barbara Haider-Wilson, William D. Godsey, and Wolfgang Mueller (eds.), *Internationale Geschichte in Theorie und Praxis: Traditionen und Perspektiven* (Vienna, 2017), pp. 349–70.
[119] Louis Joxe, 'Etienne Dennery', *Politique étrangère* 45:1 (1980), pp. 7–8; Étienne Dennery, *Foules d'Asie. Surpopulation japonaise, expansion chinoise, émigration indienne* (Paris, 1930).

ministry. Their idea was to promote the study of IR among the foreign policy community in Paris by modelling their institution after the Royal Institute of International Affairs. Dennery and Joxe ran the Centre d'études de politique étrangère as joint secretaries, while the president was the more established scholar Sebastien Charléty, rector of the University of Paris and a frequent participant of IR conferences.

In Austria, the foremost institution for the study of IR was the Konsularakademie in Vienna, founded in 1754 by Maria Theresa as a school for oriental languages. During the late nineteenth century, the Konsularakademie shifted its focus to the training of young diplomats and by the eve of the First World War, it boasted a curriculum that resembled interwar IR programmes, including classes in law, history, politics, economics, geography, military studies, and nine different languages.[120] At that point, the faculty already counted twenty professors and ten lecturers, teaching a total of fifty students.[121] After the Great War, the Konsularakademie was transformed into a republican institution, accepting up to eighty-eight students per year from more than two dozen countries across Europe, the Americas, as well as India and Egypt. From 1926, about a quarter of them were women.[122] About half of the student population lived on the premises of the Konsularakademie under boarding school conditions, which was meant to foster the communal international atmosphere. A press report called it a "college of the League of Nations".[123]

Like other institutions for the study of IR, the faculty consisted of both university professors and lecturers with first-hand diplomatic experience. The director was Anton Winter, himself a graduate of the Konsularakademie and formerly a senior diplomat at the Austrian foreign office. Other lecturers included the diplomat and lawyer Alfred Verdross, the historian Alfons Dopsch, and the international lawyer Stephan Verosta. The Konsularakademie taught a two-year postgraduate degree which prepared students for diplomatic careers

---

[120] *Programm der K. und K. Konsular-Akademie*, June 1915, OeStA, Archiv der Konsularakademie, Box 33.

[121] Overview leaflet, 1919, OeStA, Archiv der Konsularakademie, Box 35.

[122] *Jahrbuch der Konsularakademie*, January 1931, OeStA, Archiv der Konsularakademie, Box 41.

[123] G. E. R. Gedye, 'International College Flourishes in Austria: Consular Academy at Vienna Teaches Students from Many Lands the Rules of World Relationships', *New York Times*, 3 August 1931, OeStA, Archiv der Konsularakademie, Box 41.

in their respective home countries as well as for positions in trade
and business. Classes ranged from international law, diplomatic history, economics and trade to geography, foreign languages, and physical exercises.[124] Some foreign ministries, notably the German foreign
office and the US Department of State, directly sent their trainees to the
Konsularakademie on specially designed professional programmes.[125]

Throughout the interwar period, the Konsularakademie maintained
relationships with other institutions for the study of IR, such as the DHfP,
the IAP, LSE, Sciences Po, and the Royal Institute of International Affairs,
with whom the Austrians exchanged publications, lecturers, and students. Faculty members also attended international conferences, notably
the ones devoted to the teaching of IR.[126] As early as 1920, the
sociologist-economist Friedrich Hertz lobbied the Konsularakademie
with a scheme for an "Institute of International Relations", which was
not taken up at first but later fed into the academic programme at the
Konsularakademie.[127] In the 1930s, the pan-European activist Richard
Coudenhove-Kalergi suggested re-structuring the Konsularakademie as a
"European Academy of Politics and Economics" – he envisioned a collaboration of European governments not dissimilar from the European
University Institute (EUI) that the European Community established in
Florence in the 1970s.[128] As these relationships indicate, the ideological
impetus of the Konsularakademie was the same to which most early IR
institutions subscribed – the "betterment of international relations and
the outlawry of war".[129]

[124] *Questionnaire pour les universités* with answers by Konsularakademie,
December 1922, OeStA, Archiv der Konsularakademie, Box 35.
[125] Cooperation with the German government ended after a dispute about
payments during the currency disruptions of 1923. The US consulate in Vienna
arranged for two diplomatic trainees to study at the Konsularakademie. See
Memo, 14 June 1923, Archiv der Konsularakademie, Box 36; and Ernest
L. Harris to Anton Winter, 9 August 1932, OeStA, Archiv der
Konsularakademie, Box 42.
[126] Werner Picht to Anton Winter, 23 June 1931, OeStA, Archiv der
Konsularakademie, Box 41.
[127] Friedrich Hertz to Nitobe Inazō, 8 November 1920, Dossier 8425, Box R1028,
League of Nations Archives, Geneva.
[128] R. Coudenhove-Kalergi, 'Memorandum über die Reorganisation der
Konsularakademie', 17 December 1935, *Jahrbuch der Konsularakademie*,
January 1931, OeStA, Haus-, Hof- und Staatsarchiv, Sonderbestände, Archiv
der Konsularakademie, Box 45.
[129] G. E. R. Gedye, 'International College Flourishes in Austria: Consular Academy
at Vienna teaches Students from Many Lands the Rules of World

To consolidate these various endeavours in the field of IR on a
supranational level, the Swiss diplomat William Rappard and the
French historian Paul Mantoux founded the Graduate Institute of
International Studies in 1927 in Geneva.[130] The Graduate Institute
was an international, not a Swiss, institution and it was the world's
first university entirely devoted to the study of IR. The idea of the
Graduate Institute was to educate future diplomats for the League of
Nations, the headquarters of which were located just a few hundred
meters away. Though not officially affiliated with the League, it was
interpreted by some as a "League of Nations University" at the centre
of international life.[131] The Graduate Institute offered courses for
postgraduate students and professionals on political, legal, economic,
and social subjects "of an international character".[132] Only two years
after its foundation, some eighty students from nineteen countries read
for postgraduate diplomas or followed short-term courses.[133] Up to
half of them were women.[134]

This concept attracted an impressive range of renowned scholars to
the Graduate Institute, including political scientists such as Harold

Relationships', *New York Times*, 3 August 1931, OeStA, Archiv der
Konsularakademie, Box 41.

[130] Originally known as the Postgraduate Institute of International Studies (French:
Institut Universitaire de Hautes Etudes), it is today called Graduate Institute of
International and Development Studies, or simply The Graduate Institute. It is
not to be confused with the Geneva Institute of International Relations, a
summer school programme that grew out of the British LNU summer school in
1924. Nor was it identical with the Geneva Research Center, a kind of US
embassy for international affairs circles in Geneva, directed by Malcolm
W. Davis, funded by the Rockefeller Foundation, and editor of *A Monthly
Review of International Affairs*. Yet another body was the Institute of World
Affairs, founded in 1924 in Geneva. See "Geneva Institute of International
Relations", 7th year, 27 July to 1 August 1930, Graduate Institute Archives,
HEI [uncatalogued]; [unknown author], 'The Geneva Research Center', *World
Affairs* 96:4 (1933), pp. 215–18; The Rockefeller Foundation, *The Rockefeller
Foundation Annual Report for 1933* (New York, 1933), p. 262.

[131] "*Völkerbunduniversität*", Hans Wehberg to Paul Mantoux, 21 September
1927, HEI 168/4/1, Graduate Institute Archives.

[132] Brochure *Announcement for 1928–1929* (Geneva, 1928), HEI A/1 (1928/
9–1940/1), Graduate Institute Archives.

[133] Rapport de l'Institut Universitaire de Hautes Etudes Internationales pour
l'année académique 1928–9, dated 31 October 1929, HEI RA 1928/30–1939,
Graduate Institute Archives.

[134] Memo on course attendance, Pitman B. Potter, 14 January 1931, HEI 163/4–6;
and memo on seminar attendance, Maurice Bourquin, HEI 149/4–5, Graduate
Institute Archives.

Laski, Eric Voegelin, and Quincy Wright; economists Ludwig von
Mises, Friedrich August von Hayek, and Gunnar Myrdal; and lawyers
Hans Kelsen, Hersch Lauterpacht, and Albert de Geouffre de
Lapradelle. Visiting lecturers also included IR specialists, such as
Charles Manning, Philip Noel-Baker, Charles K. Webster, and Alfred
Zimmern, as well as representatives from the League apparatus, such
as Rachel Crowdy, Salvador de Madariaga and Åke Hammarskjöld.
The Graduate Institute was co-financed by the Canton of Geneva, the
Swiss government, and the Laura Spelman Rockefeller Memorial.[135]
The Rockefeller Foundation continued to support the Graduate
Institute throughout the interwar period, arguing that Geneva was an
"indispensable" site for the study of IR.[136]

Like other founders of university-based IR, Rappard and Mantoux
were driven on the one hand by the hope "to contribute to the promotion of international understanding", while emphasising at the same
time that their Graduate Institute did not subscribe to any preconceived doctrine or propaganda, and only conducted "impartial and
scientific observation, teaching and research".[137] The Graduate
Institute's location in Geneva was extraordinarily convenient. IR
scholars lent academic authority to the endeavours of the League,
while the new institutions provided an ideal job market for graduates.
As co-founder Rappard told Lucie Zimmern (Alfred's wife) in 1931,
their students were interested in "more than purely intellectual understanding" of international affairs. Instead, they wanted to "master the
problems of international life".[138] The Graduate Institute became a
pinnacle of interwar IR scholarship, merging in one place all the
academic and political components that created the discipline.

Yet, there were many more centres of scholarship across Europe.
The international lawyer Jan Hendrik Willem Verzijl organised the
Dutch Coordinating Committee for International Studies in Utrecht,
which gathered economic, legal, and colonial experts. In Italy, a set of
university faculties established the Centro Italiano Di Alti Studi

---

[135] Pitman B. Potter, 'The Graduate Institute of International Studies, Geneva',
American Journal of International Law 62:3 (1968), p. 740.
[136] Memo, 13 November 1929, Folder 915, Box 101, Series 100.S, RG 1.1, RF,
Rockefeller Archive Center.
[137] Brochure, *Announcement for 1928–1929* (Geneva, 1928), HEI A/1 (1928/
9–1940/1), Graduate Institute Archives.
[138] William Rappard to Lucie Zimmern, 3 November 1931, HEI [uncatalogued].

Internazionali, directed by the philosopher and politician Giovanni Gentile. The Hungarian Foreign Affairs Society (Magyar Külügyi Társaság), founded in 1920, was directed by the politician Count Albert Apponyi, formerly head of his country's delegation at the Peace Conference.[139] Similar centres emerged in Belgium, Czechoslovakia, Denmark, Norway, Poland, Rumania, Spain, Sweden, and Switzerland.[140] Perhaps more important than their more or less simultaneous creation was the level of exchange between them, which fostered the common disciplinary identity and which reflected that IR could be studied from anywhere. It was a universal, albeit Eurocentric, discipline that approached the same issues with an evolving set of common questions. Nowhere was the cosmopolitan feel of the young discipline more pronounced than in Europe, but in the United States, too, interest in the field was increasing rapidly.

Across the Pond

American universities were at the forefront of IR scholarship. With the help of private funds from individuals and charitable trusts, they established degrees, departments, and professional associations throughout the 1920s and 1930s. Their goal was to educate the next generation of international experts, both in diplomacy as well as in business, to allow the United States to influence world affairs despite its absence from the League of Nations.[141] Using their growing economic power, American donors invested in non-official channels of influence, including intellectual cooperation. In fact, private and public American contributions to the League of Nations were second only to Britain.[142] At the same time, the diplomatic centre of gravity was still far from

---

[139] Memo on "Ungarische Gesellschaft für auswärtige Politik", undated, GStA PK, I. HA Rep. 303, Nr. 2116.

[140] See International Institute of Intellectual Cooperation, *Handbook of Institutions for the Scientific Study of International Relations*; International Institute of Intellectual Cooperation, *The International Studies Conference: Origins, Functions, Organisation* (Paris, 1937).

[141] On the relationship between the United States and the League of Nations, see Ludovic Tourès, *Les États-Unis et la Société des Nations (1914–1946): Le système international face à l'émergence d'une superpuissance* (Berne, 2016).

[142] Daniel Gorman, *The Emergence of International Society in the 1920s* (Cambridge, 2012), pp. 183–4.

Washington, which allowed American scholars to write about international affairs "without bias", as one observer claimed.[143]
    Intellectual influences on IR were as eclectic as in Europe – ranging
from political science and economics to history, philosophy, religion,
and what was known as 'race studies'. But the purpose of US institutions was often more explicitly geared towards careers in business
rather than public offices. The principal geographic area of interest was
Europe but there was also research on the Americas, Asia, and the
Pacific theatre. Like their European colleagues, American architects of
IR argued that the field "cannot be learnt from books and documents
alone" and thus recommended "travel and the acquaintance of men of
affairs" to train future experts.[144] Ultimately, their goal was to shape
the world by creating a new discipline and by cultivating a new form
of diplomacy.
    To be sure, US scholars had worked on international affairs from at
least the early 1900s, as Robert Vitalis has pointed out.[145] *World
Politics* (1900) by political scientist Paul Reinsch was an important
milestone. A similar style was employed by Amos Hershey, professor
of European history and politics at Indiana University, in his book *The
International Law and Diplomacy of the Russo-Japanese War* (1907).
Another influential figure was John Burgess, the founder of the political science department at Columbia University (1880) and the journal
Political Science Quarterly (1886). Like later generations, these professors did not remain on the university campus but interacted with
politicians and diplomats, learning politics "directly from their own
lips", as Burgess put it.[146] Yet, their work did not amount to a
reasonably coherent whole and usually took the form of loose historical reflections. A significant part of early US scholarship was shaped
by imperial and racist ideology. In his revisionist history of American
IR, Vitalis has shown how notions of white supremacy were employed
by the ancestors of the discipline, notably through the *Journal of Race*

[143] G. Stanley Hall, 'Foreword', in George H. Blakeslee (ed.), *The Problems and
Lessons of the War* (New York, 1916), p. ix.
[144] Jerome Greene to John A. Cousens, 21 August 1929, Fletcher School of Law
and Diplomacy Records, Box 1, Folder 2.
[145] Robert Vitalis, *White World Order, Black Power Politics: The Birth of
American International Relations* (Ithaca, 2015).
[146] John Burgess, Speech 'Founding of the Faculty of Political Science', read in
1930, John Burgess Papers, Box 13.

Development founded by Granville Stanley Hall and George Blakeslee, which published studies on imperial politics, trade, and race biology.[147] Vitalis has contrasted this body of thought with a set of thinkers at Howard University, a historically black college in Washington, DC, arguing that IR as a discipline should be critically re-examined for its inherent racism.[148] Vitalis' book has stimulated an important debate on the institutional context of early IR scholarship which complicates orthodox histories of the discipline based on canonical texts written by white Anglo-American men.[149]

Another characteristic of early American IR scholarship was the amount of financial support from private donors, notably the large philanthropies – the Rockefeller Foundation and the Carnegie Endowment for International Peace.[150] Founded in 1910 by steel magnate Andrew Carnegie, the Endowment built an extensive network of academic and non-academic institutions devoted to peace.[151] In 1909, Andrew Carnegie himself had published a pamphlet on how to limit armament among the eight great naval powers (Germany, France, Italy, Russia, Austria-Hungary, Japan, Britain, and the United States) through a system of arbitration.[152] Carnegie's idea was to codify political commitments in international law, even at the expense of national sovereignty.[153] From 1917, James T. Shotwell, professor of international history at Columbia University, served as director of research at the Carnegie Endowment. Like many other IR pioneers, Shotwell had attended the Paris Peace Conference and maintained a strong interest in current affairs. Along with his colleague Nicholas Murray Butler, president of Columbia and, from 1925, of the Carnegie

---

[147] See, for example, James L. Barton, 'The Ottoman Empire and the War', *The Journal of Race Development* 9:1 (1918), pp. 1–15; John C. Branner, 'Some of the Obstacles of North American Trade with Brazil', *The Journal of Race Development* 4:4 (1914), pp. 461–70; and Thorstein Veblen, 'The Mutation Theory and the Blond Race', *The Journal of Race Development* 3:4 (1913), 491–507.

[148] Robert Vitalis, *White World Order, Black Power Politics: The Birth of American International Relations* (Ithaca, 2015), p. 9.

[149] Susan Pedersen, 'Destined to Disappear', *London Review of Books* 38:20 (20 October 2016), pp. 23–4.

[150] William T. R. Fox, 'Interwar International Relations Research: The American Experience', *World Politics* 2:1 (1949), pp. 68–9.

[151] Rietzler, 'Philanthropy, Peace Research and Revisionist Politics'.

[152] Andrew Carnegie, *Armaments and Their Results* (New York, 1909), p. 6.

[153] Gorman, *The Emergence of International Society in the 1920s*, pp. 194–9.

Endowment, Shotwell became one of the leading figures of American
cultural diplomacy. Unofficial actors such as the Carnegie Endowment,
represented by Butler and Shotwell, became enormously influential in
shaping foreign policy debate.[154] Carnegie money funded the publication and circulation of IR books, conferences, and professorships.
Similarly, the Rockefeller Foundation and the Laura Spelman
Rockefeller Memorial sponsored research institutes for the study of
IR throughout the 1920s.[155] It was obvious that these philanthropies
did not pursue exclusively academic goals. "This, of course, is *not*
research", one Rockefeller officer remarked about William Rappard's
suggestion for an exchange of speakers.[156]

Like in Europe, the First World War was the key impulse for the
institutional formation of IR. The first American university institution
devoted specifically to the study of IR was the School of Foreign
Service at Georgetown University in Washington. Founded in
1919 by the Jesuit priest Edmund A. Walsh (and later so named in
his honour), the School of Foreign Service was an attempt to train
experts for the world of international politics and business. Walsh
himself had served as an advisor to the US government during the
First World War and noticed a lack of systematic training for international experts. After the war, he won the support of "leaders of
public thought and commerce", notably $20,000 from the president of
US Steel, James Augustine Farrell, to establish a university institute at
Georgetown.[157] Some 600 students applied for the first semester in
February 1919, 300 of whom were accepted, and began reading
courses in politics, law, economics, languages, and maritime affairs.
Located at the seat of government, Walsh envisioned his School to
become "the West Point of foreign service".[158]

[154] Rietzler, 'Before the Cultural Cold Wars'.
[155] Grant Report, RF 33009, Folder 952, Box 105, Series 100.S, RG 1.1, RF;
Grant Report, RF 32130, 13 April 1932, Folder 177, Box 19, Series 717, RG
1.1, RF; Beardsley Ruml to Albrecht Mendelssohn Bartholdy, 16 November
1925, Folder 561, Box 52, Series 3.06, LSRM, Rockefeller Archive Center.
[156] Selskar M. Gunn to Edmund E. Day, 31 December 1931, [emphasis in the
original], Folder 60, Box 7, Series 910, RG 3, RR, Rockefeller Archive Center.
[157] Edmund A. Walsh, 'The Aims of the School of Foreign Service', Academic
Exercises in Gaston Hall, 25 November 1919, p. 10, available at https://
georgetown.app.box.com/s/vlbdbjsx2b48p8m3ew8p [accessed 15
January 2019].
[158] Ibid., p. 11.

The first non-academic institution in the field of IR was the Foreign Policy Association (FPA) established in 1918 as the League of Free Nations Association.[159] Its original goal was to campaign for and inform about Woodrow Wilson's internationalist policy at the Paris Peace Conference. However, after the United States failed to join the League, the FPA adopted a more general programme. Supported by the Rockefeller, Carnegie, and Ford foundations, the FPA sought to improve public understanding of international affairs through a network of local branches and educational materials. Its first chairman was the diplomat and university professor James Grover McDonald. Claiming to be strictly "non-partisan and educational", the FPA offered several publication series – bi-weekly foreign policy reports, a weekly foreign policy bulletin, and about ten pamphlets per year – as well as free bibliographies, posters, and radio programmes.[160] The FPA was endorsed, among others, by political scientist Parker Thomas Moon and the banker-philanthropist Jerome D. Greene who later became IR professor at Aberystwyth in the 1930s. Greene thought that "the benefits to public opinion ... through the educational influence of the Foreign Policy Association [were] beyond calculation".[161] This notion, that education in foreign affairs was of "utmost importance" in a democracy, was reiterated by Robert Cecil on the occasion of the FPA's tenth anniversary in 1928.[162]

Around the same time as the formation of the FPA, a group of scholars, lawyers, and businessmen led by the former Secretary of State Elihu Root established the Council on Foreign Relations in New York. Formally registered in 1921, the Council was the product of the same meetings at the Paris Peace Conference in May 1919 which inspired the British Institute of International Affairs in London.[163] Among the members of the original nucleus at Paris – all of whom were members of Woodrow Wilson's set of advisors The Inquiry – were historian Archibald Cary Coolidge, international lawyer James

---

[159] David Allen, *Every Citizen a Statesman: Building a Democracy for Foreign Policy in the American Century*, PhD thesis (New York, 2019).
[160] Brochure, 'Your Organization and the Foreign Policy Association', 1931, James T. Shotwell Papers, Box 213.
[161] Ibid.
[162] 10 Years of FPA booklet, 1918–28, James T. Shotwell Papers, Box 213.
[163] 'Draft Report for consideration by the Provisional Committee appointed to prepare a Constitution, and select the original members of the British Branch of the Institute of International Affairs', James T. Shotwell Papers, Box 43.

Brown Scott, and historian James T. Shotwell. When they came back from Paris, they transformed Elihu Root's foreign affairs dinner club, founded in 1918, into a full-blown research institute. It was a symbiosis of New York's wealth and intellectual energy.[164] Over the following years, the Council on Foreign Relations developed into the foremost American IR institute and from 1922 it published the influential journal *Foreign Affairs*, which was the successor of the *Journal of Race Development*, though not to be confused with *Foreign Affairs: A Journal of International Understanding*, published by the Union of Democratic Control in Britain since 1919. Although not university-based, the Council on Foreign Relations counted many of the leading professors among its members, such as geographer Isaiah Bowman, lawyer Manley Ottmer Hudson, and economist Edwin F. Gay. Besides academics, it gathered influential figures, such as publicist Walter Lippmann, legal advisor David Hunter Miller, and the German-born banker Paul Warburg (brother of Max Warburg, the sponsor of Hamburg's IAP). The Council on Foreign Relations captured the key message of early American IR – it was possible to influence international affairs through unofficial means.

From 1921, the Institute of Politics at Williamstown, Massachusetts, ran an influential series of lectures.[165] The Institute was founded by Harry Garfield, a law professor and president of Williams College as well as the incumbent president of the American Political Science Association.[166] Co-sponsored by the financier and philanthropist Bernard Baruch and, from 1924, by the Carnegie Endowment, the Williamstown lectures featured speakers from Europe, Latin America, Russia, and the United States. Among them were British politician Philip Kerr, German law professor Albrecht Mendelssohn Bartholdy, Italian diplomat Carlo Sforza, and Swiss diplomat William Rappard. Guests also included women, such as the American librarian Mary Elizabeth Wood, the Irish civil servant Thekla Beere, and Maria Lanzar, a political scientist from the Philippines. The sessions covered

---

[164] Peter Grose, *Continuing the Inquiry: The Council on Foreign Relations from 1921 to 1996* (New York, 1996, 2006), pp. 1–9.
[165] Arthur Howland Buffington, 'Institute of Politics, Williamstown, MA, Its First Decade', 1931, James T. Shotwell Papers, Box 151.
[166] James McAllister, *Wilsonian Visions: Harry Garfield, the Williamstown Institute of Politics, and Liberal Internationalism in the Interwar Era* (Ithaca, 2021).

issues from peace settlement to trade, raw materials, and demographics. The idea was to provide academic-style commentary congruent with the "shifting panorama of world affairs". By 1925, the Institute of Politics had some 280 members from twenty-one countries, almost half of whom were women.[167] While not a degree-awarding institution, the Institute of Politics did offer courses taught by G. L. Ridgeway and it became a widely respected venue for foreign policy debate during the interwar period.

Chicago was another centre of IR scholarship in the United States. In 1922, a group of foreign policy enthusiasts founded the Chicago Council on Foreign Relations which was similar to, though independent from its New York-based namesake. The Chicago Council was presided over by the former secretary of war Jacob M. Dickerson. The Council launched a journal *Foreign Notes*, a book series *American Policies Abroad*, and invited a set of prominent international speakers, including Norwegian explorer and diplomat Fridtjof Nansen, the director of the International Labour Organization Albert Thomas, social reformer Jane Addams, the German feminist Adele Schreiber-Krieger, the economist Moritz Julius Bonn, the pacifist writer Norman Angell, the pan-Europeanist Richard Coudenhove-Kalergi, the IR professor Alfred Zimmern, and the Spanish diplomat Salvador de Madariaga. By 1925, the Chicago Council had more than 1,000 members.[168] In addition to the Council, the University of Chicago received a grant in 1923 to set up the Norman Wait Harris Memorial Foundation, which organised public and private lecture series as well as teaching in IR. Its purpose was to promote better understanding between Americans and foreigners – in short, an "enlightened world-order".[169] To this end, the Memorial invited foreign speakers, such as international lawyers Herbert Kraus and Charles de Visscher. In 1927, the Laura Spelman Rockefeller Memorial financed a study by Chicago professor Quincy Wright on the causes of war.[170] The interplay of these academic and

---

[167] 'Membership Statistics', Institute of Politics, 1921–5, James T. Shotwell Papers, Box 151.
[168] Booklet, Chicago Council on Foreign Relations, 1928, James T. Shotwell Papers, Box 213.
[169] Booklet, Norman Wait Harris Memorial Foundation, 24 June to 18 July 1924, James T. Shotwell Papers, Box 151.
[170] 'Local Community Research Committee', annual report, 1927–8, to LSRM, James T. Shotwell Papers, Box 167, 168.

practical initiatives made Chicago the centre of IR in the mid-western United States.

In 1924, Harvard University and Radcliffe College established a joint Bureau of International Research. The Bureau, funded by a five-year grant from the Laura Spelman Rockefeller Memorial, offered grants to researchers and helped to disseminate their work.[171] Affiliated faculty included the IR specialist Raymond Leslie Buell, economist Eleanor Lansing Dulles, and Sarah Wambaugh, an expert on plebiscites.[172] Research topics ranged from international law and trade to so-called 'race studies', such as "The native African under self-government, colonial administration, and mandates".[173] In Massachusetts, too, emphasis was put on current international issues to promote academic interventions in ongoing policy debates. A decade later, in 1936, Harvard established the Graduate School of Public Administration thanks to a $2 million donation by the businessman and politician Lucius N. Littauer, offering a one-year training course. It was renamed in honour of John F. Kennedy in 1966.

There were plans at Johns Hopkins University from 1924 to establish a school of IR, to be named after the journalist-diplomat Walter Hines Page.[174] After an endowment from editor Edward W. Bok, the school opened in October 1930 with John Van Antwerp MacMurray, a former assistant secretary of state, as director. Among the teaching staff were international lawyer Frederick Dunn and historian John H. Latané. The Walter Hines Page School of International Relations was meant to train experts for foreign service and to promote research in foreign policy, though it did not award degrees.[175] Both MacMurray and his successor Owen Lattimore intermittently left the School for government service. Eventually, in 1951, after Joseph McCarthy had accused Lattimore of being a Soviet spy, the School was closed and replaced by the School of Advanced International Studies (SAIS).[176]

---

[171] W. G. Wilson to J. David Thompson, 7 June 1926, James T. Shotwell Papers, Box 136 (a), (b).
[172] Booklet, 'Bureau of International Research: Researches: 1924–1929', James T. Shotwell Papers, Box 136 (a), (b).
[173] W. G. Wilson to J. David Thompson, 7 June 1926, James T. Shotwell Papers, Box 136 (a), (b).
[174] 'Back First School of International Relations', *Harvard Crimson*, 22 May 1924.
[175] Plans for a "Walter Hines Page School of International Relations" at Johns Hopkins University, May 1926, James T. Shotwell Papers, Box 136 (a), (b).
[176] John C. French, *A History of the University Founded by Johns Hopkins* (Baltimore, 1946), pp. 240–3.

In October 1927, the American Association of University Women presented an IR programme, specifically aimed to educate women about international affairs. Led by the historian and civil servant Esther Caukin Brunauer, they produced a set of studies on topics such as disarmament, arbitration, and raw materials, on which Alfred Zimmern commented he had seen "nothing better of the kind".[177] The Association organised round-table discussions, invited lecturers, and organised a cooperative library. Members included the dean of Barnard College, Virginia Gildersleeve, as well as the public health and international affairs specialist Emma McLaughlin (née Moffat). They understood their purpose as serving "the practical political needs of a democracy".[178] While still largely sidelined in the male-dominated field of diplomacy, American women were clearly ready to work on these subjects.

Some of the now-famous IR schools followed in the late 1920s and early 1930s. In 1930, Princeton University established the School of Public and International Affairs, later re-named in honour of Woodrow Wilson. Based on the donation of trustees and friends, the School began to offer courses in IR, sponsored field studies, and invited visiting speakers – "men of practical experience in world affairs".[179] Although ostensibly not a vocational school, its purpose was to train "men who expect to enter public life", future diplomats and businessmen representing American interests abroad. Associated faculty included the historian Thomas J. Wertenbaker, the president of the American Political Science Association Edward Samuel Corwin, and the diplomat De Witt Clinton Poole. Students, both undergraduate and postgraduate, were taught in history, law, politics, economics, and foreign languages. In addition to that, a programme leaflet argued that "an understanding of the racial characteristics of foreign peoples is an essential part of the equipment of men being trained for the international field".[180]

---

[177] Alfred Zimmern to J. David Thompson, 24 May 1929, James T. Shotwell Papers, Box 155, 156.
[178] AAUW, International Relations Office, *Handbook for Leaders of International Relations Round Tables*, October 1928, James T. Shotwell Papers, Box 155, 156.
[179] Booklet, 'School of Public and International Affairs, Princeton University', 22 February 1930, James T. Shotwell Papers, Box 151.
[180] Ibid.

In 1931, the Social Science Research Council formed a division on
International Relations. The Council advocated a scientific approach
to the subject, arguing that it must achieve what natural scientists were
doing in physics. They regarded IR literally as a "laboratory" of the
political world.[181] Gathering leading scholars, such as Shotwell, Jacob
Viner, and Quincy Wright, the Council provided an infrastructure for
the study of IR in the United States as well as for field study abroad.
Crucially, it elevated IR to a social *science*, welcoming the new discipline into the company of economics, sociology, and political science.
The study of IR was no longer a codename for political journalism but,
so the founders hoped, a form of systematic research based on an
evolving set of common topics, methods, and terminology. The representation of IR at the level of universities and professional associations
helped to cultivate the new discipline, and gave it academic authority.

Tufts University opened its Fletcher School of Law and Diplomacy
in 1933, a graduate school built upon the bequest of a former trustee
and organised in close alliance with Harvard University.[182] An original
endowment was made by Austin Barclay Fletcher in 1923, suggesting
to put up "a School of Law and Diplomacy".[183] Lengthy negotiations
with other sponsors and Tufts' governors delayed its establishment and
put its very purpose in question. In 1928, they considered merging the
Fletcher School with the business school to form the "Fletcher-Braker
School of Business and Government Services".[184] The head of the
history department Arthur Irving Andrews, too, envisioned the
Fletcher School to be a preparatory course for diplomats and businessmen alike. He modified his classes "according to the best advice
attainable from … the United States Government, from great banks,
and from great commercial corporations".[185] Eventually though, upon
James Shotwell's and Jerome Greene's advice, the School took its

181 Social Science Research Council, 'Report of the Director of the Program of
     Research in International Relations for the Year 1931', 'confidential', 2 January
     1932, James T. Shotwell Papers, Box 136 (a), (b).
182 'Tufts to Establish School of Diplomacy', *Washington Star*, 24 May 1930.
183 John A. Cousens to Chas. Neal Barney, 7 August 1923, Fletcher School of Law
     and Diplomacy Records, Box 6, Folder 1.
184 Raymond Vincent Phelan to Frank George Wren, 30 September 1928, Fletcher
     School of Law and Diplomacy Records, Box 6, Folder 1.
185 Arthur Irving Andrews (Tufts, History Department), Memo, 'Preparatory
     Steps', 16 February 1924, Fletcher School of Law and Diplomacy Records,
     Box 6, Folder 1.

current form and began offering courses on international law, diplomacy, international relations, economics, and trade, taught by lecturers such as historian George Blakeslee, lawyer William Langer, and economist Seymour Harris. "Dispassionate analysis", so the intention of the Fletcher School, would help to find "practicable solutions ... for crises arising in the community of nations".[186]

In 1935, Yale University established the Institute of International Studies with the help of a $100,000 grant from the Rockefeller Foundation. It was directed by the political scientist Nicholas J. Spykman who had been a professor of International Relations at Yale since the mid-1920s. The creation of the Institute went along with new hires and the formation of a department of IR which offered a major for undergraduates as well as graduate degrees. Spykman's co-founders were the international lawyer Frederick Dunn, previously a legal advisor at the Department of State and a lecturer at Johns Hopkins University, and the Swiss-born IR specialist Arnold Wolfers who had fled Europe after having worked at the Deutsche Hochschule für Politik in Berlin during the 1920s and early 1930s. Other associated faculty included economist Jacob Viner, historian Samuel Flagg Bemis, and German emigré Hajo Holborn who, like Wolfers, had taught at the Hochschule until 1933. There were a number of women among the faculty and graduate students, including political scientist Helen M. Moats and food-trade expert Ada F. Wyman.[187]

They offered courses on topics such as "Objectives and Methods of Foreign Policy" (Spykman), "Foreign Policy and the Strategy of Peace" (Wolfers), "International Organisation" (Dunn), and "International Economics" (Wolfers) – Spykman claimed that their programme was "probably the best in the country".[188] While the courses were run and paid for by Yale, the Rockefeller grant allowed professors to pursue extensive research projects. This resulted in numerous studies and books, such as Dunn's *Peaceful Change* (1937) and Spykman's *America's Strategy in World Politics* (1942). Members of the Institute

---

[186] Halford Lancaster Hoskins to John A. Cousens, 27 December 1935, Fletcher School of Law and Diplomacy Records, Box 1, Folder 5.
[187] Statement of Budget Allowances and Expenditures, 30 June 1938, Box 3, Folder 20, Institute of International Studies, Yale University, Records.
[188] Nicholas Spykman, Preface to Report for 1938–1939, Box 3, Folder 21, Institute of International Studies, Yale University, Records.

of International Studies identified as taking a 'realist' approach to IR. Founded during a time of international crisis, Spykman and his colleagues had no illusions about the state of the collective security apparatus, and advocated a national approach to politics, rather than an international one.[189] In the 1938–9 report, Spykman stressed the "realistic approach to the subject at Yale" which, despite the general popularity of IR among students, "sometimes shocked their youthful idealism".[190] On the other hand, the Institute claimed to be primarily interested in strategies for peace and supported many research projects traditionally associated with the 'idealist' camp.

The most striking feature of Yale's approach, however, was its practical focus. The goal of the Institute, as Dunn explained, was not merely to accumulate knowledge but to "assist in the formulations of policies" and to provide the "basis for action".[191] Spykman agreed that IR was not aimed at "theoretical analysis" but had developed "in response to the practical requirements" of their times.[192] In particular, the Institute sought to train young diplomats for a new age of US foreign policy. Indeed, many graduates ended up in leading positions in government or business. In this sense, they resembled their professors who worked as advisors to non-academic institutions throughout their careers. They were "practical men" as well as scholars, searching for the *"possible* rather than the *ideal"*.[193] Even the two German emigrés, Holborn and Wolfers, worked for the US government, notably the Office of Strategic Services during the Second World War.

These patterns were replicated at countless other American universities during the interwar period. In 1919, the University of California, Berkeley, established a Bureau of International Relations in response to the First World War which offered a library, put up conferences, and

---

[189] Report 'New Program', 1936, Box 2, Folder 18, Institute of International Studies, Yale University, Records.
[190] Nicholas Spykman, Preface to Report for 1938–1939, Box 3, Folder 21, Institute of International Studies, Yale University, Records.
[191] Frederick Dunn, 'Report of the Institute of International Studies, 1940–1941', Box 7, Folder 47, Institute of International Studies, Yale University, Records.
[192] Nicholas Spykman, Preface to Report for 1938–1939, Box 3, Folder 21, Institute of International Studies, Yale University, Records.
[193] Lawrence H. Chamberlain on a book written by members of the Yale Institute of International Studies. Lawrence H. Chamberlain, 'Reviewed Work: The Absolute Weapon: Atomic Power and World Order by Frederick S. Dunn, Bernard Brodie, Arnold Wolfers, Percy E. Corbett, William T. R. Fox', *Political Science Quarterly* 61:3 (1946), p. 443.

welcomed international visitors.[194] In 1930, the American Friends
Service Committee (Quakers) together with Haverford College
launched an annual Institute of International Relations, offering a
two-week school for "peace workers" with lectures by Thomas
Parker Moon, Bishop Frances John McConnell, and Quaker historian
Rufus Jones.[195] By the 1930s, IR had become so popular in the United
States that Arthur Charles Watkins of the National Student Forum
organised an "International Relations Observation Tour" across
Europe, with visits to The Hague Peace Palace, Westminster, and the
League of Nations in Geneva.[196]

A Global Discipline?

While it is important to appreciate the geographical spread of early IR
institutions across the United States and Europe, it is also true that the
discipline was largely a Western enterprise. Most professorships,
departments, and research institutes were located in the Western
world, as was most of the political, military, and economic power.
The intellectual repercussions of this geo-political bias were undeniable. Political circumstances shaped the institutional and intellectual
formation of IR. Perhaps the most notable absence was Soviet Russia
which for ideological reasons refused to engage in international organisation, especially economic cooperation, for much of the 1920s and
allowed only sporadic interactions with the IR community.[197] As a
result, interwar IR scholarship considered international affairs almost
exclusively from the perspective of (and to the benefit of) Western

---

[194] University of California, Berkeley, 'General Catalogue: Fall and Spring
Semesters 1959–1960', *Bulletin* 53:28 (Berkeley, 1959), pp. 155–6.
[195] Booklet, ' Institute of International Relations', 9–20 June 1930, James
T. Shotwell Papers, Box 136 (a), (b).
[196] Prospectus "International Relations Observation Tour", 1932, James
T. Shotwell Papers, Box 136 (a), (b).
[197] The International Institute of Intellectual Cooperation (IIIC) recorded only one
Soviet delegate at the International Studies Conference in 1935. IIIC, *The
International Studies Conference*, p. 48. See Gleb J. Albert, 'International
Solidarity With(out) World Revolution: The Transformation of
"Internationalism" in Early Soviet Society', *Monde(s)* 10:2 (2016), pp. 33–50;
Kazimierz Grzybowski, 'International Organizations from the Soviet Point of
View', *Law and Contemporary Problems* 29:4 (1964), pp. 882–95.

governments and, more fundamentally, presupposed a system of the 'international' which was based on Western political philosophy. What is nonetheless remarkable about early IR scholars is their attempt at wide geographical coverage and their conviction that the study of IR was in itself a genuinely international, or, more precisely, a universal endeavour. In other words, their approach to the discipline rested on the possibility of global truths, global laws, and global institutions. This tension between global claims on the one hand and national (or at best regional) realities on the other was reflected in the institutional architecture of early IR. Even programmes that explicitly addressed an international audience – exchange programmes, summer schools, and conferences – largely failed to include non-European perspectives. IR was a discipline available only to the 'civilised world', as it was then called. Although the architects of IR understood themselves as internationalists, they were also imperialists to varying degrees.[198]

One of the earliest extra-European formats for the study of IR was the Institute of Pacific Relations (IPR). The IPR was a private organisation devoted to the study of international affairs among the countries of the Pacific region. It was founded by American YMCA officials Frank C. Atherton and Edward Clark Carter alongside Stanford University president Ray Lyman Wilbur.[199] They saw themselves as promoters of peaceful cooperation, in an "entirely unofficial capacity", for the peoples of the Pacific theatre.[200] To them, the lack of mutual understanding between nations was the key source of conflict. They launched a range of studies on regional, economic, sociological, and anthropological subjects.[201] From 1925, they organised meetings at varying locations – Honolulu (1925), Kyoto (1929), Shanghai (1931), etc. Notable participants included American IR pioneers George Blakeslee, Jerome D. Greene, James T. Shotwell, Westel W. Willoughby as well as avant-garde women, including French-Canadian politician Thérèse

---

[198] David Long and Brian C. Schmidt (eds.), *Imperialism and Internationalism in the Discipline of International Relations* (New York, 2005).
[199] Paul F. Hooper, 'The Institute of Pacific Relations and the Origins of Asian and Pacific Studies', *Pacific Affairs* 61:1 (1988), pp. 98–101.
[200] The Rockefeller Foundation, *The Rockefeller Foundation Annual Report for 1929* (New York, 1929), p. 251.
[201] Minutes of Meeting of Subcommittee on Program, 29 October 1926, James T. Shotwell Papers, Box 29.

Casgrain and the economist Elizabeth Boody Schumpeter.[202] Among the non-Western scholars was the Chinese social scientist Han-Seng Chen, Japanese economist Tadao Yanaihara, and Sophia H. Chen Zen (Chen Hengzhe), a writer, historian, and the first female professor in China. From 1928, the IPR published the journal *Pacific Affairs*.

Recent accounts have described the IPR as one of the most influential conferences in interwar foreign policy.[203] Thanks to generous funding from the Carnegie Endowment and the Rockefeller Foundation, the IPR was able to host meetings across continents and gathered an impressive number of international scholars. Participants came from Japan, China, the Philippines, Indonesia, India, Pakistan, Australia, New Zealand, Canada, Britain, France, the Netherlands, the United States, and, for some time, the Soviet Union and Burma. They studied IR on the basis of racial equality and generally took an anti-imperialist approach. Like most early IR actors, members of the IPR often crossed the boundaries between academia and diplomacy, such as its research secretary J. B. Condliffe, a New Zealand economist and consultant for the League of Nations' Economic and Financial Organisation. Although the format of the IPR was innovative and inspired other conferences in the field, it ultimately lost influence after the Japanese invasion of Manchuria and later in the United States as a result of Joseph McCarthy's accusations of communist subversion.

Religious internationalists, too, were important advocates of a universalist perspective in the study of IR. Simply put, if God existed then God existed for everyone, in the same sense as the rules of international politics applied to everyone. Although many scholars were Christians, only some authors made this influence more explicit.[204] Examples included Christian student groups, charitable organisations, and church councils.[205] The most influential group were the Society of

202 List 'Committees of the American Group of the Institute of Pacific Relations', 1929, James T. Shotwell Papers, Box 29; W. L. Holland and Kate L. Mitchell (eds.), *Problems of the Pacific, 1936: Aims and Results of the Social and Economic Policies in Pacific Countries* (Oxford, 1937).
203 Priscilla Roberts, 'The Institute of Pacific Relations: pan-Pacific and pan-Asian Visions of International Order', *International Politics* 55:6 (2018), p. 838.
204 Minutes of Meeting of Subcommittee on Program, 29 October 1926, James T. Shotwell Papers, Box 29.
205 For example, the World's Student Christian Federation and the World Union of Jewish Students. See International Institute of Intellectual Cooperation, *University Exchanges in Europe: A Handbook* (Paris, 1928).

Friends (Quakers), a liberal Christian offshoot with roots in seventeenth-century England. Members included the pacifist writer Horace Alexander, the diplomat John Henry Barlow, the IR lecturer Karlin Capper-Johnson, the activist Corder Catchpool, the social reformer Joan Mary Fry, the IR professor Philip Noel-Baker, and the lawyer Harold Evans. Wealthy Quaker families became important sponsors of liberal causes in international affairs, most notably the chocolate producers Cadbury, Fry, and Rowntree. In the wake of the First World War, they were among the first to revive exchange with German intellectuals, such as Mendelssohn Bartholdy.[206] Their network provided an infrastructure but also contributed to the mindset of early IR scholarship as a participatory, liberal project.

Women internationalists shared this perspective on international politics. They made a strong case for the universalist study of IR and attempted to build a global network of women, who saw themselves first and foremost as *women* in international politics, and therefore as independent from national attachments. Having started a series of conferences in 1915, the Women's International League for Peace and Freedom (WILPF) became the principal institutional home for female IR thinkers. Seeking to become truly global, WILPF offered summer schools, publications, and conferences. By 1924, it welcomed non-Europeans from China, Bolivia, Cuba, Ecuador, Guatemala, India, Japan, Liberia, Mexico, the Philippines, Ukraine, and Turkey.[207] Members included the Indian diplomat Begum Shareefah Hamid Ali, the Ecuadorian historian Pastoriza Flores, and the Japanese professor-activist Tano Jodai. Other organisations, such as the International Council of Women (ICW) or the International Woman Suffrage Alliance (IWSA) counted members from Chile, Brazil, Egypt, Jamaica, Palestine, Turkey, Mexico, and South-West Africa. Yet, as Leila Rupp has shown, feminist pacifism was nonetheless dominated by Western women from privileged backgrounds.[208] The vast majority of WILPF associates, and certainly the most influential ones, came from Europe and the Anglo-American world.

---

[206] Joan Mary Fry to Albrecht Mendelssohn Bartholdy, 6 July 1919, Albrecht Mendelssohn Bartholdy Papers, 2,26,102.

[207] Women's International League for Peace and Freedom, *Report of the Fourth Congress of the WILPF, Washington, May 1 to 7, 1924* (Geneva, 1924).

[208] Leila Rupp, *Worlds of Women: The Making of an International Women's Movement* (Princeton, 1997), p. 5.

On the other hand, there was a remarkable number of quasi-global IR initiatives, in the sense that they covered the world as far as it would have been covered by any comparable academic institution at the time. Western institutions welcomed colleagues from across the globe, such as the Deutsche Hochschule für Politik which received student applications from Ukraine, Armenia, Georgia, the Soviet Union, and China.[209] As early as 1919, the *American Political Science Review* featured non-European authors, such as Indian social scientist Benoy Kumar Sarkar.[210] Out of the eighty students reading at the Graduate Institute in Geneva during the late 1920s there were nineteen nationalities, including students from China, Colombia, India, Japan, Palestine, and Syria.[211] By the 1930s, the world's most important IR association, the International Studies Conference, gathered delegates from up to forty countries, including representatives from all continents.

Despite these efforts, the dominant institutions were in the Anglo-American world. British Dominions followed the example of Chatham House. The Canadian Institute of International Affairs was founded in 1928 by the former Prime Minister Robert Borden together with the military officer Arthur Currie, the journalist John Wesley Dafoe, and the businessman Joseph Flavelle.[212] The Australian Institute of International Affairs was created in 1933 by the politician Thomas Bavin and the IR scholar Stephen Henry Roberts.[213] An Indian Institute of International Affairs was established in 1936 with the lawyer and politician Muhammad Zafarullah Khan as chairman.[214] Across all these places, the study of IR shared similar motivations, organisational forms, and intellectual spirit. What is more, they were connected through a network of transnational cooperation. While IR

[209] List of foreign applicants since 1922, GStA PK, I. HA Rep. 303, Nr. 2113.
[210] Benoy Kumar Sarkar, 'Hindu Theory of International Relations', *American Political Science Review* 13 (1919), pp. 400–14.
[211] Annex, Student Numbers, RA 1928/30–1939, Graduate Institute Archives.
[212] E. D. Greathed, 'The Antecedents and Origins of the Canadian Institute of International Affairs', in Harvey L. Dyck and Peter Krosby (eds.), *Empire and Nations: Essays in Honour of Frederic H. Soward* (Toronto, 1969).
[213] Diana Stone, 'A Think Tank in Evolution or Decline?: The Australian Institute of International Affairs in Comparative Perspective', *Australian Journal of International Affairs* 50:2 (1996), p. 117.
[214] Vineet Thakur and Alexander E. Davis, 'A Communal Affair over International Affairs: The Arrival of IR in Late Colonial India', *South Asia: Journal of South Asian Studies* 40:4 (2017), pp. 691–3.

was not a global discipline it achieved a remarkable geographical spread during the interwar period, in some respects better than today.

Conclusion

The period from the First World War to the mid-1930s was a formative time for the study of IR. Over the course of less than two decades, the architects of IR turned a set of loosely associated authors and ideas into a coherent academic discipline, represented at dozens of institutions in more than thirty countries across the globe. IR professors began teaching at IR departments and universities awarded IR degrees. Scholars published in IR journals, spoke at IR conferences, and mingled in IR societies. As early as 1920, the British writer G. Lowes Dickinson put together a series of *Handbooks on International Relations*.[215] By 1934 in the United States alone, there were 384 student societies – so-called International Relations Clubs – funded by the Carnegie Endowment.[216] Thanks to the generous support of wealthy donors and political leaders, IR quickly became a respected university discipline and reproduced itself over the following decades.

More remarkable than the sheer number of new institutions was their common purpose and organisational design. Almost without exception, early IR institutions promoted both the study and practice of international politics. They focused on professional training for aspiring diplomats and businessmen. They closely collaborated with future employers to develop suitable curricula. Few scholars devoted their intellectual energy to theory. The vast majority used IR as a gateway to participate in policy debates in order to change international politics rather than to understand it. Several programmes were specifically designed to train personnel for foreign offices and the League of Nations. What is more, their underlying motivation was geared towards the concept of international cooperation and peace. Finally, they were funded by the same sources – large philanthropic trusts, wealthy individuals, and governments – which, although not imposing intellectual restrictions, carved out a certain space for IR scholars to operate in.

[215] See Graham H. Stuart, 'Handbooks on International Relations by G. Lowes Dickinson', *The Journal of International Relations* 12:2 (1921), pp. 294–6.
[216] Carnegie Endowment for International Peace Records, Columbia University, Boxes 310–3.

Perhaps the most striking characteristic of early IR scholarship was its geographic spread across Europe, North America, and the rest of the globe. Although the now-famous Anglo-American institutions were clearly among the principal IR centres, they were complemented by a range of professorships, departments, and conferences in other parts of the world. Crucially, as this chapter has highlighted, European scholars played a vital role in shaping the young discipline. It is significant, for instance, that German professors began to set up IR institutions at the same time as their Anglo-American colleagues, and in close collaboration with them. But non-Western authors, too, contributed to the emerging field and challenged the Eurocentric perspective that dominated the interwar period. International exchange allowed students and professors to test their research in front of diverse audiences and thereby to form a disciplinary identity. IR was the fastest growing and most international social science, although, as the following chapters show, it had not yet established a fixed theoretical basis.[217]

At the end of the first decade of IR scholarship, the historian James T. Shotwell reflected upon the remarkable rise of the discipline as well as its inherent shortcomings. On the one hand, he thought, IR provided a much-needed critical perspective on government policy, allowing systematic investigations of foreign affairs which were previously inaccessible and unintelligible to the public. In this sense, IR was an important tool for the spread of democracy. On the other hand, Shotwell recognised that most questions of war and peace rested "upon an emotional rather than a factual basis".[218] The solution was to lift these questions from the emotional into the factual realm – the "Geneva technique", as Shotwell called it. The fate of this technique depended on whether military intimidation could be replaced by rational debate. In other words, the mission of IR scholars such as Shotwell was to rationalise international politics, to make questions of war and peace fit into university degrees, academic journals, and conferences. Ultimately the goal was to convince decision-makers that IR was a social science like economics or sociology. So building reputable institutions was an important step to take.

---

[217] Alfred Zimmern, *University Teaching of International Relations* (Paris, 1939), pp. ix–x.
[218] James T. Shotwell, 'Scientific Method in Research and Discussion in International Relations: A Proposal for Institutes of International Relations', confidential, 6 June 1933, James T. Shotwell Papers, Box 155, 156.

All their efforts in establishing IR as an academic discipline were based on the dual assumption that international affairs could actually be studied and that research in the field could lead to practical change. But did war and peace allow scientific investigation? Could scholars develop a language to describe and explain these phenomena? How would they translate research results into applicable recommendations for politicians? The architects of IR were optimistic about all of these questions. They believed that through the "mastery of scientific principles" they would be able to learn, teach, and apply their insights.[219] By turning their research field into an academic discipline, represented at universities around the globe, they created at once an institutional home and the professional authority required for a social science with practical ambitions. They entertained close relations between university departments, private foundations, and foreign ministries, deliberately blending the boundary between academia and diplomacy. In doing so, they relied on the high-profile support of leading intellectuals, statesmen, and philanthropists. Yet, contrary to orthodox historiography, they did not pursue a fixed ideological agenda or subscribe to a consistent theory.

If anything, the discipline was marked by its international spread, reflecting as it did the international system itself. Having gained experience as government advisors at the end of the First World War, the architects of IR envisioned their discipline as the intellectual backbone of the 'new diplomacy'. The founding declarations of IR institutions read like official mission statements. The Aberystwyth professor was supposed to research "justice in the world" and "to be of general public service" in the spirit of the League of Nations.[220] The Deutsche Hochschule für Politik aspired to be "an important tool for the reconstruction of the German state".[221] The architects of IR saw themselves as diplomatic interlocutors on semi-official missions, often at the expense of scientific quality. In doing so, they relied not only on the institutions examined in this chapter but also on the growing transnational networks explored in Chapter 3.

---

[219] Walsh, 'The Aims of the School of Foreign Service', p. 14.
[220] Ellis, *The University College Wales*, p. 187; and Alfred Zimmern to Thomas Jones, 8 December 1918, Thomas Jones Papers, Vol. 12.
[221] Pamphlet on establishment of DHfP, 1920(?), GStA PK, I. HA Rep. 303 (neu), Nr. 1.

3 | *Peace in the Minds of Men and Women*

One of the fields in which intellectual cooperation seems to us most urgently needed is that of the scientific study of international relations ... nothing is more essentially international than these investigations.

Alfredo Rocco (1932)[1]

Introduction

In the wake of the First World War, a number of professors and politicians suggested establishing an international organisation for education and culture. By cooperating in cultural diplomacy, they wanted to foster international peace more generally. They pictured students attending foreign universities, libraries sharing their collections, and artworks being circulated across the globe. One of the schemes proposed in 1920 was a "University of the Nations", an international academy to be associated with the League of Nations, specialising in social sciences and International Relations (IR).[2] That particular idea never materialised, but intellectual cooperation in the field of IR became a major preoccupation for the architects of the discipline. By the 1930s, their community spanned more than thirty countries and offered anything from research directories to quasi-diplomatic conferences. Intellectual networks played an essential role in the formation of IR, both because of the institutional infrastructure they provided and because of the universalist spirit that underpinned

---

[1] International Institute of Intellectual Cooperation, *A Record of a First International Study Conference on the State and Economic Life* (Paris, 1932), p. 4.
[2] H. C. Andersen, Brochure 'University of the Nations', 13 October 1920, Dossier 7480, Box 1028, League of Nations Archives. A similar proposal was put forward by Paul Otlet and Henri La Fontaine. See La Fontaine and Otlet to Eric Drummond, 8 May 1920, Dossier 4646, Box R1008, League of Nations Archives.

them. In short, the goal was peace in the minds of men and women – the same *leitmotiv* that UNESCO continues to use until today.[3]

Among the earliest to suggest intellectual cooperation in the field of IR – an awkward translation from the French *coopération intellectuelle* – was a group of feminist pacifists who founded the Women's International League for Peace and Freedom (WILPF).[4] At their 1915 conference in The Hague, attended by hundreds of women from twelve countries, they issued a resolution calling for international conferences on "the scientific study and elaboration of the principles and conditions of permanent peace".[5] These conferences, the resolution went on, were to be organised by government-approved commissions and open to women. WILPF argued that studying peace in theory was essential to achieving peace in practice, and began to organise summer schools and publish educational material. At the government level, however, WILPF's proposal was ignored and the Covenant of the League of Nations did not provide for a technical organisation for education and culture, such as it did for economics and health.

It was in 1922 then, upon proposals by Belgian internationalists Henri La Fontaine and Paul Otlet as well as by French academics Paul Appell and Julien Luchaire, that the League of Nations decided to set up an International Committee on Intellectual Cooperation (ICIC) in Geneva. The ICIC comprised of a prominent board, including Nobel laureates Albert Einstein and Marie Curie, and took up a number of projects, ranging from bibliographic exchanges to intellectual property rights. It was primarily a European enterprise, akin to the League itself, although members came from across the (non-colonised) world. Due to its chronic lack of funding, the ICIC was complemented in 1926 by the Paris-based International Institute of Intellectual

---

[3] "Since wars begin in the minds of men, it is in the minds of men that the defences of peace must be constructed". UNESCO, *Constitution of the United Nations Educational, Scientific and Cultural Organization*, 16 November 1946 (London), available at http://portal.unesco.org/en/ev.php-URL_ID=15244&URL_DO=DO_TOPIC&URL_SECTION=201.html [accessed 30 May 2017].

[4] Joyce Goodman, 'Women and International Intellectual Co-operation', *Paedagogica Historica* 48:3 (2012), pp. 357–68.

[5] Women's International League for Peace and Freedom (WILPF), *Extract from the Forthcoming Report of the International Congress of Women: Held at Zurich, May 12–17, 1919* (Geneva, 1919), quoting 'Resolutions adopted at the Congress at the Hague, 1915', resolution xiv.

Cooperation (IIIC), an institution controlled by the League but largely financed by the French government. The IIIC essentially became the executive branch of intellectual cooperation at the League and it was particularly invested in the field of IR. The IIIC sponsored conferences, edited handbooks, and coordinated research projects. Several architects of IR, including Gilbert Murray, James T. Shotwell, and Alfred Zimmern, served in senior positions at the ICIC and IIIC.[6]

More important than the somewhat puzzling organisational architecture of intellectual cooperation at the League of Nations, however, was the internationalist mindset of its protagonists. Murray, Zimmern, and their colleagues believed that collaboration in science and arts would cultivate a peaceful spirit among political elites. In particular, they supported the study of IR to promote a rational approach to international politics. If international affairs could be studied on an academic level, they thought, then foreign policy makers could learn from professors. To this end, the IIIC organised from 1928 to 1939 the International Studies Conference which became the principal interwar meeting for IR scholars and practitioners. Intellectual cooperation was "more essential in the field of political education than in any other branch of academic training", the Italian jurist and ICIC member Alfredo Rocco emphasised.[7] It is impossible therefore to understand the formation of IR without this symbiotic and highly productive relationship between academia and the League of Nations.

On the other hand, the universalist spirit of intellectual cooperation collided with partisan politics and an increasingly hostile international environment. The protagonists of intellectual cooperation presupposed that it was possible to debate international affairs on the basis of common discursive standards – accepting factual evidence, avoiding preconceived biases, applying rational arguments, and respecting the equality of human beings. But the extremist politicians who gained power in the 1930s put those very standards into question, showing that intellectual cooperation was not a "non-political sphere", as has

---

[6] On Murray, see Peter Wilson, 'Gilbert Murray and International Relations: Hellenism, Liberalism, and International Intellectual Cooperation as a Path to Peace', *Review of International Studies* 37:2 (2011): 881–909.
[7] IIIC, *Handbook of Institutions for the Scientific Study of International Relations* (Paris, 1929), p. 3.

often been assumed.[8] The architects of IR who wanted to engage in "disinterested" intellectual cooperation found themselves confronted with fanatic doctrines that undermined any sense of rationality.[9] Struggling to find clear answers to fascism, they launched propaganda campaigns of their own.[10] Activism in favour of the League, however, was as detrimental to the idea of intellectual cooperation as right-wing extremism. Even before the crises of the 1930s, political debates affected the intellectual output of the IIIC which depended on the funds of sponsors and on the support of governments. The mere choice of promoting the study of IR rather than spending resources on, say, art history or biology was a political statement. Simply put, the architects of IR faced the fundamentally political nature of their field.

Historiography on intellectual cooperation, scarce as it is, has portrayed the League's specialised agencies as bureaucratic experiments and organisational failures – a correct albeit incomplete assessment. Jean-Jacques Renoliet's *L'UNESCO oubliée* (1999) outlines the complex institutional apparatus and showcases a range of its ill-fated activities.[11] A set of recent publications has added valuable case studies on certain individuals and organisational dynamics.[12] Using a digital humanities approach, Martin Grandjean has provided a social

[8] Zara Steiner, *The Lights that Failed: European International History, 1919–1933* (Oxford, 2005), p. 368.

[9] IIIC, *The State and Economic Life* (Paris, 1932), pp. xxii–xxiii.

[10] Henri Bonnet, 'Intellectual Cooperation', in American Council on Public Affairs (ed.), *World Organization: Balance Sheet of the First Great Experiment* (Washington, 1942), p. 209.

[11] Jean-Jacques Renoliet, *L'UNESCO oubliée: La Société des Nations et la coopération intellectuelle, 1919–1946* (Paris, 1999).

[12] Jimena Canales, 'Einstein, Bergson, and the Experiment that Failed: Intellectual Cooperation at the League of Nations', *Modern Language Notes* 120 (2005), pp. 1168–91; Cormac Shine, 'Papal Diplomacy by Proxy? Catholic Internationalism at the League of Nations' International Committee on Intellectual Cooperation, 1922–1939', *Journal of Ecclesiastical History* 69:4 (2018), pp. 785–805; Goodman, 'Women and International Intellectual Co-operation'; and Jo-Anne Pemberton, 'The Changing Shape of Intellectual Cooperation: From the League of Nations to UNESCO', *Australian Journal of Politics and History* 58:1 (2012), pp. 34–50; Jo-Anne Pemberton, *The Story of International Relations: Cold-Blooded Idealists*, parts 1–3 (Cham, 2020); Jonathan Voges, 'Eine Internationale der "Geistesarbeiter"? Institutionalisierte intellektuelle Zusammenarbeit im Rahmen des Völkerbundes', in Christian Heinrich-Franke et al. (eds.), *Grenzüberschreitende institutionalisierte Zusammenarbeit von der Antike bis zur Gegenwart* (Baden-Baden, 2019), pp. 355–84.

network analysis of intellectual cooperation at the League.[13] The critical question of what 'technical' cooperation really meant is addressed in Daniel Gorman's study of 1920s internationalism.[14] However, the most comprehensive interpretation remains F. S. Northedge's (unpublished) 1953 doctoral thesis which reveals the IIIC's systematic mistakes and attests interwar internationalists an inflated sense of self-importance.[15] Above all, Northedge teased out the tension between technical cooperation and political constraints within the environment of the League – a relationship that he called an "uneasy marriage between imaginative thought and political action".[16] It was this relationship that shaped the formation of IR as a young discipline during the interwar period.

This chapter explores the relationship between intellectual cooperation and the formation of IR scholarship. It begins by briefly chronicling the idea of intellectual cooperation. The second section traces the origins of the ICIC at Geneva, while the third one deals with the IIIC and its activities in Paris. The next section demonstrates how their projects became politicised, particularly those in the field of IR. Finally, the last section discusses the universalist motives of interwar intellectual cooperation and contrasts those ambitions with the political realities of the 1930s. The chapter concludes that IR benefitted enormously from the League of Nations but, at the same time, suffered from its political context and ultimately fell prey to the kind of aggressive foreign policy it set out to prevent.

From the Republic of Letters to the League of Nations

Intellectual collaboration across borders was not invented in the twentieth century. Its history is much older, perhaps as old as scientific inquiry itself. Most historians would trace it back to the

---

[13] Martin Grandjean, *Les réseaux de la coopération intellectuelle: La Société des Nations comme actrice des échanges scientifiques et culturels dans l'entre-deux-guerres* (Lausanne, 2018).
[14] Daniel Gorman, *The Emergence of International Society in the 1920s* (Cambridge, 2012), p. 203.
[15] F. S. Northedge, *International Intellectual Co-operation within the League of Nations: Its Conceptual Basis and Lessons for the Present*, PhD thesis (London, 1953).
[16] Ibid., p. viii.

seventeenth-century Republic of Letters, others to scholasticism and the medieval universities or even to Plato's dialogues.[17] Intellectual elites have long moved across borders, learned foreign languages, and shared cosmopolitan ideals, often underpinned by religious claims to universal truth. They travelled widely, corresponded with colleagues across the globe, and socialised in salons and learned societies. Their reference framework was not tied to a specific polity. Up until the eighteenth century, intellectual life was a universalist enterprise and Latin was the dominant vehicle of scientific communication in the Western world – the *unitas intellectus*.[18]

Only the advent of the modern nation-state in Europe, during the eighteenth and nineteenth centuries, together with advances in science and technology, changed the dynamics of scholarly collaboration. National academies and cultural boards increasingly segregated a community previously considered global. Universities drew up national curricula. Poets became national poets. In some places, the role of the intellectual became, as Tony Judt observed, "almost by definition, the representative, spokesperson, theorist of a nation".[19] By the mid-nineteenth century, new scientific fields and increasing student numbers turned small intellectual circles into education systems, often subject to state regulation. Governments pursued romantic nationalist campaigns in pursuit of political or military goals. That type of nationalism culminated in 1914 when ninety-three German intellectuals signed the infamous manifesto in support of German war aims.[20]

---

[17] Alfred Zimmern, *The Study of International Relations: An Inaugural Lecture Delivered before the University of Oxford on 20 February 1931* (Oxford, 1931); Joseph Needham, *Science and International Relations* (Oxford, 1948), p. 6; Anthony Grafton, *Worlds Made by Words: Scholarship and Community in the Modern World* (Cambridge, MA, 2009); Samuel Moyn and Andrew Sartori (eds.), *Global Intellectual History* (New York, 2013). See also, David Armitage, *Foundations of Modern International Thought* (Cambridge, 2013).

[18] Alfred Zimmern, *Internationale Politik als Wissenschaft* (Berlin, 1933), p. 3.

[19] Tony Judt, 'Nineteen Eighty-Nine: The End of Which European Era', in Vladimir Tismaneanu (ed.), *The Revolutions of 1989* (New York, 1999), p. 174.

[20] *An die Kulturwelt*, 4 October 1914, Archiv der Berlin-Brandenburgischen Akademie der Wissenschaften, Bestand Preußische Akademie der Wissenschaften, II-XII-31, Bl. 41–42, available at http://planck.bbaw.de/onlinetexte/Aufruf_An_die_Kulturwelt.pdf [accessed 28 October 2015]; see also Max Planck, 'German Scholars Explain Their Manifesto', *Current History* 4:5 (1916), p. 876.

In response to the fragmentation of academia, the first transnational organisations were founded during the second half of the nineteenth century. They were used by scholars to transcend borders in a variety of unofficial ways, not just as national representatives. Their work rested on the assumption that some problems were best solved above the national level, an approach that became known as 'international-ism' from the nineteenth century.[21] This included conferences, such as the Congress of Authors and Artists, held in Brussels in 1858; scholarly societies, such as the Chemical Society, founded in 1841 in London; and technical organisations, such as the International Bureau of Weights and Measures, established in Sèvres in 1875. According to calculations by Belgian internationalists Henri La Fontaine and Paul Otlet, the total number of international congresses increased from only nine between 1840 and 1849 to more than 1,000 during the first decade of the twentieth century.[22] In 1911, another statistic counted some 614 organisations in the sciences and humanities alone, ranging from the International Rubber Testing Committee to the International Commission for the Study of Clouds.[23] Some of these organisations were specifically aimed at transnationalising education and science. For example, the Dutch lawyer and teacher Hermann Molkenboer proposed in 1888 to form a "permanent council on education", establishing universal standards for schools.[24] In 1899, members of British, French, and German learned societies founded the International Association of Academies, which served as an umbrella organisation

---

[21] Robert Fox, *Science without Frontiers: Cosmopolitanism and National Interests in the World of Learning, 1870–1940* (Corvallis, 2016); Martin H. Geyer and Johannes Paulmann, 'Introduction', in Martin H. Geyer and Johannes Paulmann (eds.), *The Mechanics of Internationalism: Culture, Society, and Politics from the 1840s to the First World War* (Oxford, 2001), p. 2; Mark Mazower, *Governing the World: The History of an Idea* (New York, 2012), pp. 95–104; Davide Rodogno, Bernhard Struck, and Jakob Vogel, 'Introduction', in Rodogno et al. (eds.), *Shaping the Transnational Sphere: Experts, Networks, Issues* (New York, 2015), p. 7.

[22] Union of International Associations, *Conceptions et programmes de l'internationalisme: organismes internationaux et UAI*, 98 (1921).

[23] P. H. Eijkman, *L'Internationalisme Scientifique* (The Hague, 1911).

[24] Hermann Molkenboer, 'Aufruf des Vereins für Einsetzung eines bleibenden Internationalen Erziehungsrates', *Schweizerisches Schularchiv* 9:11 (1888), pp. 189–90.

to seventeen national academies from three continents and which was a predecessor of the International Science Council.[25]

Most of these organisations had a private or unofficial character. Some were based on religious beliefs, such as the World Student Christian Federation, founded in 1895, others represented political causes, such as the International Council of Women, formed in 1888. Academics established a number of professional associations, such as the Institut de Droit International, founded in 1873, and the International Institute of Sociology, founded in 1893. By the eve of the First World War, the American journalist Louis P. Lochner observed, there was an "ever-increasing tendency" to recognise the mutual inter-dependence by "organising and federating internationally".[26] This trend included political science, as Paul Reinsch highlighted in 1911.[27] But governmental internationalism, too, expanded during the late nineteenth and early twentieth centuries in the form of technical cooperation, such as the Universal Postal Union, founded in 1874, or political exchange, such as the Inter-Parliamentary Union, founded in 1889 – both origin-ally located in Berne, Switzerland.[28] Meanwhile, the champions of international law tried to expand on the 1864 Geneva Convention at the two Hague Conferences in 1899 and 1907. Internationalism became so widespread that in 1907 La Fontaine and Otlet founded the Union of International Associations, an umbrella organisation based in Brussels.

It is not true therefore that internationalism only flourished after 1919, as is sometimes suggested.[29] There were important precursors to the organisations that emerged in the 1920s, a fact acknowledged even by contemporaries.[30] The architects of IR knew that "scholarship [was] in its very nature international" long before its institutional

[25] Peter Alter, 'The Royal Society and the International Association of Academies 1897–1919', *Notes and Records of the Royal Society of London* 34:2 (1980), pp. 241–64.

[26] Louis P. Lochner, 'Internationalism among Universities', *World Peace Foundation Pamphlet Series* 3 (1913), p. 3.

[27] Paul Reinsch, 'Avant-Propos', in P. H. Eijkman (ed.), *L'Internationalisme Scientifique* (The Hague, 1911).

[28] C. C. Eckhardt, 'The Old Internationalism and the New League of Nations', *The Scientific Monthly* 8:5 (1919), pp. 437–41.

[29] Gorman, *The Emergence of International Society in the 1920s*, p. 3.

[30] League of Nations, 'The International Institute of Intellectual Cooperation', *Brochures de Propagande, 1926–1927* (Paris, 1926), p. 2.

manifestation.[31] The first wave of internationalism may have been a "casualty of World War I", as Elizabeth Crawford has put it, but its ideas and practices lived on.[32] The novelty in the 1920s was that the League of Nations gave intellectual cooperation an official character. The memoirs of former IIIC directors Henri Bonnet and Jean-Jacques Mayoux, written during and immediately after the Second World War, offer a good impression of the fruitful atmosphere of the new organisations.[33] Subsequent studies by Jan Kolasa, Jean-Jacques Renoliet, and Daniel Laqua have added to our understanding of the structure, personnel, and activities of both the IIIC and ICIC.[34] Yet, these works reveal more about the mechanics of cooperation than about the inherent tensions and conflicts.

What distinguished intellectual cooperation during the interwar period was the collision between the ideals of a universal scholarly community and state-sponsored institutions vulnerable to political controversy. This was a particular challenge for IR scholars whose own research rested on the assumption that international relations were accessible by scientific inquiry and, inversely, that rational arguments could inform practical politics. In other words, the experience of interwar intellectual cooperation at the League of Nations undermined the premise of a workable nexus between academia and politics. The architects of IR were either unaware of or willing to ignore this

[31] Lochner, 'Internationalism among Universities', p. 3.
[32] Elizabeth Crawford, *Nationalism and Internationalism in Science, 1880–1939: Four Studies of the Nobel Population* (Cambridge, 1992), p. 49.
[33] Bonnet, 'Intellectual Cooperation', p. 191; Jean-Jacques Mayoux et al., *L'Institut International de Coopération Intellectuelle* (Paris, 1946). See also, H. R. G. Greaves, *The League Committees and World Order* (London, 1931), pp. 111–39; John Eugene Harley, *International Understanding* (Stanford, 1931); Robert Richter, *Die internationale geistige Zusammenarbeit im Rahmen des Völkerbundes*, PhD thesis (Würzburg, 1930); and Margarete Rothbarth, *Geistige Zusammenarbeit im Rahmen des Völkerbundes* (Münster, 1931).
[34] Jan Kolasa, *International Intellectual Cooperation: The League Experience and the Beginnings of UNESCO* (Wroclaw, 1962); Renoliet, *L'UNESCO oubliée*; Daniel Laqua, 'Transnational Intellectual Cooperation, the League of Nations, and the Problem of Order', *Journal of Global History* 6:2 (2011), pp. 223–47. See also, Canales, 'Einstein, Bergson, and the Experiment that Failed'; Pemberton, 'The Changing Shape of Intellectual Cooperation'; Goodman, 'Women and International Intellectual Co-operation', pp. 357–68; Corinne A. Pernet, 'Twists, Turns and Dead Alleys: The League of Nations and Intellectual Cooperation in Times of War', *Journal of Modern European History* 12:3 (2014), pp. 342–58.

problematic relationship and continued to blur the line between science and diplomatic practice. Political representatives attended academic conferences (and vice-versa), thereby opening a new sphere of quasi-diplomacy or, as Madeleine Herren has called it, "a back door to power".[35] The key problem, addressed in the next sections, is how the League's framework provided both an institutional and an intellectual home to thinkers of IR.

Beginnings in Geneva: The International Committee on Intellectual Cooperation (ICIC)

In February 1919, Henri La Fontaine and Paul Otlet submitted a petition to the Peace Conference via Belgian Foreign Minister Paul Hymans, proposing an organisation for intellectual cooperation as part of the League of Nations.[36] Their idea, called *Commission internationale de relations intellectuelles*, was to build scientific and artistic relationships in order to generate "an international mentality".[37] To the disappointment of the Belgians, none of their proposals was welcomed or even discussed in Paris. A similar proposal by the International Council of Women, suggesting to install a permanent bureau of education, was turned down with the remark that the League could not care for all aspects of human life.[38] It is interesting to note that both initiatives came from non-governmental, pre-war bodies. Internationalists were used to working with pressure groups, private individuals, and philanthropists. Now they wanted to establish their work on the official level.

A few months later, in July 1920, the rector of the University of Paris, Paul Appell sent a letter to the newly elected secretary-general of the League, Eric Drummond, proposing an "Office for Intellectual

---

[35] Madeleine Herren, 'Governmental Internationalism and the Beginning of a New World Order in the Late Nineteenth Century', in Martin H. Geyer and Johannes Paulmann (eds.), *The Mechanics of Internationalism: Culture, Society, and Politics from the 1840s to the First World War* (Oxford, 2001), p. 123.

[36] Renoliet, *L'UNESCO oubliée*, p. 12. There were also informal discussions between members of the American Board on Education and their British counterparts in May 1919. See Stephen T. Duggan to Gilbert Murray, 2 May 1919, Gilbert Murray Papers, Box 39.

[37] David Hunter Miller, *The Drafting of the Covenant* (New York, 1928), p. 350.

[38] Northedge, *International Intellectual Co-operation within the League of Nations*, p. 270.

Intercourse and Education".[39] Appell's letter was endorsed by the French League of Nations Association and contained a detailed programme drawn up by Julien Luchaire, then chief of staff to the French education minister.[40] Similar to the Belgian plan, Luchaire and Appell argued that cooperation in education and culture was a prerequisite for solving political disputes.[41] More detailed than previous plans, Luchaire and Appell outlined a feasible project at an inter-governmental level, including a governance structure that largely foresaw the future institutions. It included an educational branch for the exchange of teachers and students, book translations and conferences, a scientific branch intended to create laboratory and documentary centres for cost-intensive research, and a literary and cultural branch which would organise the circulation of books, art publications, mediate in art disputes, and help to safeguard precious works of art – perhaps an early forerunner of UNESCO's cultural heritage programme.[42]

Appell's letter was picked up by the League of Nations Assembly in December 1920, where it initially received mixed reactions. Eventually the Council was asked to consider the proposal and to "report on the advisability of forming a Technical Organisation attached to the League".[43] The Council was not enthusiastic either. Some members, notably the British delegate George Barnes, declared that the idea was premature and should be left to private actors.[44] There was little political need to establish a new agency which, in the eyes of some diplomats, seemed fairly remote from urgent tasks, such as reparations, borders, and minorities.[45] On the other hand, the Council members thought it could not do any harm.

[39] Letter by Paul Appell, dated 8 July 1920, published as 'Institution of an International Bureau for Intellectual Intercourse and Education', *League of Nations Official Journal*, Vol. 1 (October 1920), p. 445.
[40] Rothbarth, *Geistige Zusammenarbeit im Rahmen des Völkerbundes*, p. 31.
[41] Appell's letter read: "A moral union of hearts and consciences is an essential preliminary to an agreement of interests, a juridical settlement of conflicts and political organisation for peace". See also Northedge, *International Intellectual Co-operation within the League of Nations*, p. 276.
[42] Letter by Paul Appell, dated 8 July 1920, published as 'Institution of an International Bureau for Intellectual Intercourse and Education', pp. 447–50.
[43] Oliver Brett (ed.), *The First Assembly: A Study of the Proceedings of the First Assembly of the League of Nations* (London, 1921), p. 259.
[44] Kolasa, *International Intellectual Cooperation*, p. 21.
[45] Bonnet, 'Intellectual Cooperation', pp. 190–1; Renoliet, *L'UNESCO oubliée*, pp. 15, 18.

After overcoming opposition in the Council, a revised report was written up under the direction of Léon Bourgeois who was one of the most prominent French supporters of the League of Nations, a recipient of the Nobel Peace Prize, and sometime president of the Council of the League.[46] His authority lent crucial support to the plan and after preliminary approval by the fifth committee of the Assembly, Gilbert Murray was asked to present the draft in the plenary session. It was accepted on 21 September 1921, and was confirmed by the Council in January 1922.[47] The motion provided for an inaugural committee of twelve experts, both men and women, to investigate potential fields of international intellectual cooperation. They were appointed by the Council in May and held their first meeting in August, marking the 'birth' of what became known as the International Committee on Intellectual Cooperation (ICIC).[48]

Among the members of the ICIC were a range of well-known academics, most notably the physicists Albert Einstein and Marie Curie as well as the philosopher Henri Bergson who had been in touch with US President Woodrow Wilson during the war and who now went on to serve as the ICIC's inaugural president.[49] Apart from Curie, the Norwegian biologist Kristine Bonnevie was the only woman on the ICIC.[50] There were also two representatives from non-member states (Einstein and the American physicist Robert Millikan), following a suggestion by Murray, who was himself elected an ICIC member and from 1927 to 1939 its president.[51] In 1933, the American IR scholar James T. Shotwell succeeded Millikan. Besides an array of liberally minded intellectuals, the ICIC also consisted of more right-wing, nationalist, or even fascist members. The conservative Swiss literature and history professor Gonzague de Reynold was a case in point.

[46] Northedge, *International Intellectual Co-operation within the League of Nations*, pp. 279–80.
[47] Mayoux et al., *L'Institut International de Coopération Intellectuelle*, p. 15.
[48] Léon Bourgeois, *L'Œvre de la Société des Nations* (Paris, 1923), pp. 406–10.
[49] Kolasa, *International Intellectual Cooperation*, pp. 167–8; Pemberton, *The Story of International Relations*, p. 38.
[50] To the regret of the Council for the Representation of Women in the League of Nations, their other nominee, Scottish geologist Maria Ogilvie Gordon, was not elected. L. de Alberti to Nitobe Inazō, 20 June 1922, Dossier 14297, Box R1029, League of Nations Archives.
[51] Gilbert Murray was a long-time advocate of German accession to the League of Nations. Letter by Nitobé to Murray, 19 December 1921, Gilbert Murray Papers, Box 265.

He was later joined by the Italian fascists Alfredo Rocco and Balbino Giuliano as well as the nationalist historian Heinrich von Srbik.[52] Rocco openly acknowledged that the fascist state had its own morality and, consequently, its own political mission in the world.[53] Despite persistent claims that the ICIC was a technical organisation committed to disinterested and neutral goals, it was clear from the outset that political questions could not be ignored. The selection of ICIC members, for example, was achieved by "sounding" government representatives, thus imitating practices usually reserved for high politics.[54]

While receiving enthusiastic reactions from senior diplomats, notably from Secretary-General Drummond, the ICIC immediately faced financial constraints.[55] The League Secretariat provided only a single office assistant and very limited financial support.[56] Funds promised to the ICIC became unavailable just shortly after its inception.[57] This left the young committee in an awkward position torn between a grandiose mission and feeble support.

For the time being, the ICIC established a provisional working order. Meetings were held once a year in either Geneva or Paris. All proposals and resolutions were presented at these annual meetings, while the substantive work was assigned to sub-committees staffed with external experts. The Polish historian Oskar Halecki was in charge of the ICIC secretariat.[58] He reported to the Council and the Assembly, which authorised the ICIC's programme, and also entertained ties with the League Secretariat where the Japanese diplomat Nitobe Inazō (in the rank of under-secretary-general) was in charge of the International Bureaux section. Hierarchically speaking, the ICIC was on the same level as other permanent advisory commissions of the

[52] Kolasa, *International Intellectual Cooperation*, pp. 169–71.
[53] Pemberton, *The Story of International Relations*, p. 62.
[54] Nitobe Inazō to Gilbert Murray, 19 December 1921, Gilbert Murray Papers, Box 265.
[55] Pham Thi-Thu, *La Coopération Intellectuelle sous la Société des Nations* (Geneva, 1962), p. 27.
[56] Mayoux et al., *L'Institut International de Coopération Intellectuelle*, p. 16; Renoliet, *L'UNESCO oubliée*, p. 18.
[57] Rothbarth, *Geistige Zusammenarbeit im Rahmen des Völkerbundes*, p. 35.
[58] Andrzej M. Brzezinski, 'Oskar Halicki – Sekretarz Komisji Miedzynarodowej Wspólpracy Intelektualnej Ligii Narodów (1922–1924)', *Kwartalnik Historii Nauki i Techniki* 55:1 (2010), pp. 7–35.

League, such as the Mandates Commission or the Financial and Economic Committees.[59] Soon after the administration had been set up, member states began to form national commissions of intellectual cooperation in order to bundle their interaction with Geneva. By July 1923, eleven such national commissions were in contact with the ICIC.[60]

Subsequent changes to the original structure (and the bi-lingual administration) have led to confusion among contemporaries and historians, who have referred to the ICIC under a variety of names.[61] Some non-French speakers thought that '*coopération intellectuelle*' was an ill-chosen name, as it sounded pretentious and misleading in its English and German translations.[62] Others argued that the entire purpose of intellectual cooperation was unclear.[63] Although it can be tedious to uncover the subtleties of institutional arrangements, they inform our understanding of how technical cooperation was integrated into an inter-governmental organisation. Daniel Laqua has stressed the significance of organisational layers and argued that the ICIC developed an influence on international cooperation more generally. As various concepts of cooperation circulated among intellectuals, Laqua argues, the ICIC became "a tool for transforming the international order".[64] Northedge made a similar point, arguing that the true achievements of intellectual cooperation at the League lay in the bureaucratic machinery that it established, not so much in fulfilling its goals.[65] Both authors have drawn attention to the framework, as opposed to the substance, of intellectual cooperation. It is as important, however, to see the

---

[59] Formally this was only recognised in 1926 in a resolution by the League Assembly. See Bonnet, 'Intellectual Cooperation', pp. 193–5.

[60] Renoliet, *L'UNESCO oubliée*, p. 32.

[61] Among the erroneous variations are 'International Commission for Intellectual Cooperation', 'International Commission on Intellectual Cooperation', 'Intellectual Committee', 'CIC', and 'International organization of intellectual cooperation'. See Bonnet, 'Intellectual Cooperation', p. 195; Canales, 'Einstein, Bergson, and the Experiment that Failed'; Pemberton, 'The Changing Shape of Intellectual Cooperation'; and Alexandra Pita González, 'A Case Study: México and the International Intellectual Cooperation in the Interwar Period', *Relationes Internationales* 6:2 (2014), pp. 117–34.

[62] Rothbarth, *Geistige Zusammenarbeit im Rahmen des Völkerbundes*, pp. 25–7.

[63] Mayoux et al., *L'Institut International de Coopération Intellectuelle*, pp. 16–17.

[64] Laqua, 'Transnational Intellectual Cooperation, the League of Nations, and the Problem of Order', p. 226.

[65] Northedge, *International Intellectual Co-operation within the League of Nations*, p. 687.

connections between actual projects, often loaded with lofty expectations, and the institutional fabric that surrounded them.

Despite financial constraints, the ICIC took on a relatively ambitious
programme in the autumn of 1922. One project was a survey on the
conditions of "intellectual workers" – academics, artists, journalists, and
similar professions – across the various member states. Other sub-
committees worked on bibliographical questions, intellectual property
rights, and the organisation of a congress of universities.[66] All of these
projects began with extensive surveys, delegated to experts and national
representatives, which often took years to be completed. In many cases the
only service that the ICIC ever provided was to "facilitate the coordination
between existing organisations" or to publish overviews of existing
works.[67] Bernard Shaw satirised this habit in his play *Geneva* (1938) in
which the ICIC typist drily says, "we all do a lot of writing to one
another".[68] The most common reflex of ICIC officers, when confronted
with an inquiry, was to redirect them to others. In one rather odd case, for
example, Gonzague de Reynold responded to a request from students for
high school exchanges to "be organised by the students themselves".[69] On
another occasion, the ICIC simply ignored a well-intended offer from the
International Federation of University Women.[70] Given the lack of secretarial resources and regular meetings, many projects took up to a decade or
longer to produce results. The bibliographical study, for instance, resulted
in a survey of periodical titles as well as a handbook of educational
literature, published in 1930 and 1935 respectively.[71] The study on intellectual property, meagre as it was, appeared no earlier than 1938.[72]

[66] Bourgeois, *L'œuvre de la Société des Nations*, p. 410; Gorman, *The Emergence of International Society in the 1920s*, pp. 203–8.
[67] Julien Luchaire, 'Exposé sur la situation et les travaux de l'institut international', 21 May 1926, CICI.CD.1-18, IIIC Records.
[68] Rather than intellectual cooperation, "it is mere compilation", the visitor responds. Bernard Shaw, *Geneva: A Fancied Page of History in Three Acts* (London, 1938, 1946), p. 31.
[69] Report on the Exchange of Students, by Professor de Reynold, 21 July 1923, Dossier 28306, Box R1055, League of Nations Archives.
[70] Theodora Bosanquet to Oskar Halecki, 12 October 1923, Dossier 28306, Box R1055, League of Nations Archives.
[71] IIIC, *Code international d'abréviations des titres de périodique* (Paris, 1930); IIIC, *Bibliographie pédagogique internationale* (Paris, 1935).
[72] IIIC, *Le dépot légal: son organisation et son fonctionnement dans les divers pays* (Paris, 1938). See Draft Convention on Protection of Scientific Property, Dossier 31393, Box R1061, League of Nations Archives.

What the ICIC was exceptionally good at, however, was propaganda – a term that did not yet carry the negative connotation that it assumed in the 1930s and 1940s. The ICIC members relentlessly advertised their own cause and that of the League of Nations more generally. This included handbooks, educational films, lantern slides as well as information material, and exchange programmes for children.[73] Another idea was to establish an international teachers' college and to issue a teacher's handbook on *The Aims and Organisation of the League of Nations*.[74] By planting internationalist ideas in the minds of children, the ICIC sought to counter nationalist traditions. The goal was to formulate a master narrative of internationalism by building bridges in education and culture.

A flagship project in this regard was the revision of textbooks, particularly history books on the recent war.[75] The Japanese teachers' association had submitted a proposal to this effect as early as September 1920, even before the ICIC was founded. Two years later, ICIC member Robert Millikan picked up the idea and suggested "the teaching of history from an international point of view" in primary and secondary schools.[76] His French colleague Luchaire proposed a common textbook edited under the auspices of the League.[77] These hopes received little sympathy from member-states and threatened to vanish in sub-committees. A preliminary report spanning fifteen countries resulted in nothing but endless reports on national particularities.[78] Eventually the working group proposed a four-stage procedure: (i) national committees had the right to express concern about a foreign textbook and ask for changes; (ii) the national

---

[73] ICIC minutes, 10–11 July 1935, Dossier 19930, Box R4062, League of Nations Archives; and 4th Assembly, Resolutions adopted on 27 September, 1923, Dossier 30862, Box R1059; and ICIC minutes, 10 July 1933, Dossier 5625, Box 4060, League of Nations Archives.

[74] Walther Gimmi to Eric Drummond, 1 September 1922, 'Vorschlag zur Schaffung & Einrichtung einer internationalen Lehrerbildungsanstalt', Dossier 23074, Box R1712; and annotated copy of 'The Aims and Organisation of the League of Nations', Dossier 5286, Box R4059, League of Nations Archives.

[75] Ken Osborne, 'Creating the "International Mind": The League of Nations Attempts to Reform History Teaching, 1920–1939', *History of Education Quarterly* 56:2 (2016), pp. 213–40.

[76] Kolasa, *International Intellectual Cooperation*, pp. 68–9.

[77] ICIC, *Minutes of the Second Session* (Geneva, 1923), p. 35.

[78] Report by International Historical Institute, 1932[?], Dossier 319, Box R4049, League of Nations Archives.

committee accused then had to either accept the amendment or explain why it chose not to; (iii) complaints had to be based on objective facts, not moral, political, or religious values; (iv) national committees were invited to recommend the most suitable textbooks for teaching the history of their country. However, this procedure remained entirely voluntary and was only rarely used.[79]

International cooperation in the field of education was not unprecedented. The revision of textbooks, for example, had been pioneered by Hermann Molkenboer and his campaign for an international education council in the 1880s.[80] Other projects, such as the work on bibliographies or intellectual property, had also been tried before.[81] But the ICIC gave those projects an official platform and, perhaps more importantly, an ideological guideline. Its projects served as vehicles for the internationalist agenda of the League of Nations which were inevitably at odds with government interests. It is no coincidence that some of the more controversial projects, such as history curricula, are still subject to debate today.[82]

"The twelve apostles of 1922", as Northedge called the original set of ICIC members, were academics and public intellectuals, not technocratic managers.[83] They had little experience in directing an intergovernmental organisation, and almost no administrative help. The ICIC resembled "an international Senior Common Room in Geneva" more than an inter-governmental agency.[84] Crucially, they had to deal with national interests. For instance, the French vehemently rejected Esperanto as the main working language.[85] Although ICIC members were deliberately not labelled 'national delegates', there were dynamics to this effect. Einstein considered several times to resign, and eventually did, since he felt that the ICIC was too anti-German but also because

[79] Kolasa, *International Intellectual Cooperation*, pp. 71–2.
[80] Molkenboer, 'Aufruf des Vereins für Einsetzung eines bleibenden Internationalen Erziehungsrates', pp. 189–90.
[81] See Isabella Löhr, *Die Globalisierung geistiger Eigentumsrechte: neue Strukturen internationaler Zusammenarbeit, 1886–1952* (Göttingen, 2010).
[82] David D'Avray et al., 'Plan for History Curriculum Is Too Focused on Britain', *The Observer*, 16 February 2013, available at www.theguardian.com/theobserver/2013/feb/16/history-curriculum-letters [accessed 8 October 2015]; Rachel Donadio, 'Revisiting the Canon Wars', *The New York Times*, 16 September 2007.
[83] Northedge, *International Intellectual Co-operation within the League of Nations*, p. 291.
[84] Ibid., p. vi.   [85] Renoliet, *L'UNESCO oubliée*, pp. 21, 25, 33–4.

"as an Israelite" he would not adequately represent German interests.[86] The ICIC thus became a site of what Glenda Sluga has described
as "internationalism in the age of nationalism".[87]

Revival in Paris: The International Institute of Intellectual Cooperation (IIIC)

The ICIC could not afford to gather the twelve members more regularly, let alone to employ a standing committee, and there was almost
no permanent work. The sub-committees had to rely on the goodwill
of external experts and occasional government grants. Having operated on a minimal budget for two years, the ICIC decided to look for
external funding and issued an official appeal in September 1923.[88]
A few months later, the French government responded with a generous
offer to establish an institute in Paris along with an annual grant of two
million francs. The preliminary proposal, conveyed in a letter by the
French Education Minister François Albert to ICIC president Henri
Bergson, was swiftly adopted by the ICIC and then passed the League
Council and Assembly.[89] By August 1925, the French parliament, too,
had given its approval for the new agency. It was called the
International Institute of Intellectual Cooperation (IIIC).[90]

Formally an institution under French law, the IIIC was put at the
disposal of the League of Nations as an executive agency for intellectual cooperation. The ICIC simultaneously served as the IIIC's
governing body, appointed its director and chiefs of section, drew up

---

[86] After having re-joined, Einstein confessed to Murray: "Whatever the failures of
the League of Nations in the past, it must be regarded as the one institution
which holds out the best prospect of beneficent action in these sad times". Albert
Einstein to Gilbert Murray, 20 May 1924, Dossier 14297, Box R1029, League
of Nations Archives. See also, Gilbert Murray to Albert Einstein, 20 April 1923,
Gilbert Murray Papers, Box 265; Canales, 'Einstein, Bergson, and the
Experiment that Failed', pp. 1174–5.
[87] Glenda Sluga, *Internationalism in the Age of Nationalism* (Philadelphia, 2013).
[88] Approval was granted by the fourth Assembly in September 1923. Mayoux
et al., *L'Institut International de Coopération Intellectuelle*, p. 21.
[89] Communiqué to the Council and the delegates of the Assembly, document
A.64.1924.XII, dated 12 September 1924, A.I.9, IIIC Records.
[90] *Journal Officiel*, 9 August 1925, A.II.1, IIIC Records. Taken together, the ICIC, IIIC,
and the Intellectual Cooperation Section of the League Secretariat were sometimes
referred to as the Organisation of Intellectual Cooperation (OIC). Eric Drummond,
'Message' in IIIC (ed.), *Information Bulletin* 1:1 (Paris, 1932), p. 4.

a budget, and approved its programme. To overcome the problem of scattered meetings and institutional instability, a sub-group of the ICIC, the so-called committee of directors, met every two months and passed lower-level decisions. There were six sections in the original IIIC structure: a university relations section, one on bibliography and scientific relations, an artistic and literary section, a legal section, an information section, and a general section responsible for taking up new topics.[91] It is worth noting that the IIIC, just like the ICIC, employed experts from non-member countries, notably the German historian Margarete Rothbarth. By December 1928, the IIIC employed eighty-nine people from twenty nationalities.[92] It was housed in the west wing of the *Palais Royal* in Paris, a residence that reflected much of the perceived grandeur of the IIIC.[93]

Julien Luchaire, the author of the 1920 report that had inspired the ICIC, was elected inaugural director of the IIIC for a term of seven years – after which a non-French person was to take over. An education specialist and experienced political functionary, Luchaire was an ambitious, though, at times unpredictable visionary who sought to turn the IIIC into an "advertising agency for intellectual co-operation", as Northedge put it.[94] He was eager to attract additional funding by selling tailored services to individual governments. In 1926 alone, the IIIC received 100,000 francs from the Polish government for "a special study of assistance to universities".[95] Luchaire's 1926 report on the IIIC's first year, suitably called *Brochure de Propagande*, read more like a marketing strategy than an official document. He also installed a press section that published a bulletin and managed media enquiries. At the same time, however, he reassured his colleagues that the IIIC would not become a competitor to existing organisations. He

[91] 'Internal Regulations of the International Institute of Intellectual Cooperation', dated 12 August 1925, C.432.1925.XII, IIIC Records.
[92] Harley, *International Understanding*, p. 152.
[93] At the inaugural ceremony on 16 January 1926, League Secretary-General Drummond jokingly commented that the League Secretariat in Geneva would for ever be inferior to the grand residence of the IIIC. Programme leaflet '*Inauguration de l'IICI*', 16 January 1926, A.I.6, IIIC Records.
[94] Northedge, *International Intellectual Co-operation within the League of Nations*, pp. 355–6.
[95] League of Nations, 'The International Institute of Intellectual Cooperation', in *Brochures de Propagande*, 1926–1927 (Paris, 1926), p. 6. See also negotiations with other governments for additional funding, A.II.7–30, IIIC Records.

envisaged the IIIC as a sort of social club where professors mingled with diplomats under the auspices of the League, enjoying the comfort of gala dinners at the *Palais Royal* in Paris.

In practice this meant that the IIIC adopted ICIC projects on a larger scale and with a more permanent character. Study groups were created, for example, on bibliographies and scientific nomenclatures, the circulation of books, cooperation between libraries and museums, the exchange of professors and students, the equivalence of degrees, intellectual property rights as well as on regulations protecting art-work, archaeological sites, and historic buildings. Most of these studies resulted in the publication of lengthy reports, handbooks, or periodicals. The press section published a list of "remarkable books", essentially a literary review. The university relations section compiled a handbook on student exchanges in Europe.[96] And from 1927, the museum journal *Mouseion* was published under the auspices of the IIIC. At the end of its lifetime in 1946, there were half a million copies of IIIC publications in circulation around the world.[97]

Apart from written work, the IIIC regularly invited experts for conferences, luncheons, and dinners. Among the meetings were the International Congress of Dramatic and Musical Critics, a congress of the International Federation of Journalism, the annual session of the International Academy of Comparative Law, and the International Cinema Congress.[98] To facilitate dialogue between younger generations, the IIIC suggested establishing "travelling scholarships for university students" to visit the League headquarters in Geneva.[99] It also housed representatives from the World Youth Organization in its Paris offices. In addition to that, the IIIC entertained close relations to the International Educational Cinematographic Institute in Rome which was funded by the Italian government but associated with the League.[100]

[96] IIIC, *University Exchanges in Europe: A Handbook* (Paris, 1928).
[97] Mayoux et al., *L'Institut International de Coopération Intellectuelle*, p. 599.
[98] IIIC, 'The First Six Months of the International Institute of Intellectual Cooperation', *Bulletin of the Information Section* No. 1 (Paris, 1926), pp. 3–4.
[99] 'Report by Sub-Committee of Experts for the Instruction of Children Youth in the Existence and Aims of the League of Nations', 21 March 1927, Dossier 54891, Box R1025, League of Nations Archives.
[100] Report on IIIC premises covering 1927–1946, A.IV.22, IIIC Records. The Cinematographic Institute was conceived, supervised and administered by the ICIC in Geneva. See James Marchant, 'Cinema in Education', *The Times*

Women were involved in intellectual cooperation in a variety of ways. They served on the board as well as on the staff of the IIIC, including the Chilean poet Gabriela Mistral and the German historian Margarethe Rothbarth who wrote the first official history of the IIIC.[101] Female ICIC members after Curie and Bonnevie included the Norwegian chemist Ellen Gleditsch and the Hungarian writer Cécile Tormay – the election of whom feminist organisations had heavily campaigned for.[102] Besides struggling for representation, however, women worked on a number of issues, such as compulsory continuation schools, educational cinematography, and a "convention for the suppression of obscene publications".[103]

Despite persistent pressure from feminist groups to appoint women to senior positions at the League of Nations, Rachel Crowdy remained the only woman to head a section – on social questions and opium traffic, as gender clichés would have it.[104] When feminist-pacifist Helena Swanwick went to Geneva as a British delegate to the fifth Assembly in 1924, she noticed that women were assumed to be well informed only about "opium, refugees, protection of children, relief after earthquakes, prison reform, municipal cooperation, alcoholism, traffic in women".[105] But, contrary to stereotypes, Swanwick was interested in security questions, such as disarmament and sanctions.[106] Other women worked on imperialism and the rights of natives, often critical of colonial governments. At a 1927 summer school, they

11 June 1924; letter to Eric Drummond, Dossier 37604, Box R1069, League of Nations Archives; and http://atom.archives.unesco.org/international-educational-cinematographic-institute-ieci [accessed 19 April 2016].
[101] U. Lemke, '"La femme, la clandestine de l'histoire" Margarete Rothbarth – ein Engagement für den Völkerbund', *Lendemains* 146:7 (2012), pp. 51–3; Rothbarth, *Geistige Zusammenarbeit im Rahmen des Völkerbundes*.
[102] See, for instance, Margery Corbett Ashby (International Woman Suffrage Alliance) to Eric Drummond, 1 March 1922, Dossier 14297, Box R1029, League of Nations Archives.
[103] President's Memorandum Regarding the Business Transacted by the ICW Executive held at Geneva, 7–17 June 1927; and Gertrud M. Günther (ed.), *Bulletin International Council of Women*, special number (1927), Dossier 43088, Box R1022, League of Nations Archives.
[104] President's Memorandum Regarding the Business Transacted by the ICW Executive held at Geneva, 7–17 June 1927, Dossier 43088, Box R1022, League of Nations Archives.
[105] Helena Swanwick, *I Have Been Young* (London, 1935), p. 385.
[106] E. Horscroft to Eric Drummond, 11 March 1931, Dossier 11078, Box R2182, League of Nations Archives.

collected evidence in support of "native races" to "bring pressure upon their governments to effect reforms" and to work for the "liberation of those who are oppressed".[107] In 1931, the International Cooperative Women's Guild brought to the attention of the ICIC "the struggle for freedom of the extra-European nations".[108]

In the masculine world of diplomacy, intellectual cooperation was an access point for marginalised actors and ideas. Through this channel women were able to contribute to political education and practice. Their conferences and summer schools were advertised in IIIC bulletins. Their publications were circulated in League circles. For example, a 1930 booklet by the International Council of Women, titled *How Women can Promote Good International Understanding*, outlined a plan to educate the public about the causes of war and strategies for conflict prevention.[109] A 1929 meeting on intellectual cooperation earned them a flattering mention in the press – "Brilliant Women meet in London".[110] While women and feminist thought were still widely underrepresented, they gradually managed to enter the male domain of diplomacy through cultural events, conferences, and publications.[111]

International Relations and the Politics of Intellectual Cooperation

More than any other field, the study of IR benefitted from international cooperation under the auspices of the League of Nations. It was the perfect opportunity for scholars to discuss their research and to interact with diplomats and government officials. In other words, they became part of the very world that they were studying. Meanwhile,

---

[107] WILPF summer school on 'Some Aspects of the Relations between White and Coloured Races', 25 August to 8 September 1927, James T. Shotwell Papers, Box 155, 156.

[108] Statutes of the International Cooperative Women's Guild, 1930, Dossier 21115, Box R2184, League of Nations Archives.

[109] International Council of Women, 'How Women can Promote Good International Understanding between the Nations', public meeting, 2 June 1930, Dossier 10659, Box R2182, League of Nations Archives.

[110] *Paris Times*, 2 May 1929, Dossier 11078, Box R2182, League of Nations Archives.

[111] Final Programme for the Meetings of the Executive and Standing Committees of the ICW, 7–17 June 1927, Dossier 43088, Box R1022, League of Nations Archives.

officials at the League of Nations could draw on the expertise of IR scholars. It was a welcome symbiosis. Proposals to embed IR in the context of intellectual cooperation had first been made in the early 1920s. They suggested, for example, for the League to sponsor "the establishment of chairs in international relations".[112] In 1925, the feminist-pacifist Maude Miner Hadden summarised the underlying motivation:

[t]he establishment of an International Institute in Geneva under supervision of the Committee on Intellectual Cooperation [sic!], for study and research concerning international questions, would promote in an effective way the ideals of the League of Nations and the extension of world peace.[113]

At that time, IR scholars were already cooperating unofficially across borders. Professors exchanged publications, universities invited guest lecturers, and students attended summer schools gathering up to thirty nationalities.[114] The potential for intellectual cooperation in the field of IR was unmistakable.

It was Alfred Zimmern who facilitated the IIIC's support of IR scholarship during the second half of the 1920s. Having left his professorship, Zimmern served as IIIC deputy director in Paris from 1926 to 1930. In this position he co-organised in March 1928 the first international conference for the study of IR, hosted by the Deutsche Hochschule für Politik (DHfP) in Berlin and sponsored by the IIIC.[115] It was attended by fifteen IR experts from Austria, Britain, France, Germany, Italy, the United States, as well as representatives of

[112] Northedge, *International Intellectual Co-operation within the League of Nations*, p. 274; Eleanor M. Cargin to Henri Hoffer, 6 April 1921, Dossier 295, Box R1004, League of Nations Archives. Other proposals for the study of IR and diplomacy were received from Frank S. Hacket, founder of Riverdale Country School, New York, and from A. Frangulis, founder of the Académie Diplomatique Internationale, Paris. See Frank S. Hacket to ICIC members, 25 July 1922, Dossier 22137, Box R1012; and A. Frangulis to Eric Drummond, 25 May 1927, Dossier 59663, Box R1025 League of Nations Archives.

[113] Memorandum by Maude Miner Hadden, 26 July 1925, Dossier 45478, Box, R1080, League of Nations Archives.

[114] Alfred Zimmern, 'General Introduction', in Ernst Jäckh (ed.), *The New Germany: Three Lectures by Ernst Jäckh* (Oxford, 1927), p. 7.

[115] See David Long, 'Who Killed the International Studies Conference?', *Review of International Studies* 32:4 (2006), pp. 603–22; and Michael Riemens, 'International Academic Cooperation on International Relations in the Interwar Period: The International Studies Conference', *Review of International Studies* 37:2 (2011), pp. 911–28.

international institutions, such as the Academy of International Law. The participants discussed a number of arrangements, such as the equivalence of degrees and diplomas, the exchange of teaching staff, the establishment of reference centres, and collaboration in research projects. Crucially, they emphasised that international politics "constitute a field for scientific study and that this field ... needs appropriate forms of organisation".[116] The 1928 Berlin conference was followed up by meetings in London, Paris, and Copenhagen which became known as the International Studies Conference (ISC). It became the principal platform for informal foreign policy debates during the interwar period, as the next chapters show.

The apparent success of intellectual cooperation in the field of IR spurred the ambitions of IIIC director Luchaire. His vision of the IIIC as the centre of cultural diplomacy was compromised, however, both by its chronic lack of funds and by its ill-designed administration. Luchaire himself had a reputation to be an eager and at times difficult character.[117] By 1930, he had fallen out of favour with the ICIC for running the IIIC too independently, and consequently had to step down.[118] He was replaced by the French diplomat Henri Bonnet, who had previously worked for the League Secretariat.[119] Luchaire's premature departure came on top of Zimmern's resignation in 1929 who went on to become Montague Burton Professor of IR at Oxford. The change in leadership prompted a restructuring of the IIIC, introducing a new governing organ (the executive committee) that would supervise IIIC activities more closely. It also re-defined the role of the director to that of a more administrative position.[120] Staff and scope were to be limited to programmes of "immediate interest or

---

[116] Report submitted by Alfred Zimmern, 11 July 1928, Dossier 5B.6178.2423, Box R2224, League of Nations Archives.

[117] Northedge, *International Intellectual Co-operation within the League of Nations*, p. 360; Renoliet, *L'UNESCO oubliée*, p. 77; Pemberton, *The Story of International Relations*, p. 67.

[118] See, for instance, George Oprescu to Julien Luchaire, confidential, 25 October 1928, Dossier 2072, Box R2222, League of Nations Archives.

[119] Northedge, *International Intellectual Co-operation within the League of Nations*, p. 379.

[120] Report by the Committee on the work of its twelfth plenary session (submitted to the Council and to the Assembly), dated 11 August 1930, session held on 23–29 July 1930, Official No.: A.21.1930.XII., IIIC Records.

undoubted importance within the financial resources available" the report urged.[121]

The appointment of Bonnet, however, met the scorn of Dutch Foreign Minister Frans Beelaerts van Blokland who was frustrated that the ICIC had appointed another French director despite the provision in the statutes for national rotation. "This re-organisation", Blokland complained, "will not contribute to the realisation of the lofty aims of the Institute".[122] Like his predecessor, Bonnet faced the accusation that the IIIC was "a body of internationalists prepared to manipulate national interests to serve their own utopian ideas".[123] What the IIIC was missing was a flagship product – such as the UNESCO world heritage programme – a tangible project attracting sufficient interest from member states, donors, and the public while not arousing political controversy.

During the 1930s, however, the IIIC continued to run a portfolio of activities celebrating the cosmopolitan lives of intellectuals – a milieu that French poet Paul Valéry once called a "league of minds".[124] Two publication series, the *Entretiens* and the *Correspondances*, reflected this tendency towards less tangible outcomes.[125] *Entretiens* were essentially proceedings of conversations of up to sixty intellectuals on wide-ranging subjects, such as 'realism in the arts' or 'the future of European identity'. *Correspondances* were collections of letters between eminent intellectuals, including the Spanish diplomat Salvador de Madariaga and the Indian philosopher Rabindranath Tagore, on such monumental subjects as 'spirit, ethics, and war'.[126] It was an intellectual catwalk for a (largely Western) cultural elite, dwelling on the latest philosophical trends and political debates.

---

[121] Ibid.
[122] Letter by Frans Beelaerts van Blokland to Eric Drummond, 24 December 1930, Documents du CICI A. Documents du Conseil de la Société des Nations (Box 499), IIIC Records.
[123] Bonnet, 'Intellectual Cooperation', p. 197.
[124] IIIC, *A League of Minds: Letters of Henri Focillon, Salvador de Madariaga, Gilbert Murray, Miguel Ozorio de Almeida, Alfonso Reyes, Tsai Yuan Pei, Paul Valéry* (Paris, 1933).
[125] UNESCO, *Publications de l'Institut International de Coopération Intellectuelle* (Paris, 1945), pp. 2–3.
[126] Johan Bojer, Johan Huizinga, Aldous Huxley, André Maurois, and Robert Waelder, *L'esprit, l'éthique et la guerre* (Paris, 1934).

Did the intelligentsia have anything to contribute to world peace? Was there any way "to deliver mankind from the menace of war"?[127] That was Einstein's question in his 1932 *Correspondance* with Sigmund Freud. Since nation-states were unwilling, as Einstein observed, to surrender any sovereignty in favour of collective security, one had to find other ways to prevent war at a deeper, psychological level. Was there a way, he asked the psychoanalyst, to control the hatred and destructiveness of the human psyche? As much as Freud enjoyed Einstein's stimulating question, he had to disappoint him. "There is no likelihood of our being able to suppress humanity's aggressive tendencies ... better it were to tackle each successive crisis with means that we have ready to our hands".[128] In other words, Freud admitted that the international community could at best design corrective institutions to prevent the inevitable human aggression from turning into full-blown wars. He recommended a "supreme court of judicature", supported by an "adequate executive force".

Ignoring Freud's comments, Bonnet placed increasing emphasis on symbolic projects. 'Moral disarmament' became one of the key programmes in preparation of the World Disarmament Conference during the first half of the 1930s.[129] Again, the idea was that political peace required intellectual peace or, as Valéry put it, "a League of Nations implies a league of minds".[130] A 1931 memorandum by the Polish government, entitled *Moral Disarmament*, spelt out the details of this line of thought.[131] If politicians were unwilling to agree on arms reductions, then soft diplomacy would have to accompany their effort and enshrine peaceful thinking, via cultural policies, into the minds of people. School teachers had to prevent ill-will towards other nations; schoolbooks had to be re-examined for political biases; and the press had to refrain from chauvinistic propaganda. The Polish memorandum also suggested making the work of the League of Nations a compulsory school subject and installing special League of Nations chairs at

---

[127] Albert Einstein and Sigmund Freud, *Why War* (Paris, 1933).

[128] Ibid., pp. 16–17. See also, Seyom Brown, *The Causes and Prevention of War*, 2nd ed. (New York, 1994), pp. 10–11.

[129] IIIC, *Information Bulletin* 1:1 (Paris, 1932), p. 12. See Heidi Tworek, 'Peace through Truth? The Press and Moral Disarmament through the League of Nations', *Medien & Zeit* 25:4 (2010), pp. 16–28.

[130] IIIC, *A League of Minds*.

[131] League of Nations, *Moral Disarmament*, Memorandum from the Polish Government, 17 September 1931, Official No. C. 602. M. 240. 1931. IX.

law faculties. James Shotwell, too, joined the debate on 'moral disarmament' and sent a draft resolution to his political contacts in Geneva.[132] In short, the campaign for 'moral disarmament' tried to prevent new generations of nationalist aggressors. The goal was nothing less than the "moral education of mankind".[133]

In very few cases, 'moral disarmament' resulted in actual policies or international agreements. A notable exception was the 1936 International Convention concerning the Use of Broadcasting in the Cause of Peace, which was ratified by eighteen countries.[134] It committed signatories to prohibit the spread of any broadcast transmission in their country that included propaganda, war-mongering, or false news. The convention also asked the signatories to cooperate and to provide each other with accurate factual information if requested. In the spirit of moral disarmament, the convention aimed to outlaw nationalist aggression and to make the world ready for physical disarmament. A Soviet *addendum* in October 1936 pointed out the obvious flaw that the convention was only obligatory between countries that maintained diplomatic relationships.[135] Since it was never ratified by Germany, Italy, or Japan, however, it was hardly effective.

Pressure on the IIIC increased during the second half of the 1930s as the political situation aggravated. The IIIC struggled to help refugee scholars and often did little more than referring inquiries to other organisations. The German botanist Theodor Philipp Haas, for instance, was told that nothing could be done for him.[136] He was pointed to the Society for the Protection of Science and Learning, the Emergency Committee in Aid of Displaced German Scholars, and the Notgemeinschaft Deutscher Wissenschaftler im Ausland – all three of which were relatively young, small, and spontaneous creations. At no point did the IIIC set up a special bureau or a standardised procedure for refugee academics, presumably due to a lack of resources. Having failed to establish, even to a minimal degree, the equivalence of

---

[132] James T. Shotwell to J. David Thompson, 19 July 1932, James T. Shotwell Papers, Box 155, 156.
[133] Kolasa, *International Intellectual Cooperation*, p. 42.
[134] Final Act of the Conference, 17–23 September 1936, E.X.5 (Box 191), IIIC Records.
[135] 'International Convention Concerning the Use of Broadcasting in the Cause of Peace', 23 September 1936, Dosier 1658, Box R3398, League of Nations Archives.
[136] Letter by J. Belime (interim director IIIC) to Theodor Philipp Haas, 6 March 1937, B.IV.44, IIIC Records.

diplomas and degrees – the project had stalled in 1924[137] – now proved to be a hurdle when trying to accommodate refugee scholars during the 1930s. It seems bewildering that at a time when refugee scholars, such as Haas, were appealing to the IIIC in increasing numbers, the IIIC proceeded to publish *Entretiens* on the latest literary trends. This practice was continued even during the war. In January 1940 the IIIC bulletin devoted no more than half a page to "the fate of the Polish intellectuals", and acted, at best, as an information centre.[138]

The IIIC placed more emphasis on broad, lofty subjects than on building a capable machinery to solve the pressing issues of the time. None of the high expectations for a student exchange scheme was fulfilled, not to mention inclusive education programmes, improving literacy rates or women's access to higher education. There is no evidence that the IIIC improved conditions for intellectual workers either. Regulations on intellectual property, one of the first projects and most clearly defined goals, failed to materialise.[139] The more the IIIC engaged in spin-off projects, financed by private donors or national governments, the more it became exposed to partisan influence and, inevitably, lost its reputation in Geneva.[140] Most of the technical collaboration fizzled out during the 1930s while elite-level projects, such as the ISC, continued until (and even into) the Second World War.

With few exceptions, the projects that received most support were the ones that afforded nothing but a brain and a typewriter, rather than those that could be expected to have a more immediate impact on people's lives. To be sure, there was value in them. The spread of non-European works of art, various periodicals, translations, conferences, and handbooks helped to create a space for culture in international affairs. Moreover, the dedication to a universal intellectual community and the various practical activities set new standards for diplomatic interaction. In addition to that, Northedge argued, the League's efforts in intellectual cooperation may have had an effect on the way in which

---

[137] See resolutions regarding the ICIC, adopted by the 5th Assembly, Dossier 27880, Box R1055, League of Nations Archives.
[138] IIIC, *Intellectual Cooperation Bulletin*, No. 1–8 (Paris, 1940), p. 40.
[139] F. S. Northedge, *The League of Nations: Its Life and Times, 1920–1946* (Leicester, 1986), p. 187.
[140] Northedge, *International Intellectual Co-operation within the League of Nations*, p. 291.

national conflict was thought and fought during the second half of the twentieth century.[141]

The Demise of an Experiment

Intellectual cooperation in the field of IR rested on two conflicting motives. On the one hand, there was the old philosophical idea to unify scientific standards and academic communities – quite literally for the love of wisdom. On the other hand, there was the goal to serve as supporters of, or proxies for, political negotiation. This was a new motivation, linked to the specific context of the League of Nations. In Carl Schmitt's view, this conflict between the political and the universal made the League a "contra-dictory construction", and any efforts to outlaw war were doomed.[142] But it was this balancing act that the architects of IR embarked on.

The first motive was the universalist idea that scientific truths and standards applied regardless of national borders. Originally rooted in religious faith, the idea was subsequently adopted by scientists and international bureaucrats – although, interestingly, religious inter-nationalists also used the League of Nations as a vehicle to further their interests.[143] The campaign for the protection of copyright law since the 1850s, for example, rested on the assumptions that intellec-tual property inevitably and increasingly crossed borders and that property rights could only be protected by international agreements. It also implied that intellectual property had a certain universal value, like a global currency, that could only be administered on a global level. That same argument was true for scientific societies, such as the London Chemical Society, which from its early days in the 1840s admitted "foreign members".[144] Overcoming national borders and making knowledge accessible also inspired Wilhelm Ostwald's institute *Die Brücke*, founded in 1911, which served as a global repository of scientific knowledge and industry standards.[145] Ostwald wanted *Die*

[141] Northedge, *The League of Nations*, p. 189.
[142] Carl Schmitt, *Der Begriff des Politischen*, 8th ed. (Berlin, 1932, 2009), pp. 47, 52–3.
[143] Shine, 'Papal Diplomacy by Proxy?'.
[144] Chemical Society of London, *Memoirs & Proceedings of the Chemical Society of London, 1841–1842 and 1842–1843*, Vol. 1 (London, 1843), p. 9.
[145] Ostwald became obsessed with establishing standards for almost anything, including the size of office stationary, hotel brochures, or street posters. Die

Brücke to be the world's first "enquiry desk" and advocated open access to its services for anyone from anywhere. While *Die Brücke* failed to survive the First World War, its underlying ideology did not. The universalism that inspired pre-1914 associations and movements was picked up by the protagonists of intellectual cooperation at the League of Nations. The goal here was, as a retrospective put it, to foster "ties of intellectual solidarity" and to form a "spiritual union" among thinkers from different nations.[146] If arts and sciences shared the same universal value they could be institutionalised above the national level. As French Education Minister Édouard Daladier put it in his opening speech for the IIIC in 1926, the goal of intellectual cooperation was to form a "universal consciousness".[147] The focus of that enterprise was the study of international politics itself, which made up the bulk of the documents now stored at the UNESCO archives in Paris. By applying the kind of universalism immanent in natural sciences and religions to social science, the pioneers of IR underestimated that, unlike physical or metaphysical truths, political facts were a much more controversial matter. It is interesting to note the mismatch between the number of natural scientists at the ICIC (30 out of 48 members) and the output of the IIIC, which was dominated by politics, literature, and the arts.[148]

The second motive was different. After the First World War, intellectual cooperation was re-invented in the context of the League of Nations, an inter-governmental organisation devoted to political ends. Academic debate on this platform gained a political dimension as it was forced into the framework of nation-states.[149] Unsurprisingly, the nation-state and the League of Nations became the basic units of analysis in contemporary IR scholarship. This was precisely what Luchaire had proposed in 1920 – an institution "to serve purposes intimately related to the more general objectives of the League Covenant".[150] Unlike earlier associations, the League's bodies were

Brücke, *Die Brücke: Internationales Institut zur Organisierung der Geistigen Arbeit: Satzung* (München, 1912), p. 4.
[146] IIIC, *Intellectual Cooperation Bulletin*, pp. 2–4.
[147] Address by Édouard Daladier, 16 January 1926, A.I.6, IIIC Records.
[148] See Fritz Berber, *Sicherheit und Gerechtigkeit* (Berlin, 1934), pp. 33–41.
[149] See Rodogno et al., 'Introduction', p. 3.
[150] Northedge, *International Intellectual Co-operation within the League of Nations*, p. 276.

explicitly committed to political ends. And not only that, they were considered "an essential preliminary to an agreement of interests, a juridical settlement of conflicts and political organisation for peace".[151] IR scholars almost unanimously welcomed the League and readily used its institutions, unlike French pacifists, for example, who entered into a long and difficult debate about the compatibility of their respective aims.[152]

The champions of intellectual cooperation presupposed that science, or representatives thereof, could have an effect on the world of politicians and diplomats. They assumed, as Goldsworthy Lowes Dickinson once put it, that "friends of reason" could decipher the "abstractions" of power.[153] Indeed there was a widespread assumption that intellectuals were in a position to contribute "by their example, by their teaching, by their good will and by their spirit of disinterested research in all fields, to the maintenance of peace".[154] This assumption regarded the intellectual as a good-natured ambassador of their respective country who helped to overcome prejudices, identified common interests, and cleared the ground for the actual ambassador. It was manifested, for example, in the work on 'moral disarmament', which was a public relations campaign in support of a political project. It was also present in the *Entretiens* and *Correspondances* as they dwelled upon the meaning of a culture for peace. Above all, it was true for intellectual cooperation in the field of IR where academics worked on questions directly concerned with international governance.

The new relationship between academia and diplomacy reflected the idea that science had something substantial to say about the world of politics.[155] With the advent of IR as an academic subject, scholars made politics an object of rational, scientific enquiry. In doing so, they

---

[151] Letter by Paul Appell, dated 8 July 1920, published as 'Institution of an International Bureau for Intellectual Intercourse and Education', p. 445.

[152] Jean-Michel Guieu, 'La paix par la Société des Nations? Les évolutions du pacifisme français dans les années 1920', in Stéphane Tison (ed.), *Paul d'Estournelles de Constant: Concilier les nations pour éviter la guerre* (Rennes, 2015), pp. 163–79.

[153] G. Lowes Dickinson, 'The Holy War', *The Nation*, 8 August (1914), p. 3.

[154] Miguel Ozorio de Almeida, 'Open Letter', in IIIC (ed.), *Intellectual Cooperation Bulletin*, No. 1–8 (Paris, 1940), pp. 4–5.

[155] Jan-Stefan Fritz, 'Internationalism and the Promise of Science', in David Long and Brian C. Schmidt (eds.), *Imperialism and Internationalism in the Discipline of International Relations* (New York, 2005), p. 142.

implied that the virtues of diplomacy could be studied (and taught), that peace could be achieved through the application of reason, and that the practitioners of foreign politics had something to learn from thinkers of IR. In the words of a contemporary observer, IR was not only "a new science", it became the "brain of the League of Nations".[156] This meant, in turn, that officials should consult academics, and that it would be worthwhile for the League to employ a scientific advisory board. This is precisely what the IIIC did by organising conferences for IR scholars.

During the 1930s, as the following chapters show, the International Studies Conference (ISC) became a venue for scholars, diplomats, and politicians, a sphere of political negotiation parallel to official decision-making. Their goal was to study topics of immediate interest to decision-makers at the League, such as disarmament, economic trade, or national minorities, and to prepare an academic basis for practical policies. Academic research was now situated closer to and more systematically linked with high politics than ever before. The driving factor for intellectual cooperation was no longer simply the ideal of universal scientific truth but the intention to have an impact beyond the ivory tower. With every international crisis of the interwar period, the political dimension of intellectual cooperation became more visible. By 1937, a sceptical participant of the ISC observed, "members of the conference were unable to think themselves as individuals and scientists, but were exercising unwarranted diplomacy".[157]

One of the essential concepts in the rhetoric of the IIIC was 'peace'. Whether radio broadcasting or cinema, museums or scientific congresses, schools or universities – every domain was transformed into an instrument for peace. By joining the movement for peace, the IIIC built a network of academic, political, and civil society organisations which generously contributed to the common cause but obscured actual outcomes. The Carnegie Endowment for International Peace funded publication projects, conferences, receptions, and co-sponsored the ISC.[158] American and French foundations offered

---

156 William Archer, _A New Science_, December 1918, newspaper clipping, Vol. 12, Dr Thomas Jones CH Papers, National Library of Wales.
157 Letter by J. B. Condliffe to Tracy Kittredge, 18 September 1937, K.I.4b, IIIC Records.
158 Katharina Rietzler, 'Experts for Peace: Structures and Motivations of Philanthropic Internationalism in the Interwar Years', in Daniel Laqua (ed.),

peace prizes.[159] In Germany, a Peace Academy in memory of former Foreign Minister Gustav Stresemann was devoted to the same goals – peace through research and education, international conferences and lecture tours, and publications and translations. In his introduction to the Peace Academy, Foreign Minister Julius Curtius referred to the study of IR as "a science of peace".[160] But what did this really mean?

Ironically, it were exactly these political aspirations for peace and cooperation that proved most problematic. How could one be 'neutral' in any scientific sense and at the same time serve the League of Nations which, by definition, stood for a particular concept of global order (based on nation-states and empires)? How to be 'universal' while excluding a significant part of the world population? How to be 'disinterested' when the IIIC staff themselves were opinionated political actors? These tensions arose not only because of epistemological problems inherent in the social sciences, but because the IIIC deliberately extended its mission from technical cooperation to politically sensitive terrain. The original agenda – university exchanges, the equivalence of degrees, intellectual property, and the protection of artworks – shifted into the background, whereas projects with potentially controversial content – the ISC, *Entretiens,* and *Correspondances* – gained prominence. While the IIIC became more politically charged during the 1930s, a certain ideological mission was ingrained from the start. As Daladier argued in 1926, the idea of the IIIC was to spread the "spirit of collaboration for peace, for the progress of peoples" and to further "the *grandeur* of the League of Nations".[161] An institution striving to increase its own glory, however, was at odds with the humble standards of scientific inquiry.

On paper, the IIIC was a technical organ under the control of senior bodies in Geneva – the ICIC as well as the League Council and Assembly. The directors liked to stress their "autonomous" and "disinterested" approach.[162] In the case of the World Disarmament

Internationalism Reconfigured: Transnational Ideas and Movements Between the World Wars (London, 2011), pp. 45–66.

[159] Carl Bouchard, 'Les lauréats de la paix. Les concours américain et français pour la paix de 1923–1924', *Revue d'histoire moderne & contemporaine* 54:3 (2007), pp. 118–37.

[160] Julius Curtius, 'Memorial to Gustav Stresemann', *International Conciliation* No. 263 (1930), p. 15.

[161] Address by Édouard Daladier, 16 January 1926, A.I.6, IIIC Records.

[162] Bonnet, 'Intellectual Cooperation', p. 195; de Almeida, 'Open Letter', p. 5.

Conference, for example, ISC members pledged to not engage in "propaganda for or against the ideal of disarmament" and committed themselves to the "scientific exposition" of the facts.[163] In reality, the IIIC was far from neutral but advocated a liberal internationalist agenda and reacted to current events. By 1933 disarmament had become a "very unreal thing in the light of the Nazi conquest of Germany", as James Shotwell admitted.[164] What is more, the exclusion of non-member states led to a strong bias in favour of pro-League opinions. Even within this group the IIIC collaborated more closely with some governments than others, usually allowing those more attention who covered more of the financial costs. In practice, this meant almost always French dominance, hence the repeated election of French directors. Despite all efforts to eliminate nationalism from the world of science and culture, it was clearly present throughout the interwar period.[165]

External funding further complicated the structure of interests. During the 1930s, the Rockefeller Foundation gave up to 50,000 US Dollars per year to the IIIC, with the specific purpose of promoting the study of IR.[166] In 1932, the Rockefeller trustees decided that the ISC was "a type of international scientific research of great promise", and gave an additional 1,500 US Dollars to an ISC working group on state intervention and economic life.[167] They were less interested in school exchanges or the protection of artworks. Private donors did not necessarily pursue controversial interests, but their choices were a statement in itself, and their specific targets set an agenda that may well have turned out differently.

Throughout the 1930s then, Murray and Bonnet struggled to stick to their mission of universalist, 'disinterested' study whilst accommodating increasing pressure from a range of outside actors.[168] Germany withdrew its support after 1933, Italy replaced internationalists with

---

[163] Letter by Arnold J. Toynbee to Henri Bonnet, 18 March 1931; response by Bonnet to Toynbee, 26 March 1931, K.I.1b, IIIC Records.

[164] James T. Shotwell to Henri Bonnet, 13 May 1933, K1.1h, IIIC Records.

[165] Fox, *Science without Frontiers*, pp. 81–92.

[166] Resolution RF 37117, 1 December 1937, Folder 952, Box 105, Series 100.S, RG 1.1, RF, Rockefeller Archive Center.

[167] Resolution RF 32047, 5 July 1932, Folder 952, Box 105, Series 100.S, RG 1.1, RF, Rockefeller Archive Center.

[168] On the notion of "disinterested" or "neutral" work, see for instance IIIC, *A Record of a First International Study Conference*, pp. xxii–xxiii.

fascists, and a growing share of the costs had to be covered by US philanthropists instead of member states. This made the IIIC's financial situation less reliable, decreased its geographical reach, and diverted its political stance. As Bonnet revealed in 1942, the IIIC was sometimes prevented by censorship from publishing some truthful statements about fascism because too many people, in the belligerent as well as the neutral countries, maintained incredible illusions about Mussolini's policy.[169]

Towards the late 1930s, the IIIC operated in a bubble of international bureaucrats who either failed to see the challenges facing peaceful cooperation or willingly ignored them. IIIC members kept remarkably quiet on the dangers of Nazism and Fascism, perhaps because they feared that acknowledging their true character would undermine their own venture. It was only in 1942, that Bonnet conceded that "certain projects ... did not please all governments".[170]

But instead of retreating into truly neutral and technical activities, the ICIC and IIIC actively reached out to governments and private organisations to maintain an ever more political mission. "I am still trying to interest the British Government in Intellectual Cooperation", Murray lamented in 1934, "but of course we have to interest the Foreign Office and they have to struggle with the Treasury".[171] Similar effort was made to receive funds from the Carnegie Endowment. At one point in 1932, the European director of the Carnegie Endowment was so irritated that he had to clarify the nature of their contribution – they would not provide general funds, only project-specific funding on a case-by-case basis where activities "fell within its own program of work" – that was, within the interests of the Carnegie Endowment.[172] A similar approach was taken by the Rockefeller Foundation which funded projects and individuals at the IIIC throughout the 1930s and indeed into the war.[173] It was evident that during a period of crisis and war, public and private donors would

[169] Bonnet, 'Intellectual Cooperation', p. 209.   [170] Ibid., p. 197.
[171] Letter by Gilbert Murray to Henri Bonnet, 27 October 1934, A.I.71, IIIC Records.
[172] Letter by Earle B. Babcock to Werner Picht, 13 July 1932, K.V.1–5, IIIC Records.
[173] Letter by Tracy Kittredge to Henri Bonnet, 30 September 1939, K.I.26a, IIIC Records.

make careful decisions about whom to fund, and the IIIC developed a certain skill in presenting itself as a guarantor of peace.

In some ways, the IIIC succeeded in achieving what Luchaire had envisioned. Founded in 1926 as a nucleus of scientific and cultural cooperation for peace, the IIIC became an illustrious venue for scholars and peace activists, and a phalanx of supporters of the League of Nations. It is not surprising that Bonnet thought that the IIIC was "one of the most fruitful branches of League activity".[174] Recent historical accounts, too, have argued that interwar internationalists were not "necessarily naïve or nearsighted".[175] It is also true, as Northedge noted that the IIIC cannot be held responsible for the general difficulties of the time – political extremism or the Great Depression – nor for the spineless attitude of member states in backing the League.[176] Moreover, it is important to remember that the ICIC and IIIC were unprecedented experiments of international cooperation, both in spatial scope and organisational sophistication.[177] It would be wrong therefore to declare the ICIC and IIIC outright failures. They did, after all, establish the idea of intellectual cooperation at the world's first global inter-governmental organisation.

In many respects, however, the IIIC missed its chances to become effective and to make real changes in the lives of intellectuals, let alone the general public. To some extent, this ineffectiveness can be blamed on the limited reach of its activities and, in turn, on its limited financial support. This was particularly true for the early phase when the ICIC struggled to launch permanent projects due to financial constraints. However, many projects, such as the agreement on intellectual property, would have required more willingness, not money, to succeed. In those cases, stronger backing from national governments would have helped. Other projects, such as the peaceful usage of broadcasting, were simply too ambitious. It is impossible therefore to identify a single

---

[174] Bonnet, 'Intellectual Cooperation', p. 191.
[175] Gorman, *The Emergence of International Society in the 1920s*, p. 310.
[176] Northedge, *International Intellectual Co-operation within the League of Nations*, pp. 666–77.
[177] Along with the League's Health Organisation and the ILO. See, Iris Borowy, *Coming to Terms with World Health: The League of Nations Health Organization, 1921–1946* (Frankfurt, 2009).

explanation for the IIIC's record. In the end, of course, it was the Second World War that confirmed its fate.

One of the problematic characteristics was the inherent Eurocentrism in most of what the IIIC did. Not only were most of its employees European and most of its projects designed for a European audience, it seemed as if the IIIC was completely out of touch with other parts of the world. For regions with less than twenty per cent literacy rate, such as in India, the focus on 'intellectual life' was a grotesque misinterpretation of actual needs. What is more, non-Europeans did not have the same stakes in the political crises that shaped much of the IIIC's work. A 1940 survey on the conditions of 'intellectual life' revealed that Indians, Mexicans, and Australians saw no adverse effects of the war on their situation, except that they were "finding it difficult to obtain various journals and other publications".[178] In terms of logistics alone, the physical distance to Geneva and Paris made it hard for non-Europeans to attend meetings. A crucial absentee was Soviet Russia (until 1933), which precluded any interaction with socialist internationalism.[179] To be sure, the IIIC did maintain relations with a range of non-European countries, especially in South America and Asia, including Brazil, Chile, El Salvador, Guatemala, Mexico, Peru as well as Turkey, Iran, Japan, and China.[180] But none of these places was ever at the core of what was being decided in Paris or Geneva. It is true therefore as historians have pointed out, to consider interwar intellectual cooperation as a European initiative.[181]

The regional bias of interwar intellectual cooperation was particularly noticeable in the field of IR. Whenever colonies were mentioned at the ISC, discussions almost always circled around raw materials, ethnicity, or the mandate system, rather than regarding local populations

---

[178] 'Enquête sur les conditions de la vie intellectuelle dans les différents pays'; letters by John Sargent, Luis Sanchez Ponton, and the Librarian of the Australian Parliament to Henri Bonnet, dated 22, 9, and 15 February 1940 respectively, A.XIII.1 (Box 69), IIIC Records.

[179] Soviet delegates were invited in 1933 to join the ISC. Werner Picht to Marcel Rosenberg, 1 April 1933, K.I.1i, IIIC Records.

[180] See K.IV.9–36, IIIC Records.

[181] Gorman, *The Emergence of International Society in the 1920s*, pp. 4–5; Geyer and Paulmann, 'Introduction', p. 10; Long, 'Who Killed the International Studies Conference?', pp. 604–5.

as actors in their own right.[182] Only in a few cases did participants talk
about colonialism and the "eventual development of self-government
and the gradual disappearance of outside domination", as a British
report put it in 1936.[183] At a 1924 congress of WILPF, Marie Johnson
demanded that "subject nations must be freed".[184] For the overwhelming majority, however, self-determination was not a concern. Given
the colonial interests of most major powers represented at the IIIC, this
is not surprising. However, the European condescension among the
IIIC leadership ran counter to the claim of a universal intellectual
community. To promote a *civitas mundi* was incompatible with
Eurocentric practices.[185] In this way, too, IIIC ideals were out of sync
with political realities.

Another limitation of both the ICIC and the IIIC was their elitism.
The people running the organisation – eminent scientists, public intellectuals, and technocratic elites – operated at a considerable distance to
the population. This made their mission problematic in several ways.
Many activities were deliberately tailored to educated minorities, such
as journalists, professors, or museum directors. They were never
intended to provoke a mass movement, but targeted the higher ranks
of intellectual life.[186] More inclusive projects, such as the idea of
"workers' libraries" raised in 1932, never resulted in anything more
than well-meaning reports.[187] Generally speaking, the exclusion of
vast parts of the population conflicted with the IIIC's self-ascribed
mission "to render universally accessible the contributions to the welfare of mankind which men of talent and of genius, in all countries and
in all races, have to offer".[188] There was a good deal of irony in
advocating peaceful cooperation among the peoples of the world via
science and culture, but at the same time to deny the majority of these
peoples access to better education or cultural life, let alone entering the
exclusive realm of decision-making.

[182] IIIC, *Peaceful Change* (Paris, 1938), pp. 79, 132.
[183] Report by the British Coordinating Committee, dated 18 July 1936, K.IV.30h,
IIIC Records.
[184] Marie Johnson, in WILPF, *Report of the Fourth Congress of the WILPF*
(Geneva, 1924), p. 54.
[185] Kolasa, *International Intellectual Cooperation*, pp. 57–9.   [186] Ibid., p. 54.
[187] IIIC, *Information Bulletin* 1:2–3 (Paris, 1932), pp. 76–7.
[188] de Almeida, 'Open Letter', p. 4.

Despite their intellectual distinction, the protagonists of the ICIC and IIIC were often powerless in political decision-making. They did not, as Northedge argued, "have much that was significant for international affairs to show".[189] Even the most widely regarded ICIC members, such as Einstein, could at best make public appeals and were never able to exert real force in foreign policy, or even in the cultural sector for that matter. They did not enjoy any democratic legitimacy and were too insignificant to exercise any influence at the legislative or diplomatic level. Moreover, many of them were not robust enough for a world of lies and deceit. In Northedge's reading they were "too tolerant for the intolerant world they lived in".[190]

Perhaps more problematic than its composition and administration, however, was the way in which intellectual cooperation was politicised throughout the interwar period. By the late 1930s, the IIIC had, in a style not dissimilar to high-politics, developed a strategy of downplaying and ignoring the obvious dangers to peace, while allowing fascists and nationalists to voice their opinions at ICIC governor meetings and IIIC events. This culminated in the German demand to disentangle intellectual cooperation from the League of Nations as a condition for further collaboration.[191] The German representative to the ISC, Fritz Berber, remarked in 1937 that a "systematic German treatment" of ISC topics was no longer possible.[192] Bonnet was outraged at the totalitarian approach to academia, and noted in 1942:

there is supposedly a German system of physics founded on the gift of the Aryan spirit to understand what is moving, living, and changing – as distinguished from ... Frenchmen or Jews.[193]

Hitler's interpretation of evolutionary biology was incompatible with the project of international cooperation among equals, as was Nazi cultural politics.[194] It was an "attack on rationalism".[195] The influx of

[189] Northedge, *International Intellectual Co-operation within the League of Nations*, p. 693.
[190] Northedge, *The League of Nations*, p. 189.
[191] Note on the current state of the IIIC, [undated], A.I.144/2, IIIC Records.
[192] Fritz Berber, 'Vorbemerkung', in Diedrich Westermann (ed.), *Beiträge zur deutschen Kolonialfrage* (Berlin, 1937), p. 7.
[193] Bonnet, 'Intellectual Cooperation', p. 189.
[194] Fox, *Science without Frontiers*, pp. 92–106.
[195] J. Walter Jones, 'The Nazi Conception of Law', *Oxford Pamphlets on World Affairs* 21 (1939), p. 28.

extreme political opinions and international conflict in 1939 dramatically exposed the long-standing inherent problems of interwar international cooperation, and marked the end of the ICIC and IIIC.

Conclusion

Intellectual cooperation at the League of Nations served as an important infrastructure and created an ideological environment for the
formation of IR. The leaders of the ICIC and IIIC, some of whom were
among the architects of IR, believed that international politics
should be subject to academic investigation under the auspices of an
inter-governmental organisation. They claimed that IR could be
studied from a neutral point of view and that it could deliver meaningful insights for political practice. The resulting institutions and projects, especially the ISC, shaped IR as an academic discipline
during the interwar period by demarcating a habitat for the discipline
in terms of research centres, conferences, publications, and
thematic scope.

Despite their good intentions, the approach taken by Luchaire and
Bonnet fell prey to political controversies, undermining the credibility
of the IIIC and ultimately of the League itself. Part of the problem was
rooted in financial constraints and, in turn, the limited capability to
launch large-scale projects to win the trust of governments and the
general public. In addition to that, the governance apparatus of the
ICIC and IIIC was flawed and their administrators lacked expertise.
These were unprecedented inter-governmental agencies, run by philosophers and physicists who were inexperienced in managing political
processes. The IIIC's extraordinarily ambitious and broad mission – to
spread peace in the minds of people – led to considerable confusion
about the actual goals of intellectual cooperation. The result was an
incoherent compilation of projects, rich in propaganda but rarely
bringing about any tangible results. Insufficient control over the
IIIC's output, in turn, led to internal quarrels and dissatisfaction
among member states.

Besides administrative difficulties, however, the more fundamental
problem about interwar intellectual cooperation was the assumption
that scholars and artists could contribute to international peace without antagonising national governments. This fallacy corresponded to
what Carl Schmitt wrote about the impossibility of a world-state when

he noted that the political world was a "pluriverse, not a universe".[196]
International politics remained above all *politics*, the confrontation
between friends and enemies, between friendly states and hostile states.
The IIIC sought to become a moral authority whose judgements were
superior to the claims of national governments. An interesting example
of this attitude is how the term 'propaganda' was simultaneously
criticised and employed by IIIC officials. On the one hand, the IIIC
actively used propaganda in its own work – its periodical was called
Brochures de Propagande.[197] On the other hand, they argued that
there was a harmful type of propaganda that needed to be banned,
as the 1936 broadcasting convention declared.[198] This almost schizo-
phrenic argument was echoed by the British League of Nations Union
which, having issued some 400 leaflets themselves, declared in
1935 that "the League of Nations Union ... is not engaged in propaganda".[199] What the advocates of international cooperation were
doing was of course just another kind of propaganda. The IIIC
struggled to stay neutral and at the same time to contribute something
meaningful to international life.

The contradiction between the claim to neutrality and the actual
output of intellectual cooperation was particularly startling in the field
of IR. By investing in the study of IR under its auspices, the IIIC
triggered an awkward self-referential dynamic because many IR
researchers wrote on the institutions of the League themselves. Thus,
the object of their research became the same organisation from which
that research emerged. In other words, IR scholars studied the very
world that they constituted themselves, with problematic implications
for agency and objectivity.

[196] Schmitt, *Der Begriff des Politischen*, p. 50.
[197] League of Nations, 'The International Institute of Intellectual Cooperation'; see
also Robert Jones and Stanley Simon Sherman, *The League of Nations School
Book* (London, 1928, 1934).
[198] 'International Convention Concerning the Use of Broadcasting in the Cause of
Peace', 23 September 1936, Dossier 1658, Box R3998, League of
Nations Archives.
[199] J. C. Maxwell Garnett, 'Propaganda', *The Contemporary Review* May (1935),
p. 8. By contrast, E. H. Carr argued that both totalitarian governments and
democracies engaged in propaganda, and that the contrast between them was
often "less clear-cut". E. H. Carr, *Propaganda in International Politics*
(Oxford, 1939).

The advent of UNESCO in the wake of the Second World War confirmed this picture of interwar intellectual cooperation. Activities were de-politicised and focused on technical cooperation and education programmes, including literacy rates and basic schooling.[200] The central lesson to be learned from the interwar experience was that intellectual cooperation, in an inter-governmental framework, had to refrain from political debates and focus on providing the means rather than the content of international cooperation. The League bodies were, as Northedge rightly observed, "a pioneer not so much in intellectual co-operation itself as in its native procedure".[201] As a result, UNESCO actually copied the governance structure of its predecessors and even took over some employees, whereas almost all of the former projects were dropped and replaced by less elitist and less ideology-driven programmes.[202] UNESCO also withdrew from the study of IR at an official level and stopped endorsing the ISC, thus putting an end to one of the most productive yet controversial sites of interwar cultural diplomacy.

The history of intellectual cooperation substantiates recent historiography on the interwar period that has rejected the traditional view of the League of Nations as nothing but a political failure.[203] Instead, it demonstrates how the League shaped international life more broadly and, at the very least, pioneered a range of internationalist activities that flourished during the second half of the twentieth century. The bodies examined in this chapter failed in some ways, but not because of a divergence between 'idealism' and 'realism'.[204] If anything, they were troubled by the divergence of different ideas – internationalism, nationalism, imperialism, liberalism, socialism, fascism, nazism, etc. Collaborative IR scholarship was the ambitious attempt to reconcile these beliefs and to design foreign policy instruments in the pursuit of peace.

---

[200] UNESCO, *Twenty Years of Service to Peace, 1956–1966* (Paris, 1966), pp. 19, 90–3. See Pernet, 'Twists, Turns and Dead Alleys'.

[201] Northedge, *International Intellectual Co-operation within the League of Nations*, p. 687.

[202] Renoliet, *L'UNESCO oubliée*, p. 325.

[203] Susan Pedersen, 'Back to the League of Nations', *The American Historical Review* 112:4 (2007), pp. 1091–117.

[204] Gorman, *The Emergence of International Society in the 1920s*, p. 320.

4 | *Professors as Diplomats*

> Anyone who is to teach contemporary affairs should have some practical
> connection with them.
>
> Arnold Toynbee (1929)[1]

Introduction

In June 1924, the American historian James T. Shotwell submitted a
"Draft Treaty of Disarmament and Security" to the League of
Nations.[2] The document picked up the idea of compulsory arbitration,
which had been discussed by French internationalists for some time,
and adapted it to the ongoing government talks about a general
security pact.[3] It specified that any government refusing to submit their
case to arbitration would be deemed an aggressor and held accountable by international sanctions. "The path to international security is
openness", Shotwell argued and launched a semi-official propaganda
campaign in favour of his draft treaty.[4] The document was co-signed
by a group of prominent professors, generals, and political advisors,
and was circulated as a pamphlet by the Foreign Policy Association.[5]
Shotwell lobbied his contacts in Geneva, wrote journal articles, and

---

[1] Arnold Toynbee to Gilbert Murray, 9 May 1929, Gilbert Murray Papers,
Box 415.
[2] James T. Shotwell et al., 'Text of the Draft Treaty of Disarmament and Security',
Foreign Policy Association Pamphlet No. 28 (New York, 1924).
[3] James W. Garner, 'The Geneva Protocol for the Pacific Settlement of
International Disputes', *The American Journal of International Law* 19:1 (1925),
pp. 123–32; Andrew Webster, 'International Arbitration, The Pacific Settlement
of Disputes and the French Security–Disarmament Dilemma (1919–1931)',
French History 24:2 (2010), pp. 236–61.
[4] James T. Shotwell, 'Sicherheit durch Offenheit', *Europäische Gespräche* 3 (1924),
p. 249.
[5] The co-signatories were General Tasker H. Bliss, Isaiah Bowman, Joseph
P. Chamberlain, John Bates Clark, Stephen P. Duggan, General James
G. Harbord, Frederick P. Kleppel, David Hunter Miller, Henry S. Pritchett.

162 *Professors as Diplomats*

corresponded with his European colleagues, including Albrecht Mendelssohn Bartholdy, David Mitrany, and Nikolaos Politis. A few months later, Shotwell was proud to report that the Geneva Protocol, as the official treaty became known, ended up with "a lot of the spirit and significant details" of his plan.[6]

As is well known, the Geneva Protocol was rejected by the British government and failed to materialise. London was not willing to endorse dangerous commitments in areas of limited strategic interest. Even if the Protocol had been passed, however, historians doubt that it would have solved the security problem.[7] It was just one attempt in a much longer process of restoring French confidence in Europe, which Shotwell played at best a minor part in.[8] He certainly did not invent the principle of compulsory arbitration, which had been pioneered by Léon Bourgeois years earlier at The Hague and Paris. But while the Protocol was neither the unique idea of an American professor, nor a successful one, Shotwell's campaign did stimulate diplomatic debate and, above all, it illustrated the mindset of public intellectuals in the 1920s. As his biographer put it, Shotwell saw himself as an "amateur diplomat".[9]

Over the following years, Shotwell continued to present his ideas to an audience far beyond the university campus. He taught at Alfred Zimmern's popular Geneva summer schools. He gave public speeches

---

The principal authors were Miller and Shotwell. See James T. Shotwell, *The Autobiography of James T. Shotwell* (New York, 1961), pp. 181–3.

[6] James T. Shotwell, 'Amerika und das Genfer Protokoll', *Europäische Gespräche* 6 (1924), p. 517.

[7] F. S. Northedge, *The League of Nations: Its Life and Times, 1920–1946* (Leicester, 1986), p. 93; Zara Steiner, *The Lights that Failed: European International History, 1919–1933* (Oxford, 2005), p. 382. See also, Carolyn J. Kitching, *Britain and the Problem of International Disarmament: 1919–1934* (New York, 1999).

[8] Adam Adamthwaite, *Grandeur and Misery: France's Bid for Power in Europe, 1914–1940* (London, 1995); Peter Jackson, 'Deterrence, Coercion, and Enmeshment: French Grand Strategy and the German Problem after World War I', in Jeffrey W. Taliaferro, Norrin M. Ripsman, and Steven E. Lobell (eds.), *The Challenge of Grand Strategy: The Great Powers and the Broken Balance between the World Wars* (Cambridge, 2012), pp. 37–64; Jon Jacobson, 'Strategies of French Foreign Policy after World War I', *Journal of Modern History* 55:1 (1983), pp. 78–95; Andrew Webster, '"Absolutely Irresponsible Amateurs": The Temporary Mixed Commission on Armaments, 1921–1924', *Australian Journal of Politics & History* 54:3 (2008), pp. 373–88.

[9] Harold Josephson, *James T. Shotwell and the Rise of Internationalism in America* (London, 1975), p. 118.

in Berlin and Paris. He participated at the International Studies Conference, the most important interwar platform for foreign policy experts. He served as research director of the Carnegie Endowment for International Peace, managing one of the most influential sponsors of social science research. Eventually, in 1927, he launched another attempt to craft an international agreement, a treaty to make aggressive war illegal, which became known as the Kellogg–Briand Pact.

During the 1920s, the architects of International Relations (IR) began to explore new ways to influence a broader audience. They launched training programmes and academic conferences but also ran for political offices and drafted international treaties. Shotwell's efforts were not exceptional, but reflected common practice in the discipline. For example, Helena Swanwick was appointed a British delegate to the League of Nations' Fifth Assembly.[10] Philip Noel-Baker stood as a Labour candidate in the general election of 1924, risking his professorship at LSE to which he had just been appointed.[11] In 1925, Albrecht Mendelssohn Bartholdy represented the German government at the Dawes Plan negotiations in The Hague.[12] Nikolaos Politis, the Greek law professor, became a senior diplomat and sometime foreign minister of Greece in the 1920s, but kept engaging in academic debates.[13] The type and success of these non-academic endeavours varied, but the motivation was the same. They sought to have a practical impact as "pioneers [of] world affairs", to borrow Shotwell's own words.[14]

When revisiting the disciplinary history of IR, political scientists have tended to trace and re-interpret theoretical developments. Specifically, there has been a long debate on whether the traditional

---

[10] Helena Swanwick, *I Have Been Young* (London, 1935), p. 383.
[11] LSE reserved "freedom of action in the event of his being elected a Member of Parliament during the tenure of his Chair", which happened in 1929. Edwin Daller (LSE registrar) to Noel-Baker, 22 May 1924, NBKR 8/8/1, Philip Noel-Baker Papers. In 1929, Noel-Baker resigned upon his election to the House of Commons, and became personal assistant to Arthur Henderson. Memo, [1929], Box 252, Central Filing 134/8/A,B, LSE Archives.
[12] Rainer Nicolaysen, 'Albrecht Mendelssohn Bartholdy (1874–1936): Jurist – Friedensforscher – Künstler', *Rabels Zeitschrift* 75 (2011), p. 24.
[13] Evelyne Lagrange, 'Nikolaos Politis (1872–1942)', *Société française pour le droit internationale*, available at www.sfdi.org/internationalistes/politis/ [accessed 29 July 2020]; See, for example, Nikolaos Politis, 'Das Genfer Protokoll', *Europäische Gespräche* 6 (1924), pp. 509–16.
[14] Shotwell, *The Autobiography of James T. Shotwell*, p. 11.

story of IR – the so-called 'first great debate' between "idealist" and "realist" IR scholars – is an accurate reflection of actual events.[15] While most revisionists would now deny that the 'first great debate' really occurred, there is still widespread confusion about what actually constituted IR during this period. Various explanations have been offered, from alternative debates to meta-theoretical reconstructions. But the consensus still suggests that there was an IR theory of some sort.[16]

The interpretation of interwar IR writings becomes problematic, however, when taking into account the biographies of IR pioneers, their political networks, and their non-academic interests. Many of them did not even attempt to formulate general laws or theory. In fact, the field was characterised by the "absence of a general theory", as Brian C. Schmidt has acknowledged.[17] Rather than devoting their intellectual energy to theory-building – by way of definitions, axioms, models, abstractions, methodologies, etc. – IR scholars were almost exclusively concerned with either descriptive, history-like studies or policy proposals, fuelled by partisan interests. Raymond Leslie Buell, research director of the Foreign Policy Association in New York, admitted in 1931 that "we have erected none of the elaborate statistical paraphernalia which mark so many research activities", and that it was "largely a matter of opinion" if IR was a proper science.[18]

This chapter shows how the architects of IR assumed non-academic roles and tried to influence international politics during the 1920s and early 1930s. By focusing on their lives and pursuits, it argues that IR

[15] Peter Wilson, 'Where Are We Now in the Debate about the First Great Debate?', in Brian C. Schmidt (ed.), *International Relations and the First Great Debate* (New York, 2012), pp. 133–51. See the introduction for a more extensive historiography.

[16] See, for example, Brian C. Schmidt, 'On the History and Historiography of IR', in Walter Carlsnaes et al. (eds.), *Handbook of International Relations* (London, 2002), pp. 3–28 and Lucian M. Ashworth, *A History of International Thought: From the Origins of the Modern State to Academic International Relations* (New York, 2014). A notable exception is William Wallace, 'Truth and Power, Monks and Technocrats: Theory and Practice in International Relations', *Review of International Studies* 22:3 (1996), pp. 301–21.

[17] Brian C. Schmidt, 'The Rockefeller Foundation Conference and the Long Road to a Theory of International Relations', in Nicolas Guilhot (ed.), *The Invention of International Relations Theory: Realism, the Rockefeller Foundation, and the 1954 Conference on Theory* (New York, 2011), p. 79.

[18] Raymond Leslie Buell, 'What Is Research?', *Foreign Policy Association Pamphlet* No. 75 (New York, 1931), p. 2.

came of age not in isolated research laboratories but in the diplomatic milieu of European capitals. The chapter begins with Zimmern's Geneva summer schools, a popular annual event for students and practitioners of international politics which became a fixture in the Geneva calendar. The second section surveys a range of public events that IR scholars organised to advance their ideas and to build a disciplinary community. The third section shows how James Shotwell tried to engineer international treaties, specifically the 1924 Geneva Protocol and the 1928 Kellogg–Briand Pact. The fourth section introduces the International Studies Conference (ISC) which provided a permanent platform for exchange between academics and practitioners at annual meetings from 1928 to 1939. The final section illustrates how the 1931 and 1932 ISC sessions on economic policy and free trade sparked public controversy. To understand the evolution of interwar IR scholarship, the chapter argues, it is essential to consider the various activities outside normal university contexts. It concludes that there was little coherence in interwar IR thought and certainly no clear-cut theoretical debates.

The Spirit of Geneva

By the mid-1920s, the League of Nations machinery had attained a certain working routine and enjoyed the respect of a growing number of decision-makers. Germany was invited back into the international community after a successful test run at Locarno. It was the "golden age" of the League of Nations, as Jean-Michel Guieu has put it.[19] National governments accepted the League's role in hosting diplomatic debates and used it as a channel to express their security interests, cultivating a new venue of international politics. The politicians and diplomats who assembled in Geneva developed a sense of a "transnational community" as they worked on the dual challenges of disarmament and security.[20] For the French in particular this offered a

---

[19] Jean-Michel Guieu, *Le rameau et le glaive: Les militants français pour la Société des Nations* (Paris, 2008), p. 150; See also Alfred Zimmern, *The League and the Old Diplomacy* (London, 1929), p. 198 (originally published in the *Contemporary Review*, February 1924); Northedge, *The League of Nations*, p. 119.
[20] Andrew Webster, 'The Transnational Dream: Politicians, Diplomats and Soldiers in the League of Nations' Pursuit of International Disarmament, 1920–1938', *Contemporary European History* 14:4 (2005), p. 497. See also,

chance to "enmesh" their neighbours in a web of laws and norms.[21] Member states from across the globe presented a myriad of claims and petitions – all under the eyes of the world press. Geneva thus became a world capital, being home not only to the League itself but also to a range of non-governmental associations, conferences, and private meetings. Some observers called this "the spirit of Geneva", capturing the "optimistic, almost mystical" atmosphere which surrounded those who worked for world peace from the vantage point of a cosmopolitan city.[22]

Among the various groups that used Geneva as a platform for their work were young students of IR who wanted to benefit from the proximity of, and interaction with, the new institutions. In 1924, the IR professor Alfred Zimmern received a request from the Fédération Universitaire Internationale, a student organisation in support of the League of Nations, asking if he would help them to organise a series of lectures on foreign affairs.[23] Zimmern agreed and set up a small summer school in Geneva at the occasion of the Fifth Assembly of the League of Nations in September that year. The idea was to gather students from various national and disciplinary backgrounds and to offer courses by academics as well as political, diplomatic, and military experts.

The format proved so popular that Zimmern turned the summer school into a regular event – the Geneva School of International Studies.[24] For the 1925 edition, held from July to September, he was able to attract prominent lecturers and more funding. A total of 579 students from 44 countries came to attend classes by a range of international scholars, such as British IR specialist Charles Manning, French philosopher Félicien Challaye, and US lawyer Manley Ottmer

Andrew Webster, 'From Versailles to Geneva: The Many Forms of Interwar Disarmament', *Journal of Strategic Studies* 29:2 (2006), pp. 225–46.
[21] Jackson, 'Deterrence, Coercion, and Enmeshment'.
[22] See Ethel L. Jones, *The Spirit of Geneva* (London, 1929); Robert de Traz, *L'Esprit de Genève* (Paris, 1929); Otto Hoetzsch, *Germany's Domestic and Foreign Policies* (New Haven, 1919), p. 76.
[23] Brochure of the Geneva School of International Studies, 1927, p. 13, Alfred Zimmern Papers, Box 87/1-21.
[24] It went under various names, most commonly "Geneva summer schools" or "Geneva schools". See brochure of the "Geneva School of International Studies", 1927, Alfred Zimmern Papers, Box 87. Guieu, *Le rameau et le glaive*, p. 195.

Hudson. They were joined by politicians and diplomats, such as the Irish Foreign Minister Desmond FitzGerald and the Spanish diplomat Salvador de Madariaga.[25] One of these "distinguished statesmen and scholars" was James T. Shotwell who became a regular speaker at the Geneva summer schools.[26] The schedule was divided into academic lectures, public events, and dinner discussions. They covered general introductions to IR, international law, and economic relations but also touched upon philosophical, cultural, and regional subjects – much like contemporary university syllabi.[27] On various occasions, the students visited the League of Nations headquarters. During the first week of September, when the Assembly was in session, Zimmern would give special seminars covering the proceedings. For him, Geneva was "a laboratory of realistic political science".[28]

Over the following years, the Geneva summer schools became a must-go for anyone interested in the study of IR, or indeed its practice, as the *New York Times* reported.[29] Scholars such as Louis Eisenmann, Ernst Jäckh, Paul Mantoux, and Arnold J. Toynbee taught alongside a variety of 'public men' such as Edvard Beneš, Lord Cecil, Paul Hymans, Fridtjof Nansen, and Arthur Salter. An American board of governors was formed, including David Hunter Miller, John Foster Dulles, Charles P. Howland, Thomas W. Lamont, and Edwin F. Gay.[30] From the early 1930s, William Rappard and Paul Mantoux offered the premises of the Graduate Institute of International Studies to Zimmern's students over the summer months.[31]

[25] List of Lecturers, 1925, Alfred Zimmern Papers, Box 88.
[26] Booklet, 'The Geneva School of International Studies', 1927, James T. Shotwell Papers, Box 169/170.
[27] See, for instance, 'Lecture syllabus', 1927, Philip Noel-Baker Papers, NBKR 8/12/2; or Parker Thomas Moon, *Syllabus on International Relations* (New York, 1925).
[28] Memo for *Fédération Universitaire Internationale*, October 1924 to April 1925, by Zimmern, Alfred Zimmern Papers, Box 88.
[29] "A Geneva School for Peace: Students from Many Lands to Gather in Capital of the League of Nations to Hear Lectures by Eminent Scholars", *New York Times*, 21 April 1929, section 10, p. 5.
[30] Brochure, *Bureau d'Etudes internationales de Genève*, by Daniel Lagache, 1927 [?], Alfred Zimmern Papers, Box 87/1–21.
[31] Brochure entitled *The Postgraduate Institute of International Studies, Geneva: Announcement for 1931–1932*, HEI A/1 (1928/1929–1940/1941), Archives of the Graduate Institute of International Studies.

In addition to prominent lecturers, however, the summer schools achieved a reputation for their underlying mission. Zimmern wanted to invite the most capable and promising young students – including up to 80 women per year[32] – to educate them, in the best possible setting, for careers in government and diplomacy. He tried to fundraise grants to support students without the necessary financial means and asked colleagues around the world to handpick the most suitable candidates.[33] Zimmern was sensitive to issues of class, having worked as an inspector at the Board of Education and in working-class education.[34] If there was one remedy for international conflict, he argued, it was travelling and making friends abroad.[35] His profound commitment to education was reflected in his students' comments who valued the international atmosphere, eminent lecturers, and the choice of pressing topics.[36] The classical scholar and internationalist Gilbert Murray, too, applauded Zimmern's Geneva summer schools: "I ... cannot speak too highly of the work done and of the spirit that pervades it".[37]

Zimmern's initiative was not the only one of its kind. From 1926, the International Institute of Intellectual Cooperation (IIIC) entertained a section for student exchanges, hoping to generate an internationalist spirit among the next generation of decision-makers.[38]

---

[32] Student list, 1927, Alfred Zimmern Papers, Box 95.

[33] Memo for *Fédération Universitaire Internationale* October 1924 to April 1925, by Alfred Zimmern, Alfred Zimmern Papers, Box 88.

[34] D. J. Markwell, 'Zimmern, Sir Alfred Eckhard (1879–1957)', *Oxford Dictionary of National Biography* (Oxford, 2004), available at http://ezproxy-prd.bodleian.ox.ac.uk:2167/view/article/37088 [accessed 5 February 2016].

[35] Alfred Zimmern, *Learning and Leadership: A Study of the Needs and Possibilities of International Intellectual Cooperation* (Oxford, 1928), p. 47; Alfred Zimmern, *Education and International Goodwill* (Oxford, 1924), pp. 13–14.

[36] See, for example, Corlies Lamont to J. K. Newman, 3 August 1925: "I can report without exaggeration that I have never seen a student project of this kind go so well. Zimmern *gets* the students and holds them", Alfred Zimmern Papers, Box 18. See also Paul Rich, 'Alfred Zimmern's Cautious Idealism: The League of Nations, International Education, and the Commonwealth', in David Long and Peter Wilson (eds.), *Thinkers of the Twenty Years' Crisis: Inter-war Idealism Reassessed* (Oxford, 1995), p. 85.

[37] Gilbert Murray to Montague Burton, undated [1930–2?], Gilbert Murray Papers, Box 415.

[38] League of Nations, 'The International Institute of Intellectual Cooperation', in *Brochures de Propagande, 1926–1927* (Paris, 1926), pp. 6–8.

In 1928, LSE director William Beveridge announced a scholarship for the best IR student to travel to Geneva and visit the seat of the League of Nations.[39] In the early 1930s, the American educator Arthur Charles Watkins offered an "International Relations Observation Tour", a guided journey through Europe for IR students from the United States.[40] These programmes allowed students to interact with foreigners, to explore different political cultures, to learn foreign languages, or even to find employment abroad. Transnational biographies were common among students of IR. For them, working across national borders was both a logistical necessity as well as an expression of their professional ethos.

Women established similar programmes. The Women's International League for Peace and Freedom (WILPF) held summer schools at Salzburg in 1921 and at Lugano in 1922, attended by some 100 women and men.[41] The International Federation of University Women argued that "nothing will contribute more to international peace and goodwill than the constant interchange of the professors and graduate students of the universities of the world".[42] Women played a greater role in this field than is usually acknowledged. A 1923 report by Kristine Bonnevie, the Norwegian biologist and internationalist, listed vacation courses with up to 600 students from all over the world, stressing in particular the value of teaching IR in this context.[43] Women often used informal settings to bypass the diplomatic establishment dominated by men, and summer schools were a convenient way to do so. Meanwhile, it is important not to forget that many of these women were themselves members of the elite and enjoyed high levels of education, and sometimes wealth. These resources certainly helped them on their mission to increase female representation in government and diplomacy, but it also reflected a fundamental inconsistency.

[39] Nicholas Sims, 'Foundation and History of the International Relations Department', in Harry Bauer and Elisabetta Brighi (eds.), *International Relations at LSE: A History of 75 Years* (London, 2003), available at www.lse.ac.uk/internationalRelations/aboutthedepartment/historyofdept.aspx [accessed 4 February 2016].
[40] Prospectus by Arthur Charles Watkins, Director of the National Student Forum, 1932, James T. Shotwell Papers, Box 136 (a), (b).
[41] Program Leaflet, 1922, WILPF/5/7, LSE Archives.
[42] Theodora Bosanquet to Nitobe Inazō, 24 July 1922, Dossier 7759, Box R1008, League of Nations Archives.
[43] "Report on Intellectual Vacation Courses", by Kristine Bonnevie, 17 July 1923, Dossier 27944, Box R1055, League of Nations Archives.

Although the architects of IR were members of the elite themselves, they claimed to be educating a broader public. They wrote for "the ordinary man and woman", as a 1933 edited volume promised.[44] Ernst Jäckh, the founder of the Deutsche Hochschule für Politik in Berlin, took pride in the diversity of the student body at the Hochschule who came from a wide range of professional and partisan backgrounds.[45] The Institut des Hautes Etudes Internationales in Paris invited non-degree students to public lectures.[46] The Hungarian Foreign Affairs Society adopted similar means in the hope to "foster the interest for IR education".[47] The broad range of educational programmes in IR was summarised in a 1928 handbook, listing more than forty institutions across a dozen countries.[48] The surge in IR education coincided with a general worldwide increase in the university student population. From the beginning of the twentieth century until the Second World War, global university enrolment figures grew almost twentyfold.[49]

The underlying motivation for this trend, however, was not just education in itself. It was the belief in democratic control of foreign policy that substantiated the need for instruction in IR. "If democratic government is to continue under modern conditions", Zimmern explained in 1927, "it must be provided with leaders adequately trained to deal with problems of international relations, and a public opinion well enough informed to support and control an enlightened

---

[44] Leonard Woolf (ed.), *The Intelligent Man's Way to Prevent War by Lord Cecil, Gilbert Murray, W. Arnold-Forster, C. M. Lloyd, Sir Norman Angell, H. J. Laski, C. R. Buxton* (London, 1933), dust jacket. See also Eleanor Rathbone, *War Can Be Averted: The Achievability of Collective Security* (London, 1938), p. vii.

[45] Pamphlet on the founding of DHfP, undated [1921?], pp. 9–10, GStA PK, I. HA Rep. 303 (neu), Nr. 1. See also Antonio Missiroli, *Die Deutsche Hochschule für Politik* (Sankt Augustin, 1988), p. 30.

[46] Declaration IHEI, undated [1921?], Boîte 1, Archives Institut des Hautes Etudes Internationales (IHEI).

[47] Memo on *Ungarische Gesellschaft für auswärtige Politik*, undated, GStA PK, I. HA Rep. 303, Nr. 2116.

[48] IIIC, *Handbook of Institutions for the Scientific Study of International Relations* (Paris, 1929). See also Memorandum Concerning an Enquiry into the various activities of the Institutions for the Scientific Study of International Relations, 14 January 1932, Dossier 24210, Box R2275, League of Nations Archives.

[49] In 1900, approximately 500,000 students were enrolled in higher education worldwide. Evan Schofer and John W. Meyer, 'The Worldwide Expansion of Higher Education in the Twentieth Century', *American Sociological Review* 70 (2005), pp. 897–9.

foreign policy".[50] This argument was related to the original impulse for IR, the international campaign championed by the Central Organisation for a Durable Peace and its allies during the First World War who argued that decisions over war and peace should be made by an educated public rather than a small unelected elite.[51] Women were at the heart of that movement, as the writer and political activist Violet Paget (better known under her pen name Vernon Lee) argued.[52] The role of IR scholars was to train the personnel for this new system of democratic foreign policy. To this end, several IR institutions offered special courses for members of foreign ministries who began to recruit on the basis of merit rather than social status.[53]

Democratic control of foreign policy required information and education. The conduct of foreign policy had to shift into the public sphere where scholars could investigate and criticise it. This was something novel, Zimmern argued.[54] While there had been diplomatic conferences before 1914, they had been held infrequently and the public had not followed them very closely. A crucial impulse came from the first of Woodrow Wilson's Fourteen Points – "open covenants of peace, openly arrived at", although it remained a somewhat unfulfilled promise.[55] But gradually, the democratisation of national and international government took hold. It triggered a sort of political enlightenment, "an awakening ... of the self-consciousness of the masses due to popular education", as the German diplomat Harry Kessler put it.[56] William Rappard noted the rising public interest: "most of the world's keenest minds are constantly watching, and many of its most active

50 Brochure of the Geneva School of International Studies, 1927, Alfred Zimmern Papers, Box 87/1–21.
51 A. J. P. Taylor, *The Trouble Makers: Dissent over Foreign Policy, 1792–1939* (London, 1957), pp. 132–66; Harry Hanak, 'The Union of Democratic Control during the First World War', *Historical Research* 36:94 (1963), pp. 168–80; Marvin Swartz, *The Union of Democratic Control in British Politics during the First World War* (Oxford, 1971); Sally Harris, *Out of Control: British Foreign Policy and the Union of Democratic Control, 1914–1918* (Hull, 1996).
52 Violet Paget to Gilbert Murray, 5 June 1933, Gilbert Murray Papers, Box 217.
53 Hans Freytag to Albrecht Mendelssohn Bartholdy, 8 November 1919, MA Nachl., 2,26,159; and Statutes, 1921[?], Boîte 1, Archives Institut des Hautes Etudes Internationales (IHEI).
54 Address by Alfred Zimmern, meeting of the New York Branch, League of Nations Association, 24 March 1930, Alfred Zimmern Papers, Box 140.
55 Woodrow Wilson, 8 January 1918, transcript available at http://avalon.law.yale.edu/20th_century/wilson14.asp [accessed 17 May 2017].
56 Harry Kessler, *Germany and Europe* (New Haven, 1923), p. 2.

pens are, from day to day, describing the flow of current events".[57] Indeed, national newspapers now regularly covered the latest news in the field of IR and their interactions with high politics.[58] Increasing transparency allowed people to take an interest in foreign affairs while, vice-versa, their interest pressed decision-makers to be more transparent.

The push for open diplomacy also motivated a new genre of writing. Arnold Toynbee's *Surveys of International Affairs*, annual editions of up to three volumes, reflected in their extent and detail how much better informed observers of foreign policy were in the 1920s compared to pre-war times. Drawing on official documents and reports, Toynbee and his team of collaborators compiled comprehensive surveys for anyone interested in international politics. For example, the 1925 edition managed to minutely recount every step in the advent of the Locarno negotiations from December 1924 to February 1925, referring even to the secret German note to Austen Chamberlain on 20 January.[59] The growing availability of primary and secondary sources allowed almost real-time study of foreign affairs. Collections of government documents, official letters, and international treaties were printed in pamphlet-style for wide distribution, supplemented by an increasing body of textbook literature.[60] Newspapers, too, devoted more space to foreign affairs and covered diplomatic conferences that were hitherto closed to the eyes of the public.[61] These developments contributed to an awareness among the general public that government decisions in foreign policy did not have to be taken for granted but could be subject to popular and academic debate.

Unsurprisingly, the democratisation of foreign policy was not a flawless process. Decisions over war and peace were not suddenly in the hands of a perfectly educated population, nor studied by perfectly rigorous academics. Sources remained limited and biased. The very

---

[57] William Rappard, *Uniting Europe* (New Haven, 1930), p. xiii.

[58] See, for instance, 'Germany Wants a Treaty: Prof. Mendelssohn-Bartholdy [sic!] Tells of Hope to Outlaw War', *New York Times*, 17 June 1927, p. 26.

[59] C. A. Macartney et al., *Survey of International Affairs 1925* (London, 1928), p. 19.

[60] See, for instance, G. M. Gathorne-Hardy, *A Short History of International Affairs, 1920–1934* (Oxford, 1934), esp. p. ix; Otto Hoetzsch and W. Betram, *Dokumente zur Weltpolitik der Nachkriegszeit* (Berlin, 1932/3).

[61] For an illustrative introduction to the world of journalism and high politics during the interwar period, see Emery Kelen, *Peace in Their Time* (London, 1964).

The Spirit of Geneva 173

concept of 'democratic control' was not defined at all. Instead, the transition from 'old' to 'new' diplomacy opened up an opportunity for the architects of IR to define themselves as intermediaries between the people and the government. These connections were fostered by a new environment of summer schools, lecture series, and pressure groups, all of which IR scholars played principal roles in. At the same time, politicians and government officials readily entered this arena and used it as a quasi-political stage. The Deutsche Hochschule für Politik in Berlin, for example, enjoyed the support of a whole range of high-ranking state representatives even before it officially opened.[62] Zimmern's summer schools, too, were aimed at filling this gap by gathering professors, aspiring diplomats, and senior statesmen in what was then seen as the capital of the world – Geneva.

Many of these elite IR networks benefitted from the Carnegie Endowment for International Peace and the Rockefeller Foundation who provided targeted funding since the early 1920s. They sponsored publications, individual scholars, conferences, and entire research centres according to their vision for the European social science landscape. The study of IR was to serve "preparation of government action, as well as research".[63] Katharina Rietzler has characterised their activities as a type of cultural diplomacy, a precursor to Cold War strategies.[64] Philanthropic projects allowed American internationalists not only to enter European academic networks but to interact with official European diplomats and statesmen.[65] This approach seems to have provided private Americans an entrée to European

---

[62] Erich Nickel, *Politik und Politikwissenschaft in der Weimarer Republik* (Berlin, 2004), p. 80.
[63] Memo by Tracy Kittredge for Sydnor H. Walker, 15 February 1935, Folder 60, Box 7, Series 910, RG 3, RF, Rockefeller Archive Center.
[64] See Katharina Rietzler, 'Before the Cultural Cold Wars: American Philanthropy and Cultural Diplomacy in the Inter-war Years', *Historical Research* 84:223 (2011), p. 148; Katharina Rietzler, 'Philanthropy, Peace Research, and Revisionist Politics: Rockefeller and Carnegie Support for the Study of International Relations in Weimar Germany', *GHI Bulletin Supplement 5* (2008), pp. 61–79; Katharina Rietzler, 'Experts for Peace: Structures and Motives for Philanthropic Internationalism in the Interwar Years', in Daniel Laqua (ed.), *Internationalism Reconfigured: Transnational Ideas and Movements between the World Wars* (London, 2011), pp. 45–66; Katharina Rietzler, 'Of Highways, Turntables, and Mirror Mazes: Metaphors of Americanisation in the History of American Philanthropy', *Diplomacy & Statecraft* 24:1 (2013), pp. 117–33.
[65] Rietzler, 'Before the Cultural Cold Wars', p. 161.

decision-making circles and opened a field for many more partnerships between private donors, academia, and politics. As internal documents indicate, the objective of the Rockefeller Foundation was not just to advance scholarship in IR but to address "government departments in Washington and abroad".[66] In at least one case, towards the late 1930s, the Foundation facilitated the recruitment of League of Nations officials, as an internal report reveals:

a representative of the League of Nations consulted an officer of the Foundation with reference to candidates for places on the League secretariat … he and his associates agreed that the best material for staff positions ought to be found among former fellows of the Rockefeller Foundation. He was provided with a selected list of former fellows.[67]

As a result, the demarcation lines between philanthropy, education, and official diplomacy became increasingly blurry and obscured the underlying personal motivations. The spirit of Geneva thus reflected two contrasting trends in interwar IR scholarship – the democratic ambition to have well-informed public debates on international politics vis-à-vis the meritocratic practice of amateur diplomacy among small elites. On the one hand, it rested on the assumption that international politics could be rationally understood and democratically governed. On the other hand, it was driven by the personal ambition of its protagonists to shape the world. In order to achieve that, the architects of IR tried to distinguish themselves as public intellectuals and entered public debates wherever possible.

From Lectures to Treaties

The 1920s provided many opportunities for IR scholars to engage with a wider audience. They were convinced that international diplomacy was a subject which "cannot be learnt from books and documents alone".[68] One site for such exchange was the Carnegie Chair at the Deutsche Hochschule für Politik in Berlin, a visiting professorship first

---

[66] Report, 14 December 1932, Folder 871, Box 96, Series 100.S, RG 1.1, RF, Rockefeller Archive Center.
[67] The Rockefeller Foundation, *Confidential Monthly Report* No. 11 (March 1938), p. 2.
[68] Jerome Greene to John A. Cousens, 2 June 1930, Box 1, Folder 2, Russell Miller Subject Files, Fletcher School of Law and Diplomacy Records.

held by James Shotwell. The chair was established in 1926 based on a proposal by Nicholas Murray Butler, the president of the Carnegie Endowment for International Peace.[69] Co-sponsored by the German foreign office, the goal was to place an acclaimed international scholar at the heart of the Berlin political scene.[70] To this end, Shotwell was put in touch, via the foreign office, with "leading personalities" in Berlin.[71] He also delivered a public "Carnegie Lecture", a format that turned into a popular annual event – subsequent speakers included Moritz Julius Bonn, Hajo Holborn, Salvador de Madariaga, and Pierre Renouvin.[72]

Institutions like the Carnegie Chair were abundant.[73] Another prominent centre was the Institute of Politics at Williamstown, Massachusetts, founded in 1921. The Institute hosted an annual lecture series delivered by European scholars on a topic of contemporary concern. Among the speakers were Otto Hoetzsch, Philip Kerr, Albrecht Mendelssohn Bartholdy, Carlo Sforza, Walter Simons, and William Rappard.[74] The Williamstown lectures provided a platform for debate that avoided the constraints of official political institutions. Yet they went beyond the purposes of a university lecture. For example, in the summer of 1923, the German author and diplomat Harry Kessler criticised the Versailles settlement for its "paralysing" effect on the German economy and suggested that French security concerns be put aside in order for Germany to be able to join the League of Nations on equal terms.[75] Kessler spoke "from a German point of view", rather than from that of an independent scholar.[76]

[69] The first holder, James T. Shotwell, assumed the chair in February 1927. GStA PK HA Rep. 303 (neu), Nr. 51 (Carnegie Lehrstuhl).
[70] Minutes of a DHfP meeting, 13 May 1930, PA AA, RZ507, R64152.
[71] Adolf Georg von Maltzan to the German Foreign Office in Berlin, 5 January 1927, PA AA, RZ507, R64152.
[72] Reports suggest that the auditorium was "crowded" and that a press photographer from the *New York Times* was present, 5 February 1931, GStA PK HA Rep. 303 (neu), Nr. 51 (Carnegie Lehrstuhl).
[73] For an overview, see IIIC, *University Exchanges in Europe: A Handbook* (Paris, 1928).
[74] See Albrecht Mendelssohn Bartholdy, *The European Situation* (New Haven, 1927).
[75] Kessler, *Germany and Europe*, p. 73.
[76] Ibid., p. v. However, Kessler was not a blind nationalist. See Harry Kessler, 'Plan zu einem Völkerbunde auf Grund einer Organisation der Organisationen (Weltorganisation)', in Harry Kessler (ed.), *Tagebuch eines Weltmannes* (Marbach am Neckar, 1988).

Similarly, a few years later, Mendelssohn Bartholdy defended the official collection of German documents on the Great War, which he had worked on himself.[77] Both speakers were making political claims in an academic setting.

Similar events were established across Europe and the United States. They included the Montague Burton lectures at Nottingham and the lecture series at the Geneva Institute of International Relations, a programme set up by the British League of Nations Union (not to be confused with the Graduate Institute). The Chicago Council on Foreign Relations hosted external speakers, such as Lord Cecil, Georges Clemenceau, and Fridtjof Nansen.[78] The University of Denver put up a speaker series featuring among others Nicholas Murray Butler, James Shotwell, and British feminist-pacifist Agnes Maude Royden.[79]

The professors who spoke at these events imitated the style and the rhetoric of diplomats. At times they identified as academic spokespeople for their governments. "The scholar in public affairs, however detached and philosophic in outlook", Zimmern declared, "is before all things a patriot".[80] By staging quasi-diplomatic debates in academic settings, the architects of IR created a new sphere of negotiation, which was neither subject to the rules of official politics nor to the standards of social science research. This peculiar environment at the intersection of academia and diplomacy shaped the careers of most early IR scholars. Their intellectual output depended, as William Rappard confessed, on their exposure to practical politics. Authors who were directly employed with the League of Nations would be biased in its favour, and those who were not connected to the League would be biased against it. Only those formerly employed were in a neutral position, Rappard argued.[81] In other words, academic scholarship was subject to the lifestyle of authors, a fact that was clearly at odds with their claim to pursue objective science.

[77] Bartholdy, *The European Situation*, pp. 39–55.
[78] Booklet, Chicago Council on Foreign Relations, 1928, James T. Shotwell Papers, Box 213.
[79] 'Program and Methods of the Foundation for the Advancement of the Social Sciences', 1929, James T. Shotwell Papers, Boxes 167, 168.
[80] Alfred Zimmern, *The Scholar in Public Affairs* (London, 1929), p. 14 (originally appeared in *George Louis Beer, a Tribute to His Life and Work in the Making of History and the Moulding of Public Opinion* (New York, 1924)).
[81] See Rappard, *Uniting Europe*, p. xiv.

It is important to stress again that the protagonists of this story belonged to a small and highly privileged milieu. Many IR scholars descended from aristocratic and intellectual families. They were educated at elitist institutions and socialised in the exclusive clubs of European capitals. "Among a certain social elite", Harvard historian William L. Langer explained, "it became fashionable to demonstrate concern with these matters [foreign policy]".[82] When on research journeys, they travelled first class and lodged at grand locations, such as the *Hôtel Lutetia* in Paris.[83] These luxuries made IR research accessible only to an extremely limited circle of people who, in some cases, were even privately related to one another – for example, Arnold Toynbee married Gilbert Murray's daughter, the writer Rosalind Murray. Protected by social status, the architects of IR manoeuvred comfortably between senior common rooms and diplomatic conferences. They conversed effortlessly in several languages and, perhaps most importantly, they shared a common cosmopolitan lifestyle.

Membership of these circles provided an *entrée* to the world of high politics. On his visits to Europe, Shotwell would routinely meet up with senior politicians. The way he interacted with figures such as German Foreign Minister Gustav Stresemann – "We just talked nonsense and had a jolly time together"[84] – or Czech President Tomáš Garrigue Masaryk – "I had a whole day with him in his country home"[85] – suggests an almost casual relationship between academics and politicians. Indeed, it was common for an IR scholar such as Mendelssohn Bartholdy to correspond with senior politicians and diplomats, both domestic and international, such as Stafford Cripps, Allen Dulles, Elco van Kleffens, and Gustav Radbruch.[86]

To be sure, interactions between scholars and decision-makers were not unprecedented. As Davide Rodogno has noted, experts acting as "representatives of specific nation-states" were common since the late

---

[82] William L. Langer, *In and Out of the Ivory Tower: The Autobiography of William L. Langer* (New York, 1977), pp. 144–5.
[83] 'Résumé des délibérations de la IXième réunion du comité exécutif', 13 February 1937, K / 73-80, IIIC Records.
[84] The meeting took place on 11 March 1927 in Geneva. Shotwell, *The Autobiography of James T. Shotwell*, p. 205.
[85] Social Science Research Council, 'Report of the Director of the Program of Research in International Relations for the Year 1931', 'confidential', 2 January 1932, p. 15, James T. Shotwell Papers, Box 136 (a), (b).
[86] See index cards, Albrecht Mendelssohn Bartholdy Papers.

nineteenth century.[87] But the new international order emerging in the wake of the Great War provided unprecedented opportunities in this regard. Professors, such as Zimmern, Shotwell, and Mendelssohn Bartholdy, systematically used their access to diplomatic circles throughout the interwar period. In 1924, for example, Zimmern was involved in discussions of Lord Cecil's Draft Treaty of Mutual Assistance.[88] In the preparation of the 1925 Locarno treaties, the British historian James Headlam-Morley was asked several times by Ambassador Lord D'Abernon as well as by Foreign Secretary Austen Chamberlain to comment on draft versions of the multi-lateral pact.[89] According to Ernst Jäckh, the founder of the Deutsche Hochschule für Politik, the Austrian ambassador to Berlin had worked out a first draft of the Locarno treaties while on a research visit at the Hochschule.[90]

Female IR authors faced significant obstacles in this environment dominated by men. Various attempts by WILPF to present their ideas to national governments or international organisations were rejected. When, for example, two representatives of the Chilean branch of WILPF introduced themselves to the League headquarters, they were put off with a pile of information leaflets.[91] When women did manage to enter the policy world, such as Helena Swanwick as a delegate to the 1924 League of Nations Assembly, they were confronted with the blatant sexism of the diplomatic establishment who expected them to work on topics such as opium, refugees, and traffic in women.[92] While Swanwick did know something about the latter, she was actually more interested in traditional security issues, such as the sanctions question. In the end, she was elected rapporteur for refugees.[93]

[87] Davide Rodogno, Bernhard Struck, and Jakob Vogel, 'Introduction', in Rodogno et al. (eds.), *Shaping the Transnational Sphere: Experts, Networks, Issues* (New York, 2015), p. 2.
[88] Arthur Balfour et al., *The Draft Treaty of Mutual Assistance: Record of Discussion at a Meeting of the British Institute of International Affairs, Held on February 18, 1924* (London, 1924).
[89] Angela Kaiser, *Lord D'Abernon und die englische Deutschlandpolitik, 1920–1926* (Frankfurt, aM, 1989), p. 335; and Sibyl Eyre Crowe, 'Sir Eyre Crowe and the Locarno Pact', *The English Historical Review* 87:342 (1972), pp. 55–6.
[90] Ernst Jäckh, address delivered on 1 June 1933 at ISC meeting in London, Folder 3, Box 317, IIIC Records.
[91] Sofia Kriman and Celinda Arregui de Rodicio to Secretary-General, 18 May 1931, League of Nations Archives, Dossier 28350, Box R2185.
[92] Swanwick, *I Have Been Young*, p. 385.   [93] Ibid., pp. 394–5.

Shotwell, on the other hand, could build on a long career of policy advising. During the 1919 Paris Peace Conference, he had served as President Wilson's senior historical consultant.[94] He participated in a series of diplomatic negotiations, often alongside other academic experts, such as Arnold Toynbee.[95] While in Paris, Shotwell also helped to conceptualise the International Labour Organisation (ILO).[96] "He fully realised that he was making history instead of writing about it", as Shotwell's biographer put it.[97] Toynbee and Zimmern, too, had advised their government during the peace negotiations. Even the German government, although not admitted to the negotiations themselves, had sent an expert delegation, one member of which was Mendelssohn Bartholdy. The founder of the Deutsche Hochschule für Politik, Ernst Jäckh, was a member of German delegations to Versailles, Genoa, Locarno, and Geneva.[98] Almost every major IR scholar of the interwar period had some interaction with senior decision-makers.

The Search for a Security Treaty

In the spring of 1924, Shotwell co-authored the "Draft Treaty of Disarmament and Security", intended as an alternative to the failed 1923 Treaty of Mutual Assistance drafted by the Temporary Mixed Commission on Armaments.[99] It specified that any state that refused to

---

[94] Josephson, *James T. Shotwell and the Rise of Internationalism in America*, p. 10; Peter Grosse, *Continuing the Inquiry: The Council on Foreign Relations from 1921 to 1996* (New York, 2006), available at www.cfr.org/about/history/cfr/inquiry.html [accessed on 3 January 2016]; Jonathan M. Nielson, 'The Scholar as Diplomat: American Historians at the Paris Peace Conference of 1919', *The International History Review* 14:2 (1992), pp. 228–51.

[95] Diary, 1919, James T. Shotwell Papers, Box 41, Folder 1.

[96] International Labour Organisation, *Edward Phelan and the ILO: The Life and Views of an International Social Actor* (Geneva, 2009), p. 20.

[97] Josephson, *James T. Shotwell and the Rise of Internationalism in America*, p. 103.

[98] 'The Spirit of the New Germany', undated article, Ernst Jäckh Papers, Box 6.

[99] Among the co-authors were General Tasker H. Bliss, Joseph P. Chamberlain, and David Hunter Miller. Shotwell et al., 'Text of the Draft Treaty of Disarmament and Security'. See Josephson, *James T. Shotwell and the Rise of Internationalism in America*, pp. 121–8; Oona A. Hathaway and Scott J. Shapiro, *The Internationalists: How a Radical Plan to Outlaw War Remade the World* (New York, 2017), pp. 116–17; Webster, 'Absolutely Irresponsible Amateurs', pp. 373–88.

submit a dispute to international arbitration would automatically be declared an aggressor. Shotwell sent the document via Arthur Sweetser at the League Secretariat to Secretary-General Eric Drummond. The latter placed it before the Council which, in turn, voted to have the proposal circulated as an official League document.[100] Within a few weeks, the professor's essay had made it to the most senior body of international governance.[101] However, Shotwell did not stop here. When it became clear that the Protocol would not come into force, Shotwell continued his activism for a general treaty through various high-level academic and political acquaintances in Germany, France, and the Netherlands. With the help of his friends Mendelssohn Bartholdy and ILO-director Albert Thomas, he set up committees to keep in touch and to plan for future policy work in the field of arbitration and security.[102] These circles were to operate "as a research agency of the Government", Shotwell imagined.[103]

By promoting his Draft Treaty, Shotwell added to the attempts that were already being made in Europe to sign a general security treaty as well as to the much older tradition of international arbitration championed by Léon Bourgeois, Paul d'Estournelles de Constant, Louis Renault, and others at the Hague in 1899 and 1907.[104] A whole range of lawyers, governments, and pressure groups had been experimenting with legal instruments to solve international conflicts.[105] From the early 1920s, more specifically, French diplomats looked for an internationalist solution to overcome their reliance on British and American support. None of their attempts succeeded, including the Treaty of

[100] James T. Shotwell, *Autobiography of James T. Shotwell* (New York, 1961), pp. 181–3.
[101] Shotwell's amateur diplomacy risked prosecution by the Logan Act, which made it illegal for US citizens to enter into negotiations with foreign governments having a dispute with the US. See Hathaway and Shapiro, *The Internationalists*, p. 117.
[102] The German committee consisted of Albrecht Mendelssohn Bartholdy, Wilhelm Cuno, Walter Simons, Konrad Adenauer, Carl Wilhelm Petersen, Theodor Niemeyer, and Otto Hoetzsch, while on the French there were Arthur Fontaine, Albert Thomas, Paul Boncour, Charles Rist, Henri Chardon, Henri Lichtenberger, Léon Jouhaux, and René Massigli. Shotwell, *Autobiography of James T. Shotwell*, p. 197.
[103] Shotwell, *Autobiography of James T. Shotwell*, p. 198.
[104] Stéphane Tison (ed.), *Paul d'Estournelles de Constant: Concilier les nations pour éviter la guerre* (Rennes, 2015), pp. 41–3.
[105] Ignacio de la Rasilla and Jorge E. Viñuales (eds.), *Experiments in International Adjudication: Historical Accounts* (Cambridge, 2019).

Mutual Assistance. In the spring of 1924, a set of political advisors to
Édouard Herriot's *Cartel des gauches* government launched another
attempt. Jacques Seydoux, director for commercial affairs at the
foreign ministry, was at the forefront of this camp who suggested
offering Germany international rehabilitation and a moratorium on
reparations in exchange for an international security pact.[106]
Unsurprisingly, these plans met with resistance from the French military and with disinterest from London. Shotwell knew about these
difficulties, but he was not discouraged, even after the failure of the
Protocol.

Three years later, in the spring of 1927, Shotwell launched another
attempt to craft an international treaty. This time, he proposed an
agreement renouncing war as an instrument of politics – a "world
Locarno", as he called it.[107] Having taken up the Berlin-based
Carnegie Chair of International Relations in February 1927, he moved
among leading politicians, journalists, and professors in Germany.
Among many others, Shotwell was proud to report, he also met
Chancellor Wilhelm Marx and President Paul von Hindenburg.
More significant, however, was his inaugural address on 1 March
1927 which dealt with the problem of war in an interconnected world
shaped by modern weapons and complex power relationships.[108]
Shotwell's idea was to outlaw war altogether. What he had in mind
was a variation of existing anti-war commitments that would be more
effective in identifying aggressors and protecting neutrals. If it worked,
Shotwell majestically concluded, "we are at the greatest turning point
in human history".[109] The lecture was well received by the high-profile
audience and the international press, so Shotwell delivered it again the
following week in Cologne and brought up the topic in Geneva where
he came together with Foreign Minister Gustav Stresemann.

---

[106] Peter Jackson, *Beyond the Balance of Power: France and the Politics of
National Security in the Era of the First World War* (Cambridge, 2013),
pp. 438–66; Peter Jackson, 'French Security and a British "Continental
Commitment" after the First World War: A Reassessment', *The English
Historical Review* 126:519 (2011), pp. 353–6.
[107] Shotwell, *Autobiography of James T. Shotwell*, pp. 201–2.
[108] Robert H. Ferrell, *Peace in Their Time: The Origins of the Kellogg-Briand Pact*
(New York, 1952), p. 67.
[109] Shotwell, *Autobiography of James T. Shotwell*, p. 203 (quoted from the
original manuscript).

Over the following weeks, Shotwell continued to advertise his idea among senior European decision-makers, well aware of their respective interests but willing to ignore that disarmament and sanctions lacked political support in Europe and the United States.[110] In Paris, he arranged for a meeting with Aristide Briand on 22 March via his friend Albert Thomas.[111] In their conversation, according to Shotwell, Briand immediately understood Shotwell's plan and asked him to draw up a memorandum that the foreign minister could use as the basis of a public statement.[112] Shotwell agreed and suggested for Briand to publish it on the occasion of the upcoming tenth anniversary of the American entry into the First World War.[113] A few days later, on 6 April, Briand indeed sent out a message to the American people, containing almost verbatim quotes from Shotwell's memo. Crucially, it suggested that "France would be willing to enter into an engagement with America mutually outlawing war".[114] When Briand's message threatened to go unnoticed, Shotwell intervened again, now back in New York, with the editor of the *New York Times*, John Finley, who agreed that the French overture should be picked up by a powerful voice in the United States. Nicholas Murray Butler was easily won for this purpose. And it was after Butler's letter to the editor appeared on 25 April that the general discussion took off on what became the Kellogg–Briand Pact.[115]

Kellogg's initial reaction was reluctant. But Shotwell intensified his efforts and began to liaise between the French and American governments. In mid-May he met with Kellogg's undersecretary of state, Robert E. Olds, to discuss the details of a potential treaty and followed up with a revised draft a week later.[116] Olds told Shotwell that Kellogg

---

[110] Steiner, *The Lights that Failed*, p. 373.
[111] Patrick O. Cohrs, *The Unfinished Peace after World War I: America, Britain and the Stabilisation of Europe, 1919–1931* (Cambridge, 2006), pp. 451–5.
[112] Eva Buchheit, *Der Briand-Kellogg-Pakt von 1928 – Machtpolitik oder Friedensstreben?* (Münster, 1998), pp. 28–9.
[113] Ferrell, *Peace in Their Time*, p. 72.
[114] 'Briand Sends Message to America On Anniversary of Entering the War', *New York Times*, 6 April 1927, p. 5.
[115] Josephson, James T. Shotwell and the Rise of Internationalism in America, pp. 158–61; Shotwell, Autobiography of James T. Shotwell, pp. 204–13; James T. Shotwell, *War as an Instrument of National Policy and Its Renunciation in the Pact of Paris* (London, 1929), pp. 39–42.
[116] James T. Shotwell to Robert E. Olds, 25 May 1927, RG 59, 711.5112, Box 6645, US National Archives.

secretly welcomed the proposed treaty but was not ready to commit publicly.[117] Meanwhile in Paris, the local officer of the Carnegie Endowment for International Peace, Earle B. Babcock, kept in touch with Briand's secretary Alexis Leger. Babcock would cable Shotwell the latest news from Paris who, in turn, passed them on to Olds. On 30 May, Babcock reported to Shotwell that Briand was "ready to make official intimation through diplomatic channels" for an international treaty on the basis of his 6 April message to the American people.[118]

Shotwell knew that his private campaign could embarrass Washington internationally, and that unauthorised negotiations with foreign governments were a felony under the Logan Act. In fact, Kellogg was informed about "certain private individuals" who "side-track[ed] diplomatic conversations", as his papers reveal.[119] But instead of silencing Shotwell the foreign secretary chose to play him off against the 'outlawry of war'– campaign led by Chicago lawyer Salmon Levinson and Senator William Borah, who pursued a similar goal although they were much more sceptical of the League of Nations.[120] Both camps eagerly lobbied for their respective version to be adopted in the treaty, but Kellogg was still hesitant. He thanked them politely and continued at his own pace.

After months of government talks, the pact was finally signed in Paris on 27 August 1928.[121] It did contain elements of Shotwell's proposal and it certainly resonated with the internationalist spirit of many scholars in the IR community. French jurist Georges Scelle, for example, welcomed the pact and suggested amending the French constitution to ensure that any future declaration of war was in line with the new international commitment.[122] But he also criticised that it contained too much of the "religious aspiration" of the Anglo-Saxon

---

[117] "[H]e heartily approves of the whole thing – although, of course, this approval is strictly confidential and to be known only by a few of us." James T. Shotwell to Nicholas Murray Butler, 18 May, Box AAA, James T. Shotwell Papers.

[118] James T. Shotwell to Robert E. Olds, 2 June 1927, RG 59, 711.5112, Box 6645, US National Archives.

[119] Frank B. Kellogg to Myron T. Herrick, 27 June 1927, RG 59, 711.5112, Box 6645, US National Archives.

[120] Robert James Maddox, 'William E. Borah and the Crusade to Outlaw War', *The Historian* 29:2 (1967), pp. 200–20.

[121] Oona A. Hathaway and Scott J. Shapiro, *The Internationalists: How a Radical Plan to Outlaw War Remade the World* (New York, 2017), pp. 116–30.

[122] Norman Ingram, *The Politics of Dissent: Pacifism in France 1919–1939* (Oxford, 1991), pp. 51–2.

opinion, rather than to establish a powerful institution capable of keeping aggressors in check.[123] As it turned out, the failure to harmonise the Kellogg–Briand Pact with the League of Nations Covenant undermined its potential benefits.[124] In the end, the pact was both more and less than Shotwell had intended – it was signed by sixty-five governments (instead of two) but it failed to prevent war.

There is an ongoing debate among historians and international lawyers as to how effective, if at all, the Kellogg–Briand Pact really was. Traditional historiography has regarded the treaty as toothless and mostly symbolic.[125] Zara Steiner argued that Kellogg's belated and evasive response rendered the French proposal "totally innocuous".[126] More recently, legal scholars Oona A. Hathaway and Scott J. Shapiro have tried to resurrect the pact, portraying it as the decisive turning point in the transformation from old to new diplomacy by outlawing wars of conquest.[127] Their account, in turn, has faced criticism from a range of historians who have argued that the Kellogg–Briand Pact neither contained a novel political idea nor actually had any noticeable impact on world peace.[128] The mere act of prohibiting war in codified law, the critics argue, was not the reason for the decline of inter-state war. Rather, it was due to the impact of the two world wars and the broader normative transformations of the twentieth century. Within that process, Shotwell only played a minor role.

The significance of Shotwell's interventions, however, lies not so much in the effect that he had on the final treaty but in his ambitions *per se*. He took enormous pride in the fact that Kellogg personally reassured him that Levinson's contribution was not as important as his

---

[123] Guieu, *Le rameau et le glaive*, p. 157.

[124] Northedge, *The League of Nations*, p. 145.

[125] See, for example, Harold Josephson, 'Outlawing War: Internationalism and the Pact of Paris', *Diplomatic History* 3:4 (1979), pp. 377–90; Sally Marks, *The Illusion of Peace: International Relations in Europe 1918–1933* (London, 1976), p. 99; Northedge, *The League of Nations*, p. 119; David Armstrong, Lorna Lloyd, and John Redmond, *From Versailles to Maastricht: International Organization in the Twentieth Century* (London, 1996), p. 36.

[126] Steiner, *The Lights that Failed*, p. 573.

[127] Hathaway and Shapiro, *The Internationalists*.

[128] Peter Jackson et al., 'H-Diplo Roundtable XXI-15 on The Internationalists: How a Radical Plan to Outlaw War Remade the World', 18 November 2019, available at https://issforum.org/roundtables/PDF/Roundtable-XXI-15.pdf [accessed 30 July 2020].

own.[129] Shotwell wanted to "shape history, not merely write about it", as Hathaway and Shapiro have put it.[130] Or, in the words of his biographer, Shotwell was an "activist-intellectual".[131] By the late 1920s, the primary goal of IR scholars was to exercise political influence and shape public debates. This attitude conflicted with traditional academic duties and raised questions about the scientific quality of their work. By interfering in the object of their research, IR scholars undermined their claim to scientific objectivity. They began to advocate what was politically desirable, not theoretically plausible. As unelected experts, they also contradicted their own ambition to make foreign policy more democratically accountable.

One might object that IR scholars such as Shotwell inflated their own sense of importance or that relying on their papers distorts the real story.[132] But that does not undermine the argument made here. The point is that Shotwell *tried* to influence policy, not necessarily that he did have an influence. His colleagues were no different. Zimmern thought that it was a duty to leave the ivory tower and engage with political affairs. Politics, he argued, could not be studied "from behind Common Room curtains".[133] It was the responsibility of scholars as patriots to apply their intellectual powers in practice. On another occasion, he described the role of IR scholars as "representatives of [their] countries".[134] Belgian lawyer Maurice Bourquin, who taught at the Geneva Graduate Institute in the early 1930s, suggested that universities should deliberately exploit their connections to the "lived reality", and argued that professors with practical experience in diplomacy would be better equipped for the study of IR.[135] The international lawyer Fritz Berber, who became a controversial IR

---

[129] Shotwell, *Autobiography of James T. Shotwell*, pp. 218–19.
[130] Hathaway and Shapiro, *The Internationalists*, p. 116.
[131] Josephson, *James T. Shotwell and the Rise of Internationalism in America*, pp. 159, 9.
[132] Lawrence E. Gelfand, 'Reviewed Work: James T. Shotwell and the Rise of Internationalism in America by Harold Josephson', *World Affairs* 138:1 (1975), pp. 72–4.
[133] See Zimmern, *The Scholar in Public Affairs*, pp. 4, 14.
[134] Alfred Zimmern, 'The Development of the International Mind', Geneva Institute of International Relations (ed.), *The Problems of Peace* (London, 1927), p. 2.
[135] Memo by Maurice Bourquin, entitled "Suggestions relatives aux travaux de recherches que l'Institut pourrait entreprendre dans le domaine des relations internationales [Suggestions concerning potential research projects for the

spokesperson for Germany in the 1930s, was remembered in a 1973 *Festschrift* as a "teacher, researcher, and practitioner".[136] As these examples show, Shotwell's ventures were not unusual but a widespread characteristic of early IR scholarship.

Building the International Studies Conference

In 1927, a group of IR specialists established the field's first academic conference. Initially intended as a small academic gathering on university-related questions, the International Studies Conference (ISC) turned into the most important annual meeting for professors, diplomats, politicians, philanthropists, and journalists who engaged in some way with the study of IR.[137] Between 1928 and 1939, the ISC became a venue for substantial debate on pressing issues such as disarmament, economic cooperation, collective security, and peaceful change. It provided a sphere of quasi-diplomatic negotiation parallel to and connected with official decision-making bodies. The list of delegates read like a *Who's Who* of contemporary IR, including E. H. Carr, Ernst Jäckh, Charles Manning, Paul Mantoux, David Mitrany, Philip Noel-Baker, William Rappard, James T. Shotwell, Arnold Toynbee, Quincy Wright, and Alfred Zimmern, as well as a range of prominent intellectuals, diplomats, and statesmen such as William Beveridge, Austen Chamberlain, Allen and John Foster Dulles, Édouard Herriot, Hersch Lauterpacht, Eelco van Kleffens, Lord Lytton, Ludwig von Mises, Oscar Morgenstern, and Gilbert Murray.[138] Among the

Institute in the field of IR]", 24 February 1938, HEI 149/4–5, Archives of the Graduate Institute of International Studies.
[136] Dieter Blumenwitz and Albrecht Randelzhofer (eds.), *Festschrift für Friedrich Berber zum 75. Geburtstag* (Munich, 1973), p. 5.
[137] The conference was originally called 'Conference of Institutions for the Scientific Study of International Relations', but changed its name in 1933. The French title was 'Conférence Permanente des Hautes Études Internationales'. It is hereafter referred to as ISC. See report submitted by Alfred Zimmern, 11 July 1928, Dossier 5B.6178.2423, Box R2224, League of Nations Archives. See also David Long, 'Who Killed the International Studies Conference?', *Review of International Studies* 32:4 (2006), pp. 603–22; and Michael Riemens, 'International Academic Cooperation on International Relations in the Interwar Period: The International Studies Conference', *Review of International Studies* 37:2 (2011), pp. 911–28.
[138] IIC, *The International Studies Conference: Origins, Functions, Organisation* (Paris, 1937), pp. 54–74.

handful of female delegates were the Foreign Policy Association researcher Vera Micheles Dean, the assistant director of the social sciences division at the Rockefeller Foundation Sydnor H. Walker, and Margot Hentze, a PhD student working with Harold Laski at the London School of Economics (LSE).

The ISC was a joint project of academics, technocrats, and politicians. Alfred Zimmern, then deputy director of the International Institute of Intellectual Cooperation (IIIC), floated the idea among his academic colleagues.[139] Julien Luchaire, director of the IIIC in Paris, and Oskar Halecki, head of university relations at the IIIC, cared for logistics and secretarial support.[140] German scholars Ernst Jäckh and Otto Hoetzsch hosted the first meeting at the DHfP in Berlin and arranged for leading politicians to be present.[141] Both the location and the audience were significant choices with a view to Germany's reintegration into the international community. Jäckh attached "highest value to close contact with relevant figures at the foreign office".[142] Albert Dufour von Féronce, a senior German diplomat and under-secretary at the League of Nations, believed the ISC to be "extraordinarily interesting".[143] Foreign Minister Gustav Stresemann was unable to attend himself but gave permission to address the ISC on his behalf.[144] The press described the ISC as an event that "captured the spirit of the time".[145] This astonishing level of public interest in the proceedings of a small academic meeting foreshadowed the potential of the ISC to contribute to foreign policy debates over the next decade.

[139] League of Nations, 'The International Institute of Intellectual Cooperation', p. 14.
[140] Otto Hoetzch to Julien Luchaire, 5 December 1927, GSta PK, I. HA. Rep. 303, Nr. 2116.
[141] The date for the Berlin ISC meeting was postponed because Foreign Minister Gustav Stresemann and key members of the foreign office were scheduled to be in Geneva for a summit until 15 March 1928. See minutes of a meeting at the DHP, 26 January 1928, PA AA, RZ507, R64152.
[142] Members of the foreign office were henceforth invited to preparatory meetings for the ISC. See Deutsche Hochschule für Politik to Freytag, 23 November 1927, PA AA, RZ507, R64152; and Jäckh to Freytag, 6 January 1928, PA AA, RZ507, R64152.
[143] Albert Dufour to Hans Freytag, 21 January 1928, PA AA, RZ507, R64152.
[144] Memorandum by Hans Freytag, 20 March 1928, PA AA, RZ507, R64152.
[145] 'Internationale geistige Zusammenarbeit', *Berliner Tageblatt*, 23 March 1928 (Morgen-Ausgabe), p. 3.

Formally speaking, the ISC was the product of the League of Nations and its bodies for intellectual cooperation – the Geneva-based International Committee on Intellectual Cooperation (ICIC) and the IIIC in Paris. The main organ of the ISC were annual plenary sessions (later divided into administrative and study meetings) which were held in rotation at different places around Europe.[146] Each year, an executive committee was elected to ensure a certain continuity between annual conferences and to keep in touch with the IIIC. Meanwhile, the IIIC provided a secretariat based in Paris which was in charge of logistics, edited and published ISC proceedings, and provided some funding.[147] Membership of the ISC was confined to scientific institutions concerned with the study of IR. Wherever possible, the ISC encouraged individual scholars to form so-called "national coordinating committees" to bundle institutions and send joint delegations to ISC sessions.[148] Despite these organisational guidelines, the ISC allowed many exceptions and it was basically up to the executive committee to invite individuals who would otherwise have been prevented from participating – from 1933 this was particularly relevant for German delegates.

On 22 March 1928 then, at around 11 am, Jäckh opened the inaugural ISC meeting in Berlin in the presence of the Prussian minister for culture, Carl Heinrich Becker.[149] Among the participants were scholars from Austria, Britain, France, Germany, and Italy, members of the Royal Institute of International Affairs (London), the Institute of Politics (Williamstown, MA), and the Graduate Institute of International Studies (Geneva), as well as representatives of the Academy of International Law (The Hague) and the European Centre of the Carnegie Endowment for International Peace (Paris).[150] Besides Zimmern, the most prominent participants were French historians Louis Eisenmann and Paul Mantoux as well as British IR specialist Arnold Toynbee. The delegates spent the first day introducing each other and presenting their various IR research institutions, followed by

[146] 1928: Berlin, 1929: London, 1930: Paris, 1931: Copenhagen, 1932: Milan, 1933: London, 1934: Paris, 1935: London, 1936: Madrid, 1937: Paris, 1938: Prague, 1939: Bergen, Norway.
[147] IIIC, *The International Studies Conference*, pp. 21–9.   [148] Ibid., pp. 30–1.
[149] Minutes of DHfP meeting, 17 March 1928, PA AA, RZ507, R64152.
[150] Minutes of the tenth session of the ICIC, 25–20 July 1928, Annex 6, p. 83, Dossier 5B.6178.2423, Box R2224, League of Nations Archives.

a banquet the same evening. The next two days were devoted to technical discussions which resulted in a number of proposals for future cooperation: equivalence of degrees and diplomas, exchange of teaching staff and students, establishment of reference centres, exchange of surplus books, and collaboration in research projects.[151] The official conference report concluded that there was "a very real corporate consciousness among its members".[152] In other words, the ISC confirmed the status of IR as an academic discipline.

During the first three years, the ISC focused on technical cooperation and largely refrained from political debate. Promoting IR as a university discipline was the primary goal. The British delegation offered to host the 1929 session in London, where new national committees from Poland and Czechoslovakia joined the ISC.[153] Among the first projects was the compilation of a list of universities and reference centres in the field of IR.[154] Another project, which seemed equally obvious and simple initially, was an internationally co-authored handbook of political terms. "Misunderstandings and disappointments between nations", so the argument ran, "occur when they use the same terms and mean different things".[155] To prevent future confusion the participants suggested drawing up a trilingual dictionary in English, French, and German compiling the most common terms of political practice, selected and evaluated by a committee of three representatives from each country. Among the proposed terms were words such as "law, morality, freedom, statutes".[156] The Carnegie Endowment donated 30,000 francs towards the handbook.[157] The project, however admirable its underlying idea, proved to be an almost complete failure.

---

[151] Riemens, 'International Academic Cooperation on International Relations in the Interwar Period', p. 917.

[152] Report, "Second Conference of Institutions for the Scientific Study of International Relations", 7 June 1929, Dossier 2072, Box R2222, League of Nations Archives.

[153] Report by M. de Halecki, Minutes of the tenth session of the ICIC, 25–20 July 1928, Annex 6, p. 71–2, Dossier 5B.6178.2423, Box R2224, League of Nations Archives.

[154] IIIC, *Handbook of Institutions for the Scientific Study of International Relations.*

[155] Wilhelm Haas, 'Memorandum Concerning a Comparative Handbook of Political and Politico-Philosophical Terms', 20 February 1929, Dossier 2072, Box R2222, League of Nations Archives.

[156] Wilhelm Haas to Werner Picht, 16 April 1931, K.I.1d, IIIC Records.

[157] Earle B. Babcock to Werner Picht, 24 June 1931, K.V.1-5, IIIC Records.

It dragged on for years and never reached publication stage.[158] Even a relatively basic collaborative exercise, agreeing on common terminology, turned out to be controversial and impractical.

Disciplinary historians have discussed the ISC as a space of interwar IR debates. Thanks to the work of David Long, Michael Riemens, and Katharina Rietzler, we now know more about some of the discourses, the philanthropic support, and the eventual demise of the ISC.[159] However, the most important contribution of the ISC seems to have been the platform that it offered to researchers and practitioners. Why did academics, diplomats, and philanthropists invest so much in a conference that hardly produced tangible results for any of these audiences? The ISC did not bring about a breakthrough in IR theory – certainly not in the way that post-1945 conferences did. Instead it was more of a "seed-bed" of new ideas, as F. S. Northedge termed it.[160] It was precisely the blurring of professional categories that made the ISC so attractive.

The participants of the ISC built a reputation both as teachers and commentators of foreign policy. On the one hand, they understood the conference as a body of technical cooperation for education and research, making resources more available to a larger community. On the other hand, it became a platform for substantial political debate and real-world influence. The ISC agenda was designed to serve "relations between universities and extra-university institutions", according to the 1929 programme leaflet.[161] Its members never claimed to host theoretical debates, let alone any showdowns between 'idealists' and 'realists'. In fact, the word 'theory' was almost entirely absent from ISC proceedings. Rather than to work out the basis of a social science, the goal of the ISC was to facilitate personal contacts, to gather expertise,

---

[158] See Summary of the Proceedings of the Fourth Meeting of the Executive Committee, 28–29 January 1933, Dossier 2381, Box R4006, League of Nations Archives.

[159] Long, 'Who Killed the International Studies Conference?', pp. 603–22; Riemens, 'International Academic Cooperation on International Relations in the Interwar Period', pp. 911–28; Rietzler, 'Before the Cultural Cold Wars', pp. 148–64.

[160] F. S. Northedge, *International Intellectual Co-operation within the League of Nations: Its Conceptual Basis and Lessons for the Present*, PhD thesis (London, LSE, 1953), p. 652.

[161] Agenda for London ISC meeting, 11–14 March 1929, Dossier 2072, Box R222, League of Nations Archives.

and to exchange opinions on specific questions. This might explain why historians of IR have struggled to identify and agree on prevalent theoretical schools.

Although ISC members did not produce any works of theory, they were anxious to stress their objectivity and impartiality. Being independent and non-partisan was an important label for early IR institutions.[162] In Zimmern's words, the goal was "to promote the objective and dispassionate study of International politics", precisely because it was so easy to drift into partisan propaganda.[163] In his view, the study of IR had to be "lifted from the sphere of propaganda", although he failed to acknowledge how ambiguous that term was, even prior to its abuse by the Nazis.[164] The ISC came to be widely regarded as a guarantor of trustworthiness.[165] This was a delicate claim, given the participation of non-academic actors at the ISC and their respective partisan goals.

Non-academic and partisan actors started to interact with the conference on a regular basis. At the London meeting, the British government sponsored a dinner attended among others by Eustace Percy, then President of the Board of Education. In his address to the delegates, Percy affirmed that the government was "greatly interested in the progress and success" of the ISC, arguing that their studies were very instrumental in narrowing the gap between opposing diplomatic positions.[166] In response to Percy, Jäckh spoke on behalf of the ISC delegates and confirmed that their ambition was to replace old balance-of-power thinking by "a new system based on scientific research".[167] Clearly, the goals of the ISC went beyond the academic realm and technical cooperation. This was a platform for intellectual-political activists who strove to change the world, not to interpret it. For the same reasons of influence and publicity, the IIIC offered press tickets to major newspapers and appointed a press officer to deal with

[162] Pamphlet on the founding of DHfP, undated 1921[?], p. 8, GStA PK, I. HA Rep. 303 (neu), Nr. 1.
[163] Memo by Alfred Zimmern, October 1924 to April 1925, Alfred Zimmern Papers, Box 88.
[164] Alfred Zimmern, 'The relations between peoples at the present time', inaugural lecture at Oxford, 1930, Alfred Zimmern Papers, Box 140.
[165] IIIC, *The International Studies Conference*, pp. 11–13.
[166] Newspaper cutting, *The Times*, 12 March 1929, Folder 3, Box 28, CEIP Records.
[167] Ibid.

inquiries.[168] The Carnegie Endowment offered a luncheon in London for all participants in 1929.[169] In a similar fashion the French government kept an eye on ISC proceedings, generously inviting all ISC delegates for lunch during the 1930 plenary session in Paris.[170] This is remarkable because the agenda in Paris was still dominated by university affairs and technicalities which would hardly catch the interest of politicians.

Evidently, the ISC served more as a platform for public intellectuals and policymakers than for purely academic researchers. Within less than two years, the conference was transformed from a small academic gathering into a quasi-diplomatic summit. Despite these practical ambitions, recent political science scholarship on the history of interwar IR has focused on "theoretical insights".[171] The implicit assumption of this literature is that interwar IR theory existed and can be identified by re-reading the discipline's early works. It takes for granted the self-proclaimed status of IR as "a branch of scientific enquiry", as the 1928 ISC report put it.[172] While there is merit in reinterpreting early IR publications, this approach has underestimated practical political aspirations as an impulse for the study of IR, or indeed other social sciences.[173] Prior to the mid-1930s there was very little theoretical work by those who have traditionally been identified as the founders of IR. It is telling that even a professor of political *theory*, such as Arthur Salter, was recruited from the ranks of practitioners – his background at the economic and financial section of the League of Nations was well reflected in his contributions to IR debates.[174]

Only on a few occasions did IR scholars reflect on their dual role as intellectuals and policy advisors, and if they did, then usually in favour

---

[168] Memorandum, 30 March 1933, Folder 2, S. H. Bailey Papers.

[169] Programme of Conference, Folder 3, Box 28, CEIDP Records.

[170] Julien Luchaire to Arnold Toynbee, 3 June 1930, Folder 1, Box 283, IIIC Records.

[171] Brian C. Schmidt, 'Lessons from the Past: Reassessing the Interwar Disciplinary History of International Relations', *International Studies Quarterly* 42 (1998), p. 433.

[172] Report of Berlin ISC meeting, 22–24 March 1928, Dossier 2071, Box R2222, League of Nations Archives.

[173] Duncan Bell, 'Writing the World: Disciplinary History and Beyond', *International Affairs* 85:1 (2009), p. 4.

[174] Arthur Salter in Arnold J. Toynbee, 'Peaceful Change or War? The Next Stage in the International Crisis', *International Affairs* 19:1 (1936), p. 51.

of more public work. "Too often", Salter lamented, scientists withdrew "to a closed world of theory, like an anchorite to his cell, sometimes inclined even to think that his professional integrity is violated by any close contact with practical affairs".[175] It was well-known, argued Toynbee in 1931, that successful diplomatic conferences required expert preparation. He was convinced "that unofficial preparation of the kind which non-governmental bodies like our Institutes can provide is hardly less important".[176] Toynbee's ambitious programme envisaged for participants of the ISC to take a stance on political questions and essentially act as government advisors.

University courses, too, lacked theoretical foundations. According to Philip Noel-Baker's personal notes, his lectures at LSE covered history, contemporary institutions, psychology, and even sports as an element of international society, but made almost no reference to major works of political theory.[177] As one of the earliest IR professors, Noel-Baker had no blueprint for syllabi or bibliographies, but he made no attempt to impose theoretical texts, neither classical nor modern, on his students. Instead, he often referenced his practical experiences at the League of Nations and did not hide his own political stance.[178] Referring to practical diplomatic experience was the norm, not an exception. IR departments in Paris, Berlin, and Geneva were staffed with former diplomats and politicians. For example, the German diplomat-politician Kurt Riezler drew on his experience in the foreign office and taught on practical questions. Riezler was sceptical whether a theoretical analysis of "power equations, formula, and causal relationships" was even possible.[179] Publications, too, reflected the orientation towards policy and were often intended as "aides to statesmen" rather than comprehensive treatises.[180] A forum such as the ISC provided an ideal venue for this approach to IR.

---

[175] Arthur Salter et al., *The World's Economic Crisis and the Way of Escape* (London, 1932), p. 18.
[176] Arnold J. Toynbee to Henri Bonnet, 18 March 1931, K.I.1b, IIIC Records.
[177] Lecture notes on International Relations, 1927–8 and 1928–9, NBKR 8/ 12/3, Philip Noel-Baker Papers.
[178] Philip Noel-Baker to Academic Registrar, 23 April 1924, NBKR 8/8/1, Philip Noel-Baker Papers.
[179] Kurt Riezler (as J. J. Ruedorffer), *Grundzüge der Weltpolitik in der Gegenwart* (Berlin, 1915), p. x.
[180] Eduard Fueter, 'Review of Survey of International Affairs 1920–23 and 1923', *Zeitschrift für Schweizerische Geschichte* vii:2 (1927), pp. 236–8.

194 *Professors as Diplomats*

Academic Spokespeople

After the 1930 plenary session in Paris, the ISC shifted its focus from academic affairs to current problems of international relations. In doing so, it adopted a conference style that had been practised by the Institute of Pacific Relations (IPR) since 1925. The IPR was a platform for political debate in the Pacific Rim co-sponsored by the Rockefeller Foundation. Its research secretary, the New Zealand economist and League of Nations consultant J. B. Condliffe, presented a report on the IPR, suggesting that the ISC, too, should discuss specific topics in IR "which are of greatest importance at the time of the meeting".[181] The idea was to use the ISC as a platform for informal diplomatic debate on current affairs. "Unlike official diplomats conferences", Condliffe explained, "those of the Institute are not burdened and restricted by fear of committing their governments and peoples".[182] Condliffe's suggestion was at once warmly welcomed. The Paris secretariat agreed with his report and asked Sir William Beveridge, then chairman of the ISC executive committee, to put the study of specific problems of international affairs on the agenda for 1931.[183] Even prior to Condliffe's report, however, many ISC delegates were already engaging with questions of immediate political concern, and it was only a matter of time until political debates would replace academic matters as the ISC's principal purpose.

By 1931, a suitable subject had been selected. In light of the Great Depression and its global repercussions, it seemed imperative for IR to find answers to economic questions of international affairs.[184] The executive committee consequently chose "The State and Economic Life" as the first theme for the biennial study cycle from 1932 to 1933, the new format now adopted by the ISC.[185] Given that few

[181] Report submitted by J. B. Condliffe, 12 June 1930, Dossier 2072, Box R2222, League of Nations Archives.
[182] Ibid.
[183] Werner Picht to Sir William Beveridge, 12 December 1930, Dossier 2072, Box R2222, League of Nations Archives.
[184] For an overview of economic cooperation at the League of Nations, see Patricia Clavin, *Securing the World Economy: The Reinvention of the League of Nations, 1920–1946* (Oxford, 2013).
[185] ICIC memorandum, 24 July 1931, Dossier 2072, Box R2222, League of Nations Archives.

participants had any economic training, this choice was problematic. Since the discussions required detailed technical knowledge, economic vocabulary was imported into IR and mixed with political terminology. Coupled with input from historians, international lawyers, and geographers, their approach resulted in a state of methodological disarray. Notwithstanding their wide interests in unknown territory, they never considered themselves dilettantes or admitted ignorance.[186]

The first study session was held from 23 to 27 May 1932 in Milan, co-hosted by the IIIC and Alfredo Rocco (the Italian Minister of Justice and a member of the Geneva ICIC).[187] Discussions started from the basic assumption that an increasingly interconnected world economy needed appropriate forms of political organisation. As governments were simultaneously driven by economic and political constraints, the opening speaker Moritz Julius Bonn lamented, their decisions were seldom determined by economic sense and more often by protectionism or monopoly power.[188] Which level of state intervention was right? Which tariff system would guarantee the highest benefits to all trading partners without risking antagonism from the excluded? The fundamental problem, as Bonn summed up, was "where to draw the limits of intervention".[189] These questions were all the more relevant as protectionism was creeping up after a period of relative openness during the 1920s. Particularly those countries that remained on the gold standard, such as Britain, hence unable to depreciate their currencies, resorted to tariff walls and thereby fuelled the upward spiral of protectionism.[190] This development ran counter, of course, to the promise of free and equal trade in Wilson's Fourteen Points.[191] A lively, at times heated debate ensued over the course of the four days in Milan between free traders and those in favour of a planned, more restrictive system.

---

[186] See Alfred Zimmern, *Internationale Politik als Wissenschaft* (Berlin, 1933), p. 3.

[187] Cable by Alfredo Rocco to IIIC, 29 February 1932, K.I.1d, IIIC Records.

[188] IIIC, *The State and Economic Life* (Paris, 1932), pp. 10–12.

[189] Ibid., p. 109.

[190] Barry Eichengreen and Douglas A. Irwin, 'The Slide to Protectionism in the Great Depression: Who Succumbed and Why?', *The Journal of Economic History* 70:4 (2010), p. 873.

[191] "The increasing burden of Tariffs is a serious factor in creating unsatisfactory international relations." E. Horscroft to Eric Drummond, 11 March 1931, Dossier 11078, Box R2182, League of Nations Archives.

The meeting started with a discussion of the origins of the economic crisis. Two Italian economists, the neoclassicist Luigi Amoroso and the former Minister of Finance Alberto De Stefani, launched an attack against liberal economic systems, the "automatic powers" of which "having failed" to make necessary adjustments in the crisis.[192] Italy's corporative system prompted considerable scepticism, as did Russian planning. But some, such as German economist Herbert von Beckerath, agreed that there was a need for government control, if possible at an international level.[193] This led to a second discussion on a more general supranational institution to supersede the fragmented and complex system of trade, still dominated by bilateral agreements and the 'most favoured nation' clause. Most representatives, with the notable exception of the British, agreed that a reduction in tariffs would go hand in hand with international cooperation and disarmament. Internationalism thus found its way into economic policy. The Romanian economist-politician Virgil Madgearu envisioned a "European Customs Union".[194] International cooperation would also allow representatives of national economic councils to regularly meet and reconcile diverging approaches. Zimmern suggested letting "the representatives of the Fascist Council meet the representatives of the Manchester School Council".[195]

As significant as the substance of their debates was the way in which the various positions were presented in Milan. On the one hand, participants insisted that the conference should not pass resolutions or take any votes.[196] On the other hand, they fed information to the press and sought to have an influence beyond the conference room. To this end, the Italian hosts took every opportunity at taking the lead and dominating the agenda with lengthy memos. They presented corporatism as if they were spokespeople of the Italian government. According to the preface of the conference volume, the goal in Milan was to "influence others, whose proper function it is to take international action", yet based on "the results of this objective and disinterested work of research".[197] In other words, ISC participants regarded themselves as academic authorities and political advisors. Labour economist Hugh Dalton, for example, found it difficult in the

---

[192] IIIC, *The State and Economic Life*, pp. 31–8.   [193] Ibid., p. 51.
[194] Ibid., p. 85.   [195] Ibid., p. 91.   [196] Ibid., p. 98.
[197] Ibid., pp. xxii–xxiii.

debates to refrain from recalling his time in government as under-secretary of state for foreign affairs.[198] Like Dalton, many ISC partici-pants regarded themselves as national delegates in an international conference setting. Zimmern at one point described himself as "both a national man and an international body".[199]

One year later, from 29 May to 2 June 1933, the Royal Institute of International Affairs and the LSE welcomed some fifty experts in London for the second study session on "The State and Economic Life". The focus of this meeting was on trade regimes – imperial preference, the 'open door' policy, and the 'most favoured nation' clause – as well as on potential reforms. For this exercise, a number of economists joined the lawyers, historians, and political scientists at the ISC, although their methodology and theory remained largely obscure. Economics was mostly regarded as distinct from and comple-mentary to IR. But given the increasingly obvious dependency of world politics on economics, a certain cross-disciplinary understanding was required from the participants. In a way, this development anticipated the role that the field of International Political Economy would later play within IR, by integrating economic relations into the analysis of political institutions.

The 1933 ISC in London was convened just a few days before, on 12 June, dozens of governments met for the London Economic Conference to discuss the restoration of the world economy. Looking to capitalise on their role as experts, ISC participants sought to provide advice to the heads of state, although their diverging political motiv-ations soon led to intense debate. A key point of disagreement was tariff walls. The Canadian economist Jacob Viner warned that regional tariff systems would be a source for political danger, whereas Arthur Salter defended the practice of partial agreements, notably British 'imperial preference' which had emerged from the 1932 Ottawa Conference.[200] Viner's view found support from smaller countries, who feared to be excluded from preferential treatment, as well as from Zimmern who agreed that any tariff bloc would cause political

---

[198] Ibid., pp. 19–20.
[199] Ibid., pp. 19, 89. It is interesting to note that feminist-pacifist Jane Addams felt the same dual identity, refusing to sacrifice the love of her country for the devotion to international goals. See Jane Addams, in WILPF, *Report of the Fourth Congress of the WILPF* (Geneva, 1924), p. 2.
[200] IIIC, *The State and Economic Life* (Paris, 1934), pp. 48–55.

friction.[201] On the other hand, S. H. Bailey and J. Coatman sided with Salter, arguing that regional agreements were necessary as a preliminary step towards more general trade partnerships.[202] By and large, ISC delegates defended their respective government positions and actually welcomed the opportunity to discuss with "representative thinkers from other countries".[203]

William Rappard noted that the delegates were "no longer discussing a matter of scientific insight into reality" but political realities themselves.[204] The delegates struggled to live up to their promise of "disinterested pursuit of objective truth" in a "scientific spirit".[205] Instead, professors interpreted their role at the ISC as policy advisors, sometimes beyond their own area of expertise. They acted like "imitation statesmen", as Viner put it.[206] The objective was not just to "to build bridges" between academic and practical experts, as Salter had announced in his introductory remarks, but actually to merge the two into a blurry synthesis of intellectual and political argument. To be sure, the problem was not that the League of Nations sponsored scientific research *per se*, in the same sense as the European Union (EU) sponsors academic research today. For one, the difference is that today's EU scholars do not occupy senior positions within the EU, as Alfred Zimmern, James Shotwell, and Gilbert Murray did at the League's institutions for intellectual cooperation. Besides, the point is not that financial support inevitably resulted in intellectual flaws, but that the framework of the League predetermined imaginations of what international politics might entail. It forced IR into the Procrustean bed of nation-states and existing institutions.

Eventually, the 1933 ISC meeting caused irritation among the highest diplomatic ranks. In a pamphlet that had quickly been put together in time for the London Economic Conference, ISC participants criticised the Ottawa trade agreement for its discrimination against non-members.[207] Canada's Prime Minister R. B. Bennett,

---

[201] Ibid., p. 61.   [202] Ibid., pp. 64, 69–78.
[203] Hugh Dalton, in IIIC, *The State and Economic Life*, p. 20.
[204] IIIC, *The State and Economic Life*, p. 84. Viner agreed that "our differences are rather those which confront statesmen than those which confront scholars." Ibid., p. 85.
[205] IIIC, *The State and Economic Life*, pp. xiii, 4.   [206] Ibid., p. 60.
[207] That is, any country outside the British Empire and the dominions. The Ottawa system of 'imperial preference' was particularly controversial as it excluded by

who had learned about the pamphlet, interpreted the statements as an undue interference in national politics and wrote a furious letter to the League's Secretary-General Joseph Avenol.[208] How could the League take such a partisan stance on the question of international trade? Avenol responded that "the opinions expressed at the Conference [ISC] do not receive the endorsement of the Institute [IIIC], of the Secretariat of the League of Nations or, of course, of the League itself".[209] Secretly, however, Avenol's secretary admitted that one could not reasonably consider ISC delegates such as Viner or Salter merely as scholars. It should have been possible, he remarked, to foresee the delicacy of the matter and to be more careful about endorsing the work of an independent conference.[210]

It is hard to estimate the ultimate impact of ISC pamphlets, treaty drafts, and public lectures. But, regardless of their actual influence on government decisions, it was obvious that political change was what IR scholars intended. This was a general trend that continued during the 1930s. Shotwell continued to "draft clauses" and to "send them over to Geneva".[211] Professors kept acting as diplomats. International lecture tours and governmental advisory positions continued to motivate IR scholars to unfold their intellectual abilities in the public realm. In addition to that, as one professor acknowledged in his memoirs, "these extracurricular activities ... provided a welcome addition to the family budget".[212] The self-conception of these men and women was that of public intellectuals who were qualified to teach, discuss, and practice foreign affairs.

Conclusion

As a result of these non-academic side-tracks, elite policy networks, and quasi-diplomatic activities, IR scholars spent less time on ordinary

definition any country that was not part of the British world. IIIC, *The State and Economic Life* (Paris, 1933).
[208] Riemens, 'International Academic Cooperation on International Relations in the Interwar Period', p. 919.
[209] Joseph Avenol to R. B. Bennett, 22 August 1933, Dossier 2381, Box R4007, League of Nations Archives.
[210] H. H. Cummings to Joseph Avenol, 3 August 1933, Dossier 2381, Box R4007, League of Nations Archives.
[211] James T. Shotwell to J. David Thompson, 19 July 1932, James T. Shotwell Papers, Box 155, 156.
[212] Langer, *In and Out of the Ivory Tower*, pp. 144–5.

academic work. When they did lecture and publish, it was usually about issues of immediate political relevance. IR scholarship during the 1920s and early 1930s was shaped by political events, and by the way in which IR scholars interacted with foreign policy actors. This entanglement raised questions about the state of the discipline. First, it created a thematic bias in favour of the League of Nations. Second, it meant that the research agenda was determined by events, rather than by analytical or methodological advances. Third, since IR scholars struggled to keep up with the speed of world affairs their studies often remained superficial. As Zimmern acknowledged, "from 1931, events moved faster than the minds of most of the members of the Conference [the ISC]".[213] As a consequence, IR debates rarely went beyond popular "catchwords", and failed to establish a set of common terms and methods, or any coherent hypotheses that could reasonably be described as a political theory.[214]

To be sure, some authors distinguished between general claims and specific applications.[215] David Mitrany, for example, stated in general terms that sanctions had to come before disarmament as a precondition for international peace. His underlying logic was that neither disarmament nor arbitration could work without the credible threat of international sanctions. National governments did not have enough incentives to comply with laws and treaties, unless they faced severe and definite punishment. To illustrate the psychological effects of sanctions, he also drew parallels between domestic and international law. That said, Mitrany was primarily interested in actual institutions and current affairs. He criticised "from [a] purely 'realistic' angle" the League Covenant for leaving crucial passages vague.[216] None of this was rooted in political theory, rather than in the experiences (often first-hand) by the architects of IR.

It is also true, as Michael Riemens has noted that "traces of the First Great Debate" can be found at ISC sessions during the 1930s,

---

[213] 'Note by Sir Alfred Zimmern on the Future of the International Studies Conference', 1946[?], Alfred Zimmern Papers, Box 102.

[214] Alfred Zimmern, *Modern Political Doctrines* (Oxford, 1939), p. ix. For an introduction to IR theory, see Steve Smith, 'Introduction: Diversity and Disciplinarity in International Relations Theory', in Tim Dunne et al. (eds.), *International Relations Theories*, 4th ed. (Oxford, 2016), pp. 1–12.

[215] See, for example, Charles Webster, *The League of Nations in Theory and Practice* (London, 1933).

[216] David Mitrany, *The Problem of International Sanctions* (Oxford, 1925), p. 18.

specifically in the statements by Italian delegates, but also in a conference report by Zimmern in which he distinguished between "idealist" planning and "realist" practice of international affairs.[217] In fact, Zimmern sometimes made references to two opposing "policies" or "schools" when he spoke about ways to control armament and aggression.[218] But he also blended the two allegedly contrasting views into what he called an "organised balance of power".[219] Again elsewhere, Zimmern seems to have had an entirely different terminology in mind: any political plan was necessarily 'idealist', because it derived from an 'idea', whereas its application was 'realist' because it referred to political realities.[220] These terminological inconsistencies have caused confusion among contemporaries and historians. Zimmern himself confessed in a 1929 lecture that "much of what is known in academic circles as 'political science' is mere planning with words".[221]

The vast majority of interwar IR scholars did not produce any works of theory at all. Their style varied between historical narratives and political polemics. Almost no author cared to provide systematic axioms, methodologies, hypotheses, or even definitions of key terms. Their work was not intended to survive scientific tests. It lacked models or predictions that could be verified or falsified. The popular claim that democracies were more peaceful, for example, was never backed up with any definition of what democratic governance meant. One of the most widely read contemporary works, Toynbee's *Surveys of International Affairs*, presented a journalistic narrative rather than an analytical interpretation. In the preface to the 1924 volume, H. A. L. Fisher called Toynbee's *Survey* a work of "contemporary history",

---

[217] Riemens, 'International Academic Cooperation on International Relations in the Interwar Period', p. 921.

[218] Address by Alfred Zimmern, Meeting of the New York Branch of the US League of Nations Association, 24 March 1930, Alfred Zimmern Papers, Box 140; and Alfred Zimmern, 'Nationality and Government', paper presented at the Sociological Society, 30 November 1915, published in *Sociological Review*, October 1915-January 1916, p. 216, Alfred Zimmern Papers, Box 166.

[219] Alfred Zimmern, untitled lecture notes, 1932, Alfred Zimmern Papers, Box 141.

[220] Alfred Zimmern, "League of Nations", in *Manchester Guardian*, 31 October 1918, Alfred Zimmern Papers, Box 179.

[221] Alfred Zimmern, "The Prospects of Democracy", lecture delivered at RIIA, 8 November 1929, Alfred Zimmern Papers, Box 140.

which did not refrain from political commentary and could be of service to politicians.[222] In essence, the *Surveys* were exactly that – historically informed summaries of current political affairs, spiced with political remarks. Similar to Toynbee, William Rappard commented on international politics with a view to policy change, rather than theoretical interpretation. His book *Uniting Europe* (1930) – bearing a normative momentum even in the title – drew heavily on his experiences as a former diplomat.[223] He was less explicit, however, about any formal characteristics that could be used to distinguish different kinds of intergovernmental or supranational institutions. Like most interwar IR scholars he avoided analytical commitments.

Recent accounts of interwar IR have nonetheless attempted to reconstruct debates and to stick new labels on old works.[224] The fundamental problem with these *ex-post* reconstructions is that they are imposing analytical categories on authors who never subscribed to any of these terms. This leaves us with what Nicolas Guilhot has called an "artificial coherence" in the history of the discipline.[225] The truth is that interwar IR scholars never really reflected on what they were doing. Was it "current history", "political science", or a "comparative study of national institutions"?[226] Depending on the setting, IR authors stylised themselves as impartial observers, experts with inside knowledge, or simply as representatives of nation-states.[227] While it is

[222] H. A. L. Fisher, 'Preface', in Arnold J. Toynbee (ed.), *Survey of International Affairs 1924* (Oxford, 1926), pp. v–vi.

[223] Rappard had served as a delegate to the Paris Peace Conference and as a member of the Permanent Mandates Commission of the League of Nations. Rappard, *Uniting Europe*, pp. 107–9.

[224] See, for instance, Andreas Osiander, 'Rereading Early Twentieth-Century IR Theory: Idealism Revisited', *International Studies Quarterly* 42 (1998), pp. 409–32; or Cameron G. Thies, 'Progress, History and Identity in International Relations Theory: The Case of the Idealist-Realist Debate', *European Journal of International Relations* 8:147 (2002), pp. 147–85.

[225] Nicolas Guilhot, 'Introduction: One Discipline, Many Histories', in Guilhot (ed.), *The Invention of International Relations Theory: Realism, the Rockefeller Foundation, and the 1954 Conference on Theory* (New York, 2011), p. 3.

[226] Arnold Toynbee, *Economics & Politics in International Life* (Nottingham, 1930), p. 1; Hans Simons and Paul Marc, 'Vorwort', in Albrecht Mendelssohn Barholdy (ed.), *Diplomatie* (Berlin, 1927), p. v; Ernst Jäckh, *The New Germany* (Oxford, 1927), p. 8.

[227] See, for instance, Otto Hoetzsch, *Germany's Domestic and Foreign Policies* (New Haven, 1929), esp. conclusion; or Kessler, *Germany and Europe*, p. v.

possible to identify individual and temporary opinions – such as
Toynbee's argument to admit Germany to the League in 1919 – it is
much more problematic to put interwar IR writers into general theoretical camps. If anything, there were loose thematic groups with partisan goals, such as the free traders at the ISC, or Noel-Baker's work on
universal disarmament, or Shotwell's campaign for what became the
Kellogg–Briand Pact.

What, if anything, was IR during those years? This chapter has
confirmed recent revisionist literature, in that E. H. Carr's allegations
of interwar 'idealism' rested on a straw man fallacy and that early IR
scholars were less of a homogeneous group than commonly assumed.
When taking their various educational and quasi-diplomatic activities
into account, however, it becomes questionable if there was any concerted attempt at writing IR theory at all. Only in exceptional cases did
authors make general claims. The vast majority of their publications
and interventions dealt with specific cases and one-off policies, paying
little attention to general theory. This was *ad hoc* political commentary
at best, polemic journalism at worst. "All knowledge today is biased",
as one member of the Institute of Pacific Relations put it.[228] The
unwillingness to engage in more basic research may in part have been
due to the disillusionment with how concepts such as 'self-determination' or 'open diplomacy' had been watered down. The political
context favoured improvisations and deal-making, and invited governments to deviate from international norms. In other words, there was
no culture for universal truths or theoretical concepts in foreign policy.

While IR was not (yet) what most would consider a social science, it
did have a close-knit community of scholars and practitioners sharing
a set of common features. First, they were committed to improving
education in foreign affairs and making foreign affairs more accessible.
Second, they boosted transnational cooperation in research, teaching,
and policymaking. Third, they valued close interaction between
scholars and non-academic actors. These activities – education,
cooperation, and policymaking – were driven by the same people and
overlapped in various ways. Those who occupied the first university
chairs in IR – Zimmern, Noel-Baker, Mendelssohn Bartholdy, Jäckh,

---

[228] Professor Willoughby, Minutes of Meeting of Subcommittee on Program,
Institute of Pacific Relations, 29 October 1926, James T. Shotwell Papers,
Box 29.

and Shotwell – were precisely the ones who built collaborative networks and advised governments. The Geneva summer schools, the Carnegie lectures, and the ISC were sites of exchange between representatives from various professions and countries. It is hard to overestimate their impact on individual academics and diplomats as well as for IR as a discipline. The next chapter will address one of the key IR issues of the interwar period – the debate on sanctions and what became known as 'collective security' – in order to show in more detail how opinions were formed, and how ideas were applied to practice.

5 | Testing Collective Security

How men do love thunder . . . they will call their war 'sanctions'; and their armies will be 'police'; and quite a number of people, women as well as men, will be persuaded that, regrettable as this array of force may be, it is the only way of attaining law and order, security and peace.

Helena Swanwick (1934)[1]

Introduction

When the efforts in the 1920s to promote peaceful cooperation failed, the architects of International Relations (IR) turned their attention to a system of mutual security guarantees which became known as 'collective security'. The idea of 'collective security' was to protect the territorial integrity and political independence of member states by imposing concerted sanctions – economic or military – on governments that refused to arbitrate peacefully in the case of an international dispute. Inversely, if a member state was under attack, its government could count on the community to assist. In other words, it was a way to outsource security from the national to the international level.[2] There was widespread debate on the methods and effectiveness of 'collective security' as the crises of the 1930s unfolded in Manchuria, Abyssinia, and eventually Czechoslovakia.[3] However, 'collective security' was never a clear-cut concept nor synonymous with an international entity.

[1] Helena Swanwick, *Pooled Security: What Does It Mean?* (London, 1934), p. 11.
[2] For a contemporary introduction, see Maurice Bourquin and Arnold Toynbee, in International Institute of Intellectual Cooperation (IIIC), *Collective Security: A Record of the Seventh and Eighth International Studies Conferences* (Paris, 1936), pp. 161–2.
[3] Hersch Lauterpacht, *Neutrality and Collective Security* (London, 1936); Eleanor Rathbone, *War Can Be Averted: The Achievability of Collective Security* (London, 1938); Quincy Wright (ed.), *Neutrality and Collective Security* (Chicago, 1936); T. P. Conwell-Evans, 'Collective Security and Germany', *The Times* (London, 5 April 1935), p. 12.

Essentially, it was a fuzzy term for a series of attempts to protect the fragile international order from increasingly blunt violations, and it became an important test case for the plausibility of IR scholarship.

No observer of international affairs could fail to notice how the institutions created since the end of the First World War were now being jeopardised by the revisionist governments in Japan, Italy, and Germany as well as by the economic repercussions of the Great Depression. During these crucial years, the plans to "finish" the peace that had inspired so much IR scholarship gradually turned into a retreat from international-ism and gave way to erratic attempts to prevent a new war.[4] The aggres-sors annexed foreign territories, ignored international law, and undermined the principles of what had become known as the new inter-national order. For IR as an academic discipline, these events posed difficult questions. How could the international community contain aggressors without risking war? Did the League of Nations have sufficient power to impose credible sanctions? And if not, was the entire system of international cooperation flawed? Like in the 1920s, the architects of IR continued to write, speak, and intervene publicly on these questions. But they struggled, by and large, to substantiate their wide-ranging activities with conceptual clarity or reliable legal definitions. By the mid-1930s, the world was in crisis, and so was the discipline of IR.

Even at the time, 'collective security' knew many critics. The British author Helena Swanwick was one of the most outspoken opponents of economic and military sanctions. A committed feminist-pacifist, Swanwick argued that sanctions affected civilians more than the deci-sion-makers.[5] Others, such as the American historian Albert J. Beveridge, were concerned about giving up national sovereignty to a superstate with executive powers.[6] The most devastating critique, however, came from 'realist' IR scholars, such as E. H. Carr, who rejected 'collective security' as a "naïve experiment" that was doomed to fail.[7] Internationalising security was an admirable state of the world,

[4] Patrick O. Cohrs, *The Unfinished Peace after World War I: America, Britain and the Stabilisation of Europe, 1919–1932* (Cambridge, 2006); Zara Steiner, *The Triumph of the Dark: European International History 1933–1939* (Oxford, 2011).
[5] Swanwick, *Pooled Security*; Helena Swanwick, *Collective Insecurity* (London, 1937).
[6] Albert J. Beveridge, 'Pitfalls of a "League of Nations"', *The North American Review* 209:760 (1919), pp. 306–14.
[7] E. H. Carr, 'The League of Peace and Freedom: An Episode in the Quest for Collective Security', *International Affairs* 14:4 (1935), p. 837.

Carr joked, but it was as unattainable as turning lead into gold.[8] In 1939, Hans Morgenthau proclaimed the death of 'collective security' and welcomed the return of partial alliances which, according to him, reflected the distribution of power more naturally and allowed smaller states to withdraw from a system that did not work in their best interest.[9] This interpretation became the 'realist' standard during the Cold War, in a bipolar world where security could be shared only among power blocs, not among a universal community.[10]

Contrary to traditional historiography, however, the debate on 'collective security' was not simply divided into proponents and critics, nor was there any coherent theory or definition. It remained essentially the same blurry concept throughout the interwar period. Ideas for multilateral security guarantees circulated since at least the 1910s. After the First World War, Article XVI of the League of Nations Covenant, the so-called 'sanctions article', set the basic, if vague conditions for mutual action against potential aggressors. IR scholars of the 1920s, such as David Mitrany, developed and modified these provisions.[11] By the early 1930s, 'collective security' was a widely known concept and, after much hesitation, sanctions were reluctantly applied against Italy in 1935. If the ambition of interwar IR scholarship was to formulate rational solutions to the problem of war then 'collective security' was the most promising candidate. However, the League never became a direct sponsor of security. If anything, as Andrew Webster has argued, it offered a framework that member states used to express their own national security interests.[12] Not willing to give up their cause, the

[8] E. H. Carr, *The Twenty Years' Crisis, 1919–1939* (London, 1939), p. 9.
[9] Hans Morgenthau, 'International Affairs: The Resurrection of Neutrality in Europe', *The American Political Science Review* 33:3 (1939), p. 478.
[10] Reinhold Niebuhr, *The Children of Light and the Children of Darkness: A Vindication of Democracy and a Critique of Its Traditional Defenders* (London, 1945); John H. Herz, 'Idealist Internationalism and the Security Dilemma', *World Politics* 2:2 (1950), pp. 157–80; Kenneth Waltz, *Man, the State, and War* (New York, 1959).
[11] David Mitrany, *The Problem of International Sanctions* (Oxford, 1925); Lucian M. Ashworth, *Creating International Studies: Angell, Mitrany and the Liberal Tradition* (Aldershot, 1999).
[12] Andrew Webster, 'The League of Nations and Grand Strategy: A Contradiction in Terms?', in Jeffrey W. Taliaferro, Norrin M. Ripsman, and Steven E. Lobell (eds.), *The Challenge of Grand Strategy: The Great Powers and the Broken Balance between the World Wars* (Cambridge, 2012).

architects of IR engaged with these debates and experienced first-hand why it was so complicated to coordinate security internationally.

This chapter examines the intellectual formation of 'collective security' during the first half of the 1930s as it informed government decision-making and shaped public debate. Rather than retrofitting it into a particular IR theory, the chapter draws attention to the contingency and fluidity of 'collective security'.[13] First, it recounts the evolution of 'collective security' as a political idea and as a policy instrument from the First World War to the 1930s. The next section explains how an institutional apparatus emerged under the umbrella of the League of Nations and how sanctions were supposed to be employed. The third section shows how the crises in Asia, Africa, and Europe tested the concept of 'collective security' and questioned the logic of IR scholarship. The final section examines how the architects of IR dealt with these challenges, and it discusses whether the failure of 'collective security' caused a 'great debate' between so-called 'idealist' and 'realist' IR authors. Ultimately, it argues that, although 'collective security' was neither well defined nor well implemented, it forced IR scholars to take a stance on important questions that have continued to shape their discipline.

The Idea of Collective Security

Historically speaking, the idea of 'collective security' marked a departure from the old nineteenth-century style of diplomacy which rested on imperial or national sovereigns and only a minimal set of international agreements. 'Old diplomacy' provided only customary legal procedures for *ad hoc* arbitration and negotiation. It largely relied on self-help, bi-lateral alliances, and armed conflict. This system of individual security fell out of favour not only because it was unable to prevent recurrent war but also because it only served the interests of the military strong. Although it had achieved relative stability between

---

[13] Lucian M. Ashworth, for example, has claimed that interwar authors constructed "a concept of global order based on the interrelationship of arbitration, sanctions, and disarmament", yet then acknowledges that it were the "gaps" that actually characterised this concept. See Lucian M. Ashworth, 'Rethinking a Socialist Foreign Policy: The British Labour Party and International Relations Experts, 1918–1931', *International Labor and Working-Class History* 75:1 (2009), pp. 38–9.

the great powers, it ignored the claims of less powerful actors, such as small countries or national minorities.[14] Most importantly, 'old diplomacy' was blamed for the outbreak of the Great War which had exposed the danger of secret and unreliable agreements. The solution therefore was to establish an international institution in order to openly conclude, administer, and enforce general security treaties.

The invention of 'collective security' ended a longstanding era in the history of violent conflict. Previously, war itself was not illegal. It might have violated a specific contract or agreement. But apart from a few rudimentary rules, notably the 1864 Geneva Convention, war itself was not regulated at all. In fact, waging war was regarded as a normal policy instrument and as a fundamental right of any sovereign state. As the British international lawyer Arnold McNair put it, war used to be "extra-legal rather than illegal".[15] The codification of 'collective security' put an end to this state of "international anarchy", as Norman Angell called it.[16] For the first time in history, governments were able to manage international disputes by means other than offensive war. The types of sanctions invented in the first half of the twentieth century ranged from economic deterrents to military interventions, but they were all intended as anti-war instruments.[17] In this sense, 'collective security' was actually more about controlling aggression – if necessary by military means – rather than about denying it, as Angell was subsequently accused of.

'Collective security' went beyond the Hague Conventions of 1899 and 1907 which had established the Permanent Court of Arbitration but provided neither for a permanent political institution nor for effective sanctions to deter potential aggressors.[18] Both were needed, however, to reassure national governments that their interests would be defended. In 1910, Theodore Roosevelt was one of the first

---

[14] Quincy Wright, 'National Sovereignty and Collective Security', *The Annals of the American Academy of Political and Social Science* 186 (1936), p. 100.
[15] Arnold McNair, 'Collective Security', *British Year Book of International Law* 17 (1936), p. 152.
[16] J. D. B. Miller, 'Norman Angell and Rationality in International Relations', in David Long and Peter Wilson (eds.), *Thinkers of the Twenty Years' Crisis: Interwar Idealism Reassessed* (Oxford, 1995), p. 112.
[17] Nicholas Mulder, *The Economic Weapon: The Rise of Sanctions as a Tool of Modern War* (New Haven, 2022).
[18] Jacques Dumas, 'Sanctions of International Arbitration', *The American Journal of International Law* 5:4 (1911).

to raise the idea of a "League of Peace" which was able to defend itself, "by force if necessary".[19] Indeed, the readiness to use force was incorporated in the name of the League to Enforce Peace, the American branch of the League of Nations Union. Soon after the outbreak of the First World War, the architects of IR came up with the first detailed proposals of an international sanctions system within the framework of an intergovernmental organisation.[20] The Central Organisation for a Durable Peace (CODP) proposed in their 1915 programme that member states were to "bind themselves to concerted action, diplomatic, economic, or military" in case an aggressor refused to arbitrate.[21] Their idea eventually found its way into the Covenant of the League of Nations.

The distinctive feature about security within the League of Nations was the idea to internationalise the protection of individual states. In principle, 'collective security' was to include *all* states of the world – akin to the hopes of the League of Nations.[22] Multinational military alliances were nothing new, of course, nor was the idea of a universal polity.[23] In fact, historical precedents such as the Allies during the First World War or the Mongol Empire were territorially much larger than the League. But the League of Nations Covenant was the first treaty that invited states to join a "potentially universal" alliance, intended as a general safeguard against any aggressor, rather than against a specific belligerent.[24] The new system did not impose security 'from above' – like Roman 'pacification' – but it arose from a joint effort of, theoretically, equals. By subscribing to 'collective security' member states relinquished the right to resort to war in return for international

[19] Theodore Roosevelt, *Nobel Lecture*, 5 May 1910, available at www.nobelprize .org/prizes/peace/1906/roosevelt/lecture/ [accessed 23 May 2019].

[20] Program Leaflet, *Internationale Zentralorganisation für einen dauerhaften Frieden*, September 1915, SPK MA Nachl. AMB, 2,24,139.

[21] Central Organisation for a Durable Peace, *Minimum Program* (The Hague, 1915).

[22] Alfred Verdross, *Die Verfassung der Völkerrechtsgemeinschaft* (Vienna, 1926), p. 112.

[23] Quincy Wright traced the idea of "universal polity" to the sixteenth century. However, the political organisations he had in mind were based on the universal imposition of one system, rather than the pluralistic co-existence of different ones. See Wright, 'National Sovereignty and Collective Security', p. 100.

[24] 'Memorandum for Discussion at Sub-Committee on the British Commonwealth and the Collective System', Alfred Zimmern, 25 June 1934, Chatham House, Alfred Zimmern Papers, Box 97.

guarantees. 'Collective security' meant, to borrow Zimmern's words, "the safety of all by all".[25]

The advantage of a universal defence alliance was that member states no longer relied on national armies and could decrease their military expenditure. Downscaling national armies, in turn, would make offensive wars less likely. So 'collective security' was an obvious corollary of disarmament. Article VIII of the Covenant actually combined both instruments in one paragraph – "reduction of national armaments" and "enforcement by common action".[26] Charles Webster called it "a system of collective disarmament".[27] A 1932 German handbook on disarmament and security made the same argument.[28] Women were particularly outspoken supporters of general disarmament and emphasised this aspect of collective security.[29] They blamed militarism for the outbreak of the Great War and opposed private arms production.[30]

Historically and conceptually, the idea of disarmament actually preceded the corrective measure of sanctions. After the First World War, the peacemakers initially advocated general disarmament as the key to peace, but soon had to scale back to more modest bi- or multilateral agreements, notably the Washington and London Naval Treaties.[31] Like most interwar diplomacy, disarmament remained a spontaneous and fragmentary business that was deliberately flexible. To overcome the fragility of disarmament, the French had asked for a defensive pact since 1922. René Cassin, a lawyer and French representative to the World Disarmament Conference, tirelessly reiterated the

---

[25] Alfred Zimmern, 'The Problem of Collective Security', in Quincy Wright (ed.), *Neutrality and Collective Security* (Chicago, 1936), p. 4.

[26] League of Nations Covenant, available at http://avalon.law.yale.edu/20th_century/leagcov.asp [accessed 22 May 2017]. All subsequent quotations of the Covenant are taken from this source.

[27] IIIC, *Collective Security* (Paris, 1936), p. 389.

[28] K. Schwendemann, *Abrüstung und Sicherheit: Handbuch der Sicherheitsfrage* (Leipzig, 1932), p. vi.

[29] Catia Cecilia Confortini, 'Links between Women, Peace, and Disarmament: Snapshots from the WILPF', in Laura Sjoberg and Sandra Via (eds.), *Gender, War, and Militarism: Feminist Perspectives* (Santa Barbara, 2010), pp. 158–60.

[30] Women's International League (British Section), First Yearly Report: October 1915–October 1916, WILPF/2/1, LSE Archives.

[31] Zara Steiner, *The Lights that Failed: European International History, 1919–1933* (Oxford, 2005), pp. 372–80.

demand to include a 'collective security' provision in the accords.[32] Having served in the First World War as a soldier, he spent the rest of his life working on international peace, first as a French delegate to the League of Nations and later as one of the co-authors of the Universal Declaration of Human Rights.[33] Cassin thought that a working 'collective security' system relied on the "altruistic" behaviour of member states, and that this altruism had to be turned into codified, enforceable law. However, Cassin's hopes were pulverised when the League failed to restore peace in Manchuria in 1931. From this point, a sense of futility dominated the World Disarmament Conference, as the British politician and appeasement critic Eleanor Rathbone observed.[34] Disarmament suffered another, final blow after Germany's withdrawal from the League of Nations in 1933. But the responsibility was not just with the dictatorships. In September 1935, at a time when the League had effectively abandoned its security commitments to Ethiopia, British Foreign Secretary Samuel Hoare admitted that "limitation and reduction of armaments by certain countries, particularly by my own, have not been followed".[35]

As a complement to 'collective security', disarmament faced multiple problems. To begin with, the League Covenant lacked precise terms mutually agreed on and committed to. The infamous formulation in Article VIII – "reduction of national armaments to the lowest point consistent with national safety" – left actual limitations open to interpretation, and hence to political will. In the absence of specific restrictions, the architects of IR launched a propaganda campaign that became known as 'moral disarmament'.[36] The logic behind 'moral disarmament' was to de-militarise people's minds before downscaling armies. "One of the main causes of war", Polish lawyer Ludwik Ehrlich pointed out, "is the mentality which makes it possible to think of war".[37] For this purpose, the League devised a comprehensive

---

[32] René Cassin, in IIIC, *Collective Security* (Paris, 1936), p. 439.
[33] Jay Winter and Antoine Prost, *René Cassin and Human Rights: From the Great War to the Universal Declaration* (Cambridge, 2013).
[34] Rathbone, *War Can Be Averted*, p. 35.
[35] Samuel Hoare, 'Collective Action for Security Demanded', address delivered on 11 September 1935, published in Carnegie Endowment (ed.), *Italy and Ethiopia* (New York, 1935), p. 9.
[36] Heidi J. S. Tworek, 'Peace through Truth? The Press and Moral Disarmament through the League of Nations', *Medien & Zeit* 25:4 (2010), pp. 16–28.
[37] IIIC, *Collective Security*, p. 273.

propaganda plan, including "popular handbooks", "propaganda films", and "lantern slides".[38] Another popular channel was educational pamphlets with self-assessment exercises, written by prominent authors for mass audiences.[39] IR scholars also published in newspapers and featured on radio broadcasts, such as Arnold Toynbee's lecture series *World Order or Downfall* for the BBC in 1930.[40] All this was part of the desperate effort to eliminate the traditions of national military culture and to replace it with some form of internationalism.

The other novelty after the First World War was the professional political apparatus governing and administrating 'collective security'. The League of Nations offered a new sphere of political discourse where international affairs were practised and normalised. Crucially, the League was a permanent institution in contrast to the intermittent conferences of the nineteenth century. This allowed its members, at least in principle, to observe and react to tensions before they escalated into armed conflict. More generally, the League's institutions – the Council, the Assembly, and the Secretariat – provided a space for the advocates of 'collective security' to cultivate an internationalist spirit and to increase the acceptance of sanctions as a normal mode of diplomacy. The 1920s had seen a series of attempts to strengthen the effectiveness of security cooperation, notably the ill-fated 1924 Geneva Protocol which proposed to make arbitration and sanctions compulsory. Although the Protocol never entered into force, there was a growing consensus that security policy had to be controlled on the international level, rather than by individual governments.

That commitment to an international authority, however, sparked a heated debate about national sovereignty.[41] Many observers worried that collective guarantees would deprive individual states of sovereign

---

[38] Minutes of the International Committee on Intellectual Cooperation (ICIC), 10–11 July 1935, Dossier 19930, Box R4062, League of Nations Archives.

[39] Gilbert Murray, *The League and Its Guarantees* (London, 1920). Other contributors in this series included Norman Angell, G. Lowes Dickinson, Leonard Woolf, Arnold Toynbee, and C. Delisle Burns.

[40] Arnold Toynbee, six broadcast talks on *World Order or Downfall?*, BBC, 10 November to 15 December 1930, Arnold Toynbee Papers, Box 80.

[41] The reason for discussing 'collective security' at the 1934–5 ISC was that participants were interested in "sovereignty" and "sanctions". Henri Bonnet to William Rappard, 27 June 1933, HEI [uncatalogued], Archives of the Graduate Institute of International Studies.

rights, including their right to declare war.[42] A superstate, the American historian Albert Beveridge warned, would force states to give up legislative sovereignty on issues such as "tariff or immigration laws", and besides, it might not even serve the purpose of preventing war.[43] American banker and philanthropist Jerome Greene agreed that the world was not ready for a superstate, neither institutionally nor sentimentally.[44]. The belief that the League of Nations resembled at least a "rudimentary superstate" was widespread above all in the United States[45] The critics saw sovereignty as a zero-sum game in which national governments would lose to the degree that the League gained authority. But even an internationalist such as Arnold Toynbee conceded that "collective security means a diminution of local sovereignty".[46] At the other end of the political spectrum, "supranational tendencies" were criticised by those who tried to circumnavigate the watchful eye of the international community in order to change the status quo in their favour, as German historian Otto Hoetzsch recognised as early as 1925.[47] The German jurist Fritz Berber spoke of the "totalitarian character" of the post- 1919 international order.[48]

Other authors dispersed this fear and advocated a 'family of nations' as a middle path between a world-state and national isolation. If every member-state voluntarily sacrificed an equal portion of sovereignty, so the German teacher and internationalist Anna B. Eckstein argued, it was possible to collectively gain both security and freedom.[49] She regarded sovereignty not as an absolute national good but as a fluid variable of international negotiation. Contrary to the zero-sum assumption by the sceptics, Ludwik Ehrlich argued, 'collective security'

---

[42] F. S. Northedge, *The League of Nations: Its Life and Times, 1920–1946* (Leicester, 1986), p. 34.
[43] Beveridge, 'Pitfalls of a "League of Nations"', pp. 305–7.
[44] Jerome D. Greene, *Idealism and Realism in Efforts toward Peace* (Aberystwyth, 1933), p. 15.
[45] Edward A. Harriman, 'The League of Nations: A Rudimentary Superstate', *American Political Science Review* 21:1 (1927), p. 137; see also J. M. Spaight, *Pseudo-Security* (London, 1928), p. 1.
[46] Arnold Toynbee, in IIIC, *Collective Security* (Paris, 1936), p. 164.
[47] Otto Hoetzsch, *Die weltpolitische Kräfteverteilung nach den Pariser Friedensschlüssen* (Berlin, 1925), p. 34.
[48] Fritz Berber, *Sicherheit und Gerechtigkeit* (Berlin, 1934), p. 32.
[49] Anna B. Eckstein, *Staatenschutzvertrag zur Sicherung des Weltfriedens* (München, 1919), pp. 27–9. See also, Salvador de Madariaga, *The Price of Peace* (London, 1935), p. 14.

created something greater than the sum of individual securities – similar to a market economy where the interplay of subjective interests translates into greater welfare for society as a whole.[50] Even proponents of centralised systems, such as an international police force, argued that national sovereignty would not necessarily decrease but rather be transformed into new kinds of sovereignty.[51] There was no need for any state to give up its national identity. Supranational coordination was just a consequence of increasing interdependence, not an attempt to impose a super-state.

In any case, real and complete sovereignty was an illusion, argued Mitrany, especially given the level of economic interdependence in the early twentieth century.[52] Some authors, such as Swanwick, went as far as to proclaim the end of the nation-state altogether, arguing that the idea of a nation-state was not only impossible but "meaningless".[53] National sovereignty was always subject to the "collective will" of those who controlled the physical force of mankind, as former US Secretary of State Robert Lansing put it.[54] Or, in the words of anthropologist Lucy Mair, sovereignty was "nothing but the residuum of rights left" after all external commitments were subtracted.[55] Individual states had no other choice but to accept their limited sovereignty and to look for ways to reconcile their own security interests with their neighbours.

Contesting interpretations of sovereignty continued to shape IR scholarship on 'collective security' throughout the 1920s and 1930s.[56] It was "the historical mission" of his age, the director of the

---

[50] Ludwik Ehrlich, in IIIC, *Collective Security* (Paris, 1936), p. 177.
[51] David Davies, *The Problem of the Twentieth Century: A Study in International Relationships* (London, 1930), p. 202.
[52] David Mitrany, *The Progress of International Government* (London, 1933), pp. 67–8.
[53] Helena Swanwick, *I Have Been Young* (London, 1935), p. 393.
[54] Robert Lansing, 'Notes on World Sovereignty', *American Journal of International Law* 15 (1921), p. 17.
[55] Lucy Mair, *The Protection of Minorities: The Working and Scope of the Minorities Treaties under the League of Nations* (London, 1923), p. 23.
[56] See, for example, James W. Garner, 'Limitations on National Sovereignty in International Relations', *American Political Science Review* 19:1 (1925); Albert Geouffre de Lapradelle, *Principes généraux du droit international* (Paris, 1930); Hans Kelsen, *Das Problem der Souveränität und die Theorie des Völkerrechts* (Tübingen, 1920); Hans Wehberg, *Grundprobleme des Völkerbundes* (Berlin, 1926).

Deutsche Hochschule für Politik (DHfP) Ernst Jäckh argued, to find
new forms of sovereignty – a "new universalism [that] acknowledges
the individuality of the nation, but at the same time understands the
community of a family of nations".[57] French jurist Louis Le Fur
invoked the same notion of a *"famille de nations"* which he regarded
as the continuation of a longer historical process. He rejected the idea
of a *"super-état"*, stating it was impossible and dangerous, but welcomed the League of Nations as a new moral and legal authority.[58]
Austrian lawyer and diplomat Alfred Verdross, too, defended the
primacy of international law, although from a perspective of natural
law.[59] Political scientist Quincy Wright suggested yet another theory of
sovereignty in which states were intermediates between international
and municipal law. A sovereign state, in Wright's view, was in control
of municipal law but subject to international law. Sanctions, then,
existed to protect weaker states from being subjected to the municipal
law of a stronger state – in other words, sanctions *preserved* sovereignty rather than undermining it.[60] The only restriction that 'collective security' implied for national sovereignty was the right to 'private
war', but that right, as most observers now agreed, ranked lower than
the benefits of peace. Wright summarised his argument in a simple
formula: "Legal sovereignty can exist with collective security; military
sovereignty cannot".[61] But the question was whether 'collective security' could be put into practice at all.

Sanctions and the League of Nations

If 'collective security' was to work, the international community
needed a viable institutional apparatus to hold states accountable
and to impose sanctions.[62] The Covenant was the first international
treaty that translated these ideas into a comprehensive legal framework. Article X protected the "territorial integrity and existing political independence of all Members of the League". The next article

---

[57] Ernst Jäckh, *The New Germany: Three Lectures by Ernst Jäckh* (Oxford, 1927),
p. 95.
[58] Louis Le Fur, *Nationalisme et Internationalisme* (Lyon, 1926), pp. 18–21.
[59] Alfred Verdross, *Die Einheit des rechtlichen Weltbildes* (Tübingen, 1923),
pp. 76–7; and Alfred Verdross, *Völkerrecht* (Berlin, 1937).
[60] Wright, 'National Sovereignty and Collective Security'.   [61] Ibid., p. 102.
[62] Mulder, *The Economic Weapon*.

introduced the condition that an attack against any one member constituted "a matter of concern to the whole League" and entrusted the League with "any action that may be deemed wise" to re-establish peace. If the dispute could not be settled by arbitration, as outlined in Articles XII–XV, and if an international intervention was inevitable, then Article XVI offered potential sanctions, both economic and military, as well as the expulsion of a member-state. Article XVI also put the Council in charge of coordinating any sanctions and thus established an international authority to replace bi- and multilateral agreements.

By the mid-1920s, the League of Nations had established a certain working routine. The Council operated a blockade commission under the chairmanship of Robert Cecil, the British wartime blockade minister who advocated a strict economic sanctions regime.[63] This allowed the League to oversee the peaceful solution of a series of disputes, including the Finnish–Swedish quarrel over the Åland Islands, the Polish-Lithuanian disagreement over Vilna, the 1923 Corfu incident, and the 1925 Greco-Bulgarian border dispute.[64] However, all of these were smaller powers that were essentially pressured into accepting terms determined by the great powers. Nor were any sanctions actually used. The real test cases were yet to come. It was questionable, to say the least, if the League's sanction system would prevent aggression on a larger scale.

The most obvious problem of the League was the (temporary) absence of key international players, including Germany, the United States, and the Soviet Union, which made the alliance anything but global. The fact that Germany was denied accession was particularly problematic as it suggested that the League was an exclusive club, not a universal alliance. What is more, the Covenant neither defined what 'collective' meant, nor did it specify a minimum number of states to consider it as such – a fact that David Mitrany found to be a "great

---

[63] B. J. C. McKercher, 'The League of Nations and the Problem of Collective Security, 1919–1945', in The United Nations Library at Geneva (ed.), *The League of Nations 1920–1946* (Geneva, 1996).

[64] James Barros, *The Corfu Incident of 1923: Mussolini and the League of Nations* (Princeton, 1965); James Barros, *The Aland Islands Question: Its Settlement by the League of Nations* (Yale, 1968); James Barros, *The League of Nations and the Great Powers: The Greek-Bulgarian Incident, 1925* (Oxford, 1970).

obstacle".[65] Without all-encompassing membership, the Swiss jurist
Dietrich Schindler warned, 'collective security' might degenerate into a
simple alliance of states, resembling pre-1919 conditions.[66] Or, worse
even, the League might turn into a supranational autocracy that legit-
imised "holy wars" on behalf of international justice, as Helena
Swanwick cautioned.[67]

As a result, the architects of IR began to invite states to join the
League or, where membership was not an option, to design alternative
agreements. The most ambitious internationalists, such as Toynbee,
demanded from 1919 that Germany should join the League of
Nations.[68] Throughout the 1920s, James Shotwell tirelessly campaigned for a transatlantic security treaty to include the United
States. The first success of their efforts was Germany's admission to
the League in 1926 which marked not just a political turn but, more
generally, revived the hope for a universal alliance. The second step
was the 1928 Kellogg–Briand Pact which extended the reach of 'collective security' beyond the League's membership, most importantly to
the United States and the Soviet Union. Widespread participation was
crucial, as Zimmern argued, because 'collective security' was a "democratic" exercise that required "common effort".[69]

By the beginning of the 1930s, most of the world was part of some
collective agreement, at least on paper. Of course, membership was
often neither permanent nor meaningful – Spain, Japan, Germany,
Italy, and later the Soviet Union being the most infamous defectors.
Membership excluded territories under colonial control, mandates,
and parts of South America, notably Argentina and Brazil. The
United States remained reluctant and Japan was often sidelined. This
made 'collective security' effectively a European-dominated enterprise
that was mostly disinterested in conflicts involving smaller powers – for
example, the Chaco War between Paraguay and Bolivia. In many
ways, it helped to transform nineteenth-century imperialism into a

---

[65] Mitrany, *The Problem of International Sanctions*, p. 75. See also John Fischer
Williams, *Sanctions under the Covenant* (Oxford, 1936), p. 134.
[66] Dietrich Schindler, 'The Notion of Neutrality in a System Including Repression
of Resort to War', in IIIC, *Collective Security* (Paris, 1936), p. 9.
[67] Helena Swanwick and W. Arnold-Forster, *Sanctions of the League of Nations
Covenant* (London, 1928), p. 22.
[68] Arnold Toynbee to Gilbert Murray, 27 July 1919, Arnold Toynbee Papers,
Box 72.
[69] Zimmern, 'The Problem of Collective Security', p. 4.

new style of Eurocentric world domination, disguised as universal collaboration. In reality, 'collective security' was a European project, just as the League was "a regional system, the region being Europe", as F. S. Northedge put it.[70]

Fluctuating membership also caused a governance problem. Having Germany or other major powers join would upset the level of relative influence of the founding members. Having major powers outside, on the other hand, risked for collective action to turn into "offensive alliances", Mitrany warned.[71] The solution was to find a middle way – to integrate as many members as possible while gently shifting national defence capacities to the international level. But this was not easy, given that partial alliances continued to shape the world. Between 1920 and 1927 alone, the League's own *Systematic Survey of the Arbitration Conventions and Treaties of Mutual Security* listed thirty-one bi- and multilateral agreements.[72] Since it proved so difficult to integrate all governments into an effective sanctions scheme, the advocates of 'collective security' settled for a less ambitious goal. According to French politician Léon Blum, security was above all "a state of consciousness".[73] The Austro-Hungarian lawyer and diplomat Stefan Osusky also employed the notion of a "collective consciousness" in his work on European security.[74] If not a universal alliance, perhaps the League could at least generate a feeling of security? But what did that mean?

Unfortunately, many passages in the Covenant left enormous room for interpretation, as Alfred Zimmern pointed out.[75] No one knew, for example, how "immediately" sanctions should be implemented, nor were the means clearly defined. Zimmern regarded the guarantees promised in Article X as "limited", and suspected Article XV to be

---

[70] Northedge, *The League of Nations*, p. 137.
[71] Mitrany, *The Problem of International Sanctions*, p. 28. See also Swanwick and Arnold-Forster, *Sanctions of the League of Nations Covenant*, p. 19.
[72] League of Nations, *Arbitration and Security: Systematic Survey of the Arbitration Conventions and Treaties of Mutual Security Deposited with the League of Nations*, 2nd ed. (Geneva, 1927), p. 353.
[73] Léon Blum, *Les Problèmes de la Paix* (Paris, 1931), p. 97.
[74] Stefan Osusky, 'L'Europe centrale et l'avenir du système collectif', *Politique étrangère* 5 (1936), p. 9.
[75] See Alfred Zimmern, *The League of Nations and the Rule of Law, 1918–1935* (London, 1936), p. 398.

no more than a "loophole for war".[76] Mitrany complained that the infamous 'sanctions article' – Article XVI – was "worded so vaguely that extraordinary things could be read into it".[77] The 'sanctions article' also banned "personal intercourse" between the nationals of the Covenant-breaking state and foreigners – an "awkward phrase", as Charles Manning noted.[78] What is more, the sanctions described in Article XVI were only to be applied in order to "prevent or stop illegal *war*", leaving a legal gap for governments violating treaties without actually waging war.[79] There was a good case, however, as French jurist Georges Scelle pointed out, to punish not only war but "any form of armed coercion".[80] As these examples show, the imprecise language of the Covenant left many scholars somewhat puzzled. On the other hand, the vagueness of the Covenant may not actually have been a lapse but an intentional way of keeping international law "fluid and undefined", primarily by the British whose legal tradition and imperial interests did not lend themselves to fixed commitments, as the writer and air ministry official J. M. Spaight suggested.[81]

Besides nebulous language, the Covenant also failed to specify a quick and transparent procedure for the implementation of sanctions. As British feminist-pacifist Ethel Williams pointed out, it was impossible to identify and punish an aggressor within a few days, which was often the critical interval.[82] The Council was both unable and unwilling to act as an international police force. Bureaucratic efficiency was not a strength of the League, as even its most ardent supporters admitted.[83] What many analysts demanded were fast executive decisions by a strong Council and a less consensual voting system. The unanimity requirement in the Council and the absence of an effective

[76] 'A Historical Note on Collective Security', Alfred Zimmern, prepared for ISC, April 1935, Alfred Zimmern Papers, Box 86.
[77] Mitrany, *The Problem of International Sanctions*, p. 9.
[78] C. A. W. Manning, *Sanctions under the Covenant: Montague Burton International Relations Lectures* (Nottingham, 1936), p. 13.
[79] Wright, 'National Sovereignty and Collective Security', p. 101 [emphasis added].
[80] Georges Scelle, 'Theory of International Government', in IIIC, *Collective Security* (Paris, 1936), p. 11.
[81] Spaight, *Pseudo-Security*, p. 4.
[82] She cited France's occupation of the Ruhr and the Corfu incident. See Ethel Williams in WILPF, *Report of the Fourth Congress* (Geneva, 1924), p. 59.
[83] League of Nations Union, World Defence No. 348 (1933), pp. 26–8.

court, so they worried, prevented any collective action at all.[84] To overcome the problem of delays, American diplomat Allen Dulles suggested appointing League of Nations "reporters" who could investigate on the spot immediately in the case of a dispute and would provide the Council with impartial information.[85] If executive functions were transferred from the national to the international level, Dulles argued, the respective authorities had to be equipped with adequate powers. On the other hand, Jäckh objected, the advantage of 'new diplomacy' was precisely the fact that going to war now took months rather than days.[86] In practice, however, sanctions took much longer to be implemented, whereas national attacks were still launched at each government's convenience. What 'collective security' required therefore was a strategic advantage over national action.

If disarmament and arbitration – the new normal modes of settling international disputes – failed, there had to be a plan for abnormal cases, a corrective instrument to control and deter potential defectors. This logic occurred to the architects of IR as it had to the authors of the Covenant. South African statesman Jan Smuts actually identified sanctions as "the most important question of all".[87] The final document, however, left room for speculation on the nature of sanctions and delegated further interpretation to the Council. The 1924 Geneva Protocol was an attempt to clarify and operationalise the sanctions scheme. It spelt out the procedure by which member states could contribute by "military, naval and air forces" to international interventions. Mitrany felt that the Protocol was "much more complete and war-tight than the Covenant".[88] By introducing binding arbitration and automatic sanctions, however, the Protocol demanded unprecedented national commitments and failed to be ratified. This highlighted, once again, concerns about national sovereignty. Whereas some feared that the League's sanctions were not deterrent enough, the British government worried that they would commit them to interventions outside their own sphere of interest.

Others opposed sanctions on humanitarian grounds. Even non-military sanctions could lead to the paralysis of entire industries and

---

[84] Mitrany, *The Problem of International Sanctions*, p. 6.
[85] Allen Dulles, in IIIC, *Collective Security* (Paris, 1936), p. 276.
[86] Jäckh, *The New Germany*, p. 92.
[87] Jan Smuts, *The League of Nations: A Practical Suggestion* (London, 1918), p. 60.
[88] Mitrany, *The Problem of International Sanctions*, p. 10.

thereby cause great harm to innocent civilians, Jerome D. Greene argued.[89] Women were often wary of sanctions, particularly military ones, fearing that they would be used either ineffectively or at the expense of the civilian population. The South African pacifist writer Olive Schreiner had long emphasised the effects of warfare on the civilian population.[90] Delegates at the 1915 conference in The Hague were split over military intervention as a last resort, but ultimately included "social, moral and economic sanctions" in their manifesto.[91] It is interesting to note that they combined sanctions and the female franchise in the same resolution of their 20-points programme.[92] By linking diplomatic reforms with long-standing suffragist demands they established the basis of a feminist approach to IR, rather than just IR scholarship written by women. Helena Swanwick defended this approach in a 1928 debate with William Arnold-Forster, commenting on gender roles in international affairs: "I have often reflected how much safer women would be if men left off protecting them".[93]

Over the following years, Swanwick became one of the most outspoken critics of sanctions. Although not a pacifist-at-all-costs, she opposed military sanctions both because of her opposition to war in general as well as because she distrusted the decision-making structures for imposing international sanctions.[94] "Pooled security", as she called it, did not solve the fundamental risks of anarchic violence. Even if the League succeeded in building some form of 'collective security' – which, by the mid-1930s, seemed increasingly unlikely – it would still risk abusing military force, and cause unnecessary human suffering as

---

[89] Greene, *Idealism and Realism in Efforts toward Peace*, p. 16.
[90] Olive Schreiner, 'Women and War' (1911), in Uys Krige (ed.), *Olive Schreiner: A Selection* (Cape Town, 1968), p. 70.
[91] Brochure, *Women's International League for Peace and Freedom, 1915–1938: A Venture in Internationalism* (Geneva: Maison Internationale, 1938), WILPF/ 20/5, folder 1, LSE Archives; Harriet Hyman Alonson (ed.), *Women at The Hague: The International Congress of Women and Its Results* (Chicago, 2013), pp. xviii–xix.
[92] WILPF, *Extract from the Forthcoming Report of the International Congress of Women: Held at Zurich, May 12–17, 1919* (Geneva, 1919[?]), WILPF/5/7, LSE Archives.
[93] Swanwick and Arnold-Forster, *Sanctions of the League of Nations Covenant*, p. 25.
[94] Lucian M. Ashworth, 'Feminism, War and the Prospect of International Government: Helena Swanwick and the Lost Feminists of Interwar International Relations', *Limerick Papers in Politics and Public Administration* 2 (2008), pp. 9–10.

well as undermine the project of international cooperation as a whole.[95]

There was a notion of essentialism in Swanwick's argument, as was the case for much of early twentieth-century feminist pacifism. Since women were the "guardians of life", so that argument went, they were naturally more sensitive to the effects of war.[96] However, many authors went beyond straightforward essentialism and acknowledged that women could be "as virulently militarist" and "as blindly partisan' as men.[97] Giving women a voice in international politics was only one among several policy proposals. As early as 1919, Anna B. Eckstein had presented a sanctions scheme to enforce compliance with international law.[98] Her concept specified various types of sanctions, ranging from the suspension of diplomatic relationships and the exclusion from the Universal Postal Union to penalty tariffs, embargoes, denial of loans, outright international boycott or, as a last resort, international military coercion.[99] Lacking access to diplomatic circles, however, Eckstein's work remained unheard and has since been largely forgotten.[100] Both Swanwick and Eckstein wrote from the perspective of a cosmopolitan elite and it is important not to forget that only a minority of women's organisations were outspokenly pacifist. Their work nonetheless highlights the diversity of the approaches to security that have subsequently been lumped together as 'idealism' or 'pacifism'.[101]

Perhaps the most radical way to realise 'collective security' was the idea of an international police force. This concept was primarily promoted by the New Commonwealth Institute, a pressure group cofounded and financed by the liberal philanthropist David Davies, the same man who had endowed the Wilson Chair at Aberystwyth and

---

[95] Swanwick, *Pooled Security*, p. 18.
[96] Agnes Maude Royden, 'War and the Women's Movement', in G. Lowes Dickinson and Charles Roden Buxton (eds.), *Towards a Lasting Settlement* (London, 1915), p. 134.
[97] Ibid., pp. 136–7.
[98] Eckstein, *Staatenschutzvertrag zur Sicherung des Weltfriedens*.
[99] Ibid., p. 26.
[100] See Rüdiger Spenlen, *Anna B. Eckstein: Coburger Pazifistin und Vordenkerin für den Völkerbund* (Coburg, 1985), Box 2, Anna B. Eckstein Collected Papers, Peace Collection, Swarthmore College.
[101] Jan Stöckmann, 'Women, Wars, and World Affairs: Recovering Feminist International Relations, 1915–39', *Review of International Studies* 44:2 (2018), pp. 215–35.

donated to the League of Nations Union. Having witnessed the failure of the 1924 Geneva Protocol and the Disarmament Conference, Davies suggested moving past verbal assurances and forming a common international military force.[102] He received support from influential public figures, including Winston Churchill, Clement Attlee, Norman Angell, Lord Cecil, Philip Noel-Baker, Montague Burton, Arthur Salter, and Harold Temperley.[103] Interestingly, the New Commonwealth Institute also boasted a range of prominent international members, including Jäckh who emigrated to London in 1934.[104] On the French side, Air Minister Pierre Cot was a prominent supporter, as was the historian and co-founder of the Geneva Graduate Institute Paul Mantoux.[105] The Vienna Konsularakademie expressed its sympathies, too, although its statutes prohibited affiliations with partisan movements.[106] The idea of an international police was discussed by the delegates of the 1932 WILPF Congress in Grenoble.[107] Headquartered at Smith Square in Westminster, the New Commonwealth Institute had members in more than forty countries. It published a monthly periodical and launched public campaigns.[108]

At the core of Davies' project was the idea that an international police force, including especially aerial forces, would increase the credibility of the League of Nations. The international police would be commanded and controlled by a common international body. It would have to be superior, in number and armament, to national forces which would be turned into domestic police services. If every state contributed to the cost of a united force, so Davies argued, the

---

[102] Davies, The Problem of the Twentieth Century, pp. 361–8.
[103] Winston Churchill, Speech Delivered at a Luncheon at the Dorchester Hotel, London, on November 25th, 1936 (London, 1936), p. 14.
[104] Index of New Commonwealth Institute Memoranda, 1935, Dossier 2381, Box R4010, League of Nations Archives.
[105] Memo, 'Military Force or Air Police', by Pierre Cot, March 1935; and Brochure, The New Commonwealth Institute, 22 March 1935, Dossier 2381, Box R4010, League of Nations Archives.
[106] Friedrich Hlavac to Ernst Jäckh, 12 April 1934, OeStA, Archiv der Konsularakademie, Box 44.
[107] Swedish aviator Tord Ångström had argued for the abolishment of air forces and for the re-allocation of air budgets to civil causes in aviation. See 'Aviation in the Service of International Life', in WILPF, Report of the Seventh Congress (Geneva, 1932), pp. 41–5.
[108] Winston Churchill, Speech Delivered at a Luncheon at the Dorchester Hotel, London, on November 25th, 1936 (London, 1936), p. 13.

total financial cost would decrease. The international police would essentially replace the League's "vague and nebulous" sanctions system, Davies argued.[109] By centralising executive authority, a common army would also improve the speed of reaction and make it easier to determine the aggressor. Most importantly, it translated 'collective security' into a physical apparatus, rather than resting on verbal assurances.

On the other hand, critics such as Quincy Wright argued, a supranational police force would undermine national sovereignty far more than inter-state collaboration.[110] What is more, it would only relocate, not abolish, the problem of militarism. Swanwick, one of its most prolific critics, accused men of disguising their militarism by calling their war "sanctions", and their armies "police".[111] She attacked Norman Angell for supporting the New Commonwealth Institute's plan and for overlooking the fact that "defensive" or "preventive" wars could never be clearly defined and that they had caused a great deal of suffering in the past. An international police would just lead to "new wars for old".[112] Or, as her colleague Kathleen Courtney put it, "Satan cannot cast out Satan".[113] Swanwick feared that an international police force would fall into the hands of irresponsible leaders, rather than constituting a genuine force of justice.[114] Moreover, she argued, the analogy between domestic and international police forces was flawed because domestic police forces were dealing with unarmed civilians whereas an international police had to deal with armed states and lacked organisational authority.[115] Swanwick's reluctance was shared by other WILPF members as well as by Gilbert Murray and Robert Cecil.[116]

The real difficulties in internationalising security, however, surfaced only when it was applied in practice. Putting up a universal alliance was complicated by the special interests of major powers, notably by Germany's geographical location, by American isolationist reluctance,

[109] Davies, *The Problem of the Twentieth Century*, p. 143.
[110] Wright, 'National Sovereignty and Collective Security', p. 101.
[111] Swanwick, *Pooled Security*, p. 11.
[112] Helena Swanwick, *New Wars for Old* (London, 1934).
[113] Kathleen Courtney, 'Preface', in Swanwick, *New Wars for Old* (London, 1934), p. iii.
[114] Swanwick, *Pooled Security*, p. 20.
[115] Swanwick and Arnold-Forster, *Sanctions of the League of Nations Covenant*, p. 21.
[116] Gilbert Murray to Toynbee, 2 March 1934, Arnold Toynbee Papers, Box 72.

and by British imperialism. Once again, the architects of IR took up the
opportunity and swapped into their roles of advisors and negotiators.
One of the seminal works on 'collective security', David Mitrany's *The
Problem of International Sanctions* (1925), grew out of a collaboration
with James T. Shotwell on a draft for the 1924 Geneva Protocol.[117]
During the Manchurian and Abyssinian crises, scholars of IR campaigned extensively with politicians and the press, though their success
was limited. Conversely, politicians and diplomats such as Pierre Cot
intervened in academic debates.[118] Proceedings at academic conferences were shaped by 'real-world' events, and in 1936 the American
lawyer Philip Jessup noted, without regret, that while theory had "not
been excluded from consideration, ... the guiding principle has been
the realistic one".[119] It were real-world test cases, then, that would
determine how 'collective security' might work, if at all.

Reactions to Manchuria and Abyssinia

Interventions by the League of Nations in international disputes were
not new. Since the Paris Peace Conference, the world had never been
static but subject to recurring disputes over territorial borders, national
minorities, and armaments. Within this environment, the architects of
IR had established themselves as authoritative commentators and
defined their intellectual programme in relation to current affairs.[120]
They discussed both successful interventions, such as the national
status of the Åland Islands in 1921 or the settlement of the Graeco-
Bulgarian dispute in 1925, and less successful ones, such as the failure
of a Polish-Lithuanian rapprochement or the escalation of hostilities
between Bolivia and Paraguay.[121] But, as Toynbee observed in the

[117] See Mitrany, *The Problem of International Sanctions*, p. v.
[118] See, for example, 'Military Force or Air Police', by Pierre Cot, March 1935,
Dossier 2381, Box R4010, League of Nations Archives.
[119] Philip Jessup, *International Security: The American Role in Collective Action
for Peace* (New York, 1935), p. viii.
[120] The Institute of Pacific Relations thought it was "important that the American
Council should clarify its position in relation to the Sino-Japanese crisis".
Minutes of the Annual Meeting, American Council, IPR, 4 February 1932,
James T. Shotwell Papers, Box 30.
[121] Georges Lechartier, 'The Useless League', *The North American Review*
213:785 (1921), pp. 457–8; Hamilton Holt, 'The League of Nations Effective',
The Annals of the American Academy of Political and Social Science 96 (1921),
p. 3; Arthur Sweetser, 'The First Year and a Half of the League of Nations', *The

Survey of International Affairs (1932), the Manchurian crisis was the first test of the security system by a major power (with the exception of the 1923 Corfu incident).[122] The Manchurian conflict exceeded previous conflicts in terms of scope and political repercussions. This conflict had "global implications", a German author noted.[123]

Italy's campaign in Ethiopia and Germany's occupation of Czechoslovakia continued this trend. These conflicts dramatically showed the effect of dictatorial regimes on the League of Nations system and they have rightly been regarded as its decisive tests. Their "evil spirit" undermined the logic of international cooperation so profoundly that it became doubtful if the League's arsenal was suited at all for protecting peace in a world of authoritarian leaders.[124] Was it possible to fight the enemies of democracy by democratic means? Could governments who violated international law be stopped by diplomacy and sanctions?

IR experts grappled with these questions throughout the 1930s as they watched the Manchurian and Abyssinian crises unfold. The majority of them correctly identified the aggressors, acknowledged the shortcomings of 'collective security', and campaigned for improvements. Some of the more critical IR observers also noted the "imperialist" elements of the two crises and framed their solutions in terms of "de-colonisation".[125] At the same time, Japanese and Italian scholars

Annals of the American Academy 96 (1921), p. 28; Edward Mead Earle, 'Problems of Eastern and Southeastern Europe', *Proceedings of the Academy of Political Science in the City of New York* 12:1 (1926), p. 268; David Mitrany, 'The Possibility of a Balkan Locarno', *International Conciliation* 11 (1926), p. 168; George de Fiedorowicz, 'Historical Survey of the Application of Sanctions', *Transactions of the Grotius Society* 22 (1936), p. 118; Robert H. Lord, 'Lithuania and Poland', *Foreign Affairs* 1:4 (1923); N. Andrew N. Cleven, 'The Dispute between Bolivia and Paraguay', *Current History* 29:4 (1929), pp. 661–3; William L. Schurz, 'The Chaco Dispute between Bolivia and Paraguay', *Foreign Affairs* 7:4 (1929), pp. 650–5. For a comprehensive survey of the more than 40 security disputes put before the Council, see James T. Shotwell, *Lessons on Security and Disarmament: From the History of the League of Nations* (New York, 1949), pp. 45–80.

[122] Arnold Toynbee, *Survey of International Affairs 1931* (Oxford, 1932), p. 475.
[123] F. W. Mohr, 'Die Grundlagen des Mandschureikonflikts', *Europäische Gespräche* 11 (1931), p. 540.
[124] Alfred Zimmern, 'The League's Handling of the Italo-Abyssinian Dispute', *International Affairs* 14:6 (1935), p. 759.
[125] Moritz Bonn, 'The Age of Counter-Colonisation', *International Affairs* 13:6 (1934), p. 845.

presented far-fetched justifications for the respective attacks.[126] Once again, academic settings served as venues for quasi-diplomatic debate. Nonetheless, most IR scholars ultimately remained optimistic about the prospects of the League and collective guarantees. Authors such as Charles Webster, Lucy Zimmern, or Charles Saroléa all affirmed their "belief" in the League.[127] Their confidence may seem misguided in retrospect, but it was neither naïve nor detached from current events. It was all about shaping the conflicts and solutions as they evolved under their eyes.

Japan's invasion of Manchuria, following the staged assault on the South Manchuria Railway near Mukden on 18 September 1931, shocked the IR community and fuelled the debate on the effectiveness of the League's machinery of 'collective security'. News from the incident reached Geneva in the midst of preparations for the World Disarmament Conference. Despite the presence of numerous government representatives, however, no resolution was quickly agreed on. One British delegate was so unprepared that he confused the Four- and Nine-Power Washington Treaties.[128] The commission entrusted by the League and headed by Victor Bulwer-Lytton took more than a year to produce its report – the Lytton Report.[129] Rather than launching quick investigations and imposing sanctions, the League lost crucial time and passed a most rudimentary resolution, Toynbee lamented.[130] The League's reluctance rested, in turn, on that of individual governments who were either indifferent or outspokenly pro-Japanese. The British ambassador in Tokyo defended the Japanese government and argued that it was "impossible [for Japan] to withdraw before negotiating".[131]

---

[126] Francesco Coppola, in IIIC, *Collective Security* (Paris, 1936), p. 166.

[127] C. K. Webster, *The League of Nations in Theory and Practice* (London, 1933); Lucy A. Zimmern, *Must the League Fail?* (London, 1932), p. 10; Charles Sarolea, *The Policy of Sanctions and the Failure of the League of Nations* (London, 1936), p. 7.

[128] Alfred Zimmern, 'Note by the Chairman', 11 March 1935, Alfred Zimmern Papers, Box 98.

[129] League of Nations, Report of the Commission of Enquiry, Official No. C.663M.320 (October 1932).

[130] Toynbee, *Survey of International Affairs 1931*, p. 486.

[131] British Embassy Tokyo, 27 October 1931, The National Archives, FO/262/1774 Japan.China, Papers 313–354.

There were no illusions amongst IR scholars about Japan's responsibility for the dispute in Manchuria. The invasion was a "clear and unmistakable" violation of the Covenant, the Kellogg–Briand Pact, and the Nine-Power Treaty, as Zimmern pointed out in a 1932 article prepared for *Headway*, the League of Nations Union's house magazine.[132] The article was, however, withdrawn at the request of the Union's president Cecil, probably because Zimmern's analysis was too openly critical of the League. Cecil himself defended the Council and put the blame on "Japanese militarism" and "Chinese anarchy".[133] Not only did Zimmern argue that "the moral authority of the Council had been greatly weakened", but he also explained that the circumstances had actually been favourable for a League-coordinated solution. The Assembly was in full session at the time of the incident and the nature of East Asian politics was not as difficult as sometimes claimed. A peaceful solution was certainly possible. Instead, consultations in Geneva adopted the character of old-fashioned diplomacy, reflecting the lack of will of the great powers, while the public was conveniently left in the dark about the course of events. By the time of the final Council meeting on 10 December 1931, the Japanese army had advanced far into Manchuria, with casualties in the hundreds.

A memorandum prepared by the New York Council on Foreign Relations in collaboration with League of Nations Secretariat member Nitobe Inazō offered similar conclusions. Japan had violated major international treaties by occupying Manchuria "beyond any defensive necessity".[134] It had shown its aggressive intentions by refusing to arbitrate which, according to the provisions of the Covenant, constituted the case for international sanctions in order to restore Chinese rights. As a solution, the memo suggested that Manchuria be put under international control, similar to the Saar or Gdańsk, and that its status be decided in a referendum after ten years. The East Asia expert F. W. Mohr, too, condemned Japan for having violated China's territorial integrity, and advocated an international economic zone in

---

[132] Alfred Zimmern, 'The Action of the Council in the Manchurian Dispute', written for *Headway* but withdrawn, 1932, Alfred Zimmern Papers, Box 98.
[133] Viscount Cecil, in League of Nations Union (ed.), *The League, Manchuria and Disarmament* (London, 1931), pp. 24, 29.
[134] Memorandum and letter by Quincy Wright to Arnold Toynbee, 20 September 1932, Arnold Toynbee Papers, Box 72.

Manchuria.[135] WILPF launched an international campaign against arms trade with Japan.[136] Most IR authors agreed with the view that Japan had inflicted undue harm on China and damaged the "spirit of the League of Nations".[137]

IR scholars were alert to the wider implications of the Manchurian crisis. In particular, they recognised the risk of creating a precedent. If Japan's occupation of Manchuria remained unanswered, future infringements of international law would be all the more difficult to punish. The most important thing to be lost in Manchuria was "confidence", as Asian specialist Victor Frêne put it.[138] In the ensuing debate, Western reactions to Manchuria received at least as much criticism as Japan's behaviour itself. Gilbert Murray called the British government's line "unwise and dishonourable", as it both harmed the League's reputation and made war more likely.[139] Zimmern blamed the "inertia of public opinion" in Britain for ruining the League's achievements of the 1920s.[140] Philip Noel-Baker heavily criticised the British government for its half-hearted opposition to Japan's foreign policy. He submitted a paper to Chatham House calling for faster enquiries, an impartial report, and a strong British-led resolution at the League of Nations Council.[141] In terms of sanctions, he demanded restrictions on loans, an arms embargo, and more diplomatic pressure by withdrawing ambassadors from Tokyo. He also criticised the lax position of the press.

[135] Mohr, 'Die Grundlagen des Mandschureikonflikts', pp. 541, 553.
[136] Camille Drevent, in WILPF, *Report of the Seventh Congress* (Geneva, 1932), p. 25.
[137] Hans Wehberg, 'Hat Japan durch die Besetzung der Mandschurei das Völkerrecht verletzt?', *Die Friedens-Warte* 32:1 (1932), p. 11. See also, H. C. Yung, 'Les Causes Profondes du Conflit Sino-Japonais', *L'Esprit International* 7 (1932); Guglielmo Ferrero, 'L'Europe, l'Extreme Orient et la Société des Nations', *L'Esprit International* 6 (1932), pp. 339–47.
[138] Victor Frêne, *The Meaning of the Manchurian Crisis* (Shanghai, 1931), p. 16.
[139] Gilbert Murray to Wignall Hodson, 9 January 1933, Gilbert Murray Papers, Box 216.
[140] Alfred Zimmern, 'Note by the Chairman', 11 March 1935, Alfred Zimmern Papers, Box 98.
[141] Philip Noel-Baker, 'Note on the Breakdown of the Collective System over the Manchurian Dispute', 26 February 1935, Alfred Zimmern Papers, Box 98. See also Kingsley Martin, 'British Opinion and the Abyssinian Dispute: A Survey of the Daily Papers during the Second Half of August, 1935', *The Political Quarterly* 6:4 (1935).

Accusations against individual governments turned into more general criticism of the League of Nations. The German pacifist lawyer Hans Wehberg argued that the League of Nations bore at least as much responsibility as Japan for the escalation of the Manchurian conflict because Geneva had failed to define a clear directive on military occupations and civil war.[142] The reason for the crises of 'collective security' during the 1930s, according to Wehberg, was its relative negligence during the 1920s. Member states had failed to equip the League with a robust sanctions apparatus. As long as collective guarantees remained vague and feeble, the incentive for potential aggressors to comply with international law decreased. By 1930, the League had settled into a comfortable *modus vivendi* which postponed pressing questions about a universal security alliance and created an illusion of security or, as the British air specialist J. M. Spaight labelled it, "pseudo-security".[143]

Every Council meeting without tangible results made the League of Nations look more like a facade and its officials like puppets. The once praised "spirit of Geneva" now took the form of "Secretariat camaraderie", preventing rigorous decisions in favour of easily agreeable but toothless resolutions.[144] Zimmern was outraged that "the Japanese delegation gave an evening party in the week following the occupation of Mukden and all the world and his wife attended it".[145] Japanese propaganda did its best to hinder international responses. Pamphlets giving one-sided accounts were sooner and more easily available than official reports.[146] Some observers concluded from these shortcomings the "futility of the League of Nations" as soon as 1931, but the majority remained in favour of international cooperation.[147]

---

[142] Hans Wehberg, 'Hat Japan durch die Besetzung der Mandschurei das Völkerrecht verletzt?', *Die Friedens-Warte* 32:1 (1932), p. 12.

[143] Spaight, *Pseudo-Security*.

[144] Alfred Zimmern, 'Note by the Chairman', 11 March 1935, Alfred Zimmern Papers, Box 98.

[145] Ibid.

[146] See, for example, Manchuria Young Men's Federation, *An Appeal by Japanese People Concerning the Manchurian People* (Dairen, 1931); The Servants' Society of the South Manchuria Railway Company, *Declaration on Sino-Japanese Clashes* (Dairen, 1931).

[147] See League of Nations Union, *The League, Manchuria and Disarmament* (London, 1931), p. 2.

Manchuria was a disappointment for the advocates of 'collective security'. But rather than causing outright despair, it inspired a new wave of scholarship and policy proposals to fix the problem. Zimmern, who had warned for years that the League would not work without the willingness of its members, was distressed about the weak response to Japan's aggression but remained confident that 'collective security' could work.[148] Despite his criticism of the Council's performance in the Manchurian crisis, he was convinced that the Covenant was not yet "dead" – it was just "sleeping".[149] Noel-Baker, too, was embittered that Britain had "sabotaged the League and refused to carry out our pledges under the Covenant in Manchuria", and announced in March 1933 that he would devote the following two years of his life to the campaign for stronger sanctions, by using his role in the Labour Party.[150] That same month, Japan withdrew from the League as the first of the future Axis powers.

Four years after the Mukden incident at the South Manchurian Railway, another border friction disrupted the Geneva idyl and prompted extensive debate among IR scholars. The clash between Ethiopian and Italo-Somali forces at the Walwal oasis in December 1934 initiated a series of complaints and negotiations at the League of Nations which resulted in a prohibition of arms sales to the region but failed to produce a comprehensive solution. When Italian Prime Minister Benito Mussolini launched a full-scale attack on Ethiopia in October 1935 the British and French governments secretly decided to partition the country and thus betrayed Ethiopian interests. British Foreign Secretary Samuel Hoare and French Prime Minister Pierre Laval, the brokers of the infamous pact, were worried about growing tensions in Europe, particularly after Germany's reoccupation of the Rhineland in March 1936. They were willing to contain Hitler at almost any price and essentially gave Italy a blank cheque in East Africa. When the agreement was leaked to the press in December

---

[148] Paul Rich, 'Alfred Zimmern's Cautious Idealism: The League of Nations, International Education, and the Commonwealth', in David Long and Peter Wilson (eds.), *Thinkers of the Twenty Years' Crisis: Inter-war Idealism Reassessed* (Oxford, 1995), p. 85.
[149] Alfred Zimmern, 'The Action of the Council in the Manchurian Dispute', written for *Headway* but withdrawn, 1932, Alfred Zimmern Papers, Box 98.
[150] Noel-Baker to Gilbert Murray, 28 March 1933, Gilbert Murray Papers, Box 217.

1935 it caused a political scandal. Once again, 'collective security' was re-interpreted according to great power interests and sanctions failed to have the desired effect.[151] Was this outcome inevitable? How, if at all, could collective guarantees credibly deter aggressors and protect smaller states?

Like other conflicts, the Abyssinia crisis did not come without warning, nor did its European implications. As early as February 1933, Kathleen Courtney had warned Gilbert Murray of the growing tension between France, Italy, and Germany.[152] Mussolini's imperial aspirations, too, had long been known.[153] The relapse into militarist muscle-flexing was well noted by contemporary IR authors. As in the Manchurian crisis, there were few illusions about the intentions of the aggressor. In June 1935, Gilbert Murray confined to Montague Burton, the sponsor of Oxford's IR chair, that if Mussolini was allowed to wage war on Abyssinia, "the League will have lost practically all its authority".[154] Chatham House picked up the topic and hosted expert debates on the issue. Zimmern made it undoubtedly clear in an October 1935 paper that the Italo-Ethiopian conflict constituted a case of "imperialism" and "power-politics" that revealed the dominance of metropolitan interests.[155]

Throughout the crisis, IR authors followed the course of events and commented upon proposed solutions. They were well informed and critically minded, yet ultimately failed to grasp the root of the problem. In a 1936 study on the state of 'collective security', international lawyer Arnold McNair surveyed the measures taken against Italy – including an arms embargo, the prohibition of loans to the Italian government, and restrictions on exports to Italy for "key materials" such as minerals and transport animals.[156] He argued that collective action on that level was entirely unprecedented and deserved time to

---

[151] See George W. Baer, *Test Case: Italy, Ethiopia, and the League of Nations* (Stanford, 1967).

[152] Kathleen Courtney to Gilbert Murray, 13 February 1933, Gilbert Murray Papers, Box 216.

[153] Robert Gale Woolbert, 'Italian Colonial Expansion in Africa', *The Journal of Modern History* 4:3 (1932), pp. 430–45; Kenneth Scott, 'Mussolini and the Roman Empire', *The Classical Journey* 27:9 (1932), pp. 645–57.

[154] Gilbert Murray to Montague Burton, 29 June 1935, Gilbert Murray Papers, Box 415.

[155] Zimmern, 'The League's Handling of the Italo-Abyssinian Dispute', p. 751.

[156] McNair, 'Collective Security', p. 153.

develop. A series of Chatham House papers made the same apologetic argument that the Abyssinian conflict marked the first time for the League to apply Article XVI and that it would take some exercise to make it work.[157]

Like in the Manchurian case, Mussolini's defendants presented what they claimed to be evidence for Italy's innocence and denounced the League's intervention as unlawful. Their propaganda did not only circulate in the press but received attention from academics, including at Chatham House where the diplomat and historian Luigi Villari portrayed Italy as the victim of East African turmoil and "xenophobia" (sic!).[158] Villari presented Italian foreign policy in the style of an ambassador and answered questions as if on behalf of Mussolini. Academic engagement with official foreign policy was also common practice at the International Studies Conference (ISC). A 1935 memo submitted by two Italian fascists, the lawyer Roberto Forges Davanzati and the journalist Francesco Coppola, provided the "scientific" backing of Mussolini's policies.[159] They demanded the revision of treaties and discredited the concept of 'collective security'. Their argument was that peace required a "real equilibrium of forces and of needs", and that strong powers, if given enough room, would ensure stability and security for all states. They essentially described the revival of the *pax romana* under fascist leadership which Mussolini envisioned.[160] This vision received the warmhearted support of the German ISC delegate, the international lawyer and political advisor Fritz Berber, who himself translated Nazi foreign policy for an academic audience.[161]

More than previous interwar crises, the Italo-Abyssinian conflict underscored the Eurocentrism of the League of Nations. Peace in Europe ranked higher than peace elsewhere. Few pointed this out as vocally as Christine Sandford, the wife of Colonel Daniel Sandford and advisor to Haile Selassie. In an address at Chatham House on

---

[157] Royal Institute of International Affairs, 'Sanctions: The Character of International Sanctions and Their Application', *Information Department Papers* 17 (1935), p. 10.

[158] Luigi Villari, 'Italian Foreign Policy', *International Affairs* 14:3 (1935), pp. 337–9.

[159] IIIC, *Collective Security* (Paris, 1936), p. 7.

[160] Francesco Coppola, in IIIC, *Collective Security* (Paris, 1936), p. 166.

[161] Fritz Berber, in IIIC, *Collective Security* (Paris, 1936), p. 277. See Chapter 6 for more details on Berber's story.

30 January 1936, she explained how Ethiopia was able to reform "from within" and protested vigorously against European countries violating its independence. She also explained that Ethiopians greatly preferred to be called Ethiopians, not Abyssinians.[162] Oxford colonial studies lecturer Margery Perham also presented an African perspective on international relations and drew attention to the "interests of natives".[163] In several letters to the editor of *The Times*, she pointed out the moral and political inconsistency of bombing a people about whom European governments claimed they needed help from the "civilised world".[164] The surgeon John M. Melly wrote a piece in *International Affairs*, reporting about the conflict "from an Ethiopian point of view", and organised an ambulance service for the region.[165] Among the IR scholars who criticised colonial policy were the international lawyers Jan Hendrik Willem Verzijl, who attacked "that fatal illusion of the superiority of our Western civilisation", and Albrecht Mendelssohn Bartholdy who wondered whether Europeans were really as "*forward* as [their] use of the words *backward races*" suggested.[166] But these were exceptions in a field dominated by Western authors and institutions.

Eurocentrism had its racist component, but it also rested on the geostrategic assumption that peace in Europe was a prerequisite for peace elsewhere. Even a liberal anti-fascist like Czech Foreign Minister Edvard Beneš argued during the Abyssinia crisis that his country had a "special mission of peace in Central Europe", rather than international justice.[167] If the Abyssinia crisis could be settled without a European war, he claimed, this would mark "the beginning of a new

[162] [Christine] D. A. Sandford, 'Ethiopia: Reforms from within versus Foreign Control', *International Affairs* XV:2 (1936), p. 192.
[163] Margery Perham, "African Criticisms of International Relations", given to the West African Student Union (WASU), London 17 March 1936, Margery Perham Papers, Box 230.
[164] Margery Perham, 'Letters to the Editor', *The Times*, 5 October 1935 and 22 November 1935.
[165] John M. Melly, 'Ethiopia and the War from the Ethiopian Point of View', *International Affairs* XV:1 (1936), pp. 103–21; John M. Melly, 'An Ambulance Service for Ethiopia', *The Lancet* 226:5846 (1935), pp. 632–3.
[166] Jan Hendrik Willem Verzijl, in IIIC, *Collective Security* (Paris, 1936), p. 180; Albrecht Mendelssohn Bartholdy, *The European Situation* (New Haven, 1927), p. 56 [emphasis in the original].
[167] Eduard Beneš, *The Struggle for Collective Security in Europe and the Italo-Abyssinian War* (Prague, 1935), p. 58.

and more tranquil phase of European politics".[168] As Ernst Jäckh had noted in the late 1920s, Franco-German rapprochement was the key to European reconciliation and in turn global peace. To be "a good German" meant to be "a good European", not a world citizen or an advocate of colonised people.[169] For imperial powers, such as Britain, the spectrum of interests was yet more complicated, having to account for its Dominions and other parts of the empire. International affairs were always seen from different angles, mostly from national or imperial points of view, rarely from the periphery, but never from an 'objective' global one.

Despite the disappointing outcomes of the first test, Quincy Wright argued, the world might learn from the Manchurian and Abyssinian experiences. Unless all great powers thoroughly supported 'collective security', it would be premature to conclude that it had failed entirely.[170] One solution was therefore to strengthen the League by enlarging its membership, although there was little hope after Japan's and Germany's withdrawals in 1933. An alternative response was to withdraw into a more modest collective alliance and, while maintaining the League as a vehicle for international pressure, only to cooperate among those member states that were genuinely prepared to uphold guarantees.[171] A less ambitious League would ensure that treaties were actually respected while commitments stayed manageable. This version was endorsed, interestingly, by Austen Chamberlain in his inaugural address to the 1935 ISC, three years before his half-brother Neville defied 'collective security' altogether.[172]

However, the most common response to the failure of 'collective security' in the wake of the Abyssinia crisis was the demand for 'peaceful change'.[173] This generally referred to a policy of making concessions to those powers who grieved for a revision of treaties or borders in order to pre-empt violent transfers of territory or outright war. Since the international community had failed to achieve either peace or territorial stability, the new plan was to secure at least the

---

[168] Ibid.   [169] Jäckh, *The New Germany*, p. 96.
[170] Wright, 'National Sovereignty and Collective Security', p. 103.
[171] Henry Rowan-Robinson, *Sanctions Begone! A Plea and a Plan for the Reform of the League* (London, 1936), p. 204.
[172] Austen Chamberlain, in IIIC, *Collective Security* (Paris, 1936), pp. 36–7.
[173] See, for instance, G. M. Gathorne-Hardy, 'Territorial Revision and Article 19 of the League Covenant', *International Affairs* 14:6 (1935), pp. 818–36.

former.[174] 'Peaceful change' has traditionally been regarded as the ill-fated attempt to deal with Mussolini's and Hitler's expansionist ambitions, a catastrophic foreign policy that reflected the surrender of Western democracies to fascism. However, as contemporary IR scholars viewed it, 'peaceful change' was not so much a desperate policy of surrender than a pro-active policy intended to control defecting powers. The British journalist E. D. Morel knew since the early 1920s that peace would not be a "static condition".[175] 'Peaceful change' was designed as a complement to 'collective security', not in opposition to it, as Arnold McNair argued. 'Collective security', he went on, required "collective and peaceful revision of treaties".[176] In fact, the practice of negotiating changes to the status quo had been used since 1919, Zimmern noted. It is also true, as Quincy Wright pointed out, that the Covenant favoured peace over static borders and that in this sense, the League had from the outset been a project of 'peaceful change'.[177] In other words, 'peaceful change' as a foreign policy instrument was invented long before the eleventh hour at Munich.

Manchuria and Abyssinia have become standard milestones in inter-war diplomatic history as they exemplify the struggle to curb aggressive foreign policy. Along with the Spanish Civil War, the 1935 Anglo-German Naval Agreement, the re-militarisation of the Rhineland, and Neville Chamberlain's appeasement policy at Munich in 1938, they chronicle the downfall of the liberal international order. Contemporary authors were not blind to this development. They warned that Manchuria was a "crucial test of [the League's] authority",[178] and that the Italo-Abyssinian conflict would become a "classic" in the history of failures of the interwar period.[179] IR scholars saw the imminent danger of these disputes as well as their broader implications for the international system. Their works covered the immediate course of events, mid-term power shifts, and long-term implications for

---

[174] Baer, *Test Case*, pp. 303–4.
[175] E. D. Morel, 'Foreword', in Helena Swanwick (ed.), *Builders of Peace: Being Ten Years' History of the Union of Democratic Control* (London, 1924), pp. 7–17.
[176] McNair, 'Collective Security', p. 158.
[177] Wright, 'National Sovereignty and Collective Security', p. 101.
[178] Zimmern, *Must the League Fail?*, p. 9.
[179] Beneš, *The Struggle for Collective Security in Europe and the Italo-Abyssinian War*, p. 16.

the prospects of 'collective security'.[180] In the end, sanctions failed, as most IR scholars agreed, mainly because they were not rigorously applied. Collective action either took too long to have a deterring effect – as in the Manchurian case – or lacked willingness to be implemented – as in the Italo-Abyssinian dispute.[181]

A Discipline in Flux

The Manchurian and Abyssinian disputes were important test cases for 'collective security' and, more generally, for the quality of IR scholarship. The architects of IR used the crises of the 1930s to advance their ideas and to comment on current affairs. Like in the 1920s, they saw themselves as public intellectuals, providing expert advice to governments and to the League of Nations. Their goal was to present solutions to a wider audience and to exercise influence on political negotiations. Non-academic activities remained essential to their agenda, especially since the role of public opinion in foreign affairs was increasing.[182] What they failed to deliver, however, was a coherent theory of 'collective security' and a rigorous evaluation of its ill-fated application. Rather than examining the shortcomings of the concept as part of a thorough analysis, they hectically adapted their work to political realities.

Like in the 1920s, the architects of IR operated in quasi-diplomatic circles, political clubs, and societies which served their purposes better than academic journals or classroom discussions. By drawing on these influential networks, they developed new forms of non-official diplomacy. For example, after the British government failed to implement sanctions on Japan, Arnold Toynbee suggested mobilising the League of Nations Union (LNU) for a general boycott of Japanese goods.[183] Gilbert Murray used his contacts to advocate LNU goals in *The Times*.[184] Having stood for parliament six times between 1918 and

---

[180] Zimmern, 'The Problem of Collective Security', pp. 3–9.
[181] Williams, *Sanctions under the Covenant*, pp. 140–6; Albert E. Highley, 'The First Sanctions Experiment', *Geneva Studies* IX:4 (1938), p. 122.
[182] See, for example, Webster, *The League of Nations in Theory and Practice*, p. 170.
[183] Arnold Toynbee to Gilbert Murray, 22 February 1932, Arnold Toynbee Papers, Box 72.
[184] Gilbert Murray, 'Letter to the Editor', *The Times*, 9 September 1933, Gilbert Murray Papers, Box 217.

1929, Murray was very familiar with the practice of politics.[185] And Davies encouraged him to employ all means available to exert pressure on the government for a tougher policy on 'collective security', including, a "deputation to the Prime Minister ... mass meetings ... debates in both Houses of Parliament [and an] invite [to] the Churches to devote a Sunday to Prayer and Intercession on behalf of the League".[186]

In the Abyssinia crisis, too, IR scholars played a significant role in shaping public debate as well as in influencing official diplomacy. Philip Noel-Baker discussed potential sanctions against Italy on a private mission to the *Quai d'Orsay* in 1935. On the same trip, he also met up with French left-wing parties. Both were "quite solid for sanctions", he reported to Toynbee.[187] Noel-Baker's excursion into Franco-British diplomacy was no exception. The influential Greek legal scholar Nikolaos Politis served as president of the Italo-Abyssinian Commission of Conciliation and Arbitration, which had been set up by the League of Nations Council.[188] The Abyssinian side was represented by Albert Geouffre de Lapradelle, founder of the Institut des Hautes Etudes Internationales in Paris, and the American lawyer Pitman B. Potter. A few months later, Norman Angell was part of the group that welcomed Haile Selassie in London after the latter was refused by Stanley Baldwin's government.[189] These private diplomatic endeavours reflected the high international profile that many IR thinkers maintained, but it also showed their willingness to react to current events rather than to engage in analytical or theoretical research.

By prioritising ad hoc interventions and political commentary, the architects of IR neglected what they themselves had set out to establish – the scientific study of international affairs. By and large, they

---

[185] Christopher Stray, 'Murray, (George) Gilbert Aimé (1866–1957)', *Oxford Dictionary of National Biography* (Oxford, 2004), available at http://ezproxy-prd.bodleian.ox.ac.uk:2167/view/article/35159?docPos=1 [accessed 1 June 2017].

[186] David Davies to Gilbert Murray, 11 January 1933, Gilbert Murray Papers, Box 216.

[187] Gilbert Murray to Arnold Toynbee, 20 September 1935, Arnold Toynbee Papers, Box 72.

[188] H. Lauterpacht (ed.), *Annual Digest and Reports of Public International Law Cases, 1935–1937* (London, 1945), p. 268.

[189] Miller, 'Norman Angell and Rationality in International Relations', p. 102.

failed to produce scholarship that could have been considered a social science. Their works lacked definitions of terms, assumptions, and verifiable arguments. No author defined, for example, how many members a security alliance required in order to be 'collective'. Nor did they examine the effects of different governance models on 'collective security', or take into account the transaction costs of operating via Geneva. From the inception of the League of Nations to the mid-1930s, 'collective security' remained essentially the same ambiguous concept that was used at the respective convenience of politicians and scholars. Instead of a common definition, the general rapporteur of the 1934 ISC Maurice Bourquin compiled a set of "national attitudes" towards international security.[190] Bourquin himself acknowledged the ambiguity in determining an aggressor.[191] When scholars attempted to induce a sense of analytical rigour, other ISC participants such as Italian author Robert Forges-Davanzati countered that they "should remain on the political level, on the level of reality".[192] The predominance of political commentary and opinions distracted IR scholars from formulating any reasonably coherent models or theories.

As a consequence, many disciplinary retrospectives have divided interwar IR discourse into those authors who were willing to give the League of Nations another chance and those who favoured a return to traditional alliances. It is this distinction that has since become known as the 'first great debate' between so-called 'idealist' and 'realist' schools of thought. E. H. Carr and his followers argued that early IR scholarship had been dominated by 'idealism', particularly by the belief in 'collective security' under the League of Nations. They criticised the 'idealists' for blending their analysis with values and normative claims, whereas 'realism' was supposed to be limited to the study of actual power relations. 'Realist' authors were firmly convinced of the analytical superiority of their approach. They even claimed that there was a natural tendency towards more 'realism' in academic studies. According to Hans Morgenthau, "all science goes through a utopian state [and] is succeeded by a period of realism".[193] In other words, they assumed that IR would periodically shift from one

---

[190] Maurice Bourquin, in IIIC, *Collective Security* (Paris, 1936), p. 4.
[191] Ibid., p. 329.
[192] Robert Forges-Davanzati, in IIIC, *Collective Security* (Paris, 1936), p. 334.
[193] Hans Morgenthau, 'The Political Science of E. H. Carr', *World Politics* 1:1 (1948), p. 128.

paradigm to the next, an assumption that has dogged the discipline ever since. Upon closer investigation of the protagonists' personal papers and correspondence, however, there is little evidence of either a pure form of 'idealism' or of a natural shift to 'realism'.

To be sure, there were occasional references to opposing ideologies, a divergence between a "system of alliances" and a "system of obligatory conference", as Charles Webster phrased it.[194] But these arguments appeared much earlier than the alleged 'realist' turn in 1939 and from within the group of so-called 'idealists' themselves. WILPF members knew in 1931 that it was an "illusion" to count on moral disarmament and a vague desire for peace.[195] At his inaugural lecture as Wilson Professor at Aberystwyth in 1933, Jerome Greene spoke on *Idealism and Realism in Efforts Toward Peace*. He interpreted 'idealism' as the inquiry into the "desirable", and 'realism' as the study of the "attainable".[196] Greene criticised 'idealists' for ignoring "material facts", but he also exposed the flawed 'realist' dictum that "war has always been and always must be".[197] His predecessor on the Wilson Chair, Charles Webster, readily described the League's handling of the Manchurian situation as the "greatest of all the failures", and he was critical of the return of secret meetings between the great powers.[198] Zimmern, too, was fully aware of the "survival of the spirit and methods of power politics".[199] In 1936, he consequently suggested forming a sub-group of democratic states which were ready for genuine cooperation – a coalition of "welfare states" as he called it.[200] Zimmern knew that such a coalition deviated from 'collective security' and relied on "power policies", just as the dictatorships did. Earlier than the self-proclaimed 'realists', he warned to ignore "the powerful forces" that determined change in world history.[201] If at all 'idealist', this made him a "cautious idealist", as one biographer has put it.[202]

[194] Webster, *The League of Nations in Theory and Practice*, p. 178.
[195] Camille Drevet, 'Report on Activities Since Prague', in WILPF (ed.), *Report of the Seventh Congress* (Geneva, 1931), p. 24.
[196] Greene, *Idealism and Realism in Efforts toward Peace*, p. 5.
[197] Ibid., p. 21.
[198] Webster, *The League of Nations in Theory and Practice*, pp. 166–7.
[199] Zimmern, 'The Problem of Collective Security', p. 31.   [200] Ibid., p. 59.
[201] 'A Historical Note on Collective Security', Alfred Zimmern, prepared for ISC, April 1935, Alfred Zimmern Papers, Box 86.
[202] Rich, 'Alfred Zimmern's Cautious Idealism'.

Thanks to more recent research on the history of IR we now know that the outright rejection of interwar concepts of 'collective security' by the self-proclaimed 'realists' was based on a heavily simplified, if not mistaken, reading of the original authors.[203] Revisionist histories have found that interwar authors never assumed that states would behave morally and cooperatively, as Carr and Morgenthau later asserted, but on the contrary that international organisations were created as an insurance against defectors. In fact, security mattered precisely *because* governments were expected to violate international law and to defy arbitration. Arguments that were later associated with 'realism' actually originated in earlier discourses and within the group of authors traditionally labelled as 'idealists'. It was Zimmern himself who blamed "sentimental idealism" for putting the League of Nations at risk.[204] He anticipated that governments would *not* always comply with international agreements and he developed 'collective security' in response to that assumption.

Zimmern's wife Lucie was just as sharp in her analysis of the League's failures. She frequently accompanied her husband to academic conferences and wrote on international affairs in her own right. Her book *Must the League Fail?* (1932) reflected her disappointment with the Council's ineffectiveness in the Manchurian dispute and suggested a number of specific solutions: (i) controversial international disputes should be discussed at the prime ministerial level to ensure due attention; (ii) the agenda should not mix technical cooperation with violent conflicts, in order to "eliminate comfortable meetings without results"; and (iii) senior positions at the Secretariat should not be filled by great power nationals.[205] Eleanor Rathbone's *War Can Be Averted* (1938) eloquently exposed the cynicism that pervaded governments in their handling of the Manchurian and Abyssinian disputes.[206] She attacked the British government for its shameless "sympathy with Japan's desire to expand" and argued that business interests as well as geopolitical strategy – "Japan as a bulwark against

---

[203] See, for example, David Long and Peter Wilson, *Thinkers of the Twenty Years' Crisis: Inter-war Idealism Reassessed* (Oxford, 1995).

[204] 'Memorandum for Discussion at Sub-Committee on the British Commonwealth and the Collective System', Alfred Zimmern, 25 June 1934, Chatham House, Alfred Zimmern Papers, Box 97.

[205] Zimmern, *Must the League Fail?*, pp. 68–76.

[206] Rathbone, *War Can Be Averted*.

Communism" – dictated foreign policy, rather than a commitment to political principles or law.[207] What was worse, Rathbone argued, Japan's invasion of Manchuria had created a precedent for other aggressors. The work of authors such as Eleanor Rathbone, Lucie Zimmern, and Helena Swanwick begs the question of what precisely the architects of IR meant when writing on and trying to establish 'collective security'. Even revisionist disciplinary histories have not fully rectified the defining features of interwar IR scholarship.[208]

If IR did not evolve as a debate between 'idealists' and 'realists', what did constitute the new discipline? The principal problem was that throughout the interwar period there was no common set of methodologies, definitions, or scientific standards. Scholars had no analytical tools for comparing or testing their work, if it included any falsifiable hypotheses in the first place. Rather than agreeing on unmistakable currencies of international politics – such as quantitative geopolitical data or assumptions about the behaviour of states – IR authors often relied on fuzzy concepts and ambiguous language. Eleanor Rathbone, for example, believed in the "spiritual conditions" for world peace and promoted the use of propaganda. "Nazi and Fascist propaganda", she argued, "should be countered by a steady infiltration of published material, lecturers, broadcasts and personal contacts".[209] Gilbert Murray, too, spoke of the "weapon of moral pressure".[210] For Zimmern, the principal reason for the breakdown of cooperative diplomacy was the lack of a "sense of social solidarity" between countries.[211] Nowhere did he specify, however, what this "sense" meant or how it could be measured.

Some of the confusion about schools of thought in interwar IR can be reduced to terminology. For example, the IR lecturer and Quaker Karlin Capper-Johnson, proudly confessed "I hope I am an idealist", by which he meant to identify as a normative political scientist who

---

[207] Ibid., pp. 33–4.
[208] Peter Wilson, 'Where Are We Now in the Debate about the First Great Debate?', in Brian C. Schmidt (ed.), *International Relations and the First Great Debate* (New York, 2012), p. 133; Lucian M. Ashworth, 'Where Are the Idealists in Interwar International Relations', *Review of International Studies* 32:2 (2006), p. 293.
[209] Rathbone, *War Can Be Averted*, p. 182.
[210] Gilbert Murray, in League of Nations Union, *The League, Manchuria and Disarmament* (London, 1931), p. 17.
[211] Zimmern, *The League of Nations and the Rule of Law, 1918–1935*, p. 418.

nevertheless "examine[d] the world realistically".[212] Others did not subscribe to a binary 'idealist' versus 'realist' distinction at all. J. M. Spaight classified approaches to interwar diplomacy into three categories: a "progressive school" who were League enthusiasts, a "conservative school" who represented a Laodicean attitude towards international cooperation, and outright "nationalists" who put militarism and national self-interest above all else.[213] Zimmern, too, distinguished between multiple "schools of thought", rather than a two-sided debate.[214]

The rhetoric employed in IR debates during the 1930s should therefore not be mistaken for what Carr labelled 'utopianism' or 'idealism'. Indeed many authors argued that a working system of international politics required a minimum "willingness to cooperate" – whatever this meant – but they did not naïvely assume that this willingness existed.[215] Nor did the collapse of 'collective security' invariably slide into appeasement. Rathbone, for example, stressed the "uselessness of offering [concessions] to avert war, so long as the aggressors know that they can get more by grabbing it".[216] The truth is that most concepts employed by IR scholars were very blurry. Rather than retrospectively labelling interwar scholars, it would be more helpful therefore to expose their diversity, fuzziness, and inconsistency. The debate about 'collective security' reflected the fuzziness of interwar IR. The debate about Nazism and 'peaceful change' – covered in Chapter 6 – continued this trend.

Conclusion

Contrary to what subsequent generations of IR scholars have since asserted about alleged schools of thought, there were no clear-cut strategies in dealing with international disputes, let alone scientific theories. The fate of 'collective security' revealed the profoundly uncertain and ambiguous nature of interwar IR scholarship. Arbitration

[212] Karlin Capper-Johnson, in IIIC, *Collective Security* (Paris, 1936), p. 401.
[213] Spaight, *Pseudo-Security*, p. 4. See also Zimmern, *Must the League Fail?*, pp. 14–19.
[214] Alfred Zimmern, *Modern Political Doctrines* (Oxford, 1939), p. xii.
[215] Edward Grey, in League of Nations Union, *The League, Manchuria and Disarmament* (London, 1931), p. 3.
[216] Rathbone, *War Can Be Averted*, p. 171.

procedures were overruled by old-fashioned bi-lateral agreements and international institutions were replaced by ad hoc committees. Rather than keeping a critical distance, the architects of IR designed and endorsed these policies themselves. In 1933, Gilbert Murray confessed to Kathleen Courtney that the real weakness of the League was that it had "no plan at all for exerting pressure on the nations that break their Covenant".[217] The fragility of interwar diplomacy was reflected in IR scholarship. There was "a great deal of confusion of thought" on how to deal with Italy's attack on Ethiopia, Zimmern admitted in October 1935.[218] A few years later, in 1939, Zimmern concluded that the state of IR as a discipline was "confusion rather than enlightenment".[219] At the New York Council on Foreign Relations, too, experts were "in a good deal of doubt" about how to deal with Japan, as Quincy Wright privately told Arnold Toynbee.[220] These were not just scattered moments of perplexity but part of a general sense of uncertainty during the 1930s.[221]

The inability of IR scholars to provide a consistent explanation for the crises of the 1930s put them in an awkward position. Over the course of two decades, the architects of IR had achieved a reputation as political and moral authorities. They had developed a certain confidence that their discipline satisfied the standards of a social science and that it was capable of producing verifiable arguments. Indeed, the "objective and dispassionate study" of international affairs was their explicit ambition.[222] On the other hand, they continued to comment on and interfere with political events. In a 1935 speech, French historian Louis Eisenmann and US diplomat Allen Dulles summarised the multi-faceted objective of their work. They wanted to conduct

---

[217] Gilbert Murray to Kathleen Courtney, 14 January 1933, Gilbert Murray Papers, Box 216.
[218] Zimmern, 'The League's Handling of the Italo-Abyssinian Dispute', p. 759.
[219] Zimmern, *Modern Political Doctrines*, p. ix.
[220] Quincy Wright to Arnold Toynbee, 30 September 1932, Arnold Toynbee Papers, Box 72.
[221] Confusion was also widespread in other areas of international politics during the interwar period, such as anti-slavery provisions. See Amalia Ribi Forclaz, *Humanitarian Imperialism. The Politics of Anti-Slavery Activism, 1880–1940* (Oxford, 2015), pp. 190–201.
[222] Alfred Zimmern, Memo, April 1925, Alfred Zimmern Papers, Box 88.

"scientific and analytical" scholarship, promote "rapprochement through mutual understanding", and give advice to "those in responsible positions of government".[223] In other words, they wanted to simultaneously be professors, internationalist activists, and government advisors. This was an ambitious programme in the face of rising international tension.

"If the universities cannot remain bulwarks of liberalism and disinterestedness during these troublous times", a worried Quincy Wright wrote to William Rappard in 1936, "it is hard to know what can".[224] By engaging with 'collective security', the architects of IR entered heated political debates and became actively involved in the very object of their research. Not everyone appreciated this mélange of academia and diplomacy. Rappard complained about the practice of diplomatic 'talking shop' at the International Studies Conference (ISC) and its lack of tangible results. He urged "to make these conferences as scientific and unpolitical as possible".[225] But 'collective security' was all about politics. It was a political instrument, designed by political actors in order to resolve political conflicts. As a result of their preoccupation with practical politics, IR scholars struggled to formulate plain analysis which, in turn, has made it difficult for disciplinary historians to decipher any theoretical patterns in their work. What this episode shows is an eclectic exchange of ideas and policy proposals, none of which solved the political or intellectual challenges of the time.

The debate about 'collective security' marked the most controversial and momentous application of IR scholarship during the interwar period. The disquieting outcomes of the Manchurian and Abyssinian crises questioned the ambitions of the discipline but, rather than leading to immediate despair, the architects of IR decided to launch one last attempt at safeguarding international peace. This attempt, examined in Chapter 6, was to introduce another instrument to the arsenal of the League, in addition to disarmament, arbitration, and

---

[223] Louis Eisenmann and Allen W. Dulles, in IIIC, *Collective Security* (Paris, 1936), pp. 38–41.

[224] Quincy Wright to William Rappard, 31 December 1936, HEI 169/2, Archives of the Graduate Institute of International Studies.

[225] William Rappard to Chalmers Wright, 7 February 1935, HEI [uncatalogued], Archives of the Graduate Institute of International Studies.

sanctions. If peace could not be achieved by law or by coercion, they argued, perhaps the international community needed more flexible means of managing the grievances of certain governments. This was the idea of 'peaceful change', a final attempt to avoid large-scale warfare in the face of aggressive nationalism.

6 | The End of World Affairs

Obviously one cannot but gamble about the future, in as much as almost everything depends on the unforeseeable decisions of the gamblers who are in authority in at least two European neighbour States.

William Rappard (1938)[1]

Introduction

On 1 June 1933, the director of the Deutsche Hochschule für Politik (DHfP), Ernst Jäckh, gave an address in London.[2] He recounted the history of the DHfP as an institution devoted to liberal democracy and international reconciliation, and he deplored its fate under the new regime. Since its creation in 1920, Jäckh told his colleagues, the DHfP had been a site for open-minded research and education, gathering scholars from across the political spectrum. Now, in the spring of 1933, under the new government, these values were at risk. In April, the DHfP was put under the control of Propaganda Minister Joseph Goebbels, which resulted in the exodus of faculty members (including Jäckh himself) and its gradual decline into dubious kinds of research. For students of International Relations (IR), from Germany and abroad, this was a critical moment that led to the demise of their discipline.

Hitler's rise to power posed serious problems for the architects of IR. Intellectually speaking, the regime undermined the basic methodological assumption that politics was subject to reason. Nazi ideology was fundamentally at odds both with the principles of scientific inquiry (by granting certain humans a privileged access to knowledge) and with the idea of an international order of equals. Hitler relied on

[1] William Rappard to Alfred Zimmern, 16 March 1938, HEI [uncatalogued], Archives of the Graduate Institute of International Studies.
[2] Address by Ernst Jäckh at the International Studies Conference, 1 June 1933, K.IV.2, IIIC Records.

248

totalitarian control at home and military power abroad, and he wiped out the rule of law. For the practice of IR scholarship, this meant the end of institutional independence and the persecution of unwelcome scholars. Research centres came under the control of bogus academics, such as the international lawyer Fritz Berber or the propagandist Franz Six, who either openly sympathised with the regime or failed to resist. Meanwhile, Germany left the League of Nations and proceeded to break international law in increasingly blunt ways, culminating in the assault on Poland in September 1939. What, if anything, could IR scholars have done to oppose this course of events? Did they fail to see the danger of nationalist extremism?

While the IR community looked for ways to deal with the new political environment and provided some assistance to refugee scholars, their intellectual response was less convincing. Many IR experts struggled to make sense of Hitler and his foreign policy which did not seem to follow any familiar patterns. Instead they devised ad hoc solutions and entered into ill-fated negotiations with senior Nazi figures, including a dubious attempt to safeguard the DHfP by Jäckh himself. British historian Arnold Toynbee, too, did not just analyse Nazi foreign policy from an academic point of view, but sought to interact with foreign policy makers "to get a reasonable discussion with the Nazis".[3] Only a few authors, many of whom women, realised the effect of totalitarianism and militarism on the international order. The historian Elizabeth Wiskemann, later Montague Burton Professor of IR at Edinburgh, was one of the most outspoken critics of the Nazi regime which she condemned as "anti-Semitic", "anti-democratic", and "racialist".[4] Ultimately, most IR scholars remained puzzled about Hitler's course of action. In 1938, the founder of the Geneva Graduate Institute William Rappard concluded that "one cannot but gamble about the future, in as much as almost everything depends on the unforeseeable decisions of the gamblers who are in authority in at least two European neighbour States".[5]

---

[3] Arnold Toynbee to Frederick Lugard, 23 June 1936, Arnold Toynbee Papers, Box 76.
[4] Elizabeth Wiskemann, *Czechs & Germans: A Study of the Struggle in the Historic Provinces of Bohemia and Moravia* (London, 1938), p. 135.
[5] William Rappard to Alfred Zimmern, 16 March 1938, HEI [uncatalogued], Archives of the Graduate Institute of International Studies.

The desperate attempts to curb German aggression during the
second half of the 1930s became known as 'peaceful change' in diplomatic circles. The idea of 'peaceful change' was to adjust territorial
borders and sovereign rights in order to soothe aggressors and to
prevent violent conflict. It was based on the conviction that the world's
interest in peace ranked higher than the claims of individual states to
their territory.[6] Specifically, IR scholars envisioned 'peaceful change' as
an instrument to respond to Hitler's colonial claims as well as to his
aspirations in Central Europe. Several professors, including Toynbee,
embarked upon semi-diplomatic missions to Germany in order to win
supposedly modest Germans for some version of peaceful transfer of
(colonial) territories.[7] Ironically, even E. H. Carr endorsed a version of
this approach which eventually culminated in Neville Chamberlain's
infamous strategy of 'appeasement'.[8] However, IR scholars did not
universally surrender to Nazi foreign policy. Nor did they naïvely
believe in the moral and legal capacities of the League of Nations to
oppose the dictatorships. They identified 'peaceful change' as a "flexible system" to manage international relations in the absence of more
effective world governance.[9]

In the end, interwar IR scholarship fell prey to its own ambitions.
The dual strategy of producing academic output and influencing foreign policy was increasingly unworkable in a world of authoritarian
governments and collapsing international institutions. Declining financial support, the spread of propaganda, and censorship made things
worse. The final blow came in June 1940 when German troops entered
Paris and seized the International Institute of Intellectual Cooperation
(IIIC), one of the principal sponsors of interwar IR scholarship. What
most IR scholars failed to understand was that the dictators were not
simply opposed to specific treaties or institutions but that they fundamentally sabotaged all rationality in international politics. On the

[6] Quincy Wright, in International Institute of Intellectual Cooperation (IIIC),
*Peaceful Change: Procedures, Population, Raw Materials, Colonies: Proceedings
of the Tenth International Studies Conference* (Paris, 1938), p. 532.
[7] Arnold J. Toynbee, *Acquaintances* (London, 1967), pp. 276–85.
[8] Randall L. Schweller, *Unanswered Threats: Political Constraints on the Balance
of Power* (Princeton, 2006), pp. 69–70; Gerhard L. Weinberg, 'Germany,
Munich, and Appeasement', in Melvin Small and Otto Feinstein (eds.), *Appeasing
Fascism* (London, 1991), p. 9; Peter Wilson, 'E. H. Carr's the Twenty Years'
Crisis: Appearance and Reality in World Politics', *Politik* 12:4 (2009), pp. 21–5.
[9] Maurice Bourquin, in IIIC, *Peaceful Change* (Paris, 1938), p. 586.

other hand, it is important to note that interwar IR authors did not religiously believe in any one system of international cooperation. They continued to adapt their opinions and eventually conceded what French jurist Georges Scelle in 1938 called the triple "defeat of the democracies" – the juridical, diplomatic, and moral failure to withstand Germany.[10] In particular, the IR scholars never subscribed to 'idealism' or any other reasonably coherent school of thought. If anything, it was the very absence of theory that shaped this phase of IR scholarship.

This chapter examines the intellectual and institutional challenges that the architects of IR faced during the 1930s. It begins by showing how the Nazi government nationalised research centres and forced scholars into exile, essentially eliminating the independent study of IR in German-speaking Europe. The second section reviews how Hitler's rise to power was perceived by the IR community and how scholars struggled to make sense of his foreign policy agenda. The third section inspects 'peaceful change' as a political idea. The fourth section explores its application as a policy instrument, notably Toynbee's quasi-diplomatic ventures to Germany. The final section traces the gradual demise of IR scholarship, from financial and political difficulties in the mid-1930s to the complete suspension of activities within the first year of the Second World War.

Attacks on Academia

One week after the *Reichstag* had passed the Enabling Act, on 1 April 1933, Jäckh was summoned to see Hitler.[11] At that time, the DHfP was the pre-eminent German school for political science and an internationally respected research institute, offering courses to several hundred students.[12] It was, by and large, a centre for liberal political thought and counted many outspoken anti-Nazis among its faculty and students, such as the publicist Georg Bernhard, the diplomat

---

[10] Norman Ingram, *The Politics of Dissent: Pacifism in France 1919–1939* (Oxford, 1991), p. 113.

[11] Memo by John Van Sickle, 22 April 1933, Folder 178, Box 19, Series 717, RG 1.1, RF, Rockefeller Archive Center.

[12] Steven D. Korenblat, 'A School for the Republic? Cosmopolitans and Their Enemies at the Deutsche Hochschule für Politik, 1920–1933', *Central European History* 39:3 (2006), p. 422.

Richard Kuenzer, and the educationalist Hildegard Wegscheider.[13] Hitler mistrusted the DHfP's pluralism and its friendly relationships with the international research community. He was especially suspicious of the influence that foreign scholars might develop on public opinion in Germany. Consequently he demanded that the DHfP be put under state control and supervised by the propaganda ministry under Joseph Goebbels. Two weeks later, on 14 April, Goebbels confirmed this decision, insisting that his ministry would gain control of all DHfP-related activities. In addition to that, the chief of the Reich chancellery Hans Heinrich Lammers was appointed to the DHfP's governing board.[14] This had expectable implications for academic freedom and the curriculum. It also meant that unwelcome professors could be easily dismissed according to the 'Aryan paragraph', decreed in April 1933.

Jäckh's initial reaction was to try to maintain control over the research section of the DHfP, while allowing the teaching branch to be taken over by Goebbels. The idea was to secure employment and academic freedom at least for some faculty members while effectively selling out the rest of the DHfP to the government. To facilitate this plan he appealed for support from the Rockefeller Foundation which had been a longtime sponsor of the DHfP.[15] When the deal failed to materialise, Jäckh gave the impression of having followed moral principles rather than an instinct of survival. The account he presented in London in June 1933, suggested that he fought for the freedom of the DHfP and resigned in protest of Hitler's demands:

I feel it necessary to say farewell to the old Hochschule . . . the Hochschule is now taken over by the state [which means] the application of the new regulations for civil servants . . . it would have meant my dismissing those

[13] Siegfried Mielke (ed.), *Einzigartig: Dozenten, Studierende und Repräsentanten der Deutschen Hochschule für Politik (1920–1933) im Widerstand gegen den Nationalsozialismus* (Berlin, 2008), pp. 53, 66, 328.
[14] Roswitha Wollkopf, *Zur politischen Konzeption und Wirksamkeit der Deutschen Hochschule für Politik (1920–1933)*, PhD thesis (Berlin, 1983), p. 148.
[15] Cable by Ernst Jäckh to John Van Sickle, 1 May 1933: 'Please do everything your power make continuation research work possible through our Institute of International Relations Stop outstanding scholars expect this Institute becoming central research institute International Relations and Political Science and are most Anxious Cooperate Sincerely Jaeckh', Folder 178, Box 19, Series 717, RG 1.1, RF, Rockefeller Archive Center.

of my tried and valued friends and fellow workers who came under those
regulations. I could not bring myself to do that, and therefore resigned.[16]

Once it became clear that his plan had failed, Jäckh tried to establish a
career outside Germany. From 1934 to 1937, he served as vice-
president at the New Commonwealth Institute in London, a pressure
group advocating an international police force. Jäckh continued to
attend international conferences and worked on a research project
commissioned by the Geneva Graduate Institute. In July 1940, he
crossed the Atlantic together with economist Ludwig von Mises, supported by the Rockefeller Foundation, to seek refuge in the United
States and became a visiting professor at Columbia University in New
York.[17] In his memoirs, Jäckh portrayed himself as a dissident and
described the DHfP as a "liberal democratic school of politics" – an
image that remained widely accepted until challenged in the 1980s.[18]

Jäckh's behaviour has since become subject to an extensive historical
debate on Nazism and political science in Germany.[19] The historian

[16] Address by Ernst Jäckh, 1 June 1933, K.IV.2, IIIC Records.
[17] Memo by Tracy B. Kittredge, 12 July 1940, Folder 3793, Box 319, Series 200,
RG 1.1, RF, Rockefeller Archive Center.
[18] Ernst Jäckh, *Der Goldene Pflug: Lebensernte eines Weltbürgers* (Stuttgart,
1954), p. 64. Rainer Eisfeld, *Ausgebürgert und doch angebräunt: Deutsche
Politikwissenschaft 1920–1945* (Baden-Baden, 1991), p. 13.
[19] Detlef Lehnert, '"Politik als Wissenschaft": Beiträge zur Institutionalisierung
einer Fachdisziplin in Forschung und Lehre der Deutschen Hochschule für
Politik (1920–1933)', *Politische Vierteljahresschrift* 33:3 (1989), pp. 443–65;
Rainer Eisfeld, '"Nationale" Politikwissenschaft von der Weimarer Republik
zum Dritten Reich', *Politische Vierteljahresschrift* 31:2 (1990), pp. 238–64;
Detlef Lehnert, '"Schule der Demokratie" oder "politische Fachhochschule"?
Anspruch und Wirklichkeit einer praxisorientierten Ausbildung der Deutschen
Hochschule für Politik 1920–1933', in Gerhard Göhler and Bodo Zeuner (eds.),
Kontinutitäten und Brüche in der Politikwissenschaft (Baden-Baden, 1991),
pp. 65–92; Alfons Söllner, 'Gruppenbild mit Jäckh: Anmerkungen zur
"Verwissenschaftlichung" der Deutschen Hochschule für Politik während der
Weimarer Republik', in Gerhard Göhler and Bodo Zeuner (eds.), *Kontinutitäten
und Brüche in der Politikwissenschaft* (Baden-Baden, 1991), pp. 41–63; Ernst
Haiger, 'Politikwissenschaft und Auslandswissenschaft im "Dritten Reich":
(Deutsche) Hochschule für Politik 1933–1939 und Auslandswissenschaftliche
Fakultät der Berliner Universität 1940–1945, in Gerhard Göhler and Bodo
Zeuner (eds.), *Kontinutitäten und Brüche in der Politikwissenschaft* (Baden-
Baden, 1991), pp. 95–130; Manfred Gangl, 'Die Gründung der "Deutschen
Hochschule für Politik"', in Gangl (ed.), *Das Politische: Zur Entstehung der
Politikwissenschaft während der Weimarer Republik* (Frankfurt, 2008),
pp. 77–96; Rainer Eisfeld, *Ausgebürgert und doch angebräunt: Deutsche
Politikwissenschaft 1920–1945*, 2nd ed. (Baden-Baden, 2013).

Roswitha Wollkopf has argued that Jäckh failed to wholeheartedly protect the DHfP and instead ingratiated himself with Goebbels by offering his contacts to American philanthropists.[20] During the crucial phase of transition, Jäckh wrote a newspaper article affirming his confidence in Hitler's peaceful intentions.[21] Wollkopf's study also claims that Jäckh subsequently forged his resignation letter in his memoirs to portray events in his favour.[22] On the other hand, there is evidence that Jäckh might have been put under pressure for having a Jewish wife, which was the reason that the Rockefeller Foundation decided to help him flee the Nazi regime.[23] In any event, as Rainer Eisfeld has demonstrated, even the DHfP's pre-1933 programme had been less liberal and Jäckh's role less heroic than previously asserted. A number of faculty members, including the political scientists Adolf Grabowsky and Arnold Bergstraesser, represented a 'functionalist' rather than 'liberal democratic' approach to politics. Carl Schmitt's famous essay '*Der Begriff des Politischen*' emerged from a talk at the DHfP in 1927. About half of the faculty stayed in their posts under Nazi rule, thus discrediting the DHfP's reputation as a bastion of resistance. Some of the professors, such as the sociologist Max Hildebert Boehm or the lawyer Fritz Berber, actually benefitted from the Nazi take-over.[24] Meanwhile, Jäckh revealed his ambiguous stance towards the regime in a newspaper article in *Berliner Tageblatt* on 13 April 1933, shortly before the fate of the DHfP had been decided:

In my extensive conversation with *Reichskanzler* Hitler last week I reassured him that I have remained the same National Social [*Nationalsozialer*] ... I was also able to repeat the conviction that I had stated at the inauguration of the DHfP: that all my life and work for Germany ... followed the guiding

[20] Wollkopf, *Zur politischen Konzeption und Wirksamkeit der Deutschen Hochschule für Politik (1920–1933)*, pp. 151–2.

[21] *Berliner Börsen-Zeitung*, Nr. 168, 8 April 1933.

[22] Wollkopf, *Zur politischen Konzeption und Wirksamkeit der Deutschen Hochschule für Politik (1920–1933)*, Annex 3, quoting from Ernst Jäckh to Hans Heinrich Lammers, 16 April 1933; See also, Detlef Lehnert, '"Schule der Demokratie' oder 'politische Fachhochschule'?: Anspruch und Wirklichkeit einer praxisorientierten Ausbildung der Deutschen Hochschule für Politik, 1920–1933', in Göhler and Zeuner (eds.), *Kontinuitäten und Brüche in der deutschen Politikwissenschaft* (Baden-Baden, 1991), p. 72.

[23] Memo by JHW [Joseph H. Willits], 14 August 1940, Folder 3793, Box 319, Series 200, RG 1.1, RF, Rockefeller Archive Center.

[24] Eisfeld, *Ausgebürgert und doch angebräunt*, p. 31.

principle of my Swabian friend Friedrich List: "Behind all my plans lies Germany".[25]

Jäckh's story is not uncommon. Rather than clearly siding with political camps or distinct schools of thought, many IR scholars remained ambiguous and vague in their response to extreme nationalism. Albrecht Mendelssohn Bartholdy, director of the Institut für Auswärtige Politik (IAP) in Hamburg and a descendent of the accomplished Jewish family, was an open-minded intellectual who maintained a high international profile. A lawyer by training, an authority on international affairs, a passionate writer and musician, he had travelled and lectured widely, and was awarded honorary doctorates from Harvard and Chicago.[26] His tendency to go beyond professorial duties and to intervene in political debates, however, seemed suspicious to the Nazis. As a result, he was pressured out of his professorship in 1933, officially on the grounds of his Jewish heritage.[27] Nazi reports denounced the IAP as "the personal work of Mendelssohn Bartholdy ... a Western, pacifist, cosmopolitan propaganda institute of foreign policy ... exercising a bad influence abroad, especially in the English-speaking world".[28] In 1934, Mendelssohn Bartholdy emigrated to England where he took up a senior fellowship at Balliol College, Oxford, with the help of William Beveridge, the Society for the Protection of Science and Learning, and the Rockefeller Foundation.[29] He continued to teach classes on IR and International Law at Oxford but died two years later, unable to publish his last manuscript – it was edited by James T. Shotwell and posthumously

[25] Ernst Jäckh, *Berliner Tageblatt*, clxxvii, 16 April (1933), newspaper cutting, Ernst Jäckh Papers, Box 16. Detlef Lehnert has quoted a similar statement by Jäckh on 27 March 1933 in which he affirms "his agreement with Hitler's [...] synthesis of all national-political forces of life". See Lehnert, '"Schule der Demokratie" oder "politische Fachhochschule"?', p. 71.

[26] Rainer Nicolaysen, 'Albrecht Mendelssohn Bartholdy (1874–1936): Jurist, Friedensforscher, Künstler', *Rabels Zeitschrift* 75 (2011), p. 24.

[27] Report on IAP, 19 July 1933, StA HH, HW II, 361–5 II, Ad 22/1, Bd. 2.

[28] Report on IAP, addressed to Staatssekretär Ahrens, 19 July 1933, StA HH HW II, 361–5 II, Ad 22/1, Bd. 2, p. 9; and report on IAP by Dr. Ing. H. Grothe (Verbindungsstelle des Aussenpolitischen Amtes der NSDAP), 28 July 1933, StA HH, HW II, 361–5 II, Ad 22/1, Bd. 2, p. 18.

[29] William Beveridge to Mendelssohn Bartholdy, 28 September 1933, 525/3, S.P.S.L. Records; and Grant report, RF 33077, 20 June 1934, Folder 863, Box 65, Series 401, RG 1, RF, Rockefeller Archive Center.

published as *The War and German Society: The Testament of a Liberal* (1937).[30]

Despite Mendelssohn Bartholdy's remarkable record as a liberal scholar and a "conciliatory diplomat", his relationship to nationalist ideology was difficult.[31] Since the First World War, his work was motivated by a deep sense of patriotism, mostly rooted in arts and culture but sometimes taking crude forms – he concluded a 1917 speech by crying *"Deutschland voran!* [Germany ahead!]".[32] Having served as a legal expert on the German delegation to Versailles, he became a staunch critic of the peace treaty and a supporter of the revisionist campaign. In the 1920s, he fought for a German-friendly interpretation of the Dawes and Young Plans as a delegate to both tribunals. Mendelssohn Bartholdy felt first and foremost as a servant of his country.[33] When confronted with Nazi accusations in 1933, a good friend and senior official at the foreign office defended Mendelssohn Bartholdy by arguing that he had done "good service for the German cause".[34] Most alarming was perhaps a polemic article written by Mendelssohn Bartholdy in 1930 which suggested that Germany should leave the League of Nations.[35] If a German withdrawal was managed cleverly and in conjuncture with Italy, Mendelssohn Bartholdy argued, it could effectively dissolve the League system and facilitate the revision of Versailles. At the same time, this would shift power to the Permanent Court of Arbitration – "as Geneva loses ... The Hague

[30] Report by Mendelssohn Bartholdy, 18 February 1936, Folder 863, Box 65, Series 401, RG 1, RF, Rockefeller Archive Center.
[31] Gisela Gantzel-Kress, 'Albrecht Mendelssohn Bartholdy: Ein Bürgerhumanist und Versöhnungsdiplomat im Aufbruch der Demokratie in Deutschland', *Zeitschrift des Vereins für Hamburgische Geschichte* 71 (1985), pp. 127–43.
[32] These were his concluding words of a speech to international lawyers on 6 October 1917. See Deutsche Gesellschaft für Völkerrecht, *Mitteilungen der Deutschen Gesellschaft für Völkerrecht* 1 (Berlin, 1918), p. 34.
[33] Jan Stöckmann, 'Studying the International, Serving the Nation: The Origins of International Relations (IR) Scholarship in Germany, 1912–33', *The International History Review* 38:5 (2016), pp. 1050–80.
[34] Memo by Bernhard Wilhelm von Bülow to Auswärtiges Amt, 9 October 1933, StA HH, HW II, 361–5 II, Ad 22/1, Bd. 2: 5253.
[35] Albrecht Mendelssohn Bartholdy, 'Soll Deutschland kündigen?', *Europäische Gespräche* 12 (1930), pp. 589–600. Compare, for example, his argument in favour of the League of Nations based on the "interdependence and entanglement [Interdependenz und Verschlungenheit]" of European states. Albrecht Mendelssohn Bartholdy, 'Pakt und Protokoll', *Der Neue Merkur* 8:8 (1925), p. 605.

gains".[36] In doing so, Mendelssohn Bartholdy advocated a different type of international order based on law rather than permanent cooperation, and on national sovereignty rather than supra-national governance.

This peculiar dialectic between internationalism and nationalism shaped much of 1930s IR scholarship. On the one hand, Jäckh and Mendelssohn Bartholdy were at the forefront of Germany's liberal academic elite and deeply committed to international cooperation. At the same time, their interpretation of foreign politics – that is, their analytical framework as well as their personal way of navigating international politics – remained fundamentally national.[37] The interplay of internationalism and nationalism, as Glenda Sluga has argued, shaped the twentieth-century world but, unlike one might assume, both forces operated alongside rather than opposing each other.[38] There was not just "good" internationalism but a variety of political constructions advocating different forms of international order.[39] This was reflected in the way IR authors employed the 'international' and the 'national' as analytical categories, and in the respective importance that they assigned to them. At a 1932 conference, Zimmern described himself as "a national man and an international body at the same time".[40]

After 1933, German centres for the study of IR were left to academics who were not prosecuted on racial or political grounds, or who skilfully disguised their views by working on less controversial topics, such as the international economist Carl Brinkmann.[41] Historian Otto Hoetzsch managed to stay at the DHfP for a little longer before retiring

---

[36] Bartholdy, 'Soll Deutschland kündigen?', p. 599. On the relationship between law and politics at the League of Nations, see Stephen Wertheim, 'The League of Nations: A Retreat from International Law?', *Journal of Global History* 7 (2012), pp. 210–32.

[37] Stöckmann, 'Studying the International, Serving the Nation'.

[38] Glenda Sluga, *Internationalism in the Age of Nationalism* (Philadelphia, 2013), p. 152.

[39] Glenda Sluga and Patricia Clavin, 'Introduction: Rethinking the History of Internationalism', in Sluga and Clavin (eds.), *Internationalisms: A Twentieth-Century History* (Cambridge, 2016), p. 10.

[40] IIIC, *The State and Economic Life* (1932), p. 89.

[41] See, for example, Carl Brinkmann, *Die Bedeutung der Allmenden im Neuen Deutschland* (Heidelberg, 1935).

into private life.[42] Others, such as the historian Martin Spahn – who had directed the right-wing Politisches Kolleg in Berlin since 1920 – now turned from conservatism to open sympathy with Nazism.[43] Mendelssohn Bartholdy's IAP was taken over by the historian and Nazi educationalist Adolf Rein who was a staunch opponent of liberal universities.[44] At the DHfP, the loyal party member Paul Meier-Benneckenstein took over from Jäckh as acting director. Among the new lecturers was the physician Walter Groß, head of the Office of Racial Purity and a staunch anti-Semite whose academic publications justified the extermination of Jews.[45] Hitler's government also bundled research centres to make it easier to control them, forming the Department for the Scientific Study of International Relations in 1935 and later, in 1940, the German Institute for Foreign Studies, directed by the SS official Franz Six.[46]

Lecturers and staff were now selected according to the *Führerprinzip* and the DHfP offered courses such as "race studies".[47] It was advertised as the "school of political leadership (*Schule des politischen Führertums*)" on large brown posters.[48] Whereas it had once been an

[42] A national conservative politician, Hoetzsch had advocated a 'greater Germany' united with Austria but later fell out of favour with the Nazis because of his interest in Soviet Russia. See, Otto Hoetzsch to Werner Picht, 18 May 1933, K.I.1i, IIIC; Otto Hoetzsch, *Die weltpolitische Kräfteverteilung nach den Pariser Friedensschlüssen* (Berlin, 1925), p. 37; and Fritz T. Epstein, 'Hoetzsch, Otto', *Neue Deutsche Biographie* 9 (1972), p. 371, available at www.deutsche-biographie.de/gnd118838180.html#ndbcontent [accessed 3 October 2016].

[43] Steven D. Korenblat, 'A School for the Republic?', *Central European History* 39:3 (2006), p. 405.

[44] "In turning against liberal ambiguity and the democratic tendency of adult education [...] we will need concentration on all levels." Adolf Rein, *Die Idee der Politischen Universität* (Hamburg, 1933), p. 36.

[45] Lecture broschure, winter term 1934/35, PA AA, RZ 507, R 64153. See, among others, Walter Groß, *Das ewige Deutschland* (Berlin, 1937); Walter Groß, *Der deutsche Rassengedanke und die Welt* (Berlin, 1939); Walter Groß, *Die rassenpolitischen Voraussetzungen zur Lösung der Judenfrage* (München, 1943).

[46] Their original German names were *Abteilung für das wissenschaftliche Studium der Internationalen Beziehungen* and *Deutsches Auslandswissenschaftliches Institut*. Fritz Berber to IIIC, 4 May 1935, Folder 10010, Box 111, Series 100.S, RG 1.1, RF, Rockefeller Archive Center. See also Gisela Gantzel-Kress and Klaus Jürgen Gantzel, 'The Development of International Relations Studies in West Germany', in Ekkehart Krippendorff and Volker Rittberger (eds.), *The Foreign Policy of West Germany: Formation and Contents* (London, 1980), p. 200.

[47] Lecture broschure, winter term 1934/35, PA AA, RZ 507, R 64153.

[48] Advertisement poster, winter term 1934/35, PA AA, RZ 507, R 64153.

institution with a diverse student body, it now came under pressure from NS youth organisations. Yet, the academic study of IR was not hijacked or steered by the Nazi government to the extent that one might expect, probably because it was not considered important enough. After all, political elites were recruited from party circles, not from universities. Foreign policy strategies were developed by Hitler himself, not by a team of academic advisors. In this sense, it was the gradual neglect of IR, rather than an outright attack on it, that put an end to liberal scholarship in Germany.

Most remarkable, perhaps, was the role played by Friedrich ("Fritz") Berber.[49] A specialist on public international law and international affairs, Berber directed the DHfP's research branch since 1932 and continued to do so after the school's *Gleichschaltung* until 1940. He published several apologetic studies on Nazi foreign policy.[50] From the mid-1930s, he served as special advisor to the senior diplomat (and later foreign minister) Joachim von Ribbentrop who valued Berber's expertise on international affairs and sent him on various semi-diplomatic missions. Even after the war, Berber bragged that Ribbentrop used to refer to him as "my encyclopaedia".[51] Ribbentrop realised that Berber was the ideal scholar–diplomat to gauge sentiments abroad at events such as the International Studies Conference (ISC).[52] The German foreign office hence paid for Berber's travel expenses and arranged for him to meet with German and foreign ambassadors.[53] This practice skilfully exploited the non-official diplomatic channels cultivated by IR experts during a time when Nazi Germany was no longer represented at the League of Nations. Berber's objective was to justify Hitler's foreign policy while coming across as a moderate academic and by maintaining friendly contacts

---

[49] Katharina Rietzler, 'Counter-Imperial Orientalism: Friedrich Berber and the Politics of International Law in Germany and India, 1920s–1960s', *Journal of Global History* 11:1 (2016), pp. 113–34.

[50] Fritz Berber (ed.), *Locarno: Eine Dokumentensammlung* (Berlin, 1936); and Fritz Berber, *Das Diktat von Versailles: Entstehung, Inhalt, Zerfall* (Berlin, 1939).

[51] Leonhard Reinisch to Arnold Toynbee, 21 June 1967, Arnold Toynbee Papers, Box 13.

[52] After the Second World War, Berber admitted that he had worked as a research assistant for Ribbentrop. Berber to Toynbee, 13 May 1967, Arnold Toynbee Papers, Box 13.

[53] Fritz Berber to Oberregierungsrat Böttger, 9 November 1937, BArch R 4901/2994, fol. 1, p. 17.

abroad.[54] Internal documents reveal how consciously Nazi leaders used forms of cultural diplomacy. "It is obvious that we will have to deal with ideological opponents", a foreign office report contemplated in January 1939, "but it would be immensely beneficial to attack the enemy in his own camp".[55] Berber's reports were read by senior officials, including the head of the cultural division at the foreign office, Friedrich Stieve, as well as Hitler's minister of culture, Bernhard Rust.[56]

As Nazi Germany's influence spread across Europe, its propaganda machinery engulfed other institutions for the study of IR, notably the Konsularakademie in Vienna. Its interwar directors, Anton Winter and Friedrich Hlavac, were both supporters of *Großdeutschland* and did little to protect the school from right-wing influence.[57] At first, during the 1933–4 academic year, the curriculum remained largely unchanged and the school even expressed concern to have German or Italian professors lecture "under current conditions".[58] But a few days after Austria's *Anschluss* in March 1938, Hlavac signed a statement on behalf of the faculty that confirmed their loyalty to Hitler.[59] In private letters he expressed the hope to safeguard the Konsularakademie in some form, similar to what Jäckh had tried five years ago in Berlin, although the true face of the regime was now much clearer.[60] At the same time, Hlavac did not have any illusions about Berlin's power in directing the future research agenda and selection of faculty members. By 20 April 1938, on Hitler's birthday, the Nazis were firmly in control of the Konsularakademie and hosted a celebration, in honour of the *Führer*, to which only "Aryan students" were invited.[61] The event turned into a propaganda show, portraying the annexation as a "great

[54] Katharina Rietzler, 'Counter-Imperial Orientalism', *Journal of Global History* 11:1 (2016), pp. 120–7.
[55] Report by German Foreign Ministry, January 1939, R61221, PA AA.
[56] Draft Letter by Bernhard Rust, 31 December 1937, BArch R 4901/2994, fol. 1, p. 22.
[57] Heinrich Pfusterschmidt-Hardtenstein, *A Short History of the Diplomatic Academy of Vienna* (2008), p. 28.
[58] Lecture plan 1933/4, Akte 44-4; and Memo, 30 December 1935, OeStA, Archiv der Konsularakademie, Box 45.
[59] Memo, 19 March 1938, OeStA, Archiv der Konsularakademie, Box 48.
[60] Friedrich Hlavac to Müller[?], 18 March 1938, OeStA, Archiv der Konsularakademie, Box 48-1.
[61] Circular to professors and students, 12 April 1938, OeStA, Archiv der Konsularakademie, Box 48-1.

fortune" for Austria and as the reverse of the "injustices" of Versailles.[62] Soon after that, Hlavac announced a major restructuring of the school and urged his students to finish their degrees before the changes would take effect.[63] In due course, all students had to be registered members of the National Socialist Party, and the curriculum listed courses on 'race theory', the history of the 'German *Volk*', and Nazi economic policy.[64]

For many opposition scholars the only solution was to seek refuge abroad. Over the following years, a considerable number of academics in IR and related fields emigrated to Britain and the United States. Besides Jäckh and Mendelssohn Bartholdy, this group included Herbert von Beckerath, Arnold Bergstraesser, Hajo Holborn, Hans Kelsen, Hans Morgenthau, Georg Schwarzenberger, Alfred Vagts, Erich Voegelin, and Arnold Wolfers. Historians have counted fifty-eight European scholars of international law and IR who emigrated to the United States during the 1930s.[65] In many cases, the Rockefeller Foundation provided funds for refugee scholars and helped to arrange for temporary academic positions. One notable host institution was the New Commonwealth Institute in London, which employed Ernst Jäckh as director and published the works of Hans Kelsen, Gustav Radbruch, Walther Schücking, Hans Wehberg, and Georg Schwarzenberger (who taught IR in London from 1938 throughout the war).[66] Even some university students were able to continue their studies abroad. In 1937, the London School of Economics counted some twenty-one German students.[67]

By the mid-1930s, the Nazi government had largely succeeded in suppressing the study of IR and forcing liberal scholars into exile. Thus came to an end the brief period of liberal political science in German-

[62] Ibid.
[63] Circular, 6 May 1938, OeStA, Archiv der Konsularakademie, Box 48-1.
[64] Circulars of 10 January and 26 February 1940, OeStA, Archiv der Konsularakademie, Box 49-18.
[65] Alfons Söllner, 'From International Law to International Relations: Emigré Scholars in American Political Science and International Relations', in Felix Rösch (ed.), *Émigré Scholars and the Genesis of International Relations: A European Discipline in America?* (New York, 2014), p. 198.
[66] Index of New Commonwealth Institute Memoranda, 1935, Dossier 2381, Box R4010, League of Nations Archives, Geneva. On Schwarzenberger, see F. S. Northedge, *Department of International History: A Brief History, 1924–1971*, p. 11, Box 12, School History, LSE Archives, London.
[67] The Rockefeller Foundation, Confidential Monthly Report No. 12 (April 1938).

speaking countries. The very premise of Nazi ideology, a *völkisch*-inspired expansionist foreign policy, ran counter to the rational conduct of international politics. IR scholarship rested on the assumption that government policies could be criticised and changed by democratic procedures, a condition that could no longer be taken for granted. Instead, the Nazis nationalised, downsized, and curbed the study of IR to ensure as little noise as possible from potential dissidents.

Making Sense of Hitler

When the architects of IR heard about the academic purges in Germany they immediately began to help refugee scholars. They saw Hitler's ideology as an attack against the core values of academic freedom, especially in the field of IR which relied on the free exchange of political ideas.[68] On 13 May 1933, the director of the London School of Economics (LSE) William Beveridge published an open letter condemning the forced resignation of professors and lecturers at German universities. It was co-signed by classicist Gilbert Murray, economist John Maynard Keynes as well as by the vice-chancellors of Oxford and Cambridge.[69] Around the same time, Beveridge set up a scheme for refugee scholars which became known as the Academic Assistance Council – it still operates today as the Council for At-Risk Academics. One of the first scholars whom Beveridge invited to England in 1933 was the economist Moritz Julius Bonn.[70] Like Beveridge, Bonn was a participant of the ISC and was widely respected in the field of IR.[71] Thanks to his international profile, Bonn took up a teaching position at LSE before emigrating to the United States in 1939.

Emigré scholars benefitted from the extensive network that they had developed in the 1920s and that now provided them with positions at

[68] Philip Noel-Baker, Violet Bonham Carter, Victor Cazalet, Joan Mary Fry, George Barker Jeffery, Gilbert Murray, 'German Refugees', *The Times* (29 June 1937), p. 12.

[69] Open letter, 12 May 1933, BArch R43-II/1431, pp. 34–5.

[70] William Beveridge to Moritz Julius Bonn, 1 May 1933, S.P.S.L. Records 229/2 (file 1933–49).

[71] Patricia Clavin, '"A Wandering Scholar" in Britain and the USA, 1933–45: The Life and Work of Moritz Bonn', in Anthony Grenville (ed.), *Refugees from the Third Reich in Britain* (Amsterdam, 2002), p. 32.

leading Anglo-American universities. The political scientist Arnold Wolfers, who had served as director of the DHfP from 1930 until 1933 (and whose wife was Jewish), secured a position at Yale University.[72] Wolfers quickly established himself as a popular lecturer and an academic authority in the United States. In February 1935, he was appointed Master of Pierson College and was given a titled professorship at Yale.[73] In February 1934, the DHfP historian Hajo Holborn decided to leave Germany and, like his colleague Wolfers, found a position at Yale.[74] The historian Alfred Vagts, who had worked with Mendelssohn Bartholdy in Hamburg, went on to teach at Harvard and Radcliffe Colleges before becoming a member of the Institute for Advanced Study at Princeton in 1938.[75] In many cases the Rockefeller Foundation contributed funds to accommodate individual refugee scholars, for example by paying for 50 per cent of Holborn's salary, whereas they withdrew funding from German institutions for the study of IR.[76]

Although they offered practical help to refugee academics, the architects of IR struggled to make sense of Nazi foreign policy on an analytical level. The key question was how to deal with non-democratic regimes in the framework of an international order based on democracy and the rule of law. Nazi Germany was no longer a member of that community. Hitler undermined the most basic conventions of international diplomacy and deliberately torpedoed the League of Nations with his aggressive outbursts and cunning tactics. Historians still discuss the extent to which Hitler pursued any coherent strategy at all. Perhaps he was impossible to predict. Perhaps his erratic opportunism was in fact part of a long-term plan of political action, as Gerhard Weinberg has suggested.[77] In any event, it is important to remember that Hitler rose to power during a time of declining confidence in international

[72] Appointment documents, 22 April 1933, Arnold Wolfers Papers, Box 4, Folder 62.
[73] President and Fellows of Yale University to Wolfers, 9 February 1935, Box 4, Folder 62, Arnold Wolfers Papers.
[74] Hajo Holborn to Alfred Vagts, 5 February 1934; and Hajo Holborn to Alfred Vagts, 21 May 1934, Box 1, Folder 5, Hajo Holborn Papers.
[75] Kelly Boyd (ed.), *Encyclopedia of Historians and Historical Writing*, vol. 1 (London, 1999), p. 1251.
[76] Hajo Holborn to Alfred Vagts, 30 April 1934, Hajo Holborn Papers, Box 1, Folder 5. Memo by Tracy Kittredge, 6 April 1936, Folder 10010, Box 111, 100. S, RG 1.1, RF, Rockefeller Archive Center.
[77] Gerhard L. Weinberg, *Hitler's Foreign Policy 1933–1939: The Road to World War II*, 3rd ed. (New York, 2010), p. 6. See also Jochen Thies, *Hitler's Plans for*

institutions, following the Manchurian crisis, the failure of disarmament, and the Great Depression. The liberal internationalist camp had
exhausted both the "funds and the energy of [its] supporters", as Gilbert
Murray confessed in January 1933.[78]

Still, it is striking how hesitantly IR scholars reacted when the Nazi
regime unfolded its programme. Instead of speaking out against its
injustices and its threat to international peace, most scholars evaded
the challenges it posed. Their correspondence often read like there was
an elephant in the room. In May 1933, for example, the German ISC
delegation reported that they might not be able to attend the next
session due to "circumstances".[79] None of the ISC study cycles – on
"The State and Economic Life" (1932–3) and "Collective Security"
(1934–5) – devoted any significant attention to Germany. Nor did
publications during the mid-1930s provide detailed analyses of Nazi
foreign policy. Still in 1937, a conference panel on "strong political
tensions" dealt with Spain and with the China–Japan conflict but
omitted Nazi Germany.[80] Did they shy away from uncomfortable
questions? Was it related to the fact that many IR scholars had personal ties to Germany – T. P. Conwell-Evans (taught in Germany),
Toynbee (sent his son to Germany in 1933), and Zimmern (had a
German father)?

IR scholars not only failed to predict or describe political developments, some actually courted Germany's foreign policy elite. One year
into Hitler's rule, Toynbee recruited Fritz Berber as a German delegate
to the ISC (when there was no longer a full German delegation).[81] He
argued that Berber was "more representative and more effective ... in
the present circumstances" than other scholars to convey a German
point of view.[82] Henri Bonnet, then director of the IIIC, assured
Toynbee that "[t]he presence of Dr. Berber ... will certainly be most
valuable", and thanked Toynbee for his initiative.[83] Neither Toynbee

---

Global Domination: Nazi Architecture and Ultimate War Aims (New York,
  2012).
[78] Gilbert Murray to David Davies, 13 January 1933, Gilbert Murray Papers,
  Box 216.
[79] Otto Hoetzsch to Werner Picht, 2 May 1933, K.I.1i, IIIC Records.
[80] WILPF, *Report of the Ninth Congress* (Geneva, 1937), p. 11.
[81] Susan Pedersen, *The Guardians: The League of Nations and the Crisis of
  Empire* (Oxford, 2015), pp. 326–8.
[82] Arnold Toynbee to Henri Bonnet, 27 June 1934, K.I.1m, IIIC Records.
[83] Henri Bonnet to Arnold Toynbee, 9 April 1935, K.I.1q, IIIC Records.

nor Bonnet saw the problem of inviting a representative whose sole mission was to sabotage international cooperation and to spread propaganda on behalf of the German government.[84]

Toynbee's advances were not limited to professors. Nor was he alone in exploring these routes. In June 1934, he corresponded with Alfred Rosenberg, the chief theorist of Nazi ideology, who complained about the "suppression of the German minorities" in Central Europe and argued that Hitler's foreign policy was an "undeniable proof of the peaceful intentions of the national socialist state".[85] Toynbee's colleague T. P. Conwell-Evans, who lectured in Königsberg during the 1930s, proudly reported about his personal interactions with leading German officials.[86] His acquaintances included Ribbentrop, Hermann Göring as well as undersecretaries Erhard Milch and Paul Körner.[87] In October 1936, James T. Shotwell was received by Friedrich Stieve, head of cultural affairs at the German Foreign Office.[88] It was not uncommon for IR scholars to seek direct contact with German officials. Meanwhile, German politicians gained an entrée to academic circles. For example, the head of the Sudeten German Party, Konrad Henlein, gave a paper at Chatham House in December 1935.[89]

The problem was not that IR scholars were ill-informed about Nazi Germany or ignored its international role, but that they failed to integrate the disturbing developments into a resolute academic response – such as Hannah Ahrendt later provided in *The Origins of Totalitarianism* (1951). They were well aware that Germany was a principal actor in European politics, even if no longer a member of the League.[90] Nor were they blind to its authoritarian nature. In

[84] Toynbee later recalled that Berber shocked everyone at the ISC "by putting to us the case for Nazi *Realpolitik*", note on a letter by Berber to Toynbee, 13 May 1967, Arnold Toynbee Papers, Box 13.

[85] Horst Obermüller to Arnold Toynbee, 22 June 1934, Arnold Toynbee Papers, Box 76.

[86] T. P. Conwell-Evans, in 'Germany and the Rhineland II', *International Affairs* 15:6 (1936), p. 41.

[87] 'Foreword', in T. P. Conwell-Evans, *None So Blind: A Study of the Crisis Years, 1930–1939, Based on the Private Papers of Group-Captain M. G. Christie* (London, 1947), pp. x–xi.

[88] Fritz Berber to Friedrich Stieve, 27 October 1936, PA AA, RZ 507, R 64153.

[89] Konrad Henlein, 'The German Minority in Czechoslovakia', *International Affairs* 15:4 (1936), pp. 561–72 [talk delivered on 9 December 1935].

[90] The Round Table, 'German Foreign Policy', *The Commonwealth Journal of International Affairs* 26:101 (1935), p. 98.

November 1933, William Rappard sent a private letter to Zimmern in which he deplored the international "mess", and warned that "one must be stricken with absolute blindness if one does not see the imminent menace of Germany's present policies".[91] Noel-Baker wrote to conservative MP Leo Amery about the connection between Nazism and the breakdown of disarmament. "The Germans' attitude is now beyond reproach", he commented in June 1933.[92] He understood that Hitler was merely "playing [the] disarmament game".[93] Noel-Baker also saw the connection of how the League's failures in Manchuria (and in the Chaco) now backfired on Europe where no one believed in 'collective security' anymore.[94]

Women were among the sharpest and most critical observers of Nazi politics. Just days after Hitler's appointment as *Reichskanzler*, Kathleen Courtney alerted Gilbert Murray about the "only too apparent" tensions between Germany, Italy, and France.[95] At a 1936 debate at Chatham House, Eleanor Rathbone warned against perceiving Germany as an underdog, pointing out that Hitler had spent twice the sum on armaments allowed in 1935 alone.[96] If unchallenged, Hitler posed a serious threat for the outbreak of another war, Rathbone argued. A year later, the historian and Conservative politician Agnes Headlam-Morley published an analysis of how democratic institutions surrendered to authoritarian regimes.[97] In particular, she criticised Germany's parliamentary system as well as the personality cult of Hitler and Mussolini. What Headlam-Morley saw clearer than others was how authoritarian leaders systematically ignored norms of government and, coupled with their "utter disregard for historical fact", gradually replaced the rules-based international order with their own propaganda.[98]

[91] William Rappard to Alfred Zimmern, 14 November 1933, HEI [uncatalogued], Archives of the Graduate Institute of International Studies.
[92] Noel-Baker to Leo Amery[?], 1 June 1933, Gilbert Murray Papers, Box 217.
[93] Ibid.
[94] Philip Noel-Baker to Gilbert Murray, 28 March 1933, Gilbert Murray Papers, Box 217.
[95] Kathleen Courtney to Gilbert Murray, 13 February 1933, Gilbert Murray Papers, Box 216.
[96] Eleanor Rathbone, in 'Germany and the Rhineland II', *International Affairs* 15:6 (1936), p. 41.
[97] Agnes Headlam-Morley, 'The Totalitarian State', in Reginald Coupland and Margery Perham (eds.), *Oxford University Summer School on Colonial Administration* (Oxford, 1937), pp. 31–3.
[98] Ibid., p. 32.

IR authors did not uniformly misconceive the intentions of Nazism and blindly endorse a liberal internationalist agenda. Even alleged 'idealists', such as Zimmern, saw the dangers of Hitler's regime. In November 1933, he called for a tough security policy on Germany and a global arms embargo.[99] By 1934 Zimmern had grown disillusioned with formal assurances of mutual peacefulness, rejecting the Kellogg–Briand Pact as "sentimental [and] misguided idealism".[100] A few years later, Philip Noel-Baker condemned the interventions of Germany and Italy in the Spanish Civil War, and called for the British Prime Minister Neville Chamberlain to resign.[101] The journalist and Fabian socialist Robert Dell concluded in 1940 that interwar governments had "played the game of power politics without the smallest regard for the general interest of the world".[102] It would be too simple therefore to cluster IR scholarship into pro- and anti-German camps, or into 'idealist' and 'realist' theory. In any event, self-declared 'realists' such as E. H. Carr also failed to appreciate the dangers of Nazi foreign policy and ended up endorsing appeasement.[103] The truth is that the architects of IR decided to counter Hitler's unpredictable course by spontaneous policy proposals (and quasi-diplomatic ventures) rather than to formulate a reasonably consistent analytical explanation.

The Idea of Peaceful Change

The perplexities of Germany's foreign policy fuelled the debate about new instruments of international politics. IR scholars looked for new ways to deal with expansionist ambitions without risking a preventive war. The solution was, broadly speaking, to satisfy the grievances of revisionist governments by adjusting international borders and legal conditions, a policy that became known as 'peaceful change'. In

---

[99] Alfred Zimmern, 'Mesures préventive contre l'Allemagne', *La Presse*, Montreal, November 1933, newspaper clipping, HEI [uncatalogued], Archives of the Graduate Institute of International Studies.

[100] Alfred Zimmern, 'Memorandum for Discussion at Sub-Committee on the British Commonwealth and the Collective System', 25 June 1934, Alfred Zimmern Papers, Box 97.

[101] 'Halifax Speech Assurance', 12 June 1939, Lionel Curtis Papers, MS. Curtis 17.

[102] Robert Dell, *The Geneva Racket, 1920–1939* (London, 1940), p. 8. Daniel Renshaw, 'The Disillusionment of Robert Dell: The Intellectual Journey of a Catholic Socialist', *Intellectual History Review* 29:2 (2019), pp. 337–58.

[103] See Wilson, 'E. H. Carr's the Twenty Years' Crisis', p. 21.

particular, 'peaceful change' was used to address the territorial (and colonial) claims of the so-called 'have-nots', those revisionist powers including Germany and Italy that protested against their lack of overseas territories. Given the ultimate failure to contain Hitler and Mussolini by diplomatic means, 'peaceful change' is often seen as a direct precursor to Neville Chamberlain's policy of 'appeasement', his fatal 1938 strategy to make concessions to Germany at almost any cost which eventually led to the Second World War.[104]

However, the idea of 'peaceful change' actually emerged from an older and more complicated history. Some have traced it back to pre-twentieth-century traditions of royal marriages, leases, annexations, exchanges of territories or population, gifts, or uncontested secession.[105] At the very latest, it was conceived during the drafting of the League of Nations Covenant.[106] The 'adjustment' Article XIX specified that "[t]he Assembly may from time to time advise the reconsideration by Members of the League of treaties which have become inapplicable and the consideration of international conditions whose continuance might endanger the peace of the world".[107] Its original version, drafted by President Woodrow Wilson in January 1919, went on to detail the reasons, procedure, and compensation for territorial change.[108] Academic advisors supported Wilson's ambition. The British historian and government advisor James Headlam-Morley hoped "that an opportunity will be made for modification" in the Covenant.[109] Throughout the 1920s, IR scholars continued to discuss

---

[104] See, for example, P. M. H. Bell, *The Origins of the Second World War in Europe*, 3rd ed. (New York, 2007), pp. 261–84; Igor Lukes and Erik Goldstein (eds.), *The Munich Crisis, 1938: Prelude to World War II* (London, 1999); Gerhard L. Weinberg, *Germany, Hitler, and World War II: Essays in Modern German and World History* (Cambridge, 1995), p. 109; or Zara Steiner, *Triumph of the Dark: European International History, 1933–1939* (Oxford, 2011), pp. 552–670.

[105] C. R. M. F. Cruttwell, *A History of Peaceful Change in the Modern World* (Oxford, 1937), pp. 1–18.

[106] 'A Historical Note on Collective Security', by Alfred Zimmern, April 1935, Alfred Zimmern Papers, Box 86.

[107] The Covenant of the League of Nations, *The Avalon Project: Documents in Law, History and Diplomacy*, available at http://avalon.law.yale.edu/20th_century/leagcov.asp [accessed 7 March 2019].

[108] G. M. Gathorne-Hardy, 'Territorial Revision and Article 19 of the League Covenant', *International Affairs* 14:6 (1935), pp. 820–1.

[109] Headlam-Morley to Alfred Zimmern, 26 May 1919, Alfred Zimmern Papers, Box Adds. 1.

"methods for change" in the context of League interventions, such as in the Leticia dispute between Colombia and Peru or with regard to Denmark's expulsion of Norwegians in East Greenland. Their underlying premise was that "the map of the world is not static".[110] The architects of IR envisaged 'peaceful change' as a pre-emptive strategy for political stability rather than as a last resort to avoid war. In February 1933, long before border revisions were seriously considered, Toynbee privately told Murray that the British government should make up its mind about German claims in Poland.[111] At this point it was hard to foresee that adjusting borders in favour of the 'have-nots' would stimulate their demand for further expansion. In fact, political theorist David Mitrany regretted in 1935 that the work on 'peaceful change' had not started earlier.[112] Even the critics of 'peaceful change', who feared that changes of frontiers would cause violent rebellion, expressed their concerns *before* Nazi Germany launched its aggressive foreign policy.[113] It is true that the second half of the 1930s became the high tide of 'peaceful change' thinking – as is reflected in numerous publications, conferences, lectures, and university courses.[114] But the original idea to create a flexible international order was much older.

As a political concept, 'peaceful change' was not limited to territorial revisions. IR scholars used the label to discuss a whole range of policy options from formal procedures to diplomatic manoeuvring. One common interpretation, suggested at the ISC, defined the term as "the peaceful settlement of international difficulties arising out of the aspirations of non-satisfied peoples".[115] By introducing 'satisfaction' as a category in international politics, however, they left enormous

---

[110] Manley O. Hudson, 'Recent Territorial Disputes before the League of Nations', in Geneva Institute of International Relations (ed.), *The Problem of Peace: Second Series: Lectures Delivered at the Geneva Institute of International Relations* (Oxford, 1928), p. 100.

[111] Arnold Toynbee to Gilbert Murray, 20 February 1933, Arnold Toynbee Papers, Box 72.

[112] 'Notes by Professor Mitrany on Professor Zimmern's Memorandum', 3 October 1935, Arnold Toynbee Papers, Box 98.

[113] Gilbert Murray, 'Introduction', in Lucy Mair (ed.), *The Protection of Minorities: The Working and Scope of the Minorities Treaties under the League of Nations* (London, 1928), p. viii.

[114] The ISC 1936–7 study cycle was themed 'Peaceful Change'. For university courses on 'peaceful change', see F. S. Northedge, *Department of International History: A Brief History, 1924–1971*, Box 12, School History, LSE Archives.

[115] IIIC, *Peaceful Change* (1938), p. 19.

room for interpretation. There was ambiguity, too, about the practical implementation of 'peaceful settlement' and about what constituted legitimate reasons for change. Frederick Lugard, the British representative on the Mandates Commission, identified three common lines of argument: (i) population pressure, (ii) access to raw materials, and (iii) national prestige.[116] As motivations for revisionism varied, he suggested, so did the corresponding policy instruments to solve disputes. Among the topics discussed by participants of the ISC were population control, migration, colonial reform, markets, and raw materials.

One contentious point was access to raw materials. The French ISC delegate and founder of the Centre d'études de politique étrangère in Paris, Étienne Dennery, presented a detailed study of natural resources that he considered essential for state survival.[117] He then outlined their spread across various countries, and the extent to which unequal access could be mitigated. Dennery concluded that colonial revision would do little to satisfy the 'have-nots' demands since, for example, the total exports of Germany's former colonies amounted to no more than 3.5 per cent of Germany's imports. The president of the International University Federation for the League of Nations, Ewan P. Wallis-Jones, presented a similar analysis at their 1936 meeting in Geneva.[118] The revisionists' demand for the transfer of territories, he argued, sprang from a desire for geopolitical control, not access to resources. Conceding to territorial demands would allow the 'have-nots' to pursue essentially warlike strategies without having to fight.

The fear of 'overpopulation' was another popular justification for revisionists. It was based on a twofold assumption: first, that there were natural limits to how many people could live in a given country, and second, that one could re-arrange borders (and people) to achieve some sort of optimum level. "Congested" countries such as Japan needed "breathing space", as New Zealand historian Guy H. Scholefield put it.[119] Leonard J. Cromie, a Carnegie research fellow

[116] Lord Lugard, 'The Basis of the Claim for Colonies', *International Affairs* 15:1 (1936), p. 3.
[117] Étienne Dennery, in IIIC, *Peaceful Change* (1938), p. 103.
[118] Ewan P. Wallis-Jones, 'Redistribution of Raw Materials', in Fédération Universitaire Interntionale pour la Société des Nations, *Problèmes Du 'Peaceful Change': Rapport Du XIIIe Congrès* (Geneva, 1936), p. 34.
[119] Guy H. Scholefield, 'Peace in the Far East and the Collective System', *Tenth Series: Lectures Delivered at the Geneva Institute of International Relations* (Geneva, 1936), p. 98.

in IR and rapporteur at the 1938 ISC, was convinced that there was "serious overcrowding" in the Far East, notably in India, China, Japan, Korea, and the Netherlands Indies.[120] At the same conference, biologist Alexander Carr-Saunders asserted that Italy, too, was "manifestly overpopulated".[121] Germany's population, on the other hand, was stagnating during the first half of the 1930s which undermined Hitler's argument for *Lebensraum*.[122] To prevent international dispute, delegates at the ISC proposed to draw up an international population policy with the goal of reaching a "synthetic optimum".[123] That exercise never materialised but population surveys nonetheless added new evidence to the study of IR. As these examples show, 'peaceful change' referred not simply to under-the-counter diplomatic deals between the 'have-nots' and the 'haves', but it drew on studies in a range of sub-fields that substantiated the claim of IR as a social science.

The most common way to employ 'peaceful change', however, was as an instrument of foreign policy within the context of a flexible international order.[124] Given that international conditions were not static, it provided governments with a simple way to re-negotiate their respective interests. While 'collective security' guaranteed the integrity of borders (by threat of sanctions) and while arbitration courts decided in cases of dispute, the goal of 'peaceful change' was to design (and re-design) the international order. In other words, 'peaceful change' was to become the legislative branch of international governance, with 'collective security' representing the executive power, and arbitration of the judiciary. This interpretation picked up Wilson's original idea to give Article XIX an authoritative rather than merely an advisory character.[125] If sanctions and arbitration were coordinated by an international authority, the argument ran, then that authority should possess non-violent powers to adjust the international order.

[120] IIIC, *Peaceful Change* (Paris, 1938), p. 132.   [121] Ibid., p. 134.
[122] Ibid., p. 135.   [123] Ibid., p. 495.
[124] See especially Arnold Toynbee, 'Peaceful Change or War? The Next Stage in the International Crisis', *International Affairs* 15:1 (1936), p. 28. See also, Jaroslav Zourek, 'La sécurité collective et la définition de l'aggresseur', in Fédération Universitaire Interntionale pour la Société des Nations, *Problèmes Du 'Peaceful Change': Rapport Du XIIIe Congrès* (Geneva, 1936); Philip C. Jessup, *International Security: The American Role in Collective Action for Peace* (New York, 1935), p. 148.
[125] IIIC, *Peaceful Change*, pp. 531, 539.

IR scholars concluded that 'peaceful change' needed a workable machinery within the existing framework of international institutions. David Mitrany, for example, proposed to integrate it into the League of Nations.[126] French lawyer Albert Geouffre de Lapradelle suggested installing an "advisory board" attached to the League of Nations Council to study questions of 'peaceful change'.[127] Pitman B. Potter, an American IR scholar working at the Geneva Graduate Institute, agreed that the League should be open to reforming itself and to consider the revisionist claims of the 'have-nots'.[128] US lawyer and diplomat John Foster Dulles urged to develop the potential for 'peaceful change' contained in Article XIX to overcome the League's attachment to the status quo.[129] The same argument was also made by IR scholars William T. Stone and Clark M. Eichelberger and, somewhat surprisingly by the British delegation to the ISC – who as a colonial power would have had an interest in preserving the status quo.[130] In all these writings, there was a strong association between security and change. Charles Webster actually described them as two sides of the same coin of international relations.[131] And Toynbee concluded that "collective security without peaceful change would be like a boiler without a safety-valve".[132] The expectations for making 'peaceful change' work were so high that French historian Henri Hauser imagined it would constitute "the most important step forward ever made by humanity".[133] But who, it is important to ask, was considered part of that humanity?

The implications of 'peaceful change' for colonial populations were controversial, to say the least. Female IR authors were among the sharpest critics of territorial transfers, arguing that the trade of colonial

---

[126] 'Notes by Professor Mitrany on Professor Zimmern's Memorandum', 3 October 1935, Alfred Zimmern Papers, Box 98.

[127] IIIC, *Peaceful Change*, p. 545.

[128] Pitman B. Potter, 'Reform of the League', in Geneva Institute of International Relations (ed.), *The Problem of Peace: Eleventh Series: Lectures Delivered at the Geneva Institute of International Relations* (Oxford, 1937), p. 205.

[129] John Foster Dulles, *War, Peace and Change* (London, 1939), p. ix.

[130] William T. Stone and Clark M. Eichelberger, *Peaceful Change: The Alternative to War* (New York, 1937), p. 42; and Memo, 4 June 1935, Alfred Zimmern Papers, Box 86.

[131] Charles K. Webster, 'What Is the Problem of Peaceful Change?', in C. A. W. Manning (ed.), *Peaceful Change: An International Problem* (London, 1937), p. 3.

[132] Toynbee, 'Peaceful Change or War?', p. 27.

[133] IIIC, *Peaceful Change*, p. 265.

possessions would be politics at the expense of native peoples. In her 1937 study on 'Colonial Policy and Peaceful Change', LSE lecturer Lucy Mair delivered a thorough critique of what she described as a cynical and immoral game played by the great powers.[134] She first debunked the economic myth that overseas territories brought economic advantages to the metropole. Then she revealed that the territorial claims of the revisionists did not match their desire for raw materials. Nor did colonial possessions guarantee 'great power'-status (see Belgium and Holland) or vice-versa (see the United States). If governments insisted on transferring territories, Mair argued, the interests of native populations had to be respected because *they* were the ones most affected. Given the Nazi ideology of racial superiority, it was difficult to believe that returning colonies to Germany would comply with the interests of people in Tanganyika, Mair concluded. Mandates specialist Freda White delivered a similar argument at a 1936 Chatham House meeting. The application of the terms 'haves' and 'have-nots' was "very silly", she argued, because if one considered poverty and overpopulation consistently, then India and China would have to be the 'have-nots', not Italy and Germany.[135]

Since representatives of colonial people were largely excluded from political debates in Europe, IR scholars pledged to take into account the rights and interests of the "absent" on their behalf.[136] Some authors, such as French political science professor Henri Labouret and British lawyer Arnold McNair, actually pressed the issue and insisted on the rights of native people, including self-government.[137] Anti-imperialist arguments were also made by the participants of the 1936 Geneva conference of the International University Federation for the League of Nations, who called for the "definite emancipation of colonies".[138] In most cases, however, the interests of European powers ranked higher than self-determination when discussing the transfer of

---

[134] Lucy Mair, 'Colonial Policy and Peaceful Change', in C. A. W. Manning (ed.), *Peaceful Change: An International Problem* (London, 1937).
[135] Freda White, in 'Germany and the Rhineland II', *International Affairs* 15:6 (1936), p. 40.
[136] IIIC, *Peaceful Change*, p. 418.
[137] Ibid., p. 436; and Arnold McNair, 'Collective Security', *British Year Book of International Law* 17 (1936), p. 159.
[138] Fédération Universitaire Interntionale pour la Société des Nations, *Problèmes Du 'Peaceful Change': Rapport Du XIIIe Congrès* (Geneva, 1936), p. 85.

sovereignty.[139] Concern for colonial people was usually no more than a footnote and failed to result in any form of general analysis.[140] Instead, IR scholars took advantage of the contingent nature of 'peaceful change' and the vague formulations in the Covenant. This was ideal territory for professors who wanted to make a difference in current affairs.

From Chatham House to the *Reichskanzlei*

In December 1935, Arnold Toynbee gave a paper at Chatham House, London, arguing that 'peaceful change' was the only alternative to war.[141] Specifically, he suggested to re-allocate territories that were then controlled by the 'haves', so that the grievances of the 'have-nots' might be resolved. The 'have-nots' (or 'dissatisfied' powers) included Italy, Japan, Hungary, Bulgaria, Lithuania, and Bolivia, but it was clear that Germany was his principal concern. Toynbee's idea was to adjust the "dangerous inequality" between the British and French empires and post-Versailles Germany.[142] To this end, he was prepared to give up British colonial possessions – "peaceful change at our own expense", as he called it.[143] Clinging on to a quarter of the world's land surface, he argued, was difficult to justify without making an effort for international reconciliation. Toynbee's proposal was in part a reaction to Foreign Secretary Samuel Hoare's plan to grant non-colonial powers access to raw materials, which the British foreign minister had raised that September at the League Assembly and which was being discussed in the British press.[144] In part, it was Toynbee's own vision for a reform of international governance. If the idea worked, British sacrifices could serve as a model for a more general system of territorial revision. If it did not, the world would soon be at war.[145]

---

[139] IIIC, *Peaceful Change*, p. 198.   [140] Ibid., p. 192.
[141] Toynbee, 'Peaceful Change or War?' [paper written on 8 December 1935, presented on 17 December 1935].
[142] Ibid., p. 30.   [143] Ibid., p. 32.
[144] See 'Reorganisation of World Resources', *The Manchester Guardian*, 3 October 1935, p. 8.
[145] On the movement for 'colonial appeasement', see Andrew J. Crozier, *Appeasement and Germany's Last Bid for Colonies* (London, 1988); and Pedersen, *The Guardians*, pp. 327–30.

Towards the end of his talk Toynbee presented a plan that he admitted might seem "utopian or revolutionary".[146] He suggested that 'peaceful change' might be achieved by internationalising territories currently controlled by the 'haves'. In practice, this meant to extend the League's mandate system to European colonial holdings and to put these territories under international administration. They would be governed by League of Nations officials and fly the League of Nations flag, Toynbee imagined.[147] Internationalising colonies would not only ensure that the dissatisfied powers received their *economic* share but also participated *politically* in the administration of non-European territories. In addition to that, it would enhance the spirit of international cooperation among European powers.[148] What threatened peace in Europe, he concluded, was:

the fear that these forcibly imposed territorial arrangements will soon be changed violently in the traditional manner unless, at this eleventh hour, we can rise to the almost unprecedented moral achievement of carrying out peaceful change in the territorial sphere.[149]

Toynbee's perspective was strictly European, not as global as the League of Nations claimed to be. He also asserted that the Versailles treaty had been unduly and "forcibly" imposed on Germany, and thus manifested a reason for revision. The alternative, he then argued, would be the return to "traditional" means, by which he meant war. In addition to that, he created a sense of urgency, telling his audience that it was the "eleventh hour". The solution, he suggested, was "territorial" revision on an unprecedented level, possibly even in Europe. He compared Italy's campaign in Abyssinia with the option for "Poland to retrocede to Germany the Polish Corridor", concluding that, while the rights of the local population should generally take priority over foreign claims, there were exceptions to the principles of international law.[150] Perhaps most interestingly, he described it as a "moral" effort for peace, which gave his plan a certain gravitas and which became a key point of contention among his critics.

[146] Toynbee, 'Peaceful Change or War?', p. 48.
[147] This proposal was echoed by Wallis-Jones, 'Redistribution of Raw Materials', p. 39.
[148] Toynbee, 'Peaceful Change or War?', p. 47.   [149] Ibid., p. 34.
[150] Arnold Toynbee, 'Note on Mr Bailey's Draft and Professor Manning's letter of October 18th, 1935', 21 October 1935, Alfred Zimmern Papers, Box 98.

Toynbee was not alone in endorsing colonial revision. Labour politician Charles Roden Buxton applauded his paper and urged the British
government to come up with responses to the "obvious injustices"
prevailing between the 'haves' and 'have-nots'.[151] Buxton had previously made a case for "concessions" to dissatisfied powers "whatever
the form of government".[152] In their 1935 book *The Price of Peace*,
the American historian Frank H. Simonds and the political scientist
Brooks Emeny argued that neither Germany nor Italy possessed the
natural resources necessary to support their populations, and that
consequently some form of 'peaceful change' might be necessary for
maintaining peace.[153] Otherwise, so Simonds and Emeny explained,
these countries had no peaceful means of altering the status quo
enshrined in international law. Meanwhile the critics, such as the
former head of the League's Economic and Financial Section Arthur
Salter, argued that making concessions to Hitler at this stage "would
whet rather than satisfy the aggressor's appetite".[154] An anonymous
member of Chatham House doubted that dictatorial regimes would be
adequate partners in the administration of colonies, and questioned
that the League would be able to set up a qualified and accountable
staff.[155]

Regardless of these concerns, participants of the 1936–7 ISC
followed Toynbee's line of argument. They saw 'peaceful change' not
only as a complement to 'collective security' but as a prerequisite for
the entire system of international cooperation.[156] In his introductory
report, Norwegian historian H. O. Christophersen argued that colonial powers had to be prepared to transfer certain territories to other
states in the interest of international peace and he identified Germany
as the principal beneficiary of this practice.[157] The delegates also
discussed the practical details of peaceful revision. Most favoured some

[151] Charles Buxton, in Arnold Toynbee, 'Peaceful Change or War?', *International Affairs* 15:1 (1936), p. 48.
[152] Charles Roden Buxton, 'The Dissatisfied Powers and the World's Resources', *The Contemporary Review*, November (1935), p. 4.
[153] Frank H. Simonds and Brooks Emeny, *The Price of Peace: The Challenge of Economic Nationalism* (London, 1935), pp. 334–5.
[154] Arthur Salter, in Arnold Toynbee, 'Peaceful Change or War?', *International Affairs* 15:1 (1936), p. 51.
[155] Anonymous, in Arnold Toynbee, 'Peaceful Change or War?', *International Affairs* 15:1 (1936), p. 50.
[156] IIIC, *Peaceful Change*, p. 11.   [157] Ibid., p. 208.

way of "gradually extending the mandate system".[158] Once again, IR scholars took on the role of quasi-diplomats, pondering an issue "of such delicacy that Governments [were] indisposed to make it one of official discussion", as ISC chairman John Foster Dulles explained.[159]

The most controversial speaker was the lawyer Fritz Berber who attended the ISC on behalf of the German government. Berber was an advocate of natural law, a "metaphysical deepening of legal theory", and saw himself as an academic spokesperson of the Nazi government.[160] In his remarks, Berber referenced Hitler's speech of 30 January 1937 in which the *Führer* had demanded the return of German colonies.[161] Drawing on official Nazi doctrine, Berber demonstrated that the reasons for denying Germany colonial status in 1919 no longer applied. Germany was now again a fully respected member of the international community and had shown its good intentions. The prospect of 'peaceful change' was vital for Germany, Berber argued.[162] What he had in mind, of course, was a practice of ad hoc political bargaining, rather than a legal framework under the League of Nations.

Berber's proposal was welcomed by British writer G. M. Gathorne-Hardy who argued that negotiations about territorial revision should be conducted in private, not at the League of Nations, because public attention would distort negotiations.[163] David Mitrany and Norwegian lawyer Frede Castberg agreed on the "political character" of territorial revisions and rejected the idea of a judicial authority.[164] Lord Lytton, on the other hand, was less sympathetic to Berber who, so Lytton commented, had "skated over some very thin ice".[165] American economist Eugene Staley agreed with Lytton. He criticised Berber for presenting the question of colonial revision as a matter of existential concern to Germany which it was evidently not.[166] Scottish

---

[158] Quincy Wright, in IIIC, *Peaceful Change* (1938), p. 459.
[159] IIIC, *Peaceful Change* (1938), p. 259.
[160] Fritz Berber, *Sicherheit und Gerechtigkeit* (Berlin, 1934), pp. 4, 159.
[161] Max Domarus, *Hitler: Speeches and Proclamations, 1932–1945*, vol. 2 (London, 1992), pp. 861–74; IIIC, *Peaceful Change* (1938), p. 465.
[162] Fritz Berber, 'Vorbemerkung', in Diedrich Westermann (ed.), *Beiträge zur deutschen Kolonialfrage* (Berlin, 1937), p. 8.
[163] Gathorne-Hardy, 'Territorial Revision and Article 19 of the League Covenant', pp. 826–7.
[164] IIIC, *Peaceful Change* (1938), pp. 534, 537.   [165] Ibid., p. 468.
[166] Ibid., p. 470.

Labour politician and colonial expert Drummond Shiels protested that Berber's way of reasoning had very much "disorganised" the debate.[167] 'Peaceful change' was by now little more than a fuzzy catchword employed by academics at their respective convenience. After some heated exchange, Berber felt it necessary to reassure his colleagues that Germany did not intend to wage war over the question of colonies.[168]

ISC delegates became so absorbed in the simulation of diplomatic talks that Lytton had to remind his colleagues that their task was not actually to redistribute colonies or mandates.[169] James Shotwell, too, insisted on the scientific character of the ISC, although there was little point in trying to disguise its political nature.[170] At a 1937 lecture in Geneva, Berber insisted that he was providing a "scientific treatment" and speaking as an "unofficial individual", yet he proceeded to defend government policies, using verbatim quotes from official documents and Hitler's speeches.[171] He made no effort to hide his political intentions and accused his colleagues of misrepresenting the nature of German foreign policy.[172] While the proximity between thinkers and practitioners of IR had shaped the discipline since its origins, the second half of the 1930s saw a new dimension of this relationship.

In February 1936, one week before the remilitarisation of the Rhineland, Toynbee embarked on an academic visit to Germany – as he had done on several previous occasions.[173] This time, he was invited by Berber to address the Nazi Law Society and, as he routinely did, he used the occasion to meet up with his friends among the liberal German intelligentsia. When he was welcomed in Berlin by Berber, Toynbee was shocked to learn that Ribbentrop knew about these personal contacts and also about the fact that Toynbee had published an unfavourable comment about Hitler in his *Survey of International Affairs for 1934* – he had compared Hitler's liquidation of the SA to

---

[167] Ibid., p. 524.   [168] Ibid., p. 481.   [169] Ibid., p. 262.   [170] Ibid., p. 547.
[171] Fritz Berber, 'The Third Reich and the Future of the Collective System', in Geneva Institute of International Relations (ed.), *The Problem of Peace: Eleventh Series: Lectures Delivered at the Geneva Institute of International Relations* (Oxford, 1937), p. 65.
[172] Ibid., p. 71.
[173] Toynbee's friends among the German intelligentsia and diplomatic elite included Richard Kuenzer and Count Albrecht von Bernstorff. See Toynbee, *Acquaintances*.

the style of "American gangsters".[174] This put Berber in an uncomfortable position since he had arranged for Toynbee's visit, which to the
Nazi leadership now looked like an instance of foreign propaganda.
Berber consequently apologised to Ribbentrop who, in turn, passed the
news to Hitler. When the latter learned that Berber was in touch with
the influential British scholar he decided to meet Toynbee and
summoned him to his office.[175]

On 28 February then, Hitler hosted Toynbee for an almost two-hour
conversation at the *Reichskanzlei*.[176] Apart from Toynbee and Berber,
the meeting was attended by Ribbentrop, Foreign Minister Konstantin
von Neurath, and Hans-Heinrich Dieckhoff, a senior diplomat and last
interwar ambassador to the United States. Their conversation was
dominated by a long monologue in which Hitler stylised himself as
an all-European "saviour from Communism" and developed a grandiose plan for Anglo-German friendship. Hitler disclaimed any hostility
to Britain and offered German support to Britain's military post in
Singapore. This, so he argued, would create a European alliance
against threats from Japan or Russia. He also promised to be open
for discussion on Eastern Europe and denied any ambition to launch
an attack on Russia, arguing that he did not want an "inferior"
population within his realm of power. Besides, he denied Germany's
military capabilities to do so. In return for his assurances, he demanded
that Germany's former colonies be returned by the victorious powers
since they had been taken away "unjustly and under false pretences" at
Versailles.[177] He also deplored the condition of Germans in Lithuania
and Danzig, and claimed that Austria's unification with Germany was
only a matter of time.

Toynbee believed that Hitler was sincere, and drafted a memorandum for Foreign Secretary Anthony Eden recommending to respond
favourably to the German overtures: "any response from our English
side to his overtures for our friendship would produce an enormous
counter-response to us from Hitler".[178] However, Eden did not read
the memo until 9 March when German troops had already entered the

---

[174] Arnold Toynbee, *Survey of International Affairs for 1934* (Oxford, 1935),
    p. 325.
[175] Toynbee, *Acquaintances*, pp. 276–85.
[176] Report by Arnold Toynbee, 8 March 1936, Arnold Toynbee Papers, Box 76,
    Folder 6.
[177] Ibid.   [178] Ibid.

Rhineland and overturned Hitler's promises. More to the point, Toynbee's mission never had any prospect of initiating a genuine European detente. It is true that Hitler was interested in British friendship – he used to call the Anglo-German Naval Agreement of 18 June 1935 the "happiest day of his life".[179] But he was never interested in non-European territories beyond their role as bargaining chips. In *Mein Kampf*, he vigorously rejected Germany's pre-war colonial policy, precisely because it risked friction with Britain.[180] So Toynbee's interview with Hitler was less an avenue for conciliatory diplomacy than a showcase of Hitler's deceitful tactics and, above all, the extent to which an internationally respected IR scholar was willing to buy into them.

Toynbee's escapade in foreign policy (and his failure to decipher Hitler's plans) was not an isolated incident. At a Chatham House event a few days later, on 18 March 1936, Labour politician and Anglo-German Fellowship member Sydney Arnold argued that Hitler's move was rooted in Versailles injustice and that it did not inflict the slightest danger on France.[181] Several members agreed, among them businessman and conservative politician William Astor. Toynbee, who spoke next, reaffirmed his perception of Hitler, insisting that the latter was sincere about peaceful cooperation with Britain and that London should respond to the German overtures to have more control over future foreign policy.[182] Chatham House co-founder Philip Kerr, now styled Lord Lothian, was convinced of Hitler's intention to maintain peace for at least twenty-five years.[183] T. P. Conwell-Evans, too, claimed to know something of "the German desire for peace" and that Hitler's character was not as bad as usually portrayed.[184] He defended Nazi foreign policy as an understandable result of being bullied by the Versailles order. Making concessions to Hitler would draw Germany

---

[179] Ian Kershaw, *Hitler 1889–1936: Hubris* (London, 1998), p. 558.

[180] See Bryce Marian Wood, *Peaceful Change and the Colonial Problem* (New York, 1940), p. 81.

[181] Sydney Arnold, in 'Germany and the Rhineland II', *International Affairs* 15:6 (1936), p. 17.

[182] Arnold Toynbee, in 'Germany and the Rhineland II', *International Affairs* 15:6 (1936), pp. 18–19.

[183] Philipp Kerr, in 'Germany and the Rhineland II', *International Affairs* 15:6 (1936), p. 51.

[184] T. P. Conwell-Evans, in 'Germany and the Rhineland II', *International Affairs* 15:6 (1936), p. 41.

back into the League of Nations, Conwell-Evans thought. With few exceptions, IR scholars failed to recognise the unscrupulous nature of the Nazi regime. They misconceived Hitler's foreign policy as a product of the "injustices … of the Versailles Treaty", and overestimated the peaceful impact of satisfying his "legitimate grievances".[185] Toynbee's 1936 visit to Berlin was just the most spectacular example of this approach.

However, IR scholars did not unanimously subscribe to a set of territorial concessions, or a coherent theory of 'peaceful change'. Norman Angell, once considered a model pacifist, was entirely opposed to the trade of colonial territories, even at the risk of antagonising Germany. He argued that colonies would not bring the 'have-nots' any advantages.[186] In fact, so Angell, there were more Germans earning their money in Paris in 1913 than in all German colonies combined. Given the illegitimacy of German claims, Angell urged the international community to resist.[187] Specifically, he argued that the British should have sent troops to France after the German violation of the demilitarised zone in March 1936. At the same time, Angell still considered himself a "pacifist".[188] As the situation aggravated in 1938, Quincy Wright, one of the most outspoken critics of appeasement, condemned Chamberlain's course – "Mr Chamberlain's policies are all wrong" – and blamed the democracies for not standing up against the dictatorships.[189] By 1939, the Dutch diplomat-professor Emanuel Moresco acknowledged that the work on 'peaceful change' was "hopelessly out of date".[190]

Subsequent generations of IR scholars found it easy to accuse Angell, Toynbee, and their colleagues of 'utopianism' because their responses to Nazi foreign policy often seemed overly optimistic in retrospect. But, upon closer investigation, their work was actually less dogmatic and more erratic. In fact, their failure lay less in overconfidence in international cooperation than in their inconsistent attitude to any robust

---

[185] G. M. Gathorne-Hardy, *A Short History of International Affairs, 1920–1938*, 2nd ed. (Oxford, 1938), p. 356.
[186] Norman Angell, 'Germany and the Rhineland II', *International Affairs* 15:6 (1936), p. 24.
[187] Ibid., p. 31.   [188] Ibid., pp. 36, 44.
[189] Quincy Wright to William Rappard, 28 March 1938, HEI 169/2, Archives of the Graduate Institute of International Studies.
[190] Emanuel Moresco, *Colonial Questions and Peace* (Paris, 1939), p. 13.

foreign policy at all. With every crisis, they modified the rules and norms of 'peaceful change', eroding the fundament of the international system in the process. Meanwhile, the dictators were not acting according to the rational or legal norms envisaged by the architects of IR. Hitler and Mussolini operated outside the realm of reasonable politics, making it close to impossible to speculate about their next moves. It was this notion of unpredictability that William Rappard described to Zimmern in March 1938 as "the unforeseeable decisions of the gamblers".[191] Rappard was not alone in this perception. Charles Manning confessed in a 1937 lecture at LSE that he knew "next to nothing about the future of peaceful change".[192] Zimmern agreed that 'peaceful change' in international affairs was "still almost virgin soil".[193] And Toynbee, too, admitted after 1945 that he was "really quite in the dark" about Berber's motives and intentions.[194]

The point is that Hitler was not simply opposed to the objectives of the League of Nations. The entire character of his regime was so fundamentally at odds with any democratic or rational standard that IR scholars found it difficult to come to terms with it. The essence of Nazi politics was "an ethic of violence, a cult of tyranny, a narrow nationalism and racism, a scorn of discussion and reasonableness", Emily G. Balch summarised at a 1937 WILPF congress.[195] By defying the principles of reason, Hitler's foreign policy became basically unintelligible for IR research. The problem was not just *what* Hitler was doing, it was *how* he was doing it. Germany's re-armament was dangerous enough in itself, but it was "the manner in which that re-armament was made" that truly puzzled and endangered the international community, Charles Webster noted.[196] Dictators did not follow consistent plans or patterns because they did not rely on public opinion or the rule of law. As Toynbee observed in March 1936,

---

[191] William Rappard to Alfred Zimmern, 16 March 1938, HEI [uncatalogued], Archives of the Graduate Institute of International Studies.
[192] C. A. W. Manning, 'Some Suggested Conclusions', in Manning (ed.), *Peaceful Change: An International Problem* (London, 1937), p. 190.
[193] 'Memorandum by Professor Zimmern on the Preparation of the next International Studies Conference: Peaceful Change', Alfred Zimmern, 27 July 1935, Alfred Zimmern Papers, Box 98.
[194] Toynbee to Corder Catchpool, 14 December 1945, Arnold Toynbee Papers, Box 76.
[195] Emily G. Balch, in WILPF, *Report of the Fourth Congress* (Geneva, 1937), p. 8.
[196] Webster, 'What Is the Problem of Peaceful Change?', pp. 6–7.

"the present rulers of Germany were extraordinarily undecided themselves".[197] But even if there was a strategy, as Andreas Hillgruber's *Stufenplan*-thesis suggests, contemporary observers were unable to decipher it and frame it in terms of IR theory. Authoritarian foreign policy, it is worth noting, has continued to challenge political scientists throughout the twentieth century, as the international community routinely addressed the claims of dictators by ad hoc deal-making rather than by stringent application of international law.

The Demise of International Relations

In addition to the political crises, the discipline began to suffer from institutional instability and financial constraints. Scholars were pressured out of their jobs, international exchange became more difficult, and governments were less generous in funding IR education. By 1937, scholars and activists had trouble finding meeting locations and obtaining passports for international travel.[198] In 1938, two months after the annexation of Austria, the economist J. B. Condliffe reported about being stopped by SS border guards at Bregenz, Austria, while en route to Geneva.[199] A year later, universities in Europe suspended teaching and IR scholars switched, once again, into their roles as government advisors – such as Arnold Wolfers for the US war department or Alfred Zimmern for the British Foreign Office via Chatham House.[200] But the gradual demise of IR had started years earlier. As early as February 1934, Murray wrote a worried letter to Arnold Toynbee, lamenting the state of the discipline:

Do you realise how much international studies are being threatened? Manning's chair [at LSE] is coming to an end. Jerome Greene has to go back to America; which leaves Aberystwyth for the moment open; and there is the doubt whether the Montague Burton chair will continue here ... and of course the poor old Hochschule is kaput.[201]

[197] Arnold Toynbee, in 'Germany and the Rhineland', *International Affairs* 15:6 (1936), p. 19.
[198] WILPF, *Report of the Ninth Congress* (Geneva, 1937), p. 9.
[199] Condliffe to Rappard, 23 May 1938, HEI 133/1, Archives of the Graduate Institute of International Studies.
[200] War Department, 3 December 1942, Arnold Wolfers Papers, Box 4 Folder 62; and D. J. Markwell, 'Zimmern, Sir Alfred Eckhard', *Oxford Dictionary of National Biography* (Oxford, 2004).
[201] Gilbert Murray to Arnold Toynbee, 23 February 1934, Arnold Toynbee Papers, Box 72.

In most cases, private sponsors helped out to fund professorships and research institutes. Montague Burton continued to finance the Oxford chair as well as endowing the professorship originally sponsored by Ernest Cassel at the LSE. At the ISC, the Rockefeller Foundation helped out with a two-year grant worth $30,000 in 1935, supplemented by a further $100,000 in 1937.[202] These endowments allowed continuity during times of political crisis, yet they also led to dependency and caused conflicts of interest. Philanthropists usually pursued a political or otherwise ideologically inspired agenda. Their intentions were not tied to specific policy goals. But by investing in IR the way they did, they made deliberate choices to fund a particular kind of social science, rather than other research. In some cases, philanthropists sought an even more direct influence on foreign policy. Confidential reports by the Rockefeller Foundation show that the trustees were interested in securing top-level government positions for former fellows of the Foundation.[203]

One incident of the problematic relationship between philanthropy and academia unfolded at Aberystwyth. After US lawyer Jerome Greene had left the Wilson Chair in 1934, a controversy ensued over its succession.[204] The selection committee recommended considering E. H. Carr and C. A. Macartney in the final round of the appointment process.[205] But the chair's sponsor David Davies desperately wanted the League of Nations specialist William Arnold-Forster, someone he believed was "whole-hearted in his devotion to the cause of international cooperation".[206] Davies repeatedly appealed with the university authorities to this effect, using his power as one of the university's principal donors and gathering authoritative support from figures such

[202] Resolution RF 35137, 27 September 1935, and resolution RF 37117, 1 December 1937, Folder 952, Box 105, 100.S, RG 1.1, RF, Rockefeller Archive Center.
[203] The Rockefeller Foundation, Confidential Monthly Report No. 11 (March 1938), p. 2.
[204] E. L. Ellis, *The University College Wales, Aberystwyth, 1872–1972* (Cardiff, 1972), pp. 245–7.
[205] Report of the Wilson Chair of International Politics Joint Selection Committee, p. 75, Council Meeting, 6 March 1936, Council & Court of Governors Minutes, University College Wales, Aberystwyth.
[206] David Davies to W. Arnold Forster, 27 February 1936, D4/5, David Davies Papers.

as Lord Cecil.[207] Gilbert Murray, too, joined Davies in insisting that the Wilson professorship should be held by someone who shared the "evangelist spirit" for which he had endowed the chair and who would teach not "merely general history".[208] Davies knew that Arnold-Forster did not match other candidates' academic credentials but he kept challenging the decision of the selection committee, the president of which he called a "dictator".[209] Despite Davies' strenuous campaign, E. H. Carr was eventually appointed on 10 March 1936, at which point Davies furiously resigned as chairman of the university council.[210] What this story reveals, apart from Davies' almost neurotic obsession with pro-League IR scholarship, is the extent to which non-academic actors interfered with university affairs, essentially for political reasons.

As research institutions came under pressure and the political climate deteriorated, some IR scholars withdrew into technical, less politicised studies. By about 1938, the focus of their work was shifting away from the most controversial issues, avoiding 'collective security' and 'peaceful change'. Instead, they wrote surveys of their own discipline, resulting in books such as S. H. Bailey's *International Studies in Modern Education* (1938) and Alfred Zimmern's *University Teaching of International Relations* (1939).[211] Both recounted the history of the discipline rather than establishing an analytical apparatus. From 1937, the ISC attracted fewer participants and turned to less ambitious goals, including a series of meetings on the 'University Teaching of International Affairs'.[212] The 1938–9 study cycle was primarily concerned with taking account of the state of the discipline.[213]

[207] Report by the Right Hon. Lord Davies, p. 76, Council Meeting, 6 March 1936, Council & Court of Governors Minutes, University College Wales, Aberystwyth; and Lord Cecil to David Davies, 4 March 1936: "I do hope Arnold-Foster will be appointed. Not only does he thoroughly deserve it, but I am sure he would make a most admirable professor", Volume: 51138, Cecil of Chelwood Papers.

[208] Gilbert Murray to David Davies, 30 July 1935, D4/4, David Davies Papers.

[209] David Davies to Gilbert Murray, 16 February 1936, D4/5, David Davies Papers.

[210] David Davies to Lisburne, 11 March 1936, D4/5, David Davies Papers.

[211] See also Paul Guggenheim and Pitman B. Potter, 'The Science of International Relations, Law, and Organisation', *Geneva Studies* XI:2 (1940), pp. 1–35.

[212] Agenda of the tenth session, Paris 28 June–3 July 1937, K/88-100, IIIC Records.

[213] Although formally entitled 'Economic Policies in Relation to World Peace'. See IIIC, *L'Enseignement universitaire des relations internationales* (Paris, 1939).

To some extent, this retreat into less controversial topics brought about elements of self-reflection. William Rappard, for example, was eager to protect the "scholarly spirit" of IR against infiltration by purely journalistic or political works.[214] Alfred Zimmern noted with regret that the discipline neither possessed a coherent body of teaching material, nor an examination syllabus, and that it was thus "a bundle of subjects" rather than a singular one.[215] He compared the conduct of IR to birds "picking up seeds of wisdom in the most unexpected quarters".[216] After more than two decades, the discipline's protagonists were still unsure as to their ultimate goal. In December 1935, the Dean of Tufts University's Fletcher School of Law and Diplomacy Halford Lancaster Hoskins described the goal of the school as "the dispassionate analysis of the mutual relations of states" as well as to "materially assist" in finding solutions to international conflicts.[217] Paul Mantoux, too, asserted that IR scholars should seek "to understand *and* to convince", an awkward combination of descriptive and normative approaches.[218]

Unfortunately, by 1938 there was little prospect for IR scholars to turn the tide of international conflict. Despite the grim outlook, however, many continued to spread a peculiar sense of optimism. "This is no time for discouragement", declared Emily G. Balch at the 1937 congress of WILPF.[219] In May 1938, Murray was convinced that the Czech situation reflected how the League was willing "to stand up for something" and succeeded in "deterring Hitler from open

---

[214] William Rappard to Pitman Potter, 18 April 1939: "your article would strike me as more enlightening if it had been written in a more scholarly and in a less controversial spirit", HEI 163/4-6, Archives of the Graduate Institute of International Studies.

[215] Alfred Zimmern, 'The University Teaching of International Relations', 5 March 1935, Alfred Zimmern Papers, Box 86. See also W. E. C. Harrison, 'The University Teaching of International Affairs', *The Canadian Journal of Economics and Political Science* 2:3 (1936), pp. 431–9.

[216] Alfred Zimmern, 'The University Teaching of International Relations', 5 March 1935, Alfred Zimmern Papers, Box 86.

[217] Halford Lancaster Hoskins to John A. Cousens, 27 December 1935, Box 1, Folder 5, Russell Miller Subject Files, Fletcher School of Law and Diplomacy Records.

[218] IIIC, *Peaceful Change* (1938), p. 572 [emphasis added].

[219] Emily G. Balch, 'Introduction', in WILPF, *Report of the Ninth Congress* (Geneva, 1937), p. 7.

aggression".[220] He thought that Germany's neighbours still had a chance "to build some system of defence" with the help of League members.[221] The most loyal supporters of the League continued to endorse some version of international cooperation until the eleventh hour. In March 1939, David Davies sent a letter to the editor of *The Times* calling for a revised version of 'collective security' which was supposed to bring out its deterrent effect by introducing "absolute certainty and complete efficiency".[222] Davies' effort was in vain of course, as was his preposterous attempt to sack cabinet ministers in April 1939: "Is there no chance of replacing John Simon and Hoare in the Cabinet with Winston and Eden?", he asked Lord Cecil.[223] Even after the war began, Murray continued to comment on current affairs and blamed the British government for not having "believe[d] in the League or Collective Security" but pursuing a policy of postponement until there was no other choice.[224]

When hostilities broke out in September 1939, some institutions for the study of IR initially tried to sustain regular activities. Henri Bonnet, director of the Paris IIIC, informed its members by a circular letter on 4 September that all work would continue as normal.[225] The 1940 ISC was being planned, academic journals continued to publish, and professors continued to correspond. In April 1940, the IIIC Secretariat still

[220] Gilbert Murray to Clifford Allen, 24 May 1938, Gilbert Murray Papers, Box 232.
[221] Gilbert Murray, 'A Statement of Policy: prepared by Dr. Murray at the invitation of the Administration and Executive Committees [of LNU]', 31 May 1938, Gilbert Murray Papers, Box 232. On the other hand, he was also worried that the British were urging the Czechs to concede too much – reflecting the typical ambiguity of interwar IR. Gilbert Murray to Clifford Allen, 24 May 1938, Gilbert Murray Papers, Box 232.
[222] He was referring to his scheme for an international police force. Copy of a letter to the editor, David Davies to Lord Cecil, 24 March 1939, Volume: 51138, Cecil of Chelwood Papers.
[223] David Davies to Lord Cecil, 14 April 1939, Volume: 51138, Cecil of Chelwood Papers.
[224] Gilbert Murry to S. C. Bartindale, 2 February 1940, Gilbert Murray Papers, Box 236. For another example of belated internationalist scholarship, see Pitman B. Potter, 'Article XIX of the Covenant of the League of Nations', *Geneva Studies* XIII:2 (1941), pp. 1–98.
[225] Bonnet to Rappard, 4 September 1939, HEI / Classeur, 'Coopération Intellectuelle', de Février 1928 [uncatalogued], Archives of the Graduate Institute of International Studies.

happily reported about the formation of new committees at the ISC.[226] A few months later, in September 1940, IIIC director Henri Bonnet was optimistic about moving the centre of intellectual cooperation to the United States.[227]

However, the war soon had undeniable effects on the study and teaching of IR. At the start of the autumn semester 1939, international lawyer Hans Wehberg decided to replace a talk he had planned to give in German with a French lecture, due to "circumstances".[228] A few months later, he lamented the decreasing numbers of students.[229] Eventually, the Geneva Graduate Institute had to cross the names of several faculty members off the lecture timetable for the 1940–1 academic year, including Hans Kelsen and Ludwig van Mises, both of whom emigrated to the United States.[230] Co-founder Paul Mantoux was on leave until further notice due to "events in France".[231] In February 1940, the Vienna Konsularakademie began to prepare its staff and students for war by exercises in air-raid shelters.[232]

In the face of yet another war, women tended to be the most vocal advocates of disarmament and peaceful arbitration.[233] Like in 1914, they protested against the war and demanded to participate in the negotiations for peace. Women deserved a "more active part in discussions on world settlement", Kathleen Courtney wrote to Murray in March 1940.[234] They continued to speak out for mothers and children during war time but also claimed their role in high politics and

---

[226] Leo Gross to William Rappard, 29 April 1940, HEI / Classeur, 'Coopération Intellectuelle', de Février 1928 [uncatalogued], Archives of the Graduate Institute of International Studies.

[227] Henri Bonnet to Gilbert Murray, 9 September 1940, Arnold Toynbee Papers, Box 117.

[228] Hans Wehberg to William Rappard, 9 September 1939, HEI 168/4/1, Archives of the Graduate Institute of International Studies.

[229] Hans Wehberg to William Rappard, 30 April 1940, HEI 168/4/1, Archives of the Graduate Institute of International Studies.

[230] The Postgraduate Institute of International Studies, Geneva: Announcement for 1940–1, p. 5, A/1 (1940/1941), Archives of the Graduate Institute of International Studies.

[231] Rapport Administratif, 1940, Archives of the Graduate Institute of International Studies.

[232] Circular, 24 February 1940, OeStA, Archiv der Konsularakademie, Box 49-18.

[233] See, for example, Laura Puffer Morgan, 'A Possible Technique of Disarmament Control', *Geneva Studies* XI:7 (1940), pp. 1–96.

[234] Kathleen Courtney to Gilbert Murray, 11 March 1940, Gilbert Murray Papers, Box 236.

diplomacy.[235] Nonetheless their principal way of participating in international life was by writing and publishing. The German literary scholar and WILPF supporter Elizabeth Rotten told Murray in March 1940 that she had turned to work "of a spiritual kind".[236] On the whole, the war was probably more detrimental to women than men since women scholars had just begun to establish themselves at universities and research institutions. It was only after the war, in 1948, that Agnes Headlam-Morley was appointed Montague Burton Professor of IR at Oxford, the first and to this day only woman on the chair. In this respect, too, interwar IR scholarship remained incomplete.

With the German invasion imminent in June 1940, the IIIC in Paris had to consider relocating. On 9 June 1940, director Bonnet sent the personnel and the archives to Guérande, a village by the Atlantic coast, as instructed by the *Quai d'Orsay*.[237] On 19 June, shortly after German troops had occupied Paris, Bonnet left for Geneva and put his colleague Paul Ristorcelli in charge of what remained of the IIIC. Two months later, Fritz Berber arrived in Paris, having been appointed *Reichskommissar* for intellectual cooperation, and tried to take control of what was left of the institute. To this effect he signed an agreement in September 1940, with former Education Minister Léon Bérard, which specified that the IIIC should remain in Paris under French direction and German funding, but detached from the League of Nations. However, this plan never materialised and by December 1940 Berber had resigned from his post as *Reichskommissar*. The IIIC was put under seal and there is no evidence of any substantial activity after this point. Attempts to relocate the IIIC to Princeton, New Jersey – where the League's Economic and Financial Organisation had been moved – or to Havana failed in 1940 and 1941.[238] And so the semi-official headquarters of interwar IR remained closed until April 1945.[239]

[235] Pamphlet, 'Work in Germany among Women and Little Children', 18 Feb 1940, by Ruth Hanbury[?], Gilbert Murray Papers, Box 236.
[236] Elisabeth Rotten to Gilbert Murray, July 1940, Gilbert Murray Papers, Box 237.
[237] Etienne Lajti, memo, March 1943, A.I.144/2, IIIC Records.
[238] Gilbert Murray to Maude Miner Hadden, 2 August 1940, Gilbert Murray Papers, Box 237; Note by Miguel Ozorio de Almeida, 30 March 1941, Dossier 41541, Box R4048, League of Nations Archives. See Corinne A. Pernet, 'Twists, Turns and Dead Alleys: The League of Nations and Intellectual Cooperation in Times of War', *Journal of Modern European History* 12:3 (2014), pp. 342–58.
[239] J. de Reynolds to LN Secretariat, 20 April 1945, Dossier 41541, Box R4048, League of Nations Archives.

Conclusion

In many ways, the study of IR came to an end in 1940 as it had started in 1914. The architects of IR collaborated, despite wartime conditions, via a wide-ranging network of professors and politicians, men and women, from the belligerents and neutrals. The same network that had given rise to IR institutions in the 1910s and 1920s now provided emergency relief as those institutions (and individuals) were in danger. Refugee scholars took up positions abroad, research centres moved to non-combatant countries, philanthropists helped to fund IR activities which governments were no longer willing or able to maintain. As in 1914, the topics of IR were shaped by the course of political events. William Rappard set up a study group on "current circumstances" in September 1939.[240] New visions of world order circulated among a similar set of individuals.[241] More than anything, this final episode of interwar IR scholarship showed that the discipline was based on people, rather than ideas, and that these people were directly exposed to world affairs. If we understand IR in this sense, the Second World War was less important as an intellectual turning point than in the way it disrupted a community of scholars and practitioners.[242] Subsequent criticism about interwar IR by so-called 'realists' actually said more about those 'realists' themselves than anything else.

In any event, the most notable activity for IR scholars during the 1940s was advising decision-makers, rather than debating political theory. In March 1940, a private but officially approved French delegation including the international lawyer René Cassin travelled to London to discuss with their colleagues – Robert Cecil, Philip Noel-Baker, and Gilbert Murray among others – the role of the League of Nations in the future peace.[243] In 1942, Toynbee was asked by the

---

[240] William Rappard, 'Idées sur une activité scientifique exceptionnelle que pourrait éventuellement exercer l'Institut dans les circonstances actuelles', 13 September 1939, uncatalogued, Graduate Institute Archives.

[241] Or Rosenboim, *The Emergence of Globalism: Visions of World Order in Britain and the United States, 1939–1950* (Princeton, 2017).

[242] David Long, 'Who Killed the International Studies Conference?', *Review of International Studies* 32:4 (2006), pp. 603–22.

[243] Jean-Michel Guieu, *Le rameau et le glaive: Les militants français pour la Société des Nations* (Paris, 2008), p. 255.

Council on Foreign Relations to advise the US government.[244] In 1943, the German lawyer Hans Simons, who had fled to the United States and was teaching at New York's New School for Social Research, took up an advisory role at the Office of Strategic Services, and then became a liaison officer in Germany after 1945.[245] Zimmern, too, continued to loyally serve the public cause by guiding the transition from the IIIC to UNESCO at the end of the war. In 1947, he was nominated for the Nobel Peace Prize – along with two other IR pioneers, Lionel Curtis, the co-founder of Chatham House, and the Carnegie Endowment for International Peace.[246]

Despite these impressive biographies, the intellectual record of the interwar period left many questions marks. Most authors adopted flexible positions in response to political realities, without identifying the factors that led them to change their minds. Toynbee's approach to 'peaceful change' was a case in point. In 1936, he recommended responding to Hitler's overtures. Two years later, he was reluctant to grant sovereign rights to Germany in Bohemia because he feared it would endanger Czech independence. He had reservations against handing over territories to another colonial power, but failed to specify consistent criteria.[247] G. M. Gathorne-Hardy defended the opposite strategy. After the remilitarisation of the Rhineland in 1936, he called for an ultimatum against Germany, whereas two years later he thought that Nazism could be overthrown by giving in to Hitler's grievances

---

[244] Arnold Toynbee to N. B. Ronald, 17 June 1942, Arnold Toynbee Papers, Box 117.

[245] Hans Simons to Alvin Johnson 11 September 1947, Alvin Johnson Papers, Yale University; Edmund Spevack, 'Ein Emigrant in amerikanischen Diensten. Zur Rolle des Politikwissenschaftlers Hans Simons in Deutschland nach 1945', in Claus-Dieter Krohn and Patrik von zur Mühlen (eds.), *Rückkehr und Aufbau nach 1945: Deutsche Remigration im öffentlichen Leben Nachkriegsdeutschlands* (Marburg, 1997), p. 328.

[246] 'Nomination Database', available at www.nobelprize.org/nomination/archive/list.php [accessed 10 November 2016].

[247] Andrew J. Crozier, 'Chatham House and Appeasement', in Bosco and Navari (eds.), *Chatham House and British Foreign Policy, 1919–1945: The Royal Institute of International Affairs during the Inter-war Period* (London, 1994), p. 239; and Christopher Brewin, 'Arnold Toynbee, Chatham House, and Research in a Global Context', in David Long and Peter Wilson (eds.), *Thinkers of the Twenty Years' Crisis* (Oxford, 1995), p. 295.

and taking away the basis for his propaganda.[248] Norman Angell shifted from non-resistance pacifism and disarmament in the 1910s and 1920s to 'collective security' and military deterrence in the 1930s.[249] Alfred Zimmern's celebration of the League of Nations in his lectures and publications was contrasted by a profound scepticism in private correspondence, where he said that "an international authority ... is unrealistic".[250]

These inconsistencies were not just individual lapses but manifestations of a general refusal to commit to a set of methods and theories. IR scholars claimed to be conducting social science but they were not ready to adopt the principles of scientific investigation that had been discussed for decades.[251] Eventually, they were unable to keep up with the speed of political events, and their discipline was undermined by the very actors that they had tried to control. Interwar IR had undeniable intellectual defects. Despite these shortcomings, it had become a serious academic field attracting remarkable levels of attention from politicians, diplomats, philanthropists, journalists, and the general public. After all, IR had taken on the most pressing question of the twentieth century – how to make the world a more peaceful place?

---

[248] Compare G. M. Gathorne-Hardy, in 'Germany and the Rhineland II', *International Affairs* 15:6 (1936), p. 39; and Gathorne-Hardy, *A Short History of International Affairs, 1920–1938*, p. 356.

[249] Ibid., pp. 21–36, 43; see Martin Ceadel, 'The Founding Text of International Relations? Norman Angell's Seminal Yet Flawed *The Great Illusion* (1909–1938), *Review of International Studies* 37:4 (2011), pp. 1679–80.

[250] Lecture Notes, by Alfred Zimmern, 1935[?], Alfred Zimmern Papers, Box 132; and Memorandum by Professor Zimmern on the Preparation of the next International Studies Conference: Peaceful Change', Alfred Zimmern, 27 July 1935, Alfred Zimmern Papers, Box 98.

[251] Munroe Smith, 'Introduction: The Domain of Political Science', *Political Science Quarterly* 1:1 (1886), pp. 1–8; Charles E. Merriam, 'Recent Advances in Political Methods', *The American Political Science Review* 17:2 (1923), pp. 275–95; A. Gordon Dewey, 'On Methods in the Study of Politics I', *Political Science Quarterly* 38:4 (1923), pp. 636–51; Charles H. Titus, 'A Nomenclature in Political Science', *The American Political Science Review* 25:1 (1931), pp. 45–60.

Conclusion

My zeal for peace caused me to turn a blind eye to ugly facts.

T. P. Conwell-Evans (1947)[1]

Looking back on the interwar period, the author and political advisor T. P. Conwell-Evans acknowledged fundamental problems with his approach to International Relations (IR). While teaching at the University of Königsberg in the 1930s he had entertained high-level contacts to the German foreign office, including the future foreign secretary Joachim Ribbentrop and Hitler's personal advisor Walther Hewel. Like many of his peers, however, Conwell-Evans was "sadly late in perceiving the real nature of the Nazi German menace", as he now admitted.[2] A dedicated Germanophile, he was willing to go to almost any length to prevent an Anglo-German war and, in the process, gave up his critical distance to decision-makers.[3] Now, after the Second World War, he urged his readers to be "more scientific in their analysis of questions of foreign affairs than was [his] generation".[4]

Conwell-Evans was right. The political ambitions of early IR scholars were greater than their analytical progress. Although they taught at universities and published in academic journals, most of their work was effectively devoted to shaping current affairs. They founded pressure groups, lobbied government officials, and stood for parliamentary elections. Most of their academic output had a normative character, rather than a descriptive one. Their activities went beyond the occasional advice that historians, lawyers, and philosophers had

---

[1] T. P. Conwell-Evans, *None So Blind: A Study of the Crisis Years, 1930–1939* (London, 1947), p. xii.
[2] Ibid.
[3] Donald Cameron Watt, 'Chamberlain's Ambassadors', in Michael Dockrill and Brian McKercher (eds.), *Diplomacy and World Power: Studies in British Foreign Policy, 1890–1951* (Cambridge, 1996), p. 146.
[4] Conwell-Evans, *None So Blind*, p. xii.

lent their governments prior to the twentieth century. It was embedded
in a transnational network of research institutes across more than forty
countries, co-sponsored by governments and private philanthropists,
which catered to a growing popular audience. International affairs had
become the "master-problem of the present age", as Arnold Toynbee
observed in 1934.[5] But what was the theoretical basis of their work?
Was it possible to study war and peace like economists studied inflation and unemployment? And what, if anything, could IR scholars do
to contribute substantially to world peace?

The formative history of IR offers important evidence on these
perennial questions about the purpose and nature of the discipline as
well as its role in shaping twentieth-century international politics more
generally. Above all, it shows how "human imagination shapes the
course and character of politics", to borrow Duncan Bell's words.[6]
Prompted by the horrors of war and the search for peace, the interwar
years were a time of extraordinary political imagination. The architects
of IR seized this moment and invented new forms of international
governance which have had a lasting impact on the twentieth century.
At the same time, however, they struggled to develop analytical standards to guide scholarly debate and to critically assess their own policy
inventions. Interwar scholars rarely attempted to determine patterns or
causal relationships in international politics, nor did they agree on
definitions and methods. In 1939, Alfred Zimmern concluded that
the terminology of IR resembled "cut flowers severed from their
roots".[7] Ultimately, therefore, the history of IR is about the relationship between political ideas and practice, an aspect which has rarely
been acknowledged in disciplinary retrospectives.[8]

If early IR scholarship has since been criticised, the reason is to be
found precisely in this tension between political ambition and

[5] Arnold Toynbee to G. G. Kullmann, 3 May 1934, Arnold Toynbee Papers, Box 117.
[6] Duncan Bell, 'Writing the World: Disciplinary History and Beyond', *International Affairs* 85:1 (2009), p. 22.
[7] Alfred Zimmern, *Modern Political Doctrines* (Oxford, 1939), p. ix.
[8] For exceptions, see Christopher Hill, 'Academic International Relations: The Siren Song of Policy Relevance', in Christopher Hill and Pamela Beshoff (eds.), *Two Worlds of International Relations: Academics, Practitioners and the Trade in Ideas* (London, 1994), pp. 3–25; and William Wallace, 'Truth and Power, Monks and Technocrats: Theory and Practice in International Relations', *Review of International Studies* 22:3 (1996), p. 302.

intellectual rigour. By pursuing political goals alongside their role as professors, the architects of IR effectively blurred the boundary between academia and diplomacy. The point of this book is not to insist on some arbitrary division line between political science and practice, which may well not exist, but to judge the architects of IR by their own standards. They were the ones who, after the outbreak of war in 1914, began to conceive of international politics as a field of rational inquiry; they regarded the problem of war as "primarily an intellectual one" that could be solved by intellectual means;[9] they established university programmes to teach students the mechanics of international cooperation; they claimed that education would lead to peace; they wanted to "render a service to the international community", as the founder of the Geneva Graduate Institute William Rappard put it.[10] In short, they regarded war as a problem that could be solved. By devoting their professional lives to the pursuit of peace, they set themselves a goal that was as difficult to achieve as it is to measure. The outcome was neither an outright failure nor a success, akin to what recent historiography has shown about international politics in the interwar period more generally.

To assess the record of early IR scholarship, this concluding essay briefly recaps its pioneers' ambitions at the outset, then summarises their achievements, and finally discusses some wider implications for the study of IR.

Ambitious Aims

The study of IR emerged during the 1910s in the context of increasing global interdependence and the search for a new political order. The most significant impulse was the outbreak of war in 1914 which inspired a flood of publications on topics related to secret diplomacy, economic interdependence, and international organisation. To the architects of IR, the war was the result of "old diplomacy", an elite-driven system of unaccountable decision-making, which

---

[9] George H. Blakeslee, 'The War Problem and Its Proposed Solutions', in George H. Blakeslee (ed.), *The Problems and Lessons of the War* (New York, 1916), p. xxvi.
[10] William Rappard, 'Idées sur une activité scientifique exceptionnelle que pourrait éventuellement exercer l'Institut dans les circonstances actuelles', 13 September 1939, uncatalogued, Graduate Institute Archives.

required radical reform.[11] Foreign policy was to become subject to democratic control and rational debate, informed by an educated public. The idea was essentially that better international understanding would lead to better international relations. The publications and institutions arising from this idea formed an embryonic field as early as 1915, while university chairs and departments were established after the war.

It is important to remember that when political thinkers first considered international relations as a subject of academic inquiry they could not foresee the crises of the 1920s and 1930s. They looked at a world of international anarchy and, above all, at a world of violent war. It is not surprising, then, that they were motivated first and foremost by the search for peace or, more specifically, means of peaceful cooperation. This was true for virtually all early IR authors, including those such as E. H. Carr who would later reject the liberal internationalist project.[12] Whichever their ideological differences or national backgrounds, they believed that it was possible (and necessary) to make changes to the international order by way of academic research. For them, the study of IR was a normative enterprise and thus dependent on more fundamental belief systems. The founders of IR followed their political preferences and their "emotional drive", as the American IR professor William T. R. Fox referred to it in 1949.[13]

That said, the architects of IR claimed to be engaged in the "scientific study" of international relations.[14] They styled themselves "objective and dispassionate" observers of international affairs, qualified to examine anything from disarmament to international migration.[15] Their work sprang not from "noble ideals" but from the "power of reason", as Greek diplomat Nikolaos Politis put it.[16] They applied "maximum objectivity", according to Belgian legal scholar Maurice

---

[11] Max Warburg to Albrecht Mendelssohn Bartholdy, 6 November 1919, Albrecht Mendelssohn Barthold Papers, 225,161.
[12] Jonathan Haslam, 'We Need a Faith', *History Today* 33:8 (1983), p. 36.
[13] William T. R. Fox, 'Interwar International Relations Research: The American Experience', *World Politics* 2:1 (1949), p. 67.
[14] 'The Conference of Institutions for the Scientific Study of International Relations', *Journal of the Royal Institute of International Affairs* 8:3 (1929).
[15] Alfred Zimmern, Memo, April 1925, Alfred Zimmern Papers, Box 88.
[16] Nikolaos Politis, 'Das Genfer Protokoll', *Europäische Gespräche* 6 (1924), pp. 515–16.

Bourquin , and worked on the basis of "accurate and impartial documentation".[17] Although they rarely substantiated this claim, it was probably inspired by contemporary developments in neighbouring social sciences, such as the invention of survey research and the increasing reliance on quantitative data.[18] They demarcated their field in relationship to those social sciences and, crucially, in contrast to non-academic activities. International affairs were no longer "something esoteric" but had become subject to the scrutiny of scholars and an increasingly interested public.[19] Some thought that the study of IR would one day match the accuracy of the natural sciences. In 1931, the American Social Science Research Council conceived of international relations as a "laboratory" and promoted the use of methods akin to the "physical sciences".[20]

Instead of having a serious debate about the potentials and limitations of IR as a social science, the architects of the discipline launched a whole array of studies, research programmes, and political campaigns – usually without defining their nature or methodology. The speed of events did not give them enough time to reflect on the basis of the discipline. They threw themselves into the drafting of official documents and the design of the post-war order. Their most immediate concern was to create a permanent institution to manage international disputes and, more generally, to organise international life in other domains, including economics and health. As a consequence, early IR scholarship came to be closely associated with the League of Nations and its various specialised agencies. Rather than regarding it as the ultimate guarantor of peace, however, the architects of IR treated the League as a work in progress and used it as a venue to test new

---

[17] Maurice Bourquin, in International Institute of Intellectual Cooperation, *Peaceful Change* (1938), p. 585.
[18] Pitman B. Potter, 'Political Science in the International Field', *The American Political Science Review* 15:3 (1923), pp. 381–91; Raymond L. Buell, 'What Is Research?', Foreign Policy Association Pamphlet No. 75 (New York, 1931), pp. 1–9; Robert M. Groves, 'Three Eras of Survey Research', *The Public Opinion Quarterly* 75:5 (2011), pp. 861–71.
[19] Arnold J. Toynbee to Henri Bonnet, 18 March 1931, IIIC Records K.I.1b.
[20] Social Science Research Council, 'Report of the Director of the Program of Research in International Relations for the Year 1931', 'confidential', 2 January 1932, James T. Shotwell Papers, Box 136 (a), (b).

international policies. It was not "an ideal or a dream", as Gilbert Murray insisted, but "a piece of practical political business".[21]

Once the basic framework had been established, the architects of IR addressed more specific problems of contemporary relevance. David Mitrany and James Shotwell, for example, tried to design a viable system of sanctions capable of coercing governments to comply with international law. Moritz Julius Bonn and Jacob Viner invented new forms of international cooperation in economics and trade. Arnold Toynbee and Freda White reconsidered the administration of former colonial territories. A typical piece of IR scholarship would recommend policy options, rather than to only assess them, such as Philip Noel-Baker's work on disarmament in the 1920s.[22] It was not driven by the quest to understand how arms proliferation worked, but how disarmament could be made to work. In doing so, the architects of IR always remained in touch with current affairs. Their research basically followed the agenda of high politics, and sometimes anticipated it; as did their teaching. To train the next generation of decision-makers, they set up professional programmes for young diplomats and international officials.[23] At academic conferences they routinely adopted the practices and the rhetoric of politicians. Viner once described them as "imitation statesmen".[24]

Throughout the interwar period, their ambition was to shape international politics, while maintaining their academic insignia. Agnes Headlam-Morley, for example, who taught IR at St Hugh's College, Oxford, confessed in 1931 that her "whole interest [was] really in the political work".[25] IR scholars provided "unofficial preparation" for diplomatic conferences.[26] They drafted articles for the Geneva Protocol, the Locarno Treaties, and the Kellogg-Briand Pact. They

---

[21] Gilbert Murray, 'Problems of the League of Nations', address given at the Liberal Jewish Synagogue, 17 November 1918, Gilbert Murray Papers, Box 179.

[22] Philip Noel-Baker, *Disarmament* (London, 1926); Philip Noel-Baker, *Disarmament and the Coolidge Conference* (London, 1927).

[23] Booklet of the School of Public and International Affairs, Princeton University, 22 February 1930, James T. Shotwell Papers, Box 151; Memo, 'The Possible Training for Diplomatic Students and Consular Representatives which could be approved at the School', April 1924, Philip Noel-Baker Papers, NBKR 8/10/2.

[24] Jacob Viner in IIIC, *The State and Economic Life* (Paris, 1934), p. 60.

[25] Barbara Gwyer to Arthur Cayley Headlam, 15 October 1931, Agnes Headlam-Morley Papers, SHG/S/2/2/11/4.

[26] Arnold J. Toynbee to Henri Bonnet, 18 March 1931, K.I.1b, IIIC Records.

interacted with high-ranking foreign officials and passed on information to their governments. In the most extreme cases, they defended
government decisions at academic conferences for propaganda purposes. The entire apparatus of early IR scholarship was directed at
making rather than analysing international affairs. This approach
dominated the discipline well into the 1930s when its flaws were long
apparent. It was not until 1940, however, that Paul Guggenheim and
Pitman B. Potter criticised the "scientific basis" of IR and questioned
the premise of the discipline.[27]

Disheartening Results

What was left of IR scholarship after the Second World War? The
architects of IR had built an impressive range of academic institutions,
drawn up university curricula, edited journals, and organised conferences. IR had become a popular university discipline across Europe
and the United States with hundreds of graduates working in government positions. Above all, international politics had become a profes-
sion that citizens could study and understand, bringing foreign policy
closer to the people and to rational debate. But after little more than
two decades, this new international order was in ruins and its main
institution, the League of Nations, was being dismantled. Had the
architects of IR failed?

Whatever the intellectual products of early IR scholarship may have
been, there is no doubt that the architects of IR established a remarkable set of institutions, many of which have had a lasting impact by
training generations of decision-makers. Places such as the Council on
Foreign Relations in New York, the Graduate Institute in Geneva, and
the Montague Burton chairs of IR in London and Oxford have
remained prestigious centres of research and continue to generate
policy advice. Whereas today's academic landscape is much larger
and more diverse, interwar institutions tended to be dominated by a
fairly small, mostly male elite who were usually involved in political
causes, such as Ernst Jäckh, the co-founder of the Deutsche
Hochschule für Politik in Berlin, who was associated with senior

---

[27] Paul Guggenheim and Pitman B. Potter, *The Science of International Relations,
Law, and Organisation* (Geneva, 1940), pp. 23, 29.

politicians such as Matthias Erzberger and Gustav Stresemann.[28] Nonetheless, these institutions helped to formalise IR as a discipline. By the mid-1920s, when Philip Noel-Baker was elected professor at the London School of Economics, the university was convinced that "the study of International Politics is an inevitable part of the general study of Political Science".[29]

An important characteristic of early IR institutions was the near-global network of intellectual cooperation, operated by the League of Nations, which connected their activities. At its peak during the early 1930s, the International Institute of Intellectual Cooperation (IIIC) coordinated research in more than forty countries, mostly in Europe and North America, but also in China, the Soviet Union, and large parts of South America. Based in Paris, the IIIC helped to spread the study of IR by facilitating student exchanges and lecture series. Perhaps most importantly, it underlined the ethos of IR as a genuinely international discipline, applying the same standards regardless of national background. The environment of early IR scholarship was "international to the core", as Alfred Zimmern put it. Incidentally, Zimmern served as deputy director of the IIIC from 1926 to 1930.[30] Its flagship project was the International Studies Conference (ISC) which annually gathered dozens of IR scholars and practitioners, such as Henri Bonnet, John Foster Dulles, and William Rappard, and thus contributed decisively to the formation of a disciplinary community.

Women were part of this community from the outset, despite the male domination in most senior positions. They taught, researched, and published on the full spectrum of IR topics. Initially, their activities were coordinated by pressure groups, most notably the Women's International League for Peace and Freedom (WILPF), which hosted conferences and summer schools. Their work appeared in journals such as *Jus Sufragii* and *L'Europe nouvelle*. But women also worked at universities, schools, and research centres, such as Lucy Mair at the London School of Economics or Sarah Wambaugh at Radcliffe College. They often adopted feminist approaches to IR, emphasising the

[28] Ernst Jäckh, *Der Goldene Pflug: Lebensernte eines Weltbürgers* (Stuttgart, 1954), p. 64.
[29] Note on International Politics in the Final BSc Degree, 1927[?], Philip Noel-Baker Papers, NBKR 8/12/2.
[30] Alfred Zimmern, 'Nationality and Government', *Sociological Review* (1916), p. 215.

interests of women and children in international affairs although their political leanings varied. Many, but not all of them, subscribed to the essentialist argument that women were naturally more peaceful than men because their "mother instinct" made them more sensitive to the effects of war.[31] Several women were also outspoken against imperialism and racism. At a time when European governments were almost exclusively concerned with their own security, scholars such as Lucy Mair urged to take into account the interests of "native inhabitants".[32] Above all, women demanded representation in government and diplomacy to make foreign policy more democratic. Apart from Rachel Crowdy, who headed the Social Section at the League of Nations, most senior diplomatic positions and virtually all IR professorships were occupied by men. When war broke out in 1939, women were still campaigning "to play a more active part" in the making of war and peace.[33] With few exceptions, such as Agnes Headlam-Morley's election to the Montague Burton Chair at Oxford in 1947, women's international thought continued to be marginalised during the second half of the twentieth century.

Besides the institutional formation of a new academic discipline, the principal achievement of interwar scholars was to set a research agenda that resonated strongly with contemporary problems of foreign policy. They worked on anything from economic sanctions to colonial reform, from 'moral disarmament' to migration. Some of the most prominent political debates of the interwar period, such as 'collective security' or 'peaceful change', were pioneered by IR scholars. By shaping debates and writing technical reports, the architects of IR nurtured their ambition that foreign policy would become a more rational field. They were glad to see that leaders could no longer govern by "muddling through" but now consulted expert advice and statistical data before formulating policies.[34] Similarly, they welcomed the gradual opening up of the foreign services to the "people

---

[31] Edith A. Waterworth, in WILPF, *Report of the Fourth Congress of the WILPF* (Geneva, 1924), p. 90.

[32] Lucy Mair, 'Colonial Policy and Peaceful Change', in C. A. W. Manning (ed.), *Peaceful Change: An International Problem* (London, 1937), p. 88.

[33] Kathleen Courtney to Gilbert Murray, 11 March 1940, Gilbert Murray Papers, Box 236.

[34] James T. Shotwell, 'Scientific Method in Research and Discussion in International Relations: A Proposal for Institutes of International Relations', 6 June 1931, James T. Shotwell Papers, Box 155, 156.

of the democracies" who began to interest themselves in greater numbers for international affairs.[35] In short, the concerns of IR became increasingly popular.

Unfortunately, few of these research projects brought about any immediate improvements in current affairs. The aim of a truly global League of Nations was crushed at once. Disarmament efforts failed definitively in 1933. Any remaining hopes for international sanctions were buried in the mid-1930s. Most of the policy instruments that IR scholars had worked on since the First World War turned out to be either impractical or ineffective, at least in the short run. But even more modest projects proved difficult. The trilingual dictionary of political terminology, edited by the IIIC, caused endless quarrels and was never published.[36] Collaborative research projects fizzled out. By the mid-1930s there was still no "single coherent body of teaching material", Zimmern lamented.[37] Nor was there any clarity on why the discipline should exist in the first place. Philip Noel-Baker simply claimed that since international activities were happening "no further justification for their academic study is required".[38]

The point is not to argue that IR's proximity to the League of Nations inevitably resulted in intellectual dishonesties, but that interwar scholars tended to conceive of international life rather narrowly within the confines of one particular institutional framework. This was reflected, for example, in their belief that elitist conferences would contribute more to international peace than, say, UNESCO's literacy work later did. The style of interwar academic life with all its pomp and circumstance was so blatantly modelled after the perceived grandeur of old diplomacy – gala dinners, social clubs, first-class travel, etc. – that ordinary citizens must have gaped at Arnold Wolfer's claim that the Deutsche Hochschule für Politik served the educational needs of an expanding democracy.[39] That decadence, by the way, helps to explain

---

[35] R. J. F. Boyer, 'Foreword', *Australian Journal of International Affairs* 1:1 (1947), p. 3.

[36] Summary of the Proceedings of the Fourth Meeting of the Executive Committee, 28–29 January 1933, Dossier 2381, Box R4006, League of Nations Archives.

[37] Alfred Zimmern, 'The University Teaching of International Relations', 5 March 1935, Alfred Zimmern Papers, Box 86.

[38] Philip Noel-Baker to Gilbert Murray, 9 November 1929, Gilbert Murray Papers, Box 415.

[39] Detlef Lehnert, '"Schule der Demokratie" oder "politische Fachhochschule"?: Anspruch und Wirklichkeit einer praxisorientierten Ausbildung der Deutschen

the transformations that IR went through, intellectually and institutionally, after the Second World War. In any event, it is difficult to deny that interwar institutions preconfigured the scope of what international politics might do and how it might be achieved.

The most obvious negligence of interwar IR, however, was theory. The architects of IR were undoubtedly intelligent and learned, but they spent almost no time on definitions, assumptions, or methodologies. Few authors made any verifiable claims that could be challenged by empirical evidence, rather than by political belief. Research was rarely published in the form of general laws or abstract analysis, even beyond a strictly positivist sense. The theoretical work of leading IR scholars such as Arnold Toynbee was unclear or mistaken, as political scientists now argue.[40] Scholars failed to establish common points of reference, they rarely cited each other, and never entered into genuine scientific debates, as their colleagues in neighbouring social sciences did. For example, John Maynard Keynes explained in the preface of *The General Theory of Employment, Interest, and Money* (1936) that the book's "main purpose is to deal with difficult questions of theory, and only in the second place with the applications of this theory to practice".[41]

It is not anachronistic, therefore, to point out these characteristics of IR, especially since some contemporary scholars, such as Raymond Leslie Buell, acknowledged shortcomings in the field as early as 1931.[42] Nor is it implausible to assume that IR scholars could have used more sophisticated empirical methods or laboratory-based studies – that is precisely what simulations and war games did in the 1950s (drawing criticism of its own).[43] The president of the American Political Science Association Edward Corwin observed as early as 1929 that there was a trend to "convert political science from a

Hochschule für Politik, 1920–1933', in Gerhard Göhler and Bodo Zeuner (eds.), *Kontinuitäten und Brüche in der deutschen Politikwissenschaft* (Baden-Baden, 1991), p. 65.

[40] Ian Hall, '"Time of Troubles": Arnold J. Toynbee's Twentieth Century', *International Affairs* 90:1 (2014), pp. 35–6.

[41] John Maynard Keynes, *The General Theory of Employment, Interest, and Money* (Cambridge, 1936), p. v.

[42] Raymond L. Buell, 'What Is Research?', Foreign Policy Association Pamphlet No. 75 (New York, 1931).

[43] Sharon Ghamari-Tabrizi, 'Simulating the Unthinkable: Gaming Future War in the 1950s and 1960s', *Social Studies of Science* 30:2 (2000), pp. 163–223.

'normative' ... into a natural science".[44] Interestingly, one of the most popular metaphors was to compare world politics with the human body, and foreign policy with medicine. "Just as it was hopeless to do away with plagues and epidemics before the mysteries of animal biology were understood", William Rappard wrote in 1931, "so it is hopeless to suppress war and to eliminate harmful friction in international relations as long as mysteries of international life still baffle the human mind".[45] Arguably, of course, both diseases and wars changed over the course of time, and so it remains questionable if either can ever be cured. New types of conflict have led IR scholars to devise new solutions. As a result, the problem of durable peace often seemed like a "disease for which there are plenty of doctors but no cures", to use another of these metaphors.[46] At the very least, then, the status of IR as a social science was debatable.

The founders of the discipline, there is no doubt, were preoccupied with practical questions and their research agenda was determined by current events. They wrote journalistic pieces or delivered speeches on topics that they had "some direct, first-hand knowledge" of.[47] Their sponsors further encouraged this approach. A 1938 Rockefeller Foundation report revealed that the trustees were looking for "direct participation in the international activities" in Geneva.[48] This was true for many of the scholars associated with the Rockefeller-sponsored Graduate Institute. Pitman B. Potter was an adviser to the Ethiopian government and a member of the Italo-Ethiopian Arbitration Commission, William Rappard was a member of the Mandates Commission, Maurice Bourquin was a Belgian delegate to the Disarmament Conference, and Carl Jacob Burckhardt was appointed High Commissioner to Danzig. Their careers leave little doubt about the political motivations behind them.

---

[44] Edward S. Corwin, 'The Democratic Dogma and the Future of Political Science', *The American Political Science Review* 23:3 (1929), p. 569.

[45] William Rappard to Lucie Zimmern, 3 November 1931, uncatalogued, Graduate Institute Archives.

[46] Don C. Seitz, 'Moral Influences in a Durable Peace', *The Annals of the American Academy of Political and Social Science* 72 (1917), p. 216.

[47] Arnold Wolfers, 'The Crisis of the Democratic Régime in Germany', *International Affairs* 11:6 (1932), p. 757.

[48] Resolution, 6 April 1938, Folder 922, Box 102, Series 100.S, RG 1.1, RF, Rockefeller Archive Center.

This kind of scholarship resulted in ambiguities and inconsistencies. Zimmern, for instance, once argued that the success of the League of Nations depended on the general "willingness to cooperate", but he was uncertain as to the existence of this "will".[49] In one article in 1936, he argued that the will existed but the means were missing.[50] In another publication, written in the same year, he claimed the exact opposite.[51] A 1935 memo by Zimmern confessed that it would be "a waste of time" to discuss 'peaceful change' or treaty revision, and that none of the debates since 1920 had been of any use whatsoever.[52] Norman Angell, once Britain's foremost pacifist, refused to endorse comprehensive disarmament in the 1930s and counted instead on the deterring effect of "certain and overwhelming" sanctions.[53] Albrecht Mendelssohn Bartholdy, widely regarded as one of Germany's foremost internationalists, suggested that Germany should withdraw from the League of Nations in 1930.[54] Every reasonable scholar would accept corrections of research results, but these were merely changes of opinion.

When the Second World War broke out, the architects of IR were left with a range of open questions about why European governments kept resorting to force and what, if anything, the students of IR could do to prevent it. It seemed that the corpus of early IR scholarship was ill-equipped to handle the authoritarian leaders who defied the institutions that were supposed to control them. Instead, political extremists used academic conferences to propagate official foreign policy, such as the German lawyer Fritz Berber who wrote several books defending Hitler's treaty violations.[55] But the political nature of IR

[49] Alfred Zimmern, 'The Problem of Collective Security', in Quincy Wright (ed.), *Neutrality and Collective Security* (Chicago, 1936), pp. 6–7.
[50] Ibid., p. 89.
[51] Alfred Zimmern, *The League of Nations and the Rule of Law* (London, 1936), p. 283.
[52] 'Memorandum by Professor Zimmern on the Preparation of the Next International Studies Conference: Peaceful Change', Alfred Zimmern, 27 July 1935, Alfred Zimmern Papers, Box 98.
[53] Norman Angell, 'Germany and the Rhineland II', *International Affairs* 15:6 (1936), pp. 26, 34.
[54] Albrecht Mendelssohn Bartholdy, 'Soll Deutschland kündigen?', *Europäische Gespräche* 12 (1930), pp. 589–600.
[55] Fritz Berber, *Sicherheit und Gerechtigkeit* (Berlin, 1934), pp. 108–10; Fritz Berber, *Diktat von Versailles: Entstehung, Inhalt, Zerfall: eine Darstellung in Dokumenten* (Essen, 1939).

was neither a surprise, nor the result of Nazi influence. The architects
of IR were not what Mark Lilla has called "philotyrannical intellectuals".[56] The fundamental flaws of the discipline were clear long before
Hitler came to power. As early as 1929, Zimmern admitted that
"much of what is known in academic circles as 'political science' is a
mere playing with words".[57] The inevitable question was if there was
something fundamentally wrong with IR.

A Doomed Discipline?

More than a hundred years after the invention of IR as an academic
discipline, there are still violent conflicts across the globe. Diplomats
still negotiate treaties behind closed doors. And international institutions still struggle to act as impartial brokers. Many of the concepts
devised by the architects of IR such as 'collective security' are still
endorsed by scholars and policymakers, albeit with questionable
results. But even if IR scholars cannot be blamed for the persistence
of wars – in the same sense that economists cannot be blamed for
unemployment or inflation – there is no doubt that current affairs have
raised difficult questions for IR scholarship. Indeed, there is now a
debate on whether IR should be an academic discipline at all.[58]
A recent introspection argued that the field was in "an existential
crisis" which exposes the "political and moral" motives underlying
the discipline.[59] What has IR scholarship done to achieve its original
goals? Do we – and the population at large – now know more about
international relations? Or is IR doomed to fail?

The most common explanation for the shortcomings of early IR
scholarship has been to blame its 'idealist' or 'utopian' ideology, the

---

[56] Mark Lilla, *The Reckless Mind: Intellectuals in Politics* (New York, 2001),
p. 197.
[57] Alfred Zimmern, 'The Prospects of Democracy', *Journal of the Royal Institute of
International Affairs* 7:3 (1928), p. 156.
[58] Dan Reiter, 'Should We Leave behind the Subfield of International Relations?',
Annual Review of Political Science 18 (2015), pp. 481–99; Helen Louise Turton,
'The Importance of Re-affirming IR's Disciplinary Status', *International
Relations* 29:2 (2015), pp. 244–50.
[59] Andreas Gofas et al., 'The Struggle for the Soul of International Relations:
Fragments of a Collective Journey', in Andreas Gofas et al. (eds.), *The SAGE
Handbook of the History, Philosophy and Sociology of International Relations*
(London, 2018), pp. 3–4.

belief that international institutions and legal guarantees would prevent violent conflict. To be sure, many architects of IR thought it was
possible to establish an international order based on peaceful cooperation, although they rejected the label 'idealism'.[60] But even scholars
who were less optimistic about the set of institutions that emerged after
1919 had a fairly clear idea of how the world should be organised. In
particular, the self-described 'realists' such as E. H. Carr formulated
their own visions for a global order, rather than merely analysing the
current state of affairs. They needed a "new utopia of [their] own", as
Carr himself acknowledged.[61] Put more starkly, in the words of
Foreign Affairs editor E. D. Morel, "every man who is not a mere
human cabbage is of necessity an idealist".[62] Variations of that
approach became apparent in Carr's *Conditions of Peace* (1942) and
in Georg Schwarzenberger's *Power Politics* (1941).[63] It was also
reflected in the government work of 'realists' such as Hans
Morgenthau and George Kennan.

Their work raised questions about the role of normative values in
IR. Where did 'realists' derive their ideas from? How did they formulate policy recommendations? If morality had no place in international
politics and if all thought was historically conditioned, as the realist
critique claimed, it was difficult to establish universal principles to
serve as guides for action (or standards of judgement).[64] Nor did the
early 'realists' explain in which ways power was more 'real' than law,
cooperation, or religious belief, as Leonard Woolf argued in one of the
most biting contemporary critiques of Carr's *The Twenty Years' Crisis*
(1939) – which Woolf denounced as an "unscientific" failure.[65] But
even if one accepted the absolute primacy of material power in international politics, it was unclear how the 'realists' proceeded from

[60] See, for example, C. A. W. Manning, in International Institute of Intellectual
Cooperation, *Peaceful Change* (1938), p. 270.
[61] E. H. Carr, *The Twenty Years' Crisis, 1919–1939* (London, 1939), p. 87.
[62] E. D. Morel, 'Foreword', in Helena Swanwick (ed.), *Builders of Peace: Being
Ten Years' History of the Union of Democratic Control* (London, 1924), p. 10.
[63] Paul Howe, 'The Utopian Realism of E. H. Carr', *Review of International
Studies* 20:3 (1994), pp. 277–97; Georg Schwarzenberger, *Power Politics: An
Introduction to the Study of International Relations and Post-War Planning*
(London, 1941).
[64] Graham Evans, 'E. H. Carr and International Relations', *British Journal of
International Studies* 1:2 (1975), pp. 88–9.
[65] Leonard Woolf, 'Utopia and Reality', *Political Quarterly* (1940), p. 172.

there. Why *should* the world be shaped according to the factors that
allegedly *did* shape the world? That argument seemed suspiciously
close to what philosophers call an 'appeal to nature' fallacy – a thing
is not good simply because it is natural. In other words, the 'realist'
response to interwar IR did not solve the problem of normative values
in the study of IR.

So the question was not whether conflicts were easier to be prevented by collective guarantees or by military supremacy, but if there
was *any* scientific method to make reliable predictions of this sort and,
as a consequence, to derive policy recommendations. What the field
needed was a general review of its epistemological foundations. That
opportunity came in 1954 when the Rockefeller Foundation sponsored
a conference gathering a group of influential figures, including George
Kennan, Hans Morgenthau, Reinhold Niebuhr, Paul Nitze, and
Arnold Wolfers, "to discuss some of the fundamental problems
involved in theoretical approaches to international politics".[66] For
the first time in the history of the discipline, they examined the "possibility, nature and limits" of IR theory as well as its relationship to the
conduct of foreign policy. They acknowledged that existing IR scholarship had not made "use of rigorous scientific technique" and failed
to provide reliable descriptive studies, let alone predictive ones. The
1954 conference was also the first time that IR scholars thoroughly
addressed the conflict between the rational analysis of political patterns
and the need for statesmen to take ad hoc decisions based on a
combination of intuition and personal beliefs. This realisation
became the founding moment of IR theory, as Nicolas Guilhot
has argued.[67]

From the 1950s, then, IR scholars devoted more attention to essential questions about the nature of their discipline which their predecessors had neglected. What was the scientific basis for promoting
international sanctions, or the transfer of colonial territories, or the
practice of international governance? If IR was to be more than

---

[66] 'Conference on Theory of International Politics', 1954[?], Arnold Wolfers Papers, Box 3, Folder 50.
[67] Nicolas Guilhot (ed.), *The Invention of International Relations Theory: Realism, the Rockefeller Foundation, and the 1954 Conference on Theory* (New York, 2011).

history, or journalism, it needed a stronger methodological apparatus.[68] But there were no easily observable factors or patterns in foreign policy that would make one theory more valid than another. Causal relationships in international affairs were hard to identify because of the sheer number of actors and variables, but also because even the most basic units of observation – nation-states, borders, treaties, etc. – were complex constructions. It was not at all clear, for example, what a state really was or how to measure its power. A simple research question about, say, the impact of relative military power on regional peace was impossible to answer without further specifying the variables at play. Any problem of international affairs eventually boiled down to profounder questions about how society should be organised. In other words, the assumptions underlying the study of IR were political preferences, philosophical ideas or, at best, psychological patterns.

After all, the agents of foreign policy were human beings with fallible minds and questionable morals. "Human ignorance, and still more human folly", Gilbert Murray warned in 1931, "are so far from being removable elements in public affairs".[69] His American colleague James Shotwell agreed that questions of war and peace rested almost always on "an emotional rather than a factual basis" – an observation that the American journalist Walter Lippmann had eloquently described a decade earlier in his landmark book *Public Opinion* (1922).[70] German-born lawyer Georg Schwarzenberger, too, argued that the secret to international conflict lay in "human nature", as did American economist Emily Greene Balch.[71] If it was true that the psychology of individuals determined the course of international affairs, rather than legal guarantees or national armies, then it would

[68] See George Lawson, 'International Relations as a Historical Social Science', in Andreas Gofas et al. (eds.), *The SAGE Handbook of the History, Philosophy and Sociology of International Relations* (London, 2018), pp. 75–89.
[69] Gilbert Murray, 'Introduction', in William Archer, *The Great Analysis: A Plea for a Rational World-Order*, 2nd ed. (London, 1931), p. iii.
[70] James T. Shotwell, 'Scientific Method in Research and Discussion in International Relations: A Proposal for Institutes of International Relations', 6 June 1931, James T. Shotwell Papers, Box 155, 156; Walter Lippmann, *Public Opinion* (New York, 1922), p. 29.
[71] Schwarzenberger, *Power Politics*, p. 430; Emily Greene Balch, 'The War in Its Relation to Democracy and World Order', *The Annals of the American Academy* 72 (1917), p. 28.

be crucial to know more about how those innermost forces played out in the international realm – a question still discussed in IR literature.[72] Was it possible, Albert Einstein asked Sigmund Freund in 1933, "to control man's mental evolution so as to make him proof against the psychoses of hate and destructiveness?"[73] Freud's response was discouraging, to say the least. He argued that there was "no likelihood of our being able to suppress humanity's aggressive tendencies". If anything, there was some hope, according to Freud, for the human intellect to "master our instinctive life".[74] The question was which role IR would play in this context.

One way in which the architects of IR tried to shape international politics was through asking questions. By challenging existing power structures, they pressed governments to better explain their policies and to make their decisions more accountable. They questioned the logic of sanctions and treaties as well as of international governance more generally. Their solution to the dilemma of IR was to bring questions of war and peace "out of the emotional and into the factual realm" or, to put it differently, "out of politics and into the atmosphere of arbitration".[75] This ambition, to translate value-based questions into empirical research, and then back to policy recommendations, has remained a disciplinary standard until today.[76] There is still a debate, for example, on the economic roots of democratic peace with wide-ranging policy implications for the promotion of democracy.[77] Many now argue that positivist and normative theory are inevitably linked and that advocates of the former just fail to make their

---

[72] Joshua D. Kertzer and Dustin Tingley, 'Political Psychology in International Relations: Beyond the Paradigms', *Annual Review of Political Science* 21 (2018), pp. 319–39.
[73] Albert Einstein and Sigmund Freud, *Why War?* (Paris, 1933), p. 7.
[74] Ibid., pp. 16, 18.
[75] James T. Shotwell, 'Scientific Method in Research and Discussion in International Relations: A Proposal for Institutes of International Relations', 6 June 1931, James T. Shotwell Papers, Box 155, 156.
[76] Stephanie Lawson, *Theories of International Relations* (Cambridge, 2015), p. 5; Henry R. Nau, 'Scholarship and Policy-Making: Who Speaks Truth to Whom?', in Christian Reus-Smit and Duncan Snidal (eds.), *The Oxford Handbook of International Relations* (Oxford, 2008), p. 636.
[77] See, for example, Michael Mousseau, 'The Social Market Roots of Democratic Peace', *International Security* 33:4 (2009), pp. 52–86.

normative premises explicit.[78] In any event, the philosophical foundations of the discipline are still subject to debate and many of the questions that interwar IR scholarship raised remain essentially unresolved.[79]

It is not for a historian to identify avenues for future research, nor to comment on their intellectual benefits, but simply to highlight some pitfalls of the past and to examine their causes. A hundred years ago, the architects of IR built an ambitious academic discipline and designed an even more ambitious world order. They established research institutions and invented policy instruments to govern an increasingly complex web of political, economic, and cultural relationships. Variations of the so-called 'realist' critique emerged during the 1930s, although they neither offered a consistent theory nor initiated a 'great debate'. By and large, IR authors failed to discuss the normative premises and the intellectual limitations of their discipline. Nor did their work predict (or prepare for) future conflicts in the way that they had hoped. In fact, none of the instruments they designed, from disarmament to 'peaceful change', brought about any immediate practical results or analytical insights. Despite these failures, or precisely because of them, they succeeded in making international affairs a matter of public concern and encouraged citizens to think critically about the political world they lived in. That is perhaps their most important achievement, and it remains a powerful inspiration today.

---

[78] Robert Jackson and Georg Sørensen, *Introduction to International Relations: Theories and Approaches*, 4th ed. (Oxford, 2010), p. 292; Chris Brown, *International Relations Theory: New Normative Approaches* (New York, 1992).

[79] Andreas Gofas et al., 'The Struggle for the Soul of International Relations: Fragments of a Collective Journey', in Andreas Gofas et al. (eds.), *The SAGE Handbook of the History, Philosophy and Sociology of International Relations* (London, 2018), pp. 3–12.

Index

Bouglé, Célestin, 67
Bourgeois, Léon, 48, 51, 61, 64, 92, 130, 162, 180
Bourgin, Hubert, 52
Bourne, Randolph, 50
Bourquin, Maurice, 93, 185, 240, 297
Bowman, Isaiah, 104
Brailsford, H. N., 33, 39
Brand, Robert, 81
Brentano, Lujo, 33, 90
Briand, Aristide, 182
Brinkmann, Carl, 257
British Institute of International Affairs. *See* Chatham House
Brunauer, Esther Caukin, 107
Bryce, James, 47, 53
Buell, Raymond Leslie, 106, 164
Bureau international de la paix, 47
Bureau of International Relations, University of California, Berkeley, 110
Bureau of International Research, Harvard University, 106
Burgess, John W., 31, 100
Burton, Montague, 85, 233
Butler, Nicholas Murray, 101, 182
Buxton, Charles Roden, 50, 276

Canadian Institute of International Affairs, 115
Capper-Johnson, Karlin, 114, 243
Capy, Marcelle, 51
Cargin, Eleanor, 81
Carnegie Endowment for International Peace, 16, 88, 93, 101, 104, 153, 173, 175
Carr, E. H., 6, 59, 70, 206, 284, 307
Carr-Saunders, Alexander, 271
Carter, Edward Clark, 112
Casgrain, Thérèse, 113
Cassel, Ernest, 82
Cassin, René, 3, 211, 290
Castberg, Frede, 277
Catchpool, Corder, 114
Cecil, Lord Robert, 61, 64, 77, 80, 167, 217
Central Organisation for a Durable Peace, 1, 20, 29, 41–2, 45, 51, 54, 171

Centre d'études de politique étrangère, 94
Centro Italiano Di Alti Studi Internazionali, 99
Challaye, Félicien, 166
Chamberlain, Austen, 236
Charléty, Sebastien, 95
Chatham House, 64, 80–2, 197, 233, 274
Chen, Han-Seng, 113
Chen Zen, Sophia H., 113
Chicago Council on Foreign Relations, 105
Christophersen, H. O., 276
Clark, John Bates, 50
Clausewitz, Carl von, 37
Clemenceau, Georges, 176
colonial revision, 274–6, 279
Concert of Europe, 37
Condliffe, J. B., 113, 194, 283
contextualism in IR, 10
Conwell-Evans, T. P., 264, 280, 293
Coolidge, Archibald Cary, 59, 103
Coppola, Francesco, 234
corporatism, 196
Corwin, Edward Samuel, 107, 303
Cot, Pierre, 224
Coudenhove-Kalergi, Richard, 96, 105
Council for the Study of International Relations, 20, 29, 46
Council on Foreign Relations, 64, 103
Courtney, Kathleen, 225, 233, 266, 288
Cremer, Randal, 44
Cromie, Leonard J., 270
Crowdy, Rachel, 98, 139
Crowe, Eyre, 64
cultural diplomacy, 75, 173
Curie, Marie, 130
Currie, Arthur, 115
Curtis, Lionel, 47, 59, 64, 80
Curtius, Julius, 151

d'Estournelles de Constant, Paul, 44, 61, 180
Dafoe, John Wesley, 115
Daladier, Édouard, 148
Dalton, Hugh, 196
Davanzati, Roberto Forges, 234
Davies, David, 17, 38, 72, 76–8, 223–5, 284, 287

For EU product safety concerns, contact us at Calle de José Abascal, 56–1°,
28003 Madrid, Spain or eugpsr@cambridge.org.

www.ingramcontent.com/pod-product-compliance
Ingram Content Group UK Ltd.
Pitfield, Milton Keynes, MK11 3LW, UK
UKHW020340140625
459647UK00018B/2237